Firing the Heather

❖

Books by Nellie McClung

Sowing Seeds in Danny (1908)
The Second Chance (1910)
The Black Creek Stopping-House and Other Stories (1912)
In Times Like These (1915)
The Next of Kin (1917)
Three Times and Out: A Canadian Boy's Experience in Germany (1918)
Purple Springs (1921)
When Christmas Crossed 'The Peace' (1923)
Painted Fires (1925)
All We Like Sheep (1926)
Be Good to Yourself (1930)
Flowers for the Living (1931)
Clearing in the West: My Own Story (1935)
Leaves from Lantern Lane (1936)
More Leaves from Lantern Lane (1937)
The Stream Runs Fast: My Own Story (1945)

Firing the Heather

❖

The Life and Times
of Nellie McClung

Mary Hallett & Marilyn Davis

FIFTH
HOUSE
PUBLISHERS

Cover photograph courtesy Glenbow Archives, Calgary (NA-273-2)
Hand-colouring of photograph by Grant Kernan/A.K. Photos
Cover design by John Luckhurst/GDL

The publisher gratefully acknowledges the assistance of The Canada
Council, Communications Canada, the Saskatchewan Arts Board, and
the University of Saskatchewan.

Printed and bound in Canada
94 95 96 97 98 / 5 4 3 2 1

Canadian Cataloguing in Publication Data

Hallett, Mary E. (Mary Elizabeth), 1924–1986

    Firing the heather

    Includes index.
    ISBN 1-895618-20-7 (bound)
    ISBN 1-895618-43-6 (pbk.)

1. McClung, Nellie L., 1873-1951. 2. Feminists -
Canada - Biography. 3. Authors, Canadian (English) -
20th century - Biography.* I. Davis, Marilyn I.,
1930– II. Title.

HQ1455.M3H34 1993   305.42'092   C93-098077-8

FIFTH HOUSE LTD.
620 Duchess Street
Saskatoon, SK
S7K 0R1

Contents

❖

For Norma

Preface

❖

$\mathbf{F}$*iring the Heather* was completed under unusual circumstances. Shortly after Mary Hallett completed her writing, with my assistance, of the historical chapters, she developed a terminal illness. It became urgent to secure academics to read, comment upon, and criticize her chapters before her death. Professor Michael Hayden of the University of Saskatchewan contributed his editorial skills along with his criticisms, and Professor Ramsay Cook of York University very kindly read and critiqued the text as it then stood. Mary and I were very grateful for the time and effort they so generously provided. By this time Mary's health prevented her from working on specific revisions, so I drafted a couple of amended versions in response to each criticism, and we would talk these over and come up with the approach Mary desired. These changes were then typed into a revised version of the manuscript.

Following Mary's death, professional readers made further suggestions: mainly cutting back on the text, and updating Mary's secondary source material. It was easy for me to do the former. Since my background is in Canadian literature, however, the latter required more guidance, and I am exceedingly grateful for the help of historian Georgina Taylor, who one day turned up at my door with four grocery bags filled with books and articles in women's history written since Mary's death. At first it seemed a daunting task, but as I worked through the texts—often with suggestions from Georgina, who also read and commented on the revised manuscript—what had once seemed overwhelming was finally completed. I write this to indicate the extent of my revising of the final text without Mary Hallett's input. In addition, I wrote the chapter *Antiromantic Fiction of a Feminist.*

MARILYN I. DAVIS

Acknowledgements

❖

The work of the biographer is always made easier and more pleasant by the generous support and assistance of both individuals and institutions. Among family members who were helpful with their time and memories, we wish to mention with particular gratitude the enthusiastic support of Nellie's youngest son, Mark McClung of Ottawa. Many recollections of life at Lantern Lane were generously provided by Margaret McClung, widow of Nellie's third son, Horace, of Victoria. We would also like to thank the estate of Nellie McClung for its co-operation in the project. In addition to lengthy interviews with family members we received the help and encouragement of many friends and others such as Estella (Mrs. H.B.) Donaldson of Wawanesa to whom we went for directions to the Millford Cairn and the old Millford Cemetery in southern Manitoba. To our pleasant surprise, Mrs. Donaldson turned out to be the local historian. She generously took us into her home for lunch and shared with us her large collection of historical clippings and photographs of Nellie McClung and the Millford-Wawanesa area.

Of considerable importance, too, were the intimate family memories of Randi Halvorsen (Mrs. P.) of Victoria. Randi had emigrated from Norway as a young girl in the early part of this century and provided domestic service for the McClungs in Calgary for several years. Similarly, Mrs. Winnie Fudger, who worked for three years as Nellie McClung's secretary and Girl Friday, was full of memories of the McClung family and Nellie. To Lois Currie (Mrs. R.G.S.), president of the Calgary Women's Canadian Club (1976–77), we owe a debt of gratitude for not only supplying the names of former friends of Nellie McClung, such as Mrs. Z.W. Dean, Mrs. A.C. Smith, and Mrs. Fudger, but also for arranging meetings with them. Mrs. Elaine M.

viii

Acknowledgements

Catley of Calgary also added Nellie McClung anecdotes to our collection. Mrs. Bessie Smith generously opened the Calgary home of McClung for our viewing in 1977. Anne Francis (Florence Bird) interviewed us for her CBC radio programme "Between Ourselves" on the subject of "The Incredible Nellie McClung" and was helpfully informative about some of her other interviews.

We also wish to thank Mr. J. Donald Wilson of the University of British Columbia's Faculty of Education, who asked a Finnish friend, Ms. Maija Kainulainen (at that time Information and Cultural Attaché of the Embassy of Finland in Ottawa) for information on the Finnish translation and reviews of Nellie McClung's last novel, *Painted Fires*. Ms. Kainulainen was in Finland at the time and was able to supply information on the translation and reception of this novel in that country. Thanks are also due to M. Ann Sunahara of Edmonton for drawing to our attention that the Japanese-Canadian newspaper *The New Canadian* (12 January 1942) had republished a Nellie L. McClung letter in defence of Japanese Canadians originally addressed to the editor of the *Victoria Times*. Professors Clara Thomas and John Lennox from the English Department at York University very kindly shared an early draft of a chapter on the Canadian Authors Association written for their book *William Arthur Deacon: A Canadian Literary Life*, and generously passed on letters they had discovered, in the course of their research, from Nellie McClung to Deacon.

This biography could not have been written without the helpful cooperation of the many librarians and archivists at the numerous locations where we carried out our research. Our seven-and-a-half months spent on the McClung Papers, lodged in the Provincial Archives of British Columbia at Victoria, were made particularly pleasurable by Kent M. Haworth, Frances Gundry, Head, Manuscripts and Government Records Division, and David B. Mason, Chief, Library and Archives Programme, who graciously and trustingly found us a comfortable working niche in the stacks, thus lightening our burden enormously and adding to general efficiency.

In Calgary at the Glenbow Library and Archives, our special thanks go to Ms. Sheilagh Jameson. Her thorough knowledge of that institute's holdings enabled her to zero in on our needs with unerring accuracy. We are also indebted to Dr. John C. Butt, Chief Medical Examiner for Alberta. Archivists at the Alberta, Saskatchewan, Manitoba, and Ontario provincial archives answered our requests for material with cheerful expediency, as did librarians at the University of British Columbia Special Collections Division, the central Toronto Reference Library, and the Thomas Fisher Rare Book Library at the University of Toronto. Susan Bellingham of the Women's Library at Waterloo University helpfully supplied materials. The Reverend Glenn Lucas at the United Church Archives in Toronto was both obliging and informative regarding our several queries. At the National Library and Archives in Ottawa the alacrity with which cart-loads of early Canadian magazines were brought to our table was truly astonishing. In the National Film, Television, and Sound Archives we are particularly grateful for the help of Jo Langham, Sharron Gleeson, and Sylvie Robitaille. Pierre Charbonneau, Director of Secretariat with the Canadian Broadcasting Corporation, smoothed the way for the examination of minutes, memoranda, correspondence, etc., of the CBC Board of Broadcast Governors from 1936 to 1942 when Nellie McClung was a member of the board. Thanks, too, are due Judy and Peter Gendron of Owen Sound, who searched out deeds to the Mooney farm in Grey County, and to Mr. Melvin McMullen, who at the eleventh hour managed to find a number of crucial photographs for the book.

Among colleagues at the University of Saskatchewan who assisted by checking the finer points of Alberta politics in 1926 and B.C. rail line connections in 1908, respectively, were professors Duff Spafford of the Department of Political Studies, and T.D. Regehr of the Department of History. Professor Ron Fritz of the College of Law provided us with material on the Dower and Child Custody laws in the West as did Professor Alison Diduck, Faculty of Law, University of Manitoba. Mere words are insufficient to thank Michael Hayden, friend, and professor in the Department of History. His kindnesses were many and varied, and he brought to the reading of our typescript his sharp editorial experience. We are indebted, also, to Professor Ramsay Cook of York University who, already deluged by "regenerators," plunged bravely into the typescript and managed to come up smiling. Our typists, Suzan Piot, Candace Bourget, and Joni Aschim, gave us their unfailing patience through all the changes we required. When proofreading became a serious problem, professors Laurence Kitzan and Joseph Fry, along with Florence Carson, and the unflagging Dr. Florence Bennee came willingly to our aid. A debt of

Acknowledgements

gratitude is also owed to Professor Dale Miquelon, head of the Department of History, University of Saskatchewan, who was instrumental in securing a grant in aid of publication from the university.

Thanks, too, to Professor Bill Waiser, Department of History, University of Saskatchewan, advisory editor to Fifth House Publishers, and to Charlene Dobmeier, the managing editor at Fifth House, whose sharp editorial skills have made this a better book.

Last, but never least, is our debt to The Canada Council for generous research grants in 1973–74 and 1978–79. Professor Mary Hallett is also grateful for the University of Saskatchewan's President's Humanities and Social Science Award in 1981–82.

MARY E. HALLETT
MARILYN I. DAVIS

Introduction

❖

Carolyn G. Heilbrun in her important *Writing a Woman's Life* (1988) indicates that the central approach to women's biography has been to document the female life of prime devotion to male destiny. For young women searching for more from a female biography, there were few other models to be found, at least before the 1970s. Despite a few exceptions in recent years, Heilbrun does not see much improvement. "There still exists little organized sense of what a woman's biography or autobiography should look like." The reason for this, she claims, is that—even though women may find it difficult to admit or defend—a woman's right to her "own story" frequently depends upon her "ability to act in the public domain." This, in turn, depends upon power: "the ability to take one's place in whatever discourse is essential to action and the right to have one's part matter." Nellie Letitia (Mooney) McClung had certainly developed enough of what Heilbrun refers to as "ego-strength" to allow her to be an instrument of change and creativity rather than a passive observer of life.[1] As an author whose works reflect her social conscience, and as a leading activist and social reformer in the public domain during the first half of the twentieth century, McClung undoubtedly deserves an in-depth study.

Maria Tippett reminds us in her biography of Emily Carr that 1871–1945 was not a period that "encouraged a woman of independent spirit to have a life of her own."[2] In spite of this, Nellie McClung not only led an autonomous and vigorous life, she chose to write about it in a two-volume autobiography, *Clearing in the West* (1935), and *The Stream Runs Fast* (1945). The first volume is a lively and generally convincing account of her life up to 1896 ending with her marriage. Apart from her personal papers it is the only available source of information about her early life as she recalled it from the perspective of sixty years of age. As a writer of fiction, McClung was keenly aware of the dramatic moment and how to create it, and one is conscious of the novelist's art at play upon careful examination of the book—especially where other sources of information are available. Nevertheless, the spirit and general outline ring true, and Nellie's older sisters—Lizzie Rae and Hannah Sweet—read and approved the manuscript, offering very few corrections of fact. Still, having *Clearing* in its early manuscript state, Lizzie wrote to Nellie: "I have finished your new book and enjoyed every word. I laughed and cried and was happy doing both . . . You were kind to all of us, very kind."[3] This implies that Nellie McClung had somewhat softened her public portrayal of family members, perhaps by concentrating on their positive traits. As Nellie matured she tended to search out the better qualities in people as a constructive, and charitable, principle of human relations. This is not to say that she falsified family portraits beyond recognition, or that her autobiography is anything but essential truth.

The second volume of Nellie McClung's autobiography was published ten years after the more memorable *Clearing in the West*. It lacks the graphic, sensuous description, the careful attention to historical detail, and the general vitality and readability of the earlier work, and it is often factually unreliable. At times one senses here—as in the earlier volume—that Nellie was attributing the ideas and feelings of her maturer years to the younger self that she presented, particularly in the earlier chapters of this book. Nor is the volume an adequately full account of the last two-thirds of the life of the unforgettable woman who wrote it. *The Stream Runs Fast* was written at a time when McClung's health was seriously declining and, as both the title and her "Introduction" intimate, it was written "with a sense of urgency," for Nellie had begun to realize that death was not far off. The biographer, then, reads both books with some degree of caution, in spite of the fact that Nellie did indeed set out to leave by means of them "some small legacy of truth." In addition to her autobiography, Nellie kept a series of diaries from the early years of her marriage to Wesley McClung right up to the end of her life. It is a misfortune for the biographer and the social historian that these diaries have been destroyed.

We can learn much about Nellie McClung from the written legacy she left behind. Unfortunately her writing has most often been underappreciated, even overlooked. The chapter "Antiromantic Fiction of a Feminist," which reexamines McClung's fiction, assumes, with feminist criticism, that women have also told the important stories of our culture[4] and that male critics, ignorant of women's values, are often poor readers of women's fiction.[5] Feminist literary criticism allows us to take a fresh look at the development of women's literary traditions. It holds that by examining the "best sellers" of a particular period, one can discover "a female countertradition" that conveys "various attempts to portray feminine consciousness and self-consciousness"; that is to say, "how we [women] live, how we have been living."[6] Fiction of McClung's like *Purple Springs*, *Painted Fires*, and "Carried Forward" could have been written only by a woman. Such criticism, which involves both genre and gender, has been called "revision": "the act of looking back, of seeing with fresh eyes, of entering an old text from a new critical direction."[7] As such, then, feminist literary criticism can be seen as a political or feminist action. Literary critic Elaine Showalter holds that "feminist criticism was the discovery that women writers had a literature of their own, whose historical and thematic coherence, as well as artistic importance, had been obscured by the patriarchal values that dominate our culture." As a consequence, feminist criticism "set out to map the territory of the female imagination" and an entire new field of enquiry into women's writing has evolved. The result has been the "recovery and rereading of literature by women from all nations and historical periods . . . hundreds of lost women writers were discovered."[8] Thus, feminist literary criticism reconsiders long-accepted attitudes and allows for a new interpretation of texts long thought of as unarguable.[9] It is in this new atmosphere that McClung's work must be considered.

Robert Craig Brown, speaking of the role of the biographer in relation to the historian, points out that the biographer is "a bit old-fashioned in his insistence that individuals can and do shape the historical process we [historians] evaluate and interpret in our work." Brown holds that "biography . . . could and should inform and enrich the study of the history of the society. But without a clear linkage to social history, biography is incomplete and its utility is vitiated." For this reason we chose "the life and times" form of biography in order to integrate McClung's character and personality with the social circumstances of her time. "But in the end," says Brown, the biographer's obligation remains what it has always been: "to disclose with sympathy and candor, and with such literary grace as he can command, as much as he can discover of his subject's private and public life";[10] or, as Carl Berger describes it: "the main task of the biographer [is] the revelation of character and personality in history."[11] This we have sought to do.

McClung certainly did not work alone in the suffrage campaigns or for other social reforms. Yet in her time, and to this present day, she stands out as the unofficial leader in those causes espoused by the reform-minded minority of her time. Then, as now, she was admired, or castigated, by those who failed to understand her in the historical and reformist circumstances of that period. It is for such reasons that Nellie L. McClung warrants a scholarly but readable biography: one that probes the strong character and lively personality of a remarkable Canadian woman; that searches out the methods through which she sought to be a catalyst for social reform; and one that places her in the context of those times, those issues, and those people, all of which helped to mould the woman who, in turn, helped shape the world we live in.

"Prohibition is a hard sounding word, worthless as a rallying cry, hard as a locked door or going to bed without your supper. It could never fire the heather, and yet the heather must be fired . . . "
Nellie L. McClung, *The Stream Runs Fast*

"The phrase [fire the heather] is a Scottish agricultural term that means getting rid of the old crop, so that new growth can begin."
Catherine Kerrigan, Edinburgh University

1

Grey County
and the Move West

❖

A mile south of Chatsworth, in Grey County, Ontario, on the west side of the Garafraxa Road, was the Mooney farm: a two storey white-washed house, surrounded by maples, a big red barn, a tidy vegetable garden, a few fruit trees near the house, and cultivated but stony fields stretching out over the rolling countryside. It is a home McClung describes with affection in the first volume of her autobiography, *Clearing in the West* (1935), a book written when she was in her sixties and looking back on her life with the help of the journals she kept. The details in this volume regarding pioneer life in Manitoba, however, are highly selective. There is no doubt that what Nellie McClung describes is essential truth, but the whole work is sentimentalized and gilded with the myth of the Golden West, so assiduously promoted by railway-builders, immigration officials, and westerners themselves. *Clearing in the West* has three layers. It is a memoir; it is a temperance tract; and it is a piece of social history written out of the Golden West myth. One has, at times, the impression that the novelist is at work. Indeed, manuscript variations of some episodes indicate that at times McClung developed and dramatized her role in specific events much as if she were writing fiction. One should say, however, in Nellie's defence, that the strategies and devices of fiction are usually employed to dramatize some larger truth. Still, *Clearing in the West* is the only readily available source of information about her early life, and the first three chapters of this biography depend on it to a considerable extent.[1]

By 1873, when Nellie Letitia Mooney was born on a stormy

1

October afternoon, her father, John Mooney, had been struggling with the land for over thirty years. He had come to Canada in 1830, an eighteen-year-old boy. He and his two brothers, William and Thomas, left a comfortable home in Tipperary, Ireland, where there was little prospect for the future, and set out with high hopes for the new world. After ten weeks on the Atlantic they arrived in Canada and went to the centre of a flourishing lumber trade, Bytown, on the Ottawa River. John became a shanty man, a rough job, where he worked with hard-drinking, hard-fighting men. After ten years he had made little economic progress, his brothers had died of typhoid, and he looked around for a more settled way of life. At this time the government of the Canadas was building a pioneer road into the newly acquired Indian lands of the Georgian country, so John signed on to work on the road so that he could get not only his free grant of fifty acres but, at the same time, work off his debt for fifty more. Later on he was able to add fifty additional acres to his holding. The land he received in Sullivan Township was heavily timbered with hard maple, hemlock, and elm, and unknown to the eager young pioneer, was situated on the stony side of the new land tract where the soil was not suitable for agricultural purposes. The first ten years were a bitter struggle for "in no portion of north-western Ontario, perhaps, did the pioneers encounter more genuine hardships, or more stubborn trials, in their struggle for existence . . . "[2] Gradually the land was brought under cultivation, and more and more settlers arrived. In 1850 the township was organized. The first treasurer was John Mooney.

Soon after his arrival in Grey County, John married his cousin Jane Shouldice, who died a little more than a year after their marriage. At this point, Judy Connor—one of the loyal family servants of John's father—came to the bush to keep house for him. She stayed with John Mooney to the end of her days, and he remained a widower for many years. In 1858, however, he married Letitia McCurdy. Letitia had recently arrived from Scotland with her mother and sister to join her aunts, who were comfortably settled in the more prosperous part of the county east of the Garafraxa Road, a distinction they never let the Mooneys forget. Letitia, twenty years younger than her husband, became his hard-working partner, and soon there was a family to care and provide for.

When Nellie was born, in 1873, the last child, she had five

brothers and sisters: Will, almost fifteen; George, thirteen; Elizabeth, six; Jack, five; and Hannah, three. One boy had died of diphtheria at the age of four. As Nellie grew up in the close family circle she had little reason to feel unwanted or unappreciated; her older brothers treated her with consideration and kindness, Lizzie was a thoughtful older sister, and Hannah was her playmate. The only sibling rivalry was with her brother Jack and that was to continue for many years.

Life in the Grey County home was simple. Looking back, Nellie remembered that almost everything was homemade: cloth woven by her mother for curtains and clothes, hand-hooked mats on the floor, pictures on the wall from the Montreal *Family Herald*. The pine floors were scrubbed every week and the inside walls whitewashed every spring. Smoked hams and dried apples were hung from the kitchen rafters. It was a typical Ontario farm emerging from the pioneer state.

Nellie's first six years on the Chatsworth farm remained a happy memory. She recalled sunny summer days in the farmyard, cozy winter evenings around the big kitchen stove, exciting rides to town in the big farm wagon, sometimes filled with fresh grass covering the kegs and crocks of butter that Letitia had for sale. Dairying, along with vegetable growing and the care of eggs and poultry, was considered women's work on the farm in addition to the many household chores. It was difficult, time-consuming work. In addition, during the planting and harvest time women were also expected to work in the fields. In the early pioneer days many farmers had to abandon farming because their wives were unable to withstand the physical strain that the endless duties of a farm house imposed on them.[3]

> They grew their own hops to make their own rising to make their own bread. They saved ashes to make their own lye to boil with collected fat to make their own soap. They made their own candles. They spun wool, they made clothes, cutting up old garments for patterns. They had complete responsibility for the dairy, the milking, the butter-making and the cheese-making. They took part in the butchering of the beasts, in the making of sausages, the smoking of hams, the salting of pork. They did great laundries, which they finished, in spite of protective bandages, with bleeding wrists. They stood through the long nights keeping the fire going under the huge potash pots and stirring the hardening mass. In the cold spring nights they tended the fires under the maple syrup . . . The women did, willingly, even harder work, such as clearing underbrush and, when things were quiet in winter, threshing . . .

3

The vegetable garden too was the woman's care, as well as the putting down of berries, pickles, fruits and preserves; the making of substitutes for teas and coffee from dandelion roots, sumach leaves and parched grain; the dying of wool and knitting; the care of poultry; the dressing and curing of fish and game. And, of course, there were three meals a day to prepare.[4]

Every member of the family had duties and even the littlest was expected to pour water over the ashes to make the lye for soap. On soap-making day Nellie would climb on the kitchen roof and watch with fascination the boiling cauldron set up in the back yard and admire her mother's skill in knowing when to remove the kettle and pour the liquid into the waxed wooden boxes so the soap would set just right—not too hard, not crumbly, not too soft. She felt sorry for those who had to buy their soap at the store. When the family was hurrying to get ready for the 24th of May picnic Nellie was allowed to help plant potatoes. Her older brothers and sisters were at school during the day and had their homework and chores when they arrived home. Before they left Chatsworth even Hannah was in school and Nellie would have joined her the next year. For the most part hers was a carefree existence. There was, however, one horror that marked her young life: the annual pig-killing. She knew with a terrible clarity when it would occur for "the gruesome scaffold" was erected, and the farmyard was immediately transformed "from a friendly playground to a place of evil." At these times the kindly Lizzie would take Nellie down to the lower meadow, but always "the terrible cry came drilling through the hill, and tore through us like a thousand poisoned arrows." Lizzie would press her hands over the sensitive child's ears, but with little effect: "I knew then," the mature McClung said, "that life was a place of horror, in spite of flowers and trees, and streams, and I flung myself down on the grass and cried my heart out in an agony of helplessness." At such times, she claimed, her young spirit rebelled against a God who permitted such pain and her words, she recalled, though "wild and wicked," brought relief. Lizzie never betrayed shock or tried to suppress her outbursts, and Nellie learned then the kindly wisdom of the friend "who has the gift of listening, and forgetting."

Nellie was also an imaginative child, quick to see the funny side—a characteristic she shared with her father. When her mother's prosperous aunts came to visit, for example, Nellie observed their patroniz-

4

ing ways and listened to the Edinburgh accents, which they implied were superior to her mother's Dundee Scottish. They talked nonstop, their steel knitting needles moving as quickly as their tongues. When they left she would go out to the barn—where John Mooney had fled—to entertain her father with a shrewd imitation of the aunts. He would double up with laughter at her clever mimicry, which encouraged her to greater efforts, but when her mother appeared at the barn door, disapproval of them both was obvious and Nellie would be sent to set the table for supper. One day Nellie asked her father if it was wrong to mock the aunts. Years later she recorded his answer as she remembered it:

> Your mother thinks it is . . . she thinks it shows disrespect. I do not think so. They are funny, queer stiff old ladies, set in their ways and right in their own eyes. It's no harm for you and me to have a laugh over them, a laugh is as good as a meal or an hour's sleep. But perhaps we had better not offend your mother. We know that would be wrong, we'll just keep it to ourselves and not be hurting anyone's feelings.

When Nellie became an adult, this childhood capacity for amusing, accurate mimicry would be directed with great effectiveness to more mature, more serious goals. Still, Letitia Mooney was not all stern and forbidding. She worked hard, but she sang as she worked, and she taught her children the joy of song.

As a child, Nellie admired her mother's skills, and she learned, through the years, to respect her strength of character and her blunt kindliness. From the beginning, however, she adored her father whose quick Irish wit and humour offset her mother's stern, Scottish Presbyterian ideas of what was proper. Letitia Mooney's strict Calvinism was also countered by John Mooney's more relaxed Methodism. He was what Nellie described as "an out-and-out Methodist" who had experienced that "strange 'warming of the heart' that John Wesley wrote about in his Journal." It was, in fact, Nellie's first childhood experience of church that provoked an argument between her parents that significantly distinguishes the religious temperament of each. Fascinated by the minister's ears, which wiggled while he preached, young Nellie tried to reciprocate with the one trick she possessed: "I kept my one eye on the minister and the other one shut," an accomplishment that set him laughing in the middle of the service. Letitia, unaware of the cause of this levity, was indignant and claimed

5

that the Methodist clergyman was "too light a man to be preaching the gospel" for if "there was a time to laugh . . . it was not in the church." John Mooney, however, more amiably considered that "there was no harm in a laugh at any time, and it would be better if there were more laughter in the churches." Her father's religious stance would be far more winning to a child, especially one like Nellie who showed signs of being a natural comic. In addition, the fact that John Mooney was sixty years older than his youngest daughter and inclined to be indulgent—more like a lovable grandfather than a stern Victorian father—probably reinforced her youthful allegiance to the Irish, rather than the Scottish, character.

As a parent, however, John Mooney was as wise as he was indulgent, and he taught this impressionable youngster that some medium point between the two extremes was more desirable. He reached her sensitive child's mind with a lesson that Nellie would never forget, by comparing the Mooneys' two dogs: Watch, who had "a stern sense of duty," "never played," and "never had any fun," and the "joyous pup" Nap, who was "light of heart," friendly, and would do nothing useful. "My father called him 'play-boy,'" Nellie recalled, "and said it was too bad that the two dogs could not be combined."

> He said old Watch did not need to be so cross and grim and suspicious, and Nap might easily learn to be useful without losing one bit of his playful ways. People were the same. And then he went on and said that was one reason why Christ was sent on earth—to show people that a Christian might be, indeed must be polite and pleasant, and full of fun and fond of music, and pretty colors and yet serious too and earnest. And he told me to think about this and try to combine the virtues of Watch and the friendliness of Nap, in my own life.

John Mooney's reasonable blend of fun and pleasure with usefulness and earnestness provided Nellie with an attainable and desirable ideal that would mould her developing character, and eventually govern her adult life. Nellie was far from being a model child—"good, meek, mild, gentle"—and it is mainly in later years that she was able to place her mother's stern Scottish ways in perspective, and recognize that her Scottish "courage and backbone" admirably sustained the Mooneys through all the hardships of those early years. Eventually, to Nellie, Letitia Mooney would typify "the pioneer woman . . . calm, cheerful, self-reliant, and undaunted."

Meanwhile, along the Garafraxa Road, Letitia Mooney set a hard pace for the family. Her wash was first on the line on Monday morning and her men were first in the fields, seed-time or harvest. "My father often said of my mother that she could keep forty people busy . . . I know now these things compensated her for the busy life she led, for everyone has to be proud of something." Even as a child Nellie used to wish that there was more time for talk and play, as did the rest of the family. What a child could not realize was that all this hard work was achieving little in economic advancement. The thin rocky soil produced only "cattle-feed and chicken-feed," and a scanty crop of these. The more rocks they picked off, the more came to the surface to interfere with the ploughing. There was little cash. When purchases had to be made—new boots, schoolbooks, a piece of harness—the money had to come from the sale of butter and eggs. Initially, the products were consumed by the family only, but as markets improved, women's dairying became an important source of income for farm families.[5] Thirty years of hard work had developed a farm that kept the family well-fed and housed but little more. Now, machinery was making the small farm even less economical. What was to become of three boys? One hundred and fifty acres could not support them. Already Will and George were growing discontented with the treadmill nature of their existence, seeing no future but that of being hired hands for other farmers.

Like many other Ontarians in the late 1870s, they were ready to receive eagerly the stories being told of the wonderful Canadian west: "One hundred and sixty acres for ten dollars as a homestead, and another one hundred and sixty as a preemption for a moderate price. You could plough a furrow a mile long and never strike a stone! . . . When ploughing, the feet of the oxen would be stained red by the wild strawberries!"[6] The thick black virgin soil would produce crops undreamed of in Ontario. Almost every day the Toronto *Globe* carried some reference to the wonders of the new land in editorials, in the "Latest from Manitoba" column, or in letters to the editor: "the best soil in the world"; "sow two bushels of wheat to the acre and reap about thirty or forty"; "the finest country the sun ever shone upon"; "the soil is rich, there are no stones or stumps to hinder operations and the prospects for settlers are magnificent."[7] The myth of the Golden West was launched. People were pouring in. One *Globe* editorial, in the spring of 1878, predicted an unprecedented migration

7

of Ontario farmers and saw it as "cause for satisfaction, not mourning." The emigrants, the editor pointed out, were not disposing of
their land at a sacrifice but getting good prices.[8] This money, in turn,
would outfit the western pioneer who did not, therefore, have to
begin all over again with nothing but the land. Reports from Manitoba told of arrivals from Ontario—four hundred arriving at one time
in the spring of 1878. During the month of May that year one
hundred thousand acres were recorded at the Emerson land office,
and on 1 June, in a single day, six thousand acres were taken up.[9] It is
no wonder that a popular song in Grey County that summer had the
chorus: "So pack up your duds: say good-bye to your Ma, and try your
luck farming in Man-ito-bah."[10]

In this period, the West was seen by many Ontarians as a kind of
agricultural wonderland whose development would provide the
means to empire. Faith in the land and the region's commercial
potential knew no limits. The West was opportunity waiting to be
realized where settlers would fulfil their dreams and prosperity was
inevitable.

The Chatsworth district farmers enthusiastically exchanged views
on the westward trend. They passed around Thomas White's articles
from the *Globe* and the Montreal *Gazette*: a glowing report of his trip
to Manitoba in the summer of 1878. And Mr. Cameron, the Presbyterian minister in Chatsworth, fired Will Mooney's imagination by
reading him passages from Butler's *Great Lone Land* with its graphic
description of the prairie west of Manitoba in the 1870s. There were
pessimistic voices, of course. The older men warned of cold and flies
and Indians and the hardships of pioneering. They had already
experienced the backbreaking toil of creating farms in a wilderness.
But the young enthusiasts laughed at such warnings and reminded
their elders that Manitoba was different. There were no trees to cut
down and no stumps to remove; the grassy plains were just waiting
for the plough. Then, in the winter of '78, Red Michael Lowery—a son
of the Mooneys' neighbours—returned from Manitoba. Now they had
a first-hand account from someone they knew. His praise for the
zesty, bawdy frontier was unlimited and the fever was catching. Will
Mooney became convinced that he was going to try his luck.

Will's decision is not surprising. More difficult to explain is the
decision that the whole family would go. Letitia Mooney did not
intend to see the family divided, and from original scepticism of the

glowing reports of the new country she became a convert to the idea that Manitoba would be the best place for all of them. Like other women who decided the West was the best place for their families, Letitia's participation in this process "is contrary to the notion that women did not affect decisions concerning their futures and the futures of their families."[11] Encouraging to her were the reports of the Presbyterian and Methodist missionaries telling of the new congregations springing up. One account spoke of fifty people turning up to hear a visiting missionary at Crystal City. The very next Sunday they met on their own to discuss building a church and having regular services.[12] Perhaps, too, she saw an opportunity to remove her boys from the temptations of the many taverns between Chatsworth and Owen Sound, although she could not have known then that they would settle outside the Manitoba borders in the prohibition area of the North-West.[13] She was certainly aware that it would not be an easy life, but she was not one to fear hard work. To Nellie's surprise her father was a more reluctant emigrant. For him, already in his late sixties, it was a hard decision to give up the farm he had worked so hard to create. Chatsworth was a settled district with schools and churches and Sunday schools. Why, therefore, should they leave all that for an unknown wilderness where they might be attacked by Indians and would certainly be eaten alive by mosquitoes? The boys, he felt, didn't know what it was like to start from nothing. But his wife's determination and Will's announcement that he was going with or without the family ended John Mooney's protests, and the great decision was made.

In the spring of 1879 Will—only nineteen years old—left for Manitoba. He was to find land for the family, who would follow the next summer. His letters kept them informed of his progress while they made preparations for their departure. When Will arrived in Winnipeg he wisely joined the surveying party of Caddy and Huston so that he could see for himself those areas that were being opened up.[14] Land was already becoming scarce in the southern Manitoba plain where much of it was held by speculators or as reserves. Besides, the wet years of 1876–78 had brought wide-spread flooding to the area, and many settlers were taking the north trail to the valley of the Whitemud. The optimism of these newcomers is revealed by the name of one of the principal settlements, Rapid City. Further south the high waters improved navigation on the Assiniboine so that the

steamer Marquette was able, for the first time, to pass through the
Sand Hills, the Grand Rapids above the mouth of the Souris River,
and reach Fort Ellice.[15] Through this event the agricultural possibilities of the great central plain became known and it was to this area,
the valley of the Souris beyond the Manitoba border, that Will
Mooney was drawn.

During the winter of 1879–80, Will Mooney, with a friend, Neil
Macdonald, lived in a log shanty in the Spruce Bush along Oak Creek,
and cut logs for houses and stables. Neither was accustomed to the
severity of the climate: frost split the trees and made them crack like
pistol-shots; wolves circled and howled about their camp; their horses,
though sheltered, died from the cold; and neither Will nor Macdonald
could keep warm though they kept their stove burning red-hot. They
had to walk more than thirty miles to Grand Valley to get their mail.[16]
Nevertheless, both men survived, and when spring came, so did many
settlers. Frank Burnett—who would soon become the Mooneys' nearest neighbour—came out from Montreal with his wife and two children: the oldest only twenty-two months. In March of 1880, he and
fifteen other western pioneers took the Qu'Appelle Trail west from
Winnipeg heading for Prince Albert, some four hundred miles distant.
He and his group soon realized that their oxen were already exhausted
by the heavy loads, and without long rest periods, would never reach
their destination in time to prepare the land for the next spring's
seeding. And the backbreaking labour of repeatedly unloading and
reloading the wagons in order to change from wheels to snow-runners,
and back again, was exhausting the men. Learning of Will's and Neil
Macdonald's winter camp, and of the "expanse of rich prairie country"
in that area, Burnett and another man—"an experienced agricultural-
ist from Ontario"—started south on the Yellow Quill Indian Trail,
braving late winter blizzards, in search of a new destination. Though
they carried with them enough provisions for ten days, they "paid
pretty dearly" for this error in judgement, for their trip lasted two
weeks. Will and Macdonald spent two days showing the area to the
newcomers, who resolved to stake out half-sections for themselves and
the others in their group for the rich black loam, they decided, was
"unsurpassed" for farming. Burnett bought logs from the boys for his
house, and returned for his family.

The group at Pine Creek—where Burnett had left his wife—had
increased enormously during his absence. "The departure of our

10

seventy-five teams . . . on the last lap of our trek," he records, was "quite an imposing sight." Included in his new party were "seven women . . . an undeterminate number of children," and a large number of men—either bachelors, or husbands preceding their families— "all eager to set eyes upon the 'Promised Land.'"[17] Once the heart-breaking toil of crossing the Assiniboine River was accomplished, they soon spread out over the newly opened territory, each making claim on the piece of land he found most attractive. The Mooneys would not lack neighbours when they arrived in the fall. Settlement had begun.

Meanwhile, the Mooney family was also en route. With characteristic foresight, Letitia Mooney had kept everyone busy that winter preparing for the years ahead: as much cloth as possible was woven; yarn was spun that would be knit into socks and stockings for several years; soap was made in double quantity. Goods were packed and repacked so that the largest number of useful articles would fill the least possible space. On 3 April 1880, John Mooney mortgaged his one-hundred-and-fifty-acre farm for one thousand dollars, Letitia freely signing away her dower rights and thereby all claim to the property upon John Mooney's death. By 5 April he had sold the property to a William Crawford who agreed to take over the mortgage and to pay Mooney an additional two hundred and forty dollars. Out of these proceeds John had to pay off what remained of a two-hundred-dollar mortgage secured on part of his farm in May of 1878.[18] With the additional sale of unnecessary chattels, and the remaining stock, crops, and farm equipment, the Mooneys started their western pioneer venture with over sixteen hundred dollars: a comfortable sum to outfit them once they reached Winnipeg. By May 1880, everything was ready and the Mooneys sailed from Owen Sound on the steamer *The City of Owen Sound*. Both the departure and the trip were a great adventure to a little girl who would soon turn eight, so it is not surprising that in the 1930s when she wrote the first volume of her autobiography, *Clearing in the West*, Nellie McClung remembered the highlights of the trip.

From Duluth the Mooneys travelled by train to St. Boniface, sleeping as comfortably as they could with their own blankets and pillows on the crowded day coach. Arriving there late one evening in May, they found that the only available accommodation was on the other side of the river, and it was too late for the ferry. They secured the use of a rowboat, however, and somehow seven people and their hand luggage were packed in and the boat's Métis owner, Timoleon Tait, made his way slowly to the other side, the water lapping dangerously close to the gunwales. To Letitia's horror they had to spend the night on the floor of a particularly dirty hotel, but next morning they moved to a tent on the riverbank at the junction of the Red and Assiniboine rivers. Here was a tent city where hundreds of settlers camped while deciding where to take up a homestead, or while gathering up their gear for the venture. And it was here that Nellie's family waited for Will, who arrived in three days full of glowing descriptions of the land he had chosen about three miles up Oak Creek near the Souris River. He had taken a half-section for his father, a half-section for himself, and a nearby quarter-section for George. Since there was no land office nearby where he could register these claims, he had written their names on the corner posts.[19] The prosaic description of the main farm—section 20, township 7, range 16—was countered by the family's sense of exuberance at their new and exciting beginning: "We had reached the Red River," Nellie says in her autobiography, "and the world was ours!"

Letitia didn't like the unsettled atmosphere of the riotous new tent city and, while she did not mind having Indian and Métis neighbours, the thought of those "jet black eyes and high cheek-bones" eventually turning up in her grandchildren caused her some concern. She preferred, therefore, to be part of an all-white settle-ment. Meantime John, with Will and George, went ahead to the homestead with all the supplies needed for housebuilding while Letitia and the children remained in a rented house in St. James, then five miles from Winnipeg. Nellie's new friends, Indian Tommy and the half-breed McMullen children, convinced Letitia of the wisdom of her decision. When Nellie innocently poured forth a blow-by-blow account of a fight on the riverbank between Mrs. Baggs and Indian Tommy's mother, she was restricted to playing in her own yard, safe from evil influences. Letitia was not idle while she waited for her husband's return. She and Jack planted and cared for a large garden, which would supply them with their vegetables for the winter. The mosquitoes, Nellie remembered, "were like all the plagues of the Old Testament." In spite of the garden produce, however, both Nellie and Hannah would suffer sore heels that winter from "not enough variety in their food."

In early September John and Will came for the family while George remained at the homestead. Within one week they would leave, and Nellie's excitement mounted. The children were taken to Winnipeg to buy sturdy new shoes. Nellie's had copper toes and were bought several sizes too large and stuffed with paper so that she could grow into them. Letitia might be making her first trek, but her practical nature ensured that the girls' clothing was suitable for the occasion. Some emigrants were not so wise. She had been busy that summer making an inventory of everything a family might need when cut off from supplies for many months—from a paper of pins to a stove. The men, too, now added to the tools they had already taken to the farm, and were preparing for every contingency along the trail with extra wagon parts, ropes and chains, shovels and axes. The Mooneys, like many western pioneers from Ontario, were starting their new life well equipped.

At sunrise, one Monday morning, the trek began. They had two wagons, each pulled by a team of oxen. In one wagon they packed the effects that would not be needed on the trip, all carefully secured so that nothing would shift on the roughest trail and covered with canvas so that rain or river water would not damage anything. In a covered wagon went all the necessities for the journey—even a bed made up in case of illness. When they reached High Bluff, they added to the procession a pony, a Red River cart, and a little black cow named Lady.

The 180-mile journey was less difficult in September than in the spring—as Frank Burnett could tell them—and they were blessed with good weather. Nevertheless, it took fourteen days and had its anxious moments. One day, for example, they made only one mile because they had to wait to be helped from a mudhole that proved too much even for their excellent oxen. It was "like a nightmare," Nellie remembered, "to see the oxen go down, down into the mud, sprawling helplessly in its treacherous depths." Sometimes it took three yokes of oxen to pull one wagon from the gumbo. Other days they managed as many as ten miles. Twice, along the trail, they called on other Chatsworth families who had preceded them to Manitoba, and were sent on their way with freshly baked food. The last stop for supplies was the Hudson's Bay store in Portage la Prairie, some eighty miles from the new homestead. "I believe my mother walked all the way," Nellie said later on, "for she liked to have her eye on the whole procession and she could only do this from the rear."

Some emigrants, too easily discouraged and beaten, lacked the courage, the hope, and resourcefulness of pioneer people. The Mooneys were rich in these virtues. Yet Nellie would recall that young Will, so burdened with the responsibility of bringing his family to an unknown country, would feel a thousand years roll away at the moment of their safe arrival. And the occasional grave marker at the side of the road was a stark reminder that tragedy was always near. They slept in a tent and ate in the open—rain or shine—and years later, at the time of Letitia Mooney's death, Will revealed that their mother dried John Mooney's socks on her own feet at night, for her husband was subject to severe bronchitis.[20] For the little girls, however, it was almost like a prolonged picnic. They could ride on the wagon or walk behind as they wished. For meals Will fried bacon and made coffee while their mother prepared bannock mixed in the mouth of the flour sack and fried in the bacon grease, a novelty enjoyed because it was part of the adventure. And although the mosquitoes were still biting, their mother had homemade "Balm of Gilhead" to soothe the itching.

After leaving Portage, the Mooneys left the main route and followed the Yellow Quill Trail southeast to their settlement. They passed through the high rolling country of the Sand Hills covered with light vegetation and raspberry brakes. Then they arrived at the steep bank of the clear blue Assiniboine. Here they paused to bathe, change their clothes, and rest overnight. The next day they forged the river, always a tense moment, but there was a good gravelly bottom and all went well. By noon "the last barrier was passed," and the long journey was over.

> No one could fail to be thrilled with the pleasant spot that Will had found for us. A running stream circled the high ground on which the log house stood. Away to the south, hazy in the distance, stood the Tiger Hills; to the northwest the high shoulder of the Brandon Hills, dark blue and mysterious, enticed the eye. Near the house there were clumps of willows on the bank of the creek and poplar bluffs dotted the prairie north of us.

Stretching to the north the country was flat and just waiting for the plough. But for Ontario folk used to trees and the hills of Grey County, this was a less frightening landscape than that faced by many pioneers: flat, unending prairie stretching as far as the eye could see. Nevertheless, Letitia Mooney had hardly set foot on their new land before she was busy deciding where to plant the Manitoba

Maple seeds she had brought from Winnipeg that would, in time, grow into the trees a house must have before it becomes a home.

A lifetime later while writing *The Stream Runs Fast* (1945), the second volume of her autobiography—and writing it swiftly, for she sensed her life drawing to its close—Nellie McClung looked back from her comfortable home at Lantern Lane on Vancouver Island, and recorded in memorable lines the southwestern Manitoba country of her childhood. It was, simultaneously, the country of her dreams and the harsh country of their pioneer reality. It was, for her, "the sting of frost, and the horror of being lost in a blizzard." It held an awesome "cold" and a terrible "loneliness," and its sudden, killing changes of weather could alter "a farmer's financial status . . . in twenty minutes." This prairie of Nellie's pioneer days was "a hard country," and it called upon "the sturdy of many lands" to tame it. But it was, too, a fine and splendid land "with its poplar groves, and great wheat fields," and its sudden springs, which brought "the first notes of the meadow lark, and . . . blue anemones carpet the pastures and headlands, and the whole countryside comes alive almost overnight."

> That was, and always will be, my country. I was one of the children who found the pussy willows, and listened for the first meadow lark, and made little channels with a hoe to let the spring water find its way to the creek, and ran swift as rabbits when the word went round that the ice was going out of the Souris, and cried if we missed it!
>
> I lay on the grassy banks in summer, and saw castles in the clouds, and dreamed great dreams of the future. I built my own raft to carry me down the creek—a raft which sometimes held, and sometimes sank—I never knew why . . . These I remember.[21]

2

Growing Up Near Millford

❖

The house to which the Mooneys came was a great deal simpler than the comfortable home they had left in Grey County. It was a log house, not well chinked, with one window facing west. "One window might be thought insufficient for a house that must lodge eight people," wrote Nellie, "but light and air came in unbidden through many openings, indeed how to keep out cold became our great problem." According to their neighbour, Frank Burnett, the pioneer method of solving this problem at freeze-up was "by throwing water all over the outside which, by immediately freezing, made [the chinks] absolutely wind proof."[1] It is likely that the Mooneys did the same, though this would not prevent water from freezing inside the house, and Nellie records that "the bed clothes were often frozen to my hair."[2] The extreme dampness inside the house that would result from the spring thaw must have been even more unpleasant. Since shingles were unavailable at that time, John Mooney, familiar with thatched roofs in Ireland, resourcefully contrived a satisfactory roof "with prairie hay," though he had never made one before. Unlike the earthen floor of many settlers' houses, the Mooneys' floor was made of rough lumber. Their stove stood in the centre of the house in order to heat all areas equally. When the furniture was unpacked from the wagon, the curtains hung at the window, the colourful quilts placed on the homemade bedsteads—"made of poplar poles and spread with planks to hold the feather ticks"—when the stove was set in place and the room filled with the smell of baking bread, the little log house sitting at the top of the hill and overlooking the wide prairie began to seem like home.

The good weather that autumn enabled the men to break the sod and back set it for spring planting. Before winter they also had a shelter ready for the animals. But this pleasant beginning was quickly followed by a very severe winter with temperatures as low as 58 below zero[3] and snow as deep as six feet on the level. At first the Mooneys had contact with neighbours, for even in December Frank Burnett, their nearest neighbour only three miles away, brought his wife for a visit travelling on a homemade bobsled pulled by an ox.[4] But in the New Year the snow got deeper and deeper, and only Will and George were able to get out using the one pair of snowshoes that Will owned. Even when the men in that area were able to move about outside, however, keeping the households supplied with firewood became a difficult, time-consuming task, for the wood "had to be procured from the banks of the Souris from three to six miles distant, according to where the settler was located, so that not more than one load could be procured and cut up daily."[5] One night in mid-December the Mooneys' little black cow, Lady, trapped her horns in the poplar poles that enclosed the hay. Trying to extricate herself she fell, broke her neck, and froze to death. This tragic event, which deprived the family of butter and milk as well as a beloved family pet, made Nellie aware of the cruelty of the country to which they had come, for her sensitive nature recoiled from the grotesque, misshapen bulk that Lady had become, with her "horribly staring eyes." "The ground, iron hard with frost, could not be dug to bury her . . . And the nights that followed were terrible when the wolves fought and cursed and cried over her . . . and they seemed to come from the four corners of the world, snarling, snapping, hungry ghouls, grey, lean and terrible." Long after the last bone was gnawed clean the wolves returned again and again like some dreadful scourge hoping, Nellie thought, "that some other evil thing had befallen us." Elsewhere in her writings, Nellie speaks of trying to make people "understand the number of wolves we used to see" at that time in the West. "They came in hundreds," and raced over the rolling, moonlit hills as numerous as "the waves of the sea."[6] This brutal event involving a family pet was one that such a child would never forget.

March of 1881 brought blizzards, and the Mooneys were completely cut off from even the nearest neighbours. During this period of isolation, Nellie's oldest sister, Lizzie, fell gravely ill. Although their mother possessed many healing skills, all were tried in vain, and even the strong-willed Letitia Mooney felt defeated by a country that seemed accursed for the white man. For her, this moment was the Indians' revenge. As she watched, helpless, knowing that the nearest doctor was eighty miles away, Lizzie's condition grew worse: "She had reached a state of coma, her jaws were locked, and her eyes though still open, did not see." But help did come, and it seemed a miracle. The Reverend Thomas Hall, a Methodist minister who had recently come to nearby Millford, and was, as yet, a stranger to the Mooneys, arrived unexpectedly at the door. He had both medicine and medical skill and, like Will Mooney, he had snowshoes to get about when others couldn't travel. He stayed for three days, treating Lizzie's illness until she began to recover. This incident, too, remained in Nellie's mind as an example of the value of the church in the pioneer community, and as an answer to a mother's prayer.

When spring came and the prairie blossomed with its colourful display of wildflowers and the land, rich and black, was ready for seeding, the misgivings of the winter months disappeared. The Mooneys had arrived in the district with the first wave of rapid settlement, and during the next spring and summer the wives of those men who had come the summer before began to arrive; and many other families, most of them from Ontario, poured into the valley and into the areas to the east and west. Towns soon emerged to serve the rural hinterland. Treherne, Manitou, and Carberry, for example, all give their founding dates as 1880–83. Near the Mooneys, the town of Millford began to develop just five miles from their farm at the junction of Oak Creek and the Souris River. Major Rogers, of Cobourg, Ontario, had drawn up plans for a sizeable town there at what he hoped would become a railroad junction. He built a saw mill and a flour mill, the government established a Registry Office, and soon there was a general store, a blacksmith shop, a boarding house, and a cobbler's. When the settlers in the area gathered the next summer and built a church in Millford with the help of the Methodist Home Mission Board, the Mooneys felt that civilization was indeed coming to the area. It was a confident and optimistic community that gathered in the new church for a harvest home festival in the fall of 1882. The new settlers were determined to create another Ontario on the open prairie, where the best features of British civilization would take root and flourish.[7]

The farm, too, seemed to fulfil the expectations of even the optimistic Will. Year by year the amount of land under cultivation on both Will's and his father's farms increased. Like most of the Ontario farmers, the Mooneys did not depend on grain alone. The first summer Will walked eighty miles to Portage to bring back two cows, and gradually they increased the herd. They raised chickens, ducks, turkeys, and pigs, and maintained a large vegetable garden. Of course, wheat soon became their main cash crop and then the difficulties of hauling grain thirty miles by horse and wagon to the new town of Brandon became an obstacle. By 1882 the Canadian Pacific Railway had been extended only that far west, and branch lines had not yet been financed to bring market outlets closer to local grain producers. As an adult Nellie McClung could write only with indignation as she recalled the western farmers' agitation at that time over the federal government railway policy.

> I knew the government at Ottawa had promised the Canadian Pacific Railway Company that no other railway would be allowed to come into Canada for twenty years. American companies were ready to come, but they could not get permission. We wanted them. It was our country! We were doing the work, but we were powerless.

Even after the long, tiring haul to Brandon and, at times, the added expense of overnight accommodation, the farmer had to waste valuable time in the long line of wagons at the elevator where he also felt unfairly at the mercy of the agent. In 1883, the CPR placed a minimum capacity of twenty-five thousand bushels on all elevators and warehouses on its line, thus, virtually creating a local "monopoly" situation since so large a size would prevent more than one or two companies from servicing any one town. Competitive prices, therefore, were nonexistent, and the farmers frequently suspected that the agents deliberately gave their wheat a lower grade than it deserved.[8]

Another source of western animosity at this time was connected with the federal government tariff barrier as it concerned farm machinery. In 1883, for example, John Mooney and Will decided to buy a binder to enable them to harvest more economically what promised to be a bumper crop. Machinery from Ontario was, with tariff protection, underselling that from the United States and, persuaded by an eloquent salesman who offered "a special concession to any neighborhood that would buy six binders," John Mooney, with many other farmers in the Millford district, bought their machines from an Ontario firm. They soon learned, however, that binders that performed well in Ontario were not adapted to the conditions of western farming as, for example, American binders built for the western United States were. "In the West the harvest came on with a terrible urgency. Everything depended upon speed, and the machinery was worked full blast from dawn at five o'clock to dusk at nine-thirty."[9] The Ontario binders were unable to stand up to the strain of normal western usage, and part after part gave way. While the company had—in good faith—promised that a supply of replacement parts would be left with the local Millford dealer, they had failed to anticipate the number of parts sufficient to meet the extraordinary demand. The result was that the farmer lost precious harvest days and often needed sleep for himself and rest for one of the horses who pulled the binder when trips to a more distant centre had to be made for the necessary part.

Far from attempting to see reason in the farmers' protests, the company believed that these farmers, unused to the equipment, were misusing it and they did not hesitate to tell them so in their caustic replies to letters of complaint. "My face burns," Nellie said, "thinking of the insults they hurled at us." Not surprisingly manufacturers of farm machinery were added to the list of eastern opportunists, joining the CPR, the elevator companies, and those eastern and American land speculators who had brought about the Winnipeg real estate boom-and-bust of 1881–82. "Lots sold and resold, without having been seen or surveyed," Nellie records, and "we heard of real estate offices opened in livery stables; money kept in tin pails and baskets, weighed down with horseshoes . . . " It seemed that "the whole population had caught the fever." By mid-summer the boom broke, and many Manitobans had lost money. "There is no doubt," says Nellie McClung, "that this spectacular boom, and its complete collapse, marked the beginning of the ill feeling between the East and the West."[10]

Many farmers—particularly the younger ones—rapidly became "westerners" in their animosity toward the eastern-based source of what they increasingly saw as deliberate abuse and exploitation. The farmers of Manitoba began organizing. In December of 1883 at the first provincial convention of the Manitoba Farmers' Protective Union, they drew up a Bill of Rights demanding provincial control of public lands as in other provinces, the lowering of tariffs, an end to the CPR monopoly and the grain "monopoly," along with the construction of branch railway lines. When the second conference of 1884 occurred, however, some extremists advocated the secession of Manitoba from Canada to the United States, and recommended an end to immigration until these grievances were settled.[11] In the minds of conservative people like John Mooney and his wife, these two ideas were almost equally treasonable. John had been a Conservative in Ontario, and remained one in Manitoba. He chose, therefore, to support the Conservative federal government policy regarding the CPR monopoly—at least as a temporary measure—and despite his neighbours' appeals, he did not support the Farmers' Protective Union. He must have felt justified in his stand when the union supported the provincial Liberal Party when Manitoba politics became partisan.[12] Although John Mooney readily understood the grievances being expressed, it was difficult for him to be seriously discontented when he compared his success in Manitoba with the many years of slow progress on his farm in Grey County. The number and size of his cultivated fields grew, a team of horses was added to the oxen, and up-to-date machinery for the farm was now economically viable.

After 1882 the Mooneys no longer lived in their small cabin. For two years logs had been gathered and squared; lumber for finishing the walls and shingles for the roof were purchased in Brandon; and on a lovely summer day the neighbours gathered for a house-raising. In Ontario, as Nellie records, pioneer "'barn raisins' were often accompanied by liquor drinking, and sometimes accidents and fights occurred as a result, but there was nothing of this at ours" where plenty of good food was set out and good will prevailed. The new house had "a big room downstairs, a bedroom for father and mother, a real stairs, and two bedrooms above, and a large kitchen with two windows and a pantry." For the first few years the kitchen could be used only in summer since, during the winter months, the stove was moved to the main room, which became the living room in the full sense of that word. Later a storm porch, storm windows, and a new layer of boards for the kitchen made it possible to use both rooms all year round and a second heating stove was purchased for the living room. Lace curtains, hand-knit, hung at the front-room windows, and handmade carpets, one hooked and one braided, decorated the floor. As money became more plentiful these attractive rugs were replaced by a carpet "full of scrolls and flowers of great beauty" and the windows received chintz curtains and blinds. Nellie remembered with pleasure the lovely silk eiderdown on her parents' bed—gold on one side and flowered with red geraniums on the other. The house did not lack for colour. In front of the house flower beds—edged with white buffalo bones—were laid, and seeds brought from Ontario were planted: magnolia, portulaca, and balsam.

Northfield School, two miles from the Mooney farm, was completed in the summer of 1883, and Nellie began her schooling that fall. She records that she had run "wild on the prairie for three years,"[13] and now, almost ten years old, felt ashamed that she could not read. Although members of the family had offered to teach her, Nellie had stubbornly refused instruction except for the limited accomplishment of learning to count to one hundred. Now, however, her self-acknowledged ignorance led her to fear humiliation. Fortunately, the teacher at the new school—a Mr. Schultz who had taken a homestead only fifteen miles away at Pelican Lake—was an understanding man. He assured Nellie that she would quickly catch up and helped her to do so. His genuine sympathy, when she had expected criticism, made Nellie feel that a "compact was sealed" between them, and that "another door had opened" in her life—an image she would use with increasing frequency in her autobiography. She would soon learn, too, that knowledge not only unlocked doors previously closed to her, but that it also "gave liberty." The desire for freedom, in fact, is a significant theme in her record of her childhood years: freedom from the petty economies practised in her home, freedom from the restrictive attitudes of her mother regarding the role of the female in society, freedom from the feeling that the private motives for her behaviour were publicly misunderstood by her family. In addition, her keen desire to learn was increased by rivalry with a more "provident" classmate named Annie Adams, who excelled in schoolwork, wore more fashionable "boughten" clothes, and mocked Nellie with this fact. "She would rue the day she taunted me!" Nellie said later, remembering her bitter feelings of that time. The practical result was that by the next spring Nellie was reading the Third Book, and sometimes being "offensively proud" of her accomplishments.

The school inspector's report for 1885 indicates that Northfield School "shows well to the front and reflects much credit on the teacher, Mr. Frank Schultz."[14] While the emphasis was on the 3-Rs and a little geography and history,[15] Schultz appears to have inspired receptive students like Nellie with a love for literature. He was also remarkable in other ways. He taught the children to think independently, and to express themselves. During the North-West Rebellion of 1885, for example, he presented to his students a remarkably enlightened explanation of the events. To the horror of the adults, Hannah and Nellie defended the Métis, trying to explain to their parents that the Métis had been neglected, that the government in Ottawa had failed to answer their legitimate grievances much as they had failed to listen to the requests of the Manitoba farmers, and that the Métis were frustrated just as the farmers had been frustrated when they were ignored by the farm implement manufacturers. Although their father recognized the truth in their arguments, Nellie remembered "a sudden tightening of the atmosphere." Years later she understood the meaning of this: "Even now, men do not like to be taught by women, but at that time for a girl of fifteen [Hannah] to presume to have an opinion, was against all tradition." And when Nellie, three years younger than Hannah, wished to be heard in the argument, she had to brave her mother's protests. Manuscript variations of this episode for Chapter Eighteen of *Clearing in the West* show Nellie speaking only a few sentences in support of Hannah. A second version extends Nellie's contribution and is closer to the published version. The implication is that Nellie would, at times, develop and dramatize her role in events much as if she were writing fiction.[16] The adult response was that Schultz was sowing dangerous, un-British attitudes at Northfield School, and that something should be done about it. Letitia Mooney threatened to go to the school trustees if nobody else did, and Nellie—knowing her mother's determination and her unreasonable set of mind in this matter—became so worried about the probable effect on her beloved Schultz that she could neither eat nor sleep for days. Torn between loyalty to the facts and loyalty to her mother, Nellie ultimately learned that deserting the parent, in this sense, was precisely "what Christ meant when he said that is just what you have to do if you swear allegiance to the truth. But I knew I wasn't ready for this." One day she would be. In the meantime it was Schultz himself who resolved the crisis with his good sense and tact during an amicable visit with Mrs. Mooney. "Looking back," Nellie said, "I wonder what power nineteenth century parents had over their children and how did they hold it. I was not a particularly meek young person, but I could not stand up to my mother, even knowing that she was wrong."

Nellie had also learned from Schultz sufficient independent thinking to question the way in which her history text ignored the common people and "what they were doing and thinking," while only the kings and prime ministers were deciding issues and making wars. His criticism pointed toward the later development of what is now loosely called "the new social history" with its emphasis on ordinary people and everyday lives. In a manuscript version of Hannah's argument against the federal government's mishandling of the Riel Rebellion is the following ironic passage—if not strictly a sentiment of the young Nellie, then certainly a reflection of her adult thought:

> But Kings and rulers have always welcomed war. You can see that all through history. It gives the young men something to do, something adventurous and thrilling, and keeps everyone from thinking about it. The people who make war do not have to risk their own skins. So it works out nicely.[17]

Even as a child, then, Nellie was certain that the common people were not so happy and contented as they were sometimes made to appear by their absence from the textbooks. Years later, as a novelist, she longed to appeal to these common people. At the same time, living in a pioneer time and a prairie place where history was in the making, young Nellie Mooney was not immune to the harsher realities of life about her, and she possessed the sensitivity and intelligence to draw significant parallels between the past and the present as Schultz had taught her.

In the summer of 1889, after only six years of formal education, Nellie wrote for her Second Class Certificate—"considered high academic achievement in those days"[18]—but in Brandon, where she wrote examinations in eight subjects during one week in July, she felt less well prepared in algebra than the city-educated students: "So many questions contained words I had never heard." The implication may be that Schultz prepared his students better in subjects like history, literature, grammar, and composition. Nevertheless, she had acquired skills that enabled her to cope with the Normal School curriculum, and she remembered with gratitude the influence that Frank Schultz had had on her young mind. In a newspaper article of 1913 she recorded that Frank Schultz "always planned a great future for me, and made me think well of myself. He and his wife now live in Baldur, Manitoba, where he is a bank manager, and they are two of my dearest friends."[19] Nellie was fortunate in having had Schultz as her teacher for the full six years of her schooling. Unlike most teachers, who stayed for only a brief period in the little prairie schools, he was a homesteader in a nearby area and taught to supplement his income. Schultz also gave every encouragement to Hannah, who was an exceptional student, but in those times school teaching was considered the only suitable occupation for young girls like Hannah and Nellie. Apparently neither one ever thought of the possibility of attending university in spite of the fact that a professor from the new college in Winnipeg lectured in Millford on the educational opportunities in the college for both boys and girls. Indeed, the chances of a farm girl going to university at that time were very slim. As an adult, however, Hannah earned her B.A. from the University of Manitoba.[20] On the other hand, although none of the boys went on to any higher education, both Hannah and Nellie were encouraged and supported in their scholastic endeavours. As the youngest, they had opportunities not available to the others, whose lives were more controlled by the demands of the farm.

The story of the developing West is a success story, but it was also marked by serious hardships as well as petty irritations. In southern Manitoba where the Mooneys lived, the spring of 1882 brought flood waters, cutting the farm off once again. Then came several years of dry summers and early frosts. In 1886 some settlers in that area experienced drought and prairie fires. That year, too, saw a drop in the price of wheat. Even though the Mooneys were among the most successful farmers of the district,[21] Nellie recalled—with some bitterness—that they were never free from "acid little economies." Lamps could not remain lit after homework was done, so that reading time was limited. New clothes were infrequent enough to remain vividly in her memory. Old clothes were dyed and made over. One of Nellie's bitter memories was of scarlet bloomers in her last year of school made from cloth that had been dyed with rag floor mats, rather than bloomers, in mind. She asserted, however, that these bloomers did have the beneficial side effect of increasing her scholarship, because she stayed in the schoolhouse reading, for fear that during an active game of "shinny" the other children might catch a glimpse of them. Her homespun coat was also a humiliation to her, particularly since the three girls had started from Owen Sound with identical green coats that Nellie had to wear one after the other until she had outgrown even Lizzie's. At the time of their move west, Letitia had been asked not to bring her loom or her spinning wheel, and Nellie remembered her mother saying, "Will was against it—he said we were getting away from all this. I know how the young people feel too, though it hurts me to see it. They are a little bit ashamed of home-made stuff. They want machine-made clothes. They are dressier and more the style." As an adult, of course, this interest in being suitably dressed—especially during public appearances—did much to counter the negative stereotype of the feminist and suffragist as a masculine woman who dressed like a frump. Those who had never met Nellie McClung were frequently surprised to find her a gracious woman with a pleasant voice and a very attractive, stylish appearance. The Saskatchewan feminist Violet McNaughton, for one, particularly noted that McClung was not uppity with the more plainly dressed farm women.[22]

Every member of the family had to play a part in the success of the pioneer venture. Will and George, of course, worked as full-time farmers from the beginning, helping to establish both their father's farm and their own. Jack, too, took on a man's work at an early age. When the Northfield School opened, he was only fourteen and might have attended, but after three years away from a classroom he had no desire to go back and pleaded the necessity of his full-time contribution to the farm work. Later on, he would confess to Nellie his regret for this childhood choice. The girls—like many other females of the time—did the housework and cooking with their mother, looked after the hens, weeded the garden, milked the cows, and, in winter, brought loads of snow to the kitchen to be melted for water. Unlike her sisters, however, Nellie also engaged in some tasks normally left to the men. In the autumn of her twelfth year, for example, she "trapped thirteen mink" and tanned one of the hides herself. This she considered one of her "proudest achievements."[23] Lizzie was particularly skilful with her needle and made many of their clothes. Nellie, too, would learn responsibility while very young. One of her tasks was to close the henhouse door at night. On one occasion, after she was in bed, she realized that she had carelessly forgotten. Terrified both of the dark and of what she might find as a result of her thoughtlessness, she crept out of bed, down the stairs, and across the dark farmyard. As she approached the henhouse she tripped over her beloved dog Nap, who was guarding the door. Greatly relieved she secured it and hurried back to bed. This chore was not a minor one in those days, and Nellie knew how deprived the family diet could be without eggs to eat or bake with. In the fall of 1882 a weasel had burrowed into the henhouse and killed their entire flock of chickens and laying hens. The Mooneys were without eggs until spring, when a helpful neighbour organized a "chicken shower" for their benefit. It is not surprising that this duty weighed heavily on Nellie's young mind.

> Responsibility is no doubt good for a child, for one has to learn sooner or later to take it. The hen-house door was my first big assignment and certainly left its mark on me. For years after I grew up and was away from the scenes of my childhood, I would waken from sleep in a panic of fright. Had I closed the hen-house door?

Nap's behaviour, on this occasion, made him even more beloved to Nellie than before. So much so that she shielded him from certain death when she discovered him, with a neighbour's dog, chasing the cows and tearing at their tails. "Tail biting was the unforgiveable sin in a dog" for "bob-tailed cattle would not sell for as much." In that community, any dog with this habit was considered "a low bred cur" fit only to be shot. Young Nellie decided that a lie was necessary to save Nap's life, for if her father—who "loved every animal on the place"—would find it difficult to kill Nap, her mother, Nellie knew, "would take the practical view, and set aside her feelings" in the matter. She knew that her action was neither admirable nor entirely truthful. Her guilt about lying was stronger than it might have been because Nap's misdeed occurred when Nellie was supposed to be carrying out her allotted chore as cattle-herder. Since the fields were not fenced, someone had to watch and keep the stock out of the grain. Ordinarily Nellie preferred such outside chores in contrast with the domestic tasks inside the house, but this quickly turned to resentment when her job required her to miss school in the fall before the grain was harvested. At these times Nellie hated the cows and wished to be free of them, for she was eager to learn, and her competitive attitude toward Annie Adams made her dread falling behind. At the time of Nap's misdeed, Nellie had been preoccupied with arithmetic lessons for Hannah to mark at the end of the day. Then, when Jack suggested that Nellie might be lying to save Nap, Letitia stoutly defended her honesty, to Nellie's further shame. Shortly she would feel "an agony of remorse" when Nap was severely wounded while fighting a boar. Had her lie merely saved Nap for pain and suffering? She sat up all night watching over her apparently dying dog. The next day Nellie appeared to her mother to be very tired: "I never thought you took anything hard; for you are Irish, like your father and light-hearted, but you mustn't worry over what you can't help. Animals will fight; their instinct drives them." The cheery morning fire in the kitchen stove, the kettle boiling, and her mother's solicitude brought some balance to Nellie's black thoughts of the previous night. The mature Nellie records:

> I couldn't put it into words, but some glimmering of life's plan swept across my mind. Sorrow and joy, pain and gladness, triumph and defeat were in that plan, just as day and night, winter and summer, cold and heat, tears and laughter. We couldn't refuse it, we must go on.

The child who vaguely sensed these things became the woman who lived them, who articulated and recorded them, and who, at times, has been accused of easy optimism. The fact is, however, that the spirit of hope which later inspired her fiction and her life's work was not won easily. It is more accurate to say of Nellie McClung that she saw life steadily and saw it whole, in both its comic and its tragic dimensions. She saw, too, a needed antidote to the pain of life: "Work! That was life's remedy. Not philosophy or explanations. There was no formula, no answer to the old problems. But we could go on, we had to go on." This strategy of hope, based on courage and hard work, was part and parcel of the pioneer spirit and one of its most important lessons. It was also a fundamental part of her own disposition, which developed somewhere between the two extremes of her mother's stern Scottish Calvinism and her father's joyful Irish humour. Certainly it also formed an essential part of her mature Christian religion whose central doctrine on the resurrection taught that optimistic hope was as valid an emotion as pessimism, and considerably more constructive for it might direct one's work toward bettering whatever had caused the pain.

For Nellie McClung, then, "there were bright spots in life's pattern" as well as tragedy, and she was conscious of this duality even as a child. Nap did not die. Nellie was allowed to stay home from school for a week to care for him, and as Nap's health and spirit returned, Nellie's burden of guilt was lifted. "I never could be gloomy in the sunshine," she says.

Life, of course, was not all farm work and school work, and Nellie recalled many of the social events that were an integral part of her pioneer community. There was the annual 1st of July picnic, a fun-filled occasion with races, games, and plenty of good food—even unfamiliar treats like bananas and chocolates. Unfortunately, the second picnic, in the summer of 1882, was spoiled by the boys in the Brandon Band who brought liquor. During the slow ox race, the rider on the Mooneys' favourite little ox—under the influence of alcohol—broke the rules by viciously spurring the animal until its sides ran with blood. Crazed by this unfamiliar treatment, the ox plunged madly off the course nearly smashing into Nellie and the baby she was caring for.

> That was my first direct contact with the liquor business and coming so early in life, it left a mark . . . I know there is a pleasant aspect to this matter of drinking, and when many people think of it they see the sunkissed vineyards . . . the happy people . . . the wine that cheers . . . I think of none of these things. I remember a good day spoiled; peaceful neighbours suddenly grown quarrelsome, and feel again a helpless blinding fear, and see blood dyeing the side of a dumb beast.

This incident strongly affected everyone present, and the next summer, no one had the heart to organize the community picnic.

Often, on such occasions, another issue proved far more puzzling to young Nellie. The "question of girls competing in races was frowned upon. Skirts would fly upward and legs would show!" Nellie was an active, and at times, competitive child, and the Victorian attitude that denied her a natural outlet for vigorous play was frustrating. Recognizing in any case, that her long dress was an impediment, she thoughtfully offered to remove it and run in her underwear. When she asked why little girls should not show their legs, she was abruptly silenced. Here, as on many other similar occasions that set an arbitrary limit on the activities of girls, she repeatedly met a "stone wall . . . that baffled me." It was her mother, in particular, who held to these very proper Victorian distinctions, and Nellie would learn to resent that many of the freedoms and privileges her brothers enjoyed were arbitrarily denied to her because of her sex. Later on, as a young adult boarding with the McClung family, Nellie was profoundly struck by the discovery that both male and female McClung children shared the same duties and privileges. Meanwhile, the feeling that she was somewhat imprisoned in her family environment increased.

29

Dances, too, became an important part of the social life of the community. When they began, at the boarding house in Millford, Nellie was too young to go, but both Will and George went and soon Lizzie was allowed to go with her brothers. Unfortunately Lizzie froze her feet on the way to one dance. No doubt pride had won out over warm footwear. Years later, when asked by Nellie to read and criticize the manuscript of *Clearing in the West,* Lizzie asked her sister to omit this passage that embarrassed her. Noting that she and her two brothers had walked the five miles to Millford, she also records that she did not dance that evening. "My feet were frozen going to the party, and Dave Young drove us all home in the morning because I could not walk. My feet were so swollen [that] I had on moccasins and sox of his" for the trip back."[24] Thus it is that Nellie, with irrepressible humour as well as kindness, set her tongue firmly in her cheek, and recorded that "they drove the oxen, in a sleigh, and were well covered with blankets and robes." There were, of course, many other dances and social occasions to follow, and by the time Will built his house and had a house-warming dance Nellie, too, was allowed to attend. Her father, who did not approve of round dancing, taught her some fancy steps for the reels, and she had a chance to perform these in the quadrille when the caller commanded "dance to your partner and corner the same." For a few minutes all eyes were on the young Nellie who thoroughly enjoyed the attention, but her mother, as always, disapproved of what she called "boldness," and Nellie was banished to the second storey to look after the babies.

Amateur school plays were also performed, often with Nellie in the leading role. On one occasion, she and a group of her schoolfriends produced T.S. Arthur's melodramatic "Ten Nights in a Bar-room," Nellie taking the role of "poor Fanny Morgan, the drunkard's wife." The play, acted with considerable gusto and ingenuity, created great hilarity. It would also help satisfy the needs of a personality that evidently required the limelight. The underlying cause of this may have been that in a busy household largely composed of adults, Nellie did not—or felt she did not—receive a fair share of family attention. Perhaps, too, it was her instinctive response to the growing feeling of being held down by her mother's restrictive attitudes. Such theatrical activity likely served to channel constructively Nellie's comic disposition and her sometimes questionable tendency to dramatize herself. These amateur plays also served as an organized extension of the wildly romantic dramas that Hannah and Nellie, as children, both concocted and enacted.

In St. James, for example, near Winnipeg, where Letitia and the children stayed until the homestead was ready for them, Nellie and Hannah, from their bedroom window, overlooked "the beautiful manor house" of Sir Donald A. Smith, chief factor in charge of Hudson's Bay Company affairs in North America. The arrival of carriages bringing "brilliantly dressed people" to dance in "the enchanted ballroom" fired the girls' already vivid imaginations. "We named them," Nellie says, "and wove romances about them." Stock characters with names like Lorelie and Sir Hector struggled through the intricacies of melodramatic plots freighted with unrequited love and sudden fortunes. They managed to be prodigal with some romantic fantasies and "carried along the story with endless epi-sodes"—to some extent an apprenticeship for her later writing career. And yet these children, never far from the harsher realities of pioneer life, conferred lumbago on Sir Hector who was made "a little stiff in the back." Bible stories, too, "flamed into reality with us. Rehoboam and Jeroboam walked with us as we crossed the prairie with our dinner pails . . . " Myth and reality existed side by side. "We could see how jealousy ate up Saul and the story of his throwing the spear at David was so well dramatized one day at noon that Billy Day nearly lost an eye." Later, when Louis Riel—leader of the Métis rebellion in the West—was sentenced to be hanged, Nellie and her friends who sympathized with the Métis planned to dramatize the expected moment of reprieve in Northfield schoolyard: "We had read about reprieves and a very thrilling business it was with a dishevelled rider on a foaming horse galloping up to the foot of the gallows waving a document and shouting 'The pardon of the King.'" Never one to leave the romantic or sentimental pose unpunctured by pedestrian reality, Nellie undermines the fantasy drama by means of Hannah's laconic statement that galloping horses were out of date: "The pardon would come by telegraph if it came at all." The stark fact of Riel's execution, however, was the harshest reality undercutting this romantic interlude: "We were shocked into silence," Nellie says tersely, "and we stopped talking about it."

No doubt the romantic tendency of Nellie's young mind was influenced by the romantic extravaganzas appearing in the Montreal *Family Herald*, to which the Mooneys subscribed. As was often the case in pioneer times, such meagre and exotic fiction was eagerly sought and read with avidity, perhaps because it relieved the harsh realities of their daily existence. Since Nellie had trained Nap as a sleigh dog—using a sled made for her by a neighbour, and a harness she devised herself from scraps of leather—each Saturday, in winter, she would travel by dogsled the five miles to Millford to get the mail, including the *Family Herald*, as well as more necessary supplies. As the *Family Herald* serial "was really the high point of interest," Nellie records, "we had a whole week to speculate on the development of the plot," and Nellie sometimes caused considerable irritation in her family who waited impatiently as she staggered along "through the snow . . . reading the story" as she walked. When she drew near home members of the family would come out and shout at her to hurry. Nellie vividly remembered one romantic tale from the *Herald* that was typical of this early fiction she was nurtured on. "It shook our neighbourhood to its foundations," she said with ironic relish, one eye on the tale's exciting intrigue and the other on its absurdities.

> It was called *Saved, or the Bride's Sacrifice*, and concerned two beautiful girls,—Jessie, fair as a lily, and Helen with blue black hair and lustrous eyes as deep as night. They each loved Herbert, and Herbert, being an obliging young fellow, not wishing to hurt anyone's feelings, married one secretly and hurriedly by the light of a guttering candle, in a peasant's hut, (Jessie), and one openly with peal of organ and general high jinks, at her father's baronial castle, (Helen).
>
> This naturally brought on complications. There were storms and shipwrecks, and secret meetings in caves, with the tide rising over the rocks and curlews screaming in the blast; there were plottings and whisperings, a woman with second sight and one with the evil eye. And did we love it?

Such tales held all the stock ingredients of the most improbable romantic and sensational fiction of the day and Nellie McClung, recording them in the 1930s for her and our amusement, reveals that in her maturity she was well aware that they were out of touch with reality as she knew it. Nor is it without self-conscious artistry that she cunningly set this account of the *Family Herald* and its elegant absurdities against the romanticized response of some of the young men in the Millford area to their role in the Métis uprising in the North-West Territories. "Every wild scheme was advocated": a fort should be built at Millford and stocked with flour and bacon in case of a siege; the men should have their guns loaded and shoot to kill. Against these exciting romantic scenarios the practical, down-to-earth Letitia Mooney advised her younger children not to listen to such "clatter." The young men, she said, were simply "having a good time . . . Jack Naismith and our Jack are killing Indians by the dozen in their minds and piling them up like cordwood and it's not hurting anyone." These young men—like the children who dramatized Riel's reprieve—were falsely converting the drab realities of their frontier existence into thrilling romantic adventure. And if, as a consequence, young Nellie dreamed of "shrieking savages with burning brands in their hands" come to massacre the Mooneys, a still small voice inside her said that "Hannah would talk them out of it, and mother would make tea for them and feed them currant buns." Soon after, Indians did come to the Millford area. They came as peacefully as they came every spring: to sell baskets. Letitia Mooney did indeed feed them tea and buttered bread. She also rubbed goose grease on a sick Indian baby, treated the sore ear of one Sioux woman with laudanum, and amicably sent them on to the next farmstead. In her autobiography, by skilfully setting the improbabilities of romance in the *Family Herald* against the highly exaggerated Indian adventures concocted in the Millford area, Nellie McClung tacitly let the absurdities of romantic fiction comment upon the unreal flights of fancy that these young Manitoba pioneers had cultivated. It reveals that a solid core of no-nonsense practicality and an ironic awareness of the realities of life about her marked Nellie McClung's mature literary consciousness. A just assessment of her fiction must take these factors into account.

As might be expected, reading material was scarce in this pioneer community. "Living as we did so far from a railway, books were a treasure eagerly desired. When a new family came into the neighbourhood we wondered what they brought: not in furniture, but books. The young Englishmen who were sent out [in the mid-1880s] to learn farming were the most productive field."[25] The Mooneys' Englishman, William, brought a book of Yorkshire sermons that Nellie read, but a neighbour's man brought more exciting fare: Kingsley's *Westward Ho!*, Burney's *Evelina*, and Marryat's *Phantom Ship*. Letitia did not think the latter was suitable reading for a child and Nellie recalled: "I had to secrete it in a hay mow and read between times . . . I knew she was right but I could not leave Philip Vanderhechin until I knew what was going to happen."[26] The first novel Nellie read, however, was *Meadow Brook,* by Mary Jane Holmes. The heroine, as Nellie remembered her, "was the youngest of her family who was misunderstood by them and criticized for talking too much. All these circumstances helped me to see myself in its glamorous pages." The heroine particularly appealed to Nellie when she "decided to lie on the dewy grass, catch cold and die, to spite her unfeeling family." Identifying with the heroine, Nellie would have liked to do likewise, "but I did not get that far. I knew what I would get if I got a cold. It would not be anything as romantic as pneumonia." It was only in imagination, therefore, that she marched her family past her coffin in a funeral that spared no expense while she "listened to their belated penitence with keen satisfaction. Especially Jack; I . . . let him repent in a big way."

Nellie also remembered reading works like Milton's "Il Penseroso," "L'Allegro," and "Lycidas," which were part of the prescribed school literature course, and she referred to fifty-five books being sent to Northfield School in the early eighties when a Sunday School was established there. These were a gift from a country church in Ontario, and included novels like *Ivanhoe, The Talisman, Swiss Family Robinson,* and *Children of the New Forest,* as well as a *Life of Livingston.* The children, as Nellie recalls, read all of them.[27] In addition, the Mooneys' immediate neighbours shared the newspapers they subscribed to from other parts of the country: "The Naismiths took the Arnprior *Chronicle,* the Ingrams, the Woodstock *Sentinel,* and we had the Owen Sound *Advertiser*" as well as the Montreal *Family Herald,* though the news was old when these arrived. The most unusual source of reading material, however, was a package of periodicals, newspapers, and books, which arrived anonymously from England every three months for ten years. Only after the death of the donor—a Miss M.E. Breasted—did the Mooneys learn her name and the fact that she had chosen one family in each township and sent reading material as her contribution to the isolated settlers in the Canadian West. It was an age when books were read aloud within the family group, and Nellie acquired a love for literature—both biblical and secular—from a very early age. In fact her first purchase, as a child, was books from Christie's Book Store in Brandon. After careful scrutiny she bought *St. Elmo* and Washington Irving's *Sketch Book of Geoffrey Crayon,* and kept both of them well on into later life. "They lasted well, too, for I rationed myself carefully on *St. Elmo* and read only ten pages a day to make it last, but I let myself go at the *Sketch Book* for I was a little bit disappointed in it and wished that I had bought *The Arabian Nights*—but I grew up to it in a couple of years."[28]

One event that particularly stood out in Nellie's memory of her childhood was her first trip to Brandon. Usually the boys hauled the grain to town and did the shopping, but on this occasion Jack was taking the grain in and Mrs. Mooney decided she and Nellie would go along. It was a long cold ride in December, but Nellie was dressed for the weather and ran along behind the sleigh when she wanted to warm up. The excitement of this adventure, to a country girl not quite twelve years old, was almost enough to prevent her noticing the slow pace of the horses and the biting prairie wind. By noon they reached the Black Creek stopping-house, which was later to become the subject of one of Nellie's short stories and the title of her third book. Already, unconsciously, she was storing memories that would furnish her with characters and incidents when she became a writer. At the stopping-house they enjoyed a good meal and a chat with Mrs. Corbett, the owner. The men—thirty or forty of them—all sat at one long table, but Nellie and her mother were served at a small separate table Mrs. Corbett had placed near her work area so she could talk to Mrs. Mooney, for she had few women visitors. But again Nellie earned her mother's displeasure by jumping up to pour tea for the men. Letitia saw this as "forward" behaviour among strangers rather than a willingness to help out where there was a need. On this occasion, too, Nellie's brother Jack said that he "felt cheap" to see her act in such a "bold" way, and he accused her of showing off. "The argument was an old one," Nellie says resignedly, "but I would be free some day."

It is perhaps a truism that the autobiographer creates in her work a public *persona*, a creation of self-defence as well as of self-revelation. Certainly McClung, in this instance and several others, depicts herself showing off while denying that she is doing so. She shows herself off against the "lout of a boy" whose job it is to pour tea for the men. He was busy washing dishes and, says Nellie with disdain, he "could not even think of two things at once," prompting her to jump up and do his job for him. It is clear from the context that the older Nellie McClung, reflecting on her past, is intent on demonstrating that even at the age of eleven she was quick and decisive, particularly in contrast to a boy-helper who may have been borderline retarded. Nellie clinches her point by having Mrs. Corbett sum Nellie up in the following laudatory way: "Look at that now, there's a girl with a quick turn, and her not more than twelve years old. I'd be a proud woman, if I had a little girl like that comin' along. By gosh, I like action." McClung from the perspective of sixty years of age was not only defending herself, she was using Mrs. Corbett to comment unfavourably on her mother and her restrictive ways. She was "getting back" at her mother and everything she stood for. On a conscious level Nellie is defending an allegedly disinterested action while unconsciously revealing the young self-centred show-off that her family knew her to be. Nellie goes on to have Mrs. Corbett speak favourably of women voicing their opinions on political and other matters, to Mrs. Mooney's horror. At this point McClung dramatizes Mrs. Corbett turning to her and saying: "Maybe you'll do it sissie, when you grow up." Young Nellie's response is purported to be: "'Maybe I will,' I said eagerly, 'I'd like to,'" thus prophesying her adult career. The situation does not ring true, and one senses once more that McClung is fictionalizing.

Nellie's more detailed manuscript version of her childhood antagonism with Jack—which she tactfully omitted from the final version of her autobiography—is, at the same time, evidence of the compassionate understanding that marked her mature years. Her manuscript attempt to explain the early bitterness between them suggests that this was not the first time she tried to understand their stormy relationship, and it also foreshadows the reconciliation that took place between them just before Nellie left home to attend Normal School. It was no accident, years later, that she would name her first child after this brother whom she grew to love and respect.

> Between Jack and me there was that enmity that often strikes brother and sister and sows the seed of much bitterness. I could do nothing that would please him. I was always wrong. We couldn't get along and there was no use trying. He just did not like me, and was always picking on me. I never understood until I read Booth Tarkington's *Seventeen* and realized that there is often real enmity between a boy of seventeen and his younger sister. It was nothing—and then I knew it was neither his fault or mine. It was just the natural antagonism.[29]

As evening approached they arrived in Brandon and Nellie saw her first big town since they had left Winnipeg when she was eight. She viewed the life, colour, and movement of urban life as a bewildering happiness. Seeing a whole street of busy stores, staying overnight in a hotel, and going on a shopping expedition the next day were new and exciting experiences for her. In her autobiography Nellie says that she had one dollar of her own to spend as she wished, and she states that she bought a bottle of tonic at a medicine show to ease her mother's headaches. Elsewhere, however, there exist both manuscript and published versions that differ from the account recorded in *Clearing in the West.* Discrepancies like this are, by themselves, insignificant, except to indicate to the biographer that Nellie McClung did, at times, alter or embroider on the facts in the writing of her autobiography.[30] Later, when the mature Nellie McClung records the fiction that both Jack and she bought a bottle of the same medicine for her mother, it is Nellie, not Jack, who is expected to return her purchase: "'You can do it more easily than Johnny. A young man can't very well seem to change his mind, but it's different with a young girl like you . . . '" "It was the old problem," Nellie says ruefully, "with the old solution."

If this small incident with the medicine is apocryphal, the larger truth it evokes was real enough to Nellie even when she was a child, and the whole chapter dramatizes the cause for, and the fact of, her spirited rebellion against the traditional, limiting role of women. In Brandon, at the age of twelve, she would long for freedom from such restrictive oppressions and the time when, for example, she could "go out alone, any time I wanted to!" A "sudden rage" kindled in her, she fictionalizes, when she saw "what fools women were" in accepting a secondary role that made them so "terribly dependent on men" and "pleased when some man, no matter how worthless, took notice of them!" There was not, in this stand, the least sign of opposition to men *per se,* and Nellie Mooney would eventually balance love and marriage and children with an independent writing career and an active public life devoted to social causes and feminism.

In 1889, Nellie Mooney wrote her examinations for entrance to Normal School and the start of her independent career as a teacher. It is very significant that this chapter of her autobiography is entitled: "When the Door Opened." By this time life, for Nellie, had resolved itself into one question: "Had I passed? If I had, I could go to the Normal." If she failed, then, "all my bright vision would fade." Her anxiety, through the summer, about the algebra exam, held her characteristically alternating between moods of exultation and discouragement. Letitia thought it might be a good thing for Nellie to fail for it might take some of the "conceit" out of her, and bluntly told her so. To Nellie's objections, her mother modified her opinion, declaring that her youngest daughter was too impulsive and talked too much. All the little irritations of Nellie's life seemed to coalesce at this time. "But in my fiercest moods of rebellion I was glad of these irritations; they kept alive my ambition. I would make my escape; I would gain my independence, and every day brought me nearer." If only Nellie could get away and get more learning and wisdom then, she thought, "maybe people will listen to me, especially strangers." It was hopeless, in her opinion, to be listened to in her own home. "Looking back," she would later say, "I can see how unfair I was to Mother . . . with the intolerance of youth, I only knew that I was being held down with bit and bridle."

Nellie must have been very difficult at this time, and the situation would not be helped by the fact that she and Jack, who still did not get along, were the only children still at home. Will had married and moved into his own home; George built, and moved into, a house on his own property even though he remained a bachelor for some time. Lizzie married a neighbour, John Rae, and moved to a farm not far away. Hannah went to Normal School in Winnipeg, and then took a school at Indian Head. These changes saddened Letitia: "She would have been glad to keep her family under her own roof, all their lives."

The day came for Nellie to learn the results of her examinations, and she went alone to Millford to get the mail. She had passed. On the way home, it seemed to her that "the road was paved with gold and every clump of silver willow burned with fire . . . " The older Nellie McClung records that she surveyed the pioneer houses of her neighbours with a new love—"brave little outposts," they were to her—and in this expansive mood "I vowed I would not forget them when I came into my kingdom. The grand mood was on me and I wanted to do something for my people here." When she reached home, however, she found everyone angry with her for she had thoughtlessly taken a much-needed wrench with her in the carriage. Resentful, she dramatized a silent, wan, and injured air that she could see was disconcerting to her mother and Jack: "At that moment I was pretty sure I would never come back. I would send a box of monkey wrenches instead. Mother and Jack were going to make it very easy for me to leave . . . The years of bondage were coming to an end . . .

I wanted out." To her surprise, Jack, fearing that she had failed, commiserated with her "in a voice that was new to me." He confided his own fears and mistakes to Nellie, and tried to encourage her, and "in that moment every bit of resentment I had ever felt against him passed away, never to return." They talked on and on, that night, and Nellie began to know this hated brother for the first time while he, too, learned of her hopes and fears. The two acquired "a mutual respect, friendship and understanding that has travelled with us down the years."

Nellie Mooney's childhood was, in many ways, similar to that of hundreds of other children in Canada at that time as revealed, for example, in the diaries of L.M. Montgomery and Elizabeth Smith Shortt: the former, like Nellie, driven by the ambition to become a famous writer, the latter, a medical doctor at a time when this was considered unfeminine. All three experienced a need to excel and a deep need for more and more education to help them achieve their respective goals. They resented having to stay away from school to do household chores, but found outside work more pleasant. All three desired marriage and children yet were forced to question whether marriage and a career are compatible. Similarly, all three saw a lifetime of mere housework as undesirable drudgery, and financial independence was attractive to them. To this end they used school teaching as a means toward their larger goals. They engaged in the usual small-town activities such as picnics and reciting in public; they all expressed a spiritual side to their natures yet questioned and rejected theological doctrines like predestination and eternal punishment; they held long and serious-minded discussions with close friends regarding these matters as well as their personal aspirations; all of them slowly awoke to a feminist consciousness.[31]

There is, then, no particular aspect about the young Nellie McClung that a biographer can single out as unique except that no person is identical with any other person, and the common experience of many may serve to fire the mature goals of only one. Certainly Nellie resented that she was allowed to go anywhere with Jack, even to a dance in nearby Wawanesa when she was fifteen, but that her mother worried about her safety when she went to Wawanesa on her own in broad daylight.[32] And from the time that Nellie learned the handicaps of running a foot race in a dress, to her dismaying discovery that her mother and Lizzie couldn't vote while her father,

Will, and George could, she began to question her mother's restrictive concept of the role of women in society. Also, Nellie was, by nature, outgoing and outspoken and very independent-minded in resisting her mother's frequent reminders that she was "too free with her tongue" and that people didn't like a girl who was "too ready with an answer." Yet these were the very traits that—cultivated with kindliness and compassion, and directed by a mature intelligence and a sense of humour—were to make Nellie L. McClung a socially responsible person who was constructively involved in the cause of women. Though she well knew, as a child, that her mother was a strong, clever woman, respected by everyone in her community for the way in which she managed her household and for her readiness to help a neighbour who was in difficulty, as an adult, Nellie could neither agree with nor accept her mother's mid-Victorian decision to remain passively in the background when it came to public affairs.

Nellie's views of just what a woman's place should be were certainly not formed at age sixteen. Nevertheless, the seeds that would stimulate her opinions were there, and a person of her background and character would be bound to formulate these in time. Nellie had, perhaps, a stronger than usual desire to be independent and earn her own money; she had a personality that not only required the limelight, but which shone radiantly in it; and she possessed an increasingly intense desire to become a writer and, by this means, carry out some as yet vague dream of helping her people. At the same time, in keeping with her training and her romantic reading, she dreamed of a handsome suitor, a happy marriage, and motherhood. It would be some time, however, before she decided that she could combine these dreams, and she had, as she confessed to a friend at the time of her Second Class examinations, certain insecurities about accomplishing her dreams. She sensed that she needed more learning and broader experience. At this time in her life, Normal School and a teaching career beckoned as a reason for leaving home and as an opportunity for further personal growth.

3

Normal School and Teaching

❖

According to Nellie, her high hopes for an independent life were almost defeated in 1889, for the Mooneys' very promising crop was nearly destroyed by an early frost. This statement conflicts with both weather and crop reports for that year.[1] Possibly this is an example of those times when she rendered the events of her life in a more highly dramatic form. In any case, it seems likely that Hannah, who had prudently saved some of her salary, was able to provide financial help; and Lizzie, always anxious to see Nellie get her chance, said that she would help with a wardrobe. By 1 September, Nellie Mooney—not yet sixteen years old—was on her way.

The Winnipeg Normal School, in 1889, was not large enough to require a building of its own, and its varied locations, during the five-month period of Nellie's attendance, were haphazard and wholly unsuitable for educational purposes.[2] The adventure in learning, however, was too exciting for her to notice any defects or inconvenience. The students were divided into two classrooms, depending on which set of examinations they had written: those for the first, or second, class certification. Nellie was "in the larger room where the second class students received instruction" from the school's principal, Mr. D.J. Goggin. He is mentioned in *Family, School, and Society in Nineteenth-Century Canada* as one of few school administrators "who were successful promoters of educational expansion and of innovations labelled 'reform.'"[3] He taught them logic and also gave talks on deportment. The latter, Nellie recalled,

> must have been miracles of tact and truth. I can't remember how he did it, but I know he inspired us with a love for the English language,

pure and undefiled, a desire to walk with dignity and grace; to love righteousness and eschew evil, even the appearance of evil, and to dignify our profession. He glorified soap and water, and impressed on us that tooth-brushes were better than face-powder. Only in one instance do I recall his words. At parting, he said "Demand decent salaries, and wear clean linen."

Normal School days were happy ones for Nellie. She enthusiastically devoured everything she was taught and sensed her "horizon widening." There was a great deal to cover in five months and she wanted to learn as much as she could in that brief time. In fact, the days went by so quickly that she began to dread their end. Every week the students had debates, and Nellie—who had always been "proud of the flow of conversation" in the Mooney family where "we always had good talk"—found debating an exciting new method of expression. It was one that, in her mature years, she would practise with great skill. She felt, too, at this time, that she was finally being taught to think for herself, although Frank Schultz at Northfield School must surely be credited with this. The talents that were now being cultivated would prove invaluable on those occasions when—as a suffragist, social reformer, and member of the provincial legislature—she addressed large and frequently hostile audiences sprinkled with hecklers who tried, in vain, to assail her logic and disturb her equanimity.

When the Normal students were sent out to the schools to observe qualified teachers, Nellie found herself much impressed by the work of a Miss Nimmons who taught grade two in the Carlton School, and of Agnes Laut in whose class Nellie taught her first lessons. Years later, as an author, McClung would meet and get to know Laut after the latter became one of Canada's noted historical novelists of the early West. Miss Nimmons, Nellie remembers, "became my ideal, with her lovely gray eyes, soft brown hair and beautiful dresses." And Nellie sensed that Laut's pupils "adored her," and that this accounted for her "perfect discipline." These were the teachers that Nellie hoped to emulate when she was on her own. She had never criticized the teaching she received from Frank Schultz, although throughout her life she tended to be uncritical of anyone she admired, but these were the first women teachers she had experienced. It is not surprising that at her age she was looking for role models, rather than principles alone, to guide her.

While at Normal School Nellie was frequently asked to do substi-

tute teaching when regular teachers were ill. She attributed her being
chosen to the fact that the principal knew she was short of money, but
it would also suggest that she was doing well as a student teacher. For
this work she received three dollars a day, and with it she was able to
buy not only Christmas presents for the family—including *The Traits
and Stories of the Irish Peasantry* for her father—but also books for her
own library from Richardson's Book Store where she was already well
known as a browser. "My greatest humiliation at this time was my lack
of knowledge. I had read so little and the others seemed to have read
everything. When they talked of D'Artagnan, Charlemagne, Ivanhoe,
and Sairy Gamp, I had to sit silent and ashamed." With purchases
from "this house of enchantment," as she called the book store, Nellie
sought to illumine her "dark estate." At this time, Nellie bought
Bellamy's *Looking Backward: 2000-1877,* Verne's *Twenty Thousand
Leagues Under the Sea,* and a volume of Longfellow's poems. Bellamy's
book, thinly disguised as an entertaining novel, was, in fact, a very
controversial portrayal of a utopian state that prophesied for the
future a state-regulated, communal economy that eliminated poverty.
It was a much-discussed book at the time. While we have no record of
Nellie Mooney's opinion of it or its ideas, it is possible to speculate
about its influence on her thinking.

One such influence would have been Bellamy's attitude to the
social relations between men and women, particularly within marriage. He called for "frankness and unconstraint" as opposed to the
artificial hiding of thoughts and feelings. A woman was to be as free
as a man to indicate her romantic interest, thus doing away with
coquetry. In this respect, Nellie Mooney was no blushing Victorian
prude, and she actively pursued her interest in young Wesley
McClung. "It would seem to follow," said Bellamy, "that wives [should
be] in no way dependent on their husbands for maintenance." Any
other arrangement denies liberty and dignity and causes humiliation.
In addition, he stated, "It was robbery as well as cruelty when men
seized for themselves the whole product of the world and left women
to beg and wheedle for their share." Similarly no man should have to
face the burden of his wife's support. In later years McClung would
argue for such independence. For her, however, a degree of fiscal
freedom in marriage was won, not through a form of socialism like
Bellamy's, but rather from the free enterprise system, by means of
book royalties. This independence, in turn, meant that women were

not to be mere beneficiaries of society. In Bellamy's words, women were to be "relieved of the burden of housework" so that their lives should not be "stunted at marriage, their narrow horizon, bounded so often, physically, by the four walls of home, and morally by a petty circle of personal interests." They should be as free as men to pursue those socially useful occupations for which they are best adapted.

In addition, Bellamy argued that in a socialist society where cooperatives existed—for example, cheap public laundries—there would be no need for menial domestic labour. While, in later years, McClung would argue occasionally for such laundry, butchering, and child care cooperatives in rural Canada, the immediate need for household domestics in a nonsocialist democracy was evident; and this she saw as freeing her from being a martyr to unpaid domesticity. The domestic, on the other hand, should have the attractive working conditions that Bellamy supported for all workers, and Nellie McClung insisted on such conditions for "her girls." While Dickens, with his love for the common people, was already Nellie Mooney's favourite author, she would have agreed with Bellamy that "he overtops all the writers of his age, not because his literary genius was the highest, but because . . . he made the cause of the victims of society his own, and devoted his pen to exposing its cruelties and shams." In her own limited way McClung sought to do much the same, particularly in her immigrant novel *Painted Fires* (1925) where the central character, Helmi Milander, is victimized by society.

In Bellamy's *Looking Backward,* McClung could also have learned opposition to large corporate structures like the powerful liquor companies, to wars (except for warfare against social evils), to mankind's "servitude to soulless machines" particularly in those factories whose working conditions were deplorable. In addition, like Bellamy, she developed the imagination to conceive of social changes from the *status quo,* and she actively sought out the means to implement such reforms. Bellamy also argued that the social qualities of men—as opposed to their self-interested, anti-social ones—"furnished the cohesive force of society." This premise of his socialist cooperative society would undoubtedly have appealed to McClung and while, throughout much of her life, her thinking was frequently close to the developing Social Gospel movement of a J.S. Woodsworth, with its emphasis on the application of Christian principles to everyday human affairs, she appears never to have seriously considered joining a socialist party. She remained a staunch Liberal to the end of her days.[4]

During her stay in Winnipeg Nellie had a brief but somewhat disturbing experience at a fundamentalist Baptist church where she acquired, as she puts it, "the sensation of a lost soul." When the minister asked all who felt the need of prayer to stand up, "I stood." At the meeting that followed "I had every sensation of spiritual sea-sickness." Youthful inexperience and a vulnerable outgoing personality may have prompted Nellie's response to this type of highly emotional religious persuasion. She possessed, too, a very sensitive but as yet immature emotional nature, and it is possible that her undirected need to be in the limelight, at this stage in her development, joined with her tendency to dramatize herself in very dubious ways when she was young, may have had some bearing on her intense sense of sin and the public acknowledgement that accompanied it. Another factor may have been that during this period of personal growth she repeatedly sought to emulate a variety of women whom she saw as role models: in this instance a fellow student and Baptist named Miss Dale whom Nellie had recently decided to board with. Miss Dale possessed a religious spirit that Nellie found attractive and that "made me want to be like her." Possibly Nellie wished also to impress her new friend with a display of her religious sensitivity to the Baptist concept of sin.[5] Although Nellie acknowledged that a psychologist might say the experience had more than a slight touch of "hypnotism" to it, she firmly rejected this kind of psychological interpretation though it is evident, in her autobiography, that she was aware of the "psychology of release," for example, and the need for an outlet for "suppressed emotion"—knowledge that she was probably learning for the first time in her psychology classes at Normal School. One senses in all of Nellie McClung's writings, however, that while she would recognize, to some extent, a psychological interpretation for the behaviour of others, she tended to avoid explaining herself in those terms. At any rate, she soon returned to Grace Methodist Church and its more moderate religious temper.

Family ties remained strong at this time, and Nellie went home for Christmas, even though her term at Normal was not completed until the end of January. Christmas was always a special time in the Mooney family and Nellie tells of several. The house was decorated with spruce boughs and streamers of red tissue paper and red and green balls. Christmas dinner meant guests and a long and laden table. Now Will and his wife had three small children to add to the excitement. There were presents, of course, more abundant than in earlier days but still practical: a dress from Lizzie—"the prettiest one I had every had"—and kid shoes with glass buttons from Jack. During the holiday season the young people had a party typical of a social gathering of that day—an evening of charades, guessing games, and singing around the piano. Nellie observed, wryly, that all the songs had sad endings: "The mortality rate among the song heroines of that day was high indeed. They snuffed out very easily . . . one breath of cold air and then crape on the door and a new mound on the hillside!" And in a brief antiromantic passage in her autobiography, reminiscent of Huckleberry Finn's comic observations about the infinite number of languishing females cut off in their prime that marked many nineteenth-century pictures, Nellie McClung does for nineteenth-century sentimental songs what Mark Twain did for the sentimental art of the same period.

At the end of January Nellie came home again. But now she felt different: she had a professional certificate, "a license to teach." Her mother, always cautious where Nellie was concerned, persuaded her not to apply for a school at that time, but to wait until the next fall. To Letitia, Nellie was still much too young to go out on her own, far too outspoken, too ready to talk to strangers, and lacking the reserve and reticence Letitia believed was the hallmark of a proper lady. Indeed, Letitia sensed qualities in Nellie she feared would land her in difficulties. According to Nellie: "She had no faith in my discretion at all, and if I were out after sundown, she had visions of disaster . . . " By contrast, she had "the Old-world reverence for men, and attributed to her sons qualities of wisdom and foresight which, no doubt, surprised them." Eventually, though, the strong-willed and conservative Letitia Mooney was compelled to free her youngest daughter. That summer Nellie heard from a Normal School friend who was leaving her position at the Hazel school near Manitou. She applied for the vacancy, was accepted, and in the middle of August 1890, she set out for her first job. She was not quite seventeen years old. As was commonly the case with Nellie, she saw the event in dramatic terms. Her departure from home "marked the end of an era. The curtain had fallen on the first act, and even if the audience grew restless, there was nothing it could do but wait. The play would go on." Letitia

Mooney sent her youngest child from home, as Nellie recalls, with the following admonition: "Don't talk, but listen, and don't believe all you hear, and don't be afraid to admit you do not know. And remember, no matter what happens to you, you can always come home, and be welcome." If this last statement worried Nellie a bit, "for it suggested a possibility I might fail," she nevertheless felt the "exaltation" of the moment: "I had longed for freedom, and now I had it!"[6]

Nellie was very fortunate in the boarding house selected for her. When her trustee and landlord, Mr. Hornsberg, first saw her sitting on her tin trunk waiting on the deserted Somerset railway platform, he could not believe that this was the new teacher—she was just a child. But as she chatted with him on the seventeen-mile ride to his farm, he came to know and like her. His farm was even more prosperous than the Mooney farm, and Nellie spotted immediately that it was well managed. She was even more happy when she discovered book cases in the parlour "filled with E.P. Rowe's and Pansy's books, and an Elsie Dinsmore or two, the *Pilgrim's Progress,* Fenimore Cooper's *Leatherstocking Tales,* and Alexandre Dumas' sombre romances"—the standard literary fare of the day. There were also numerous back issues of magazines like the *Youth's Companion* and the *Farmers' Advocate.* It was a home Nellie knew she could fit into with no trouble. Today a new teacher would probably be dismayed to discover that she was to share a bed and room with one of her pupils, but Nellie was simply pleased that Esther was a pleasant quiet girl only a few months younger than herself. This situation was, of course, common in teachers' lives.

Further acquaintance with the family only confirmed Nellie's favourable first impressions. The Hornsbergs liked to sit around in the evening while the two eldest children read aloud. Nellie was soon sharing the reading and adding new books to the repertoire. After Christmas at home Nellie had a set of Dickens, paper bound, a gift from Will. As they read these Nellie says that she became more determined than ever to become a writer "to do for the people around me what Dickens had done for his people. I wanted to be a voice for the voiceless as he had been a defender of the weak." They had begun the set by reading *Martin Chuzzlewit,* and poor Tom Pinch with his "homely face" and "awkward gait" became for Nellie a "symbol" of all the ordinary rural folk she knew in southern Manitoba, and "a token of all the unattractive people of the world whose virtue and goodness and beauty are not seen by our dull eyes." She resolved to be an "interpreter" of such people. There is no doubt that the mature Nellie McClung writing here of her early literary goal is dramatizing herself as a precocious teenager. As a young woman and aspiring author, however, she was indeed influenced by Dickens in these ways. Still, she felt ill-equipped to achieve this ambition, and read as widely as she could. In spite of Hornsberg's cheerless quip that she had better eat heartily as meals were likely to be her only pay, she was earning forty dollars a month[7] and once more could afford to buy books. One of her purchases at this time was John Ruskin's *Sesame and Lilies,* a book she felt she could really get her teeth into, but she disliked "his general attitude to women" and strongly disapproved of "his belief that they were made only to help, comfort, and inspire men, and that all their education must be to that end." Being raised by Letitia Mooney, of course, Nellie had already experienced the negative effect of this kind of Victorian counsel.

Nellie was to teach school for a total of five years. She did her job with enthusiasm and imagination and was highly rated by her inspector, Edward E. Best. Although she taught in four different schools, they were all within the same south-central Manitoba inspectorate, and Edward Best became a friend. She admired his ability as a teacher and the useful suggestions he made.[8] Her first school, Hazel School No. 365, was a typical prairie school with perhaps a little more attractive setting than some. There was no unnecessary equipment— blackboards and desks, a wall map, and of course the stove, which the teacher was expected to light on cold winter mornings. The children brought their slates and scribblers and a few books. If someone had been generous there might be a few tattered volumes in the school library. But these were the conditions Nellie had experienced herself and which she had expected to find. What was a little disconcerting on the first day, however, was to be faced by forty students—many almost as old as she was. The crops in the district had been hit by both hail and frost, and since there was no work for the young people at home, they were all at school. As Nellie faced this unexpected "peak load of students" she felt all her school management lessons slipping away, but she was fortunate to have two willing helpers in Charley and Esther Hornsberg, the eldest children of the family with whom she was boarding. They wrote lessons on the board, helped the smaller children, and handed out books while Nellie gradually got the school and the timetable for all the grades organized. Nevertheless she believed, as she struggled every afternoon after school with the next day's lessons, that she was failing, and each day on her way home to the Hornsberg farm she found herself seated "on a fine flat stone in the bottom of the coulee" where, she says, she "meditated in great humility of spirit." No doubt this change of mood would have pleased Letitia Mooney. But by the time inspector Best made his first visit, Nellie's school was progressing nicely.

Nellie was young enough to enter into the students' activities, not just supervise them. This, of course, can be a danger for a teacher, but Nellie seems to have been able to balance the dual role successfully: in the eyes of the pupils, if not in those of their parents. Shortly after school began, Nellie discovered, to her horror, that the chief recreation of the playground was vicious fighting whose roots went back to the parents and the past.

> Nearly all the families came from the same place in Ontario, and carried with them into the new life, all the sins and sorrows of the past. They knew each other too well; and some of the old grudges had their roots in the past generation. This led to fights on the school grounds, rather serious affairs that worried me. In the heat of anger, the opposing factions went deeply into the past and dragged out old skeletons, flung out old taunts and innuendoes, horrible on the lips of children. After one of these bouts my senior classes were demoralized, and even the little ones suffered from the emotional upheaval.

As might be expected, "feuds" were not discussed in Nellie's Normal School textbook on School Management and so, from the beginning, she was thrown on her own resources for an understanding of, and a solution to, the problem. "I knew the root of the trouble was in the homes where these old sins were freely discussed. Drab lives crave excitement and these neighbourhood fights were the outlet for suppressed emotions. I must find a healthier form of excitement, or the school was headed for ruin."

Nellie's method of resolving this age-old problem reveals considerable wisdom, shrewdness, and imagination. Immediately after the morning prayer she would read for ten minutes from Dr. Egerton Young's *My Dogs in the Northland*, which greatly interested the students, eliminated fighting before classes as all students wanted to arrive on time for the story, and generally "began the day pleasantly for us." At the same time she introduced a football, purchased with her own money and, playing with her students to help ensure order, soon created great enthusiasm for the game. She told her students that if a fight broke out, the ball would be locked in her desk for a day. She organized the drawing up of rules for their various football games, played by boys and girls alike, and she wisely ensured that "everyone had a voice" in the making of those rules so that each one had a personal stake in the success of the games. She discussed *Tom Brown's School Days* and the need for a "sense of fair play" and "good humor" in sporting events. She told them "about the 'Old Spites' in Ireland" and their useless bloodshed, and she "tried to make them laugh at such foolishness which belonged to the age of superstitions and ignorance, and had no place now in the lives of sensible young people."

This social evil at Hazel School had been largely resolved when some of the women of the community—much in the spirit of Letitia Mooney—decided that neither the girl students nor the teacher should play football as it "wasn't a ladies' game" and, in any case, the game should be stopped because the children "were just crazy about it." Clearly school was not to be enjoyable—even at recess. To prevent the community leader of this arbitrary and irrational dissent from undermining her good work by complaints to the school trustees, young Nellie Mooney—with considerable courage—tackled the woman head on. She put her case "plainly and bluntly" to her opponent—a Mrs. Jeffreys, who was both influential and much feared in the community—and explained the reasons for her actions. In the course of their conversation, according to Nellie, she gave a hypothetical example of the children's animosity by evoking an imaginary "post-office scandal" but discovered, to her chagrin, that she had "inadvertently stirred a bitter memory" in Mrs. Jeffreys, who was personally aggrieved by the reference. "No doubt she thought I had deliberately evoked the past to gain my point," Nellie said, while claiming that the allusion was made innocently on her part. It is difficult to accept that Nellie Mooney's allusion to so specific a scandal was as accidental as she claims. At any rate, as Nellie recalls, the allegedly "unpremeditated blackmailing" did prevent Mrs. Jeffreys from going to the trustees, and the football games—with Nellie and the girl students participating—continued unabated and schoolyard fighting was kept to a minimum.

More acceptable, in that rural community, was the Christmas concert for which Nellie not only coached the children in songs and recitations but played a leading role herself in a comic skit that punned on a train's destination—"to Morrow." She also sang "Whispering Hope" in a duet with Esther Hornsberg. Now, the teacher and the pupils were entertaining the community, and the evening ended with a memorable feast.

> A boiler of coffee had been made at Mrs. McDonald's nearby, and when it was brought over and the thick white cups borrowed from Huston and Betts store in town were passed, and two of the boys went down the aisles with blue enamel pitchers of coffee to which the cream and sugar had been added; and good thick ham and salmon sandwiches went around; followed by layer cake, spanish bun, marble cake and rolled jelly cake, and plates of home-made candy, the audience settled down into great good humour, and a truce was called on all old feuds . . . It was half-past twelve before we left the school, but what a night it had been! I couldn't sleep for thinking of it. Already I was planning what we would do next year to make the people laugh.

It is doubtful that other teachers in similar communities entered quite so wholeheartedly and enjoyably into their students' Christmas concerts. That Nellie placed herself in a starring role in what would normally be a student skit reveals her continued need to be in the limelight and to receive applause, as well as her marked inclination toward the comic and the dramatic situation: traits she would learn, as an adult, to direct outwardly and more for the benefit of others, rather than inwardly to the exclusive satisfaction of her personal needs. Still, Nellie was only seventeen years old, and probably able to get away with such unconventional behaviour.

The next day was 24 December, and Nellie caught the westbound train for Wawanesa in hope of getting home for Christmas. The passenger train came through only twice a week, so she took the early morning freight train where she was allowed to sit in the cupola of the caboose and enjoy the wide sweep of the countryside. By dark the train was into "one of the severest storms of the season," and Nellie climbed down to where the trainmen had gathered to eat. Amiably she shared the contents of her lunchbox with the men and, still in an exalted mood, performed the entire school concert for them, singing not only "Whispering Hope," but all the other children's songs as well, and acting out "all three parts in the 'Train to Morrow'"! No doubt, as Jack would have described, Nellie Mooney was showing off again. It must have been an unusual experience for the men. They made up a bunk for Nellie to sleep in overnight, and covered her with a warm fur coat. The train did not reach Wawanesa until the evening of 25 December, but the family was still gathered and Nellie ate cold turkey while she regaled them with the story of her trip. Letitia immediately "raised a storm of protest" at the idea of her too-forward daughter travelling and sleeping in a caboose with strangers. "No doubt you talked to these men," Letitia complained indignantly. When Nellie confessed that she had not only talked, but also sang and dramatized an entire play for them, and also "read aloud from a book called 'Lucille,'" Letitia must surely have thought that her youngest daughter would never grow into the proper young lady she wanted. On this occasion, however, most of the men in Nellie's family defended her, and her father even suggested that "he couldn't see that there was any harm in singing at any time." To Letitia's chagrin the matter was dropped.

Nellie's "classroom" was rural Manitoba in the late 1800s, and she gained insight here that would remain with her for a lifetime. "Laughter," she had learned, "was the cement that would heal the breaks in this neighbourhood, laughter and something to talk of other than past sins and sorrows." Nellie applied her school psychology with common sense and with a wider social sweep than her teachers at the Winnipeg Normal School could have imagined for their young charges. At the same time, she was experiencing in her very limited environment the need for, and the effects of, social reform. As well, she was cultivating her desire "to get a toe-hold on the ladder of literature," in part through her knowledge of people in her immediate environment, while defining, at the same time, what that literary role might be in terms of the happiness and betterment of people in those rural communities whose lives she knew from first hand experience.

Young Nellie Mooney looked about her and saw lives that were "drab" and, at times, dominated by "narrow, single-track minds, with no outlet," sometimes making people prisoners of their own moody "silence and temper," and somehow she wanted to help. She knew that many of her neighbours had "nothing to look forward to, or take delight in." Their lives were often limited by the pressing necessities of "sowing and reaping, cooking and washing dishes" in pioneer conditions, isolated from friendly human contact. The inner life of such people was often stunted or stifled and in desperate need of being "deepened and widened." "We can't change the facts of life," Nellie would say, "there's sorrow and sickness and death, binders break and horses get cut in barbed wire, but these things can be softened and brightened and lifted if we have a wide enough outlook . . . " Increasingly, Nellie desired to "lift the burden" from these downtrodden people with their treadmill existence, and eventually she would employ her comic and dramatic talents as one means to this end. She knew, too, that practical-minded pioneer people whose days were dominated by chores and crops and dollars had little time to "watch the sunset or raise flowers, plant trees, or do anything to make their homes beautiful," yet beauty, she also knew, "has a power to heal and comfort people and help them over the rough places in life." She wanted these, her people, to lead lives that were "not without hope." She began to feel that as an author her role might well be to feed the spirit and improve the drab lives of such people by giving them something to delight in.

The above passages are the words of the mature Nellie McClung looking back on her youthful aspirations as a writer and, no doubt, at the age of sixty she could articulate more clearly what she felt she had accomplished than the young Nellie Mooney could have foreseen. Yet the few journal manuscripts that remain from her early days as a teacher confirm her expansive, humane compassion "for that great sinsome and wayward of all children gone astray—Humanity," and also reflect her wish of that time that beyond all personal fame and praise (and these, indeed, she sought) was

> the hope that some day, some poor weary heavy-laden one would find something in those pages that would comfort and cheer them, and the sad eye would brighten and the compressed lips would smile and that one would, perhaps, steal her hand in mine and say: "you helped me, you comforted me. You made me think better of my race."[9]

In small rural communities the teacher was expected to do more than teach, and Nellie found herself cutting the hair of a pupil whose mother didn't have time, and making girls' dresses and boys' shirts with Mrs. Hornsberg's help. From the earliest days of the free Common Schools in Canada the attendance of many pupils was irregular. At times this was due to a lack of shoes or other items of clothing, an unfortunate situation for the youngsters in McClung's first novel of 1908 when not one of the Watson children owned a complete set of clothes. Obviously McClung met the same situation in the rural schools where she taught.[10] As Nellie became aware of neighbourhood problems it seemed to her that her mother's warnings were right: as long as liquor was available some men would neglect their families and their farms, and their children would go hungry and poorly clothed. Letitia had declared that there was no hope of ending this curse, but Nellie—young, naive, and a teacher—believed the solution lay in education. The trustees had been persuaded by a salesman to purchase a temperance kit for the school—a lurid chart that revealed the damage done to the body by liquor, with instructions for scientific experiments that would confirm the chart and drive the lessons home. In the classroom Nellie found that these lessons were received with great interest and trust except by one young sceptic who clung to his father's belief that "a drink of licker is better than a meal" supported by the evidence that his father had been drinking since he was ten and had never been sick a day in his life. Nellie's temperance lessons soon became a subject for debate in the community and she decided to give a public lecture with the help of some of her students. The capacity audience got the full treatment—lecture, experiments, and charts. They seemed impressed, and when the sceptic's father publicly declared that he should not have given his son bad advice Nellie was sure that temperance had won and that the drinking problems of the neighbourhood were over. Her first temperance disillusionment came that Saturday when there was no reduction in the number of men coming home late at night from the Manitou bars. She realized that education was not enough, but only after several weeks of a Methodist revival that created an uproar in the community did she understand why she had failed.

At this time, the Judd sisters—Nettie and Maude—were well advertised in the *Methodist Christian Guardian* and "fully authorized by the church." They descended in full female force on the little town of Manitou. No one was safe. They "pleaded" and "preached and sang, and had altar calls, and after-meetings" and while "their greatest appeal was to the young men," they were sufficiently "beautiful, vital, and just a little too well-dressed to escape the jealousy of the women." The ferment stirred up in the neighbourhood was shattering, according to Nellie, but only the more conservative Presbyterian and Anglican churches disapproved, alleging that cases of "insanity" resulted from all the emotional upheaval. Among all the dramatic conversions, the most spectacular was that of Silas, the town drunkard who, being "a fine looking man, and being something of a show-man, missed none of the fire-works." Unlike the conversions of many, which did not last, Silas "became a new man with a new countenance, and one of that district's best-loved citizens" to the end of his days. Nellie knew now why the temperance chart had failed her.

> It had shown certain facts, as true as the multiplication tables, and given warnings; but it had been powerless to supply the will-power to heed these warnings . . . It appealed to the head alone, and because of this it failed. This, then, was the secret of religion. It gave strength to the weak, life to the dead; it made people want to do the right thing.

Once again Nellie experienced "a high exalted feeling" and was caught by the desire to help people. She had already been impressed by two women she had heard preach—though they were not ordained clergy—and she vividly recalled the "young and beautiful" Dinah Morris preaching "up and down the lanes and greens of England" in George Eliot's *Adam Bede* and decided "I wanted to be like her!" This feeling was reinforced by the stirring dramatics of the evangelical Judd sisters. She was still the young girl trying out in fantasy a variety of roles; her high ideals still largely supported by her imaginative flair for self-dramatization and by her need for centre stage. Eventually she would fight for the right of women to be ordained clergy when they qualified through the standard university courses in theology, but she seems never to have seriously considered that by following such a profession she might easily have combined her three major interests: literature and writing, religion, and social reform.[11]

After one-and-a-half years at the Hazel school Nellie moved to the school in Manitou. Although Manitou was just a small town, about eight hundred residents, it had a four-room school and a Normal School. Soon her Division III and Intermediate classes had formed a "literary society" and every Friday afternoon her pupils took part in programmes of "music, recitation, readings, dialogues, essays, and debates."[12] The move to Manitou brought Nellie closer to people and activities she had already become familiar with while teaching at Hazel. Since Manitou was only three miles from the Hornsberg farm, she had come to town frequently, particularly after she had purchased a horse and was no longer dependent on the Hornsbergs for transportation. She had attended the Manitou Methodist Church and she and the young members of the family had come back each Sunday afternoon for Sunday School where Nellie and Esther Hornsberg were in the same Young Ladies' Bible Class. She had attended quilting bees and parties at the invitation of the Manitou teachers. Now she found herself a part of a very lively young community and enjoyed herself thoroughly.

To Nellie's delight she found she was to board with the Methodist minister's family. The McClungs had arrived in Manitou about the same time that Nellie came to the Hazel school. Mrs. McClung was the teacher of the Young Ladies' Bible Class and from the first moment Nellie set eyes on this "beautiful woman, in her late forties," who "dressed exquisitely," she was completely captivated. During the bible group's first lesson with Mrs. McClung, Nellie appears to have felt contempt for the ability of her fellow classmates, and she sought to lead the group "with fervor."

> I drew lessons, expanded thoughts, asked questions, repeated the golden text and was able to tell where it was found . . . and though I was probably detested by the others, I saw gratitude in the teacher's golden brown eyes, and came home in an exalted mood.

Of this occasion, Nellie says unabashedly that she was "the best girl in the class," and she claims that the aim of her performance was simply to help the new teacher along. That may have been part of her motivation, but it is difficult to read this passage (and others) from Nellie's autobiography without falling back on her brother Jack's frequent allegation that Nellie Mooney was just "showing off," and one is reminded, too, that Letitia Mooney felt strongly that her youngest child needed more than a little "conceit" taken out of her. It is probable that Nellie's primary motivation, on this occasion, was to impress and draw herself to the attention of this striking new role model she had just discovered.

In her autobiography Nellie made the astonishing declaration that right then she decided that Mrs. McClung was "the only woman I have ever seen whom I should like to have for a mother-in-law" since any son of Mrs. McClung's "must be the sort of man I would like." And while Nellie would indeed learn to love Wes McClung—"a tall, slim young fellow, with clear blue eyes, regular features and clear skin like his mother"—she had not yet met him and, in fact, didn't even know he existed. Mrs. McClung must have been something of a surrogate mother for young Nellie Mooney who was just sixteen when they met. "If only I could be like Mrs. McClung—sweet, placid, serene, whose life flowed on in endless song . . . who had a gift for goodness as others have for music." Her gentle beauty and her warmth must have seemed attractive substitutes for those stern and coldly practical qualities that made Letitia Mooney seem, in some ways, a somewhat arid parent.

> As long as I can remember my mother she was looking forward to her death; and had her shroud made according to the custom of her country. Many a Christmas day my young heart was saddened by her proclamation that she might not be with us next year. By her own attitude she made us feel she was on the brink of the grave all her life.

Letitia's dour, forbidding temperament was at times almost repelling. By contrast, Mrs. McClung's manner and character were far more attractive.

Living in the McClung family in Manitou only confirmed Nellie's first impression. It led also to respect and admiration—particularly regarding Mrs. McClung's "methods of training her children"—for if Mrs. McClung had the gentle qualities "of the old-fashioned woman," she also had "a fearless, and even radical, mind" that was bound to interest the spirited young Nellie Mooney.

> Her one girl, Nellie, who was my own age, did no more than one share of the work; being a girl did not sentence her to all the dishwashing and bedmaking. The two younger boys took their turn and there were no complaints from them . . . On the other hand, Nellie had no favors because she was a girl. And there was no talk of having to be accompanied by a brother every time she went out.

Mrs. J.A. McClung may have been a "gentle, soft-spoken woman," but Nellie soon learned there was steel behind the gentleness: "She had the strength of the meek—the terrible meek, who win by sweetness and gentle persuasion and the brushing away of all arguments as only the meek can." Nellie, for example, was easily won over to the cause of suffrage for women when Mrs. McClung circulated a petition. While she was still teaching at the Hazel school, Nellie had been invited to a quilting bee in Manitou where she made the shocking discovery that those present spoke only in bitter scorn of Mrs. McClung, and her petition. Upon the arrival of Mrs. McClung, the other women fled like silly school children, and Nellie was the only woman who remained present to sign the petition. At this stage of her development Nellie seems to have signed mainly because she believed "it must be right if the minister's wife believed in it." Mrs. McClung was, in Nellie's eyes, too admirable a person to lend her allegiance to an unworthy cause. As Nellie matured, she would acquire more rational grounds for supporting the women's suffrage movement, but in the meantime she was rather startled to find that the other quilters at the bee felt that in Nellie they "had harbored an anarchist." This was probably Nellie's first exposure to a major weakness in the women's movement: the capacity for mutual female antagonism.

Nellie also admired the Reverend J.A. McClung who had, as she recalled, "all the conquering fire of the circuit rider." He was outspoken in his pulpit utterances "about anything that concerned the welfare of his people" from early store-closing hours through the evils of the liquor traffic to the failings of the government of the day, and this sometimes caused his family great concern. Nellie, however, admired his "high resolves," his refusal "to take refuge behind Amos or Elijah, or any ancient authority," his "untiring energy," his "keen memory for faces and names," his refusal to be daunted by circumstances, and "his shrewd worldly wisdom"—traits that Nellie either possessed herself or would develop.

Soon after allegedly deciding that Mrs. McClung would be an ideal mother-in-law and that a man raised by her would have the right qualities for a husband, Nellie learned of the oldest McClung son, Wesley, at that time a summer clerk in the local drug store. Immediately she rode her horse in to Manitou from the Hornsberg farm to examine this boy with the red hair: "I made no pretense of being the Victorian maiden who sits on the shore waiting for a kindly tide to wash something up at her feet . . . I plunged boldly in and swam out for it." Nellie Mooney liked what she saw. In the past, she and Hannah had had many an argument about their qualifications for a husband: "Hannah put 'moral worthiness' at the head of her list . . . I had stuck out for a fine face and carriage . . . " By the time she moved to Manitou, in 1892, and began her life boarding with the McClungs, Nellie recognized that her decision was partly influenced "by the presence of the minister's eldest son" even though he would be away, during part of her stay, at the College of Pharmacy in Toronto.

Nellie was too busy to pine when Wesley went away to college. She was taking music and art lessons, studying to prepare for her First Class Certificate, sharing in all the Friday night parties and the afternoon gatherings at the Women's Christian Temperance Union (WCTU) reading room where the young people settled the problems of Manitou and the world. "We argued on annexation with the United States or the relative value of science and literature in the schools, or whether or not it is possible to live without sin, [and] we felt that we were living in the best tradition of the coffee houses of London." Her life, she felt at this time, was "uproariously, unreasonably happy . . . " Nellie loved life in the small rural towns of Manitoba, and grew to resent the condescension of those who affected to look down upon it. At the same time she was adding to the store of characters who would later appear in her books: the young Englishman exiled by family members because they thought he wasn't bright; the girl who sacrificed herself caring for her family although she dearly wanted an education; the gloomy Mrs. Brant who always saw the black cloud in the clear blue sky, and many others.

In the summer of 1892 Nellie took a trip to Alpena, Michigan, to visit her aunt Ellen—Letitia Mooney's sister. She had promised herself a long trip, once she had the money, for distant places had always fascinated her as did trains, "with their force and strength, and their minds," like hers, "set upon the far country." She was eighteen years old at this time, and still capable of dramatizing a romantic self-image to impress other people: "I wrote copious notes in a large, black-backed note book, and tried to look mysterious and important, as a young lady would who was set upon a secret mission for her country's good."[13]

Evidently Nellie planned, from the start, to work her notes up into a readable manuscript, probably for the amusement of friends but possibly with serial publication in mind. The manuscript—entitled "Six Weeks Vacation: Truth is Stranger than Fiction"—is made up of ten short chapters for a total of twenty-three hand-written pages. The manuscript breaks off in mid-sentence and is left unfinished. It is the earliest known example of Nellie McClung's prose writing and is as competent as one might expect from a young girl of her age and experience, and with her literary aspirations. Written in the style of the light travel essay that entertains with amusing observations and impressions, the manuscript stays close to Nellie's itinerary and reveals little attempt to fictionalize reality. Her prose style is generally nonpretentious, but is marred by clichés and the occasional self-conscious straining for effect. The manuscript is significant only as an early example of Nellie's comic tendency where the effect depends upon exaggeration, a down-to-earth spoofing of romantic pretensions, or on the unpredictable and erratic action.[14] Later, in her mature writing, Nellie would depend to a large extent on hyperbole and burlesque as comic devices—particularly to spoof pomposity and romantic affectation.

Another early antiromance is "The Bicycle Belle" of 1899. While it never secured a publisher, it must have delighted the young men and women of Manitou who, like Nellie and Wes, engaged in that sport. Some, in fact, may have bought their bicycles from Wes. The short story is a bicycle burlesque that spoofs the blackest-villain, whitest-hero melodrama so dear to the heart of the nineteenth century. All the clichés of extravagant melodrama—stock plot, stock characters, stock language—are mimicked and satirically cut down to realistic southern Manitoba size in a tongue-in-cheek prairie tall tale in which the traditional abduction of the heroine, and the hero's merciless pursuit of the villain, are conducted entirely on bicycle.

A mixed group of young people are bicycling back from the Brandon fair through the Pembina Valley. The characters are all named after parts of bicycles: "Pretty Polly Peddles"; "her faithful attendant" and swashbuckling hero of the tale, "Hank Kranger"; and the villainous "Flush-joint Jim." The jealous "Miss Fau de Cycle" urges the group to leave Polly and Hank behind. "Suddenly a dark shadow bore down upon them." The "wild-looking, emaciated, long-haired" villain knocks Hank down, throws the fainting Polly over his handle bars, and makes his escape. "You ar-r-r-r-re mine! I have my r-r-r-re-venge!!" The intrepid hero pursues them, shoots at Jim's tire, and the heroine—"whose faint had been a feint"—leaps free. "Now yield thee! desperate man!" Hank shouts while the villain cries: "Great handle-bars! . . . If I am discovered, I am lost!"[15]

Though her story is lacking in sophistication, Nellie's localized Manitoba bicycle burlesque is an amusing undercutting of the inflated hyperbole of melodramatic seduction romance, and she tried repeatedly to get it published between 1899 and 1901. Periodical editors called it "a clever little story" possessing "freshness and originality," but concluded it was not suitable for their magazines. Nellie still possessed too much of the enthusiasm and self-confidence of the aspiring young author to know that she was in need of sound literary criticism in spite of the indications of promise as a writer. This was an unfortunate condition of the times, however, and prairie authors like Frederick Philip Grove, and Sinclair Ross as late as the forties, paint a disheartening picture of the isolation of the prairie writer, artist, and musician, who worked well away from the major centres of publication and stimulating contact with their fellows. But by the time she approached publication of her first novel in 1906, McClung would not only recognize the need for greater knowledge of the craft of writing but receive a good deal of it from her first editor. Her antiromantic bias would continue throughout her fiction.

In January 1893, Nellie's father died while she was home for the Christmas holidays. He had just passed his eightieth birthday. Nellie had always felt a strong bond with her father, and years later, writing the first volume of her autobiography, Nellie McClung discovered that "this business of remembering is heavy work at times, so many things come back out of the past to stab me." Among these was the memory of little omissions toward her father. To the end of his life John Mooney had been "under the spell of the mystic beauty of his native land," but the family had never thought to subscribe to an Irish newspaper for him or, once there was money, they never thought to send him back to Ireland for a visit. Nellie came to feel these omissions strongly and his death, for her, was so momentous that it marked the end of an era: "And so closed the first chapter of my life." Her words are eloquent of understated grief.

In some respects there was little change on the farm following John Mooney's death. Jack took over, and Letitia continued to make it their home for some years. Nellie did not return to Manitou until the end of January. They were in mourning and could go nowhere "that might give us pleasure." In the evenings they sat quietly while Nellie read aloud from Sir Walter Scott's *The Talisman*.

Nellie probably taught in Manitou through the spring and fall of 1893 for she needed the money to finance six months at the Winnipeg Collegiate (from 1 January to 30 June 1894) where she studied for the examinations for her First Class Teaching Certificate.[16] Her Manitou school principal had permitted her to sit in on his senior mathematics classes to give her "a grounding in algebra, trigonometry and geometry . . . which made it possible for me next year at Winnipeg to win one of the Isbister Scholarships." She went to Winnipeg, however, on the 1st of December, a month before the course began, and boarded with Hannah, who was teaching in that city and being courted by a Baptist ministerial student whom she married in 1895. The summer before, Hannah had stood first in the province in these examinations, so Nellie felt extra pressure to achieve success. She and her friend Jessie McEwan were older students now competing with the city youngsters whom they found rather frivolous and indolent. But in spite of Nellie's attempts to read widely during her teaching years, she still felt ignorant compared to the younger students. This may have been more in her mind than in actual fact. Hard work paid off, though, and in August Nellie received word that she had earned her First Class Certificate. She eagerly accepted an offer to teach in Treherne, rejoicing that the opportunity had arisen to be in the town to which the McClungs had moved. Once again she was boarding with her favourite people.

Treherne was a smaller community than Manitou and about fifty miles farther north—"a busy village with four elevators and two churches"[17]—but life was much the same as in Manitou. Every community in which Nellie taught was in prosperous farm country, settled about the same time as her home district by the same sort of people—English-speaking people mostly from Ontario. During the period when Nellie taught, the Manitoba schools controversy over the question of provincial funding for separate schools raged within the province, but she does not mention it. In the districts she lived in there were no separate schools, and apparently it was not a burning local issue as it was in other parts of the province. The two Manitou papers, for example, scarcely mention it. The young people did debate the issue of provincial rights, but seem to have concentrated mainly on railway problems and the evils of the grain exchange. At this point in her life Nellie was not much concerned with political issues, although she did attend her first political meeting earlier while she was still teaching at the Hazel school. Nellie and the widow who took her to the meeting were the only females present. They were treated with patronizing indulgence at first, but when they had the temerity to pass written questions to the Liberal speaker on the issues of women's suffrage and homestead rights for women, they were "looked down" upon with an insulting if "fatherly rebuke." None of the men present, all of whom knew both women, would speak to them. It was, in fact, this dismaying experience that led Nellie to decide, for some time, that she would not involve herself in social reform. She had not yet acquired the self-confidence needed to address the social reform issues of her time. As she matured, particularly after she became a married woman, she developed the confidence to speak out bravely along with other women, such as her future mother-in-law. While still young, at this time, however, she allowed herself to be intimidated.

By mid-October of 1894, Wes had returned from the College of Pharmacy and bought two drug stores: one in Manitou—where he had previously clerked—and the other in nearby Pilot Mound. He had also begun taking an active part in the social activities of Manitou where he became known as "our popular Druggist." Nellie and Wes were probably seeing as much of each other as they possibly could over the distance of fifty miles, and the social column of the Manitou *Mercury* records the occasional visit of Wes "to his family" in Treherne where, of course, Nellie was living, or of a visit of the two Nellies—Mooney and McClung—to "friends" in Manitou.[18] Significantly, four of the five dates that Nellie tantalizingly describes in her journal as "memorable" days or nights occur at this time.[19]

During these years Nellie made scattered entries in a journal and those that survive from this period—16 September 1894, through 10 June 1896—are written in a highly romantic and overblown style much, one supposes, in the manner of the weekly letters she addressed from Winnipeg to Wes when he was at college in Toronto: "high-minded letters of theological and literary import." In general, they reveal a young person's rather ordinary emotional heights and depths: depression, seemingly caused by problems in her relationship with Wes; elation when the relationship was restored; religious doubts, followed by new conviction; much philosophizing. They came at a time when Wes "became engulfed in doubts and fears, and [was] at enmity with the doctrines of the church, and his father's stern theology, and belief in eternal punishment . . . " Nellie seems to have arrived at a more temperate theological stand, probably as a reaction to her mother's even sterner Presbyterianism. "I believed that when we are not asked whether or not we wanted to be born, God would not lightly condemn us to suffer for ever, no matter what we had done." By this time, she says, "I had welcomed the sane theology of *Robert Elsmere* and *John Ward, Preacher.*"

Both of these novels—the former written by the English novelist Mrs. Humphrey Ward, the latter by the American author Margaret Deland—published in 1888, were extremely popular in their day, and were considered theologically controversial by the mass of readers at that time. In *Robert Elsmere* a minister's scepticism triumphs over his faith, resulting in the estrangement of his wife. In *John Ward, Preacher* an austere clergyman is torn between his rigid Calvinist principles and his love for his wife, who is a kindly, charitable, and liberal-minded thinker. It is not strange that a religious spirit like Nellie's should turn to novels for the theology of her youth. This may be accounted for by the fact that Nellie Mooney was an aspiring novelist herself with a quixotic blend of romanticism and down-to-earth realism in her personal make-up, and that the didactic novel of ideas was foreign neither to her era nor to her personal taste. Indeed, theological speculation was common in the late Victorian novel.[20] She was already sufficiently a rebel, in her conventional milieu, to examine with an open mind the unorthodox ideas of the thinking minority, regardless of whether a conservative Methodist periodical like the *Christian Guardian* might advise caution. Given her personal experience of the narrow Calvinism of her mother, set against the broad-minded spirit of her father's Anglican-Methodist background, there is no doubt that Nellie would have been drawn to the Margaret Deland novel and its statement of faith in particular.

Helen, the heroine of *John Ward, Preacher*, is astonished that anyone in their day could believe in hell in any literal sense. To do so, in her opinion, is to believe in a God of cruelty. "Would I be just," she asks Ward, "if I put a little child where it was certain to fall down, and then punish it for falling?" To her, Ward's concept of God's justice is really injustice, and his Calvinist view of God is her view of the devil. Since no one has asked to be born, she says, then the doctrine of Eternal Retribution is foul. Her family hold that for Helen to conduct her life in accordance with the dictates of reason is fine until it comes to a matter of theological discussion, which is considered by them not only unfeminine, but also beyond a woman's intellectual capacity. Although Helen's episcopalian relatives also deplore Ward's perverted doctrines, they all share the hypocritical opinion that "a woman ought to think just as her husband does," and if she can't, then "it is the wife's place to yield." The cause for Helen's rational theology is laid at the door of "this new-fangled talk of women's rights . . . "[21]

How young Nellie Mooney's hackles must have risen—burdened as she had been by her mother's brand of Calvinism and her conservative attitudes toward the rights of girls and women—though Nellie was, as yet, scarcely touched by the women's rights movement of her day. Her inclination toward the self-dramatic makes it likely that Nellie identified with the abused, but not self-deluded, heroine of Deland's novel.

In her journal for 1893, while living in Manitou, Nellie Mooney records that "Wes and I walked for miles . . . threshing out our beliefs," not the least of which was Wes's quarrel with his father's doctrine of hell, and Nellie's arguments against it taken from *John Ward, Preacher*. By the spring of 1896 Nellie had resolved: "I need religion"; but like the fictional heroine of Deland's novel, Nellie formulated a simple creed to serve her daily life, though she doubted its theological soundness. "I have a sort of a [religion], but I'm afraid it's not up to much. I pray, Lord, keep me from being mean and stingy. Don't let things happen to worry me. Let me see something to laugh at, at least once a day, and give everyone else as much as you do me." If her religion at this period of her life was probably "not sound in its doctrine," Nellie said, because—as in the fictional Helen's case—it said nothing about "the laws, or aliens to the commonwealth of Israel," or other doctrines that she half-guiltily felt "should not be omitted," she was also forced to conclude: "I don't see where I can change it."[22] Nellie's religion, as summed up in the above prayer, was simple, selfless, constructive, and with a leaven of humour that—in the spirit of her father and that of the fictional Helen Ward—emphasized her sense of the joyful, over the suffering, Christ. In later years, Nellie may have expanded and developed the religion of that simple prayer, but she could never have altered its spirit and general thrust, and she would never permit a rigidly inflexible doctrinal position to undermine her reasoning where change was needed. Opposition to theological creeds and dogmas was characteristic of the times, among social reformers in particular where the emphasis was on social action and practical charity.[23]

Nellie's journal for this period seems, at times, to result from essay-like topics she had apparently set for herself to think through and express poetically. Other passages give the impression of being spontaneous outbursts. One passage is a semi-Wordsworthian reflection on childhood imagination set in opposition to the adult capacity to reason and to seek knowledge. At this point in her journal, Nellie expresses doubt in the orthodox interpretation of God. Knowledge, "the fruit of the tree of good and evil, caused Adam and Eve to fall. Is it just that that thirst for knowledge should ever be proven a curse?" In another passage she reflects on childhood days: "Weeping and wailing and gnashing of gums—these were our three languages, and we usually spoke all three at once." Reflecting upon this, she adds: "Grief that can be howled away lies principally in the mouth, and does not really hurt anyone. But when you cry with dry eyes and a quiet mouth and a sore heart—that hurts. You never cry that way," she went on to tell herself, "until you are a woman and have loved." Shortly she was to experience the truth of this.[24]

The more spontaneous passages in her journal suggest anguish in her relationship with Wes. The entry for 13 May 1896 indicates that some catastrophe had turned her world upside down: "O Lord, what an infernal world of heart-break it is! Bury it deep, away, away from the light. O how the light hurts it. Laugh and be gay. Be careless and indifferent and never, never let the world know how deep the wound was, and how sore it is. They will think your heart's cold, but it is only broken." By the 3d of June, only three months before her wedding, Nellie is still severely depressed for "everything is changed." She tries to be optimistic: "We may get it made straight and fixed over, but the marks will still be there . . . Spirit has its wounds as well as body." She shows signs of fight: "I don't want them to take pity on me . . . I'd rather be envied than pitied, like poor old Marlboro." And then we get an ironic hint of the cause for Nellie's pain: "When you ascend the hill of Prosperity, may you not meet a Friend." By 10 June she has resolved the problem. "I've come back," she confides to her journal, "I have come back to my senses . . . after having a vacation in the region of the brain." "O Lord," she muses, "keep us from ourselves and from our dear friends who have our best interest so near at heart. What a heaven on earth it would be if the people who never *meant* any harm, never *did* any. Such is Life, Dear Nellie L., and the tail of the serpent is over us all!" Time, she concludes, would heal the "bitterness" and dry up the "venom."[25]

It appears that Nellie confronted her alleged friend and got to the bottom of whatever evil had been reported about Wes. "He had suffered in reputation from being a minister's son," Nellie would later record in her autobiography, "not that he had done anything very wrong, but because he loved fun and company, and athletics, and had played cards." He did not always fit someone's conventional idea of what a Methodist minister's son should be. Whether Nellie's pseudofriend was misguided or displayed outright malice in an unjust accusation, we shall never know, but certain it is that Nellie Mooney learned a bitter truth about false friendship and about her own need to keep a level head when confronted by it.

When Nellie went home in the summer of 1895, she realised that her mother needed her. Hannah had married the Reverend H.C. Sweet, a Baptist minister, and gone to live in the United States. Lizzie, with her husband and son, had moved to a new farm near Holland, Manitoba, and her mother, although she had a woman to help her, could not cope with the harvesters that fall. Nellie very much regretted giving up her school and her pleasant life in Treherne, but she thoroughly enjoyed her last farm experience. Rural life was changing. Now there was a huge steam thresher owned by her brothers Will and Jack, and while Nellie watched this monster with keen fascination, she felt nostalgia for the older, quiet days. Large crews were still needed for the harvest, however, and they had to be fed so, for three weeks that fall, Nellie helped feed the men: at Will's, at George's, at their own place, and finally at a neighbour's.

After Christmas Nellie taught at the nearby Northfield School from January to June of 1896. Life at home was quiet compared with life in Manitou or Treherne, and once again she was teaching all grades and coping with a stubborn stove when she arrived each morning. But Nellie was content. She enjoyed skating with Jack and getting to know even better this brother with whom she had quarrelled so much as a child. In this interlude, she also looked forward to her wedding the next summer, for she and Wes had finally decided to get married: "I knew I could be happy with Wes. We did not always agree but he was a fair fighter, and I knew I would rather fight with him than agree with anyone else." It had not been an easy decision. Since her teens Nellie had set her heart and mind on being a writer and this, she felt then, was incompatible with marriage. She resolved, therefore, "to be like Queen Elizabeth and keep clear of entanglements . . . " In addition, she recognized that the conventional domestic life, which marriage generally entailed at that time, would not satisfy her. From her earliest days she had strongly resisted being kept home from school to do necessary chores, and she had long rejected the usual female pursuits of fancy work, knitting, and crocheting. When she found herself about to be freed from the confines of home to attend Normal School, she observed her sister Lizzie very closely within her domestic environment and wondered "if this little house felt like a prison to Lizzie as it would to me." Nellie aspired to a larger and grander life.

By the time Nellie had reached her early twenties, however, she had to face the depth of her feelings for Wes McClung, and at this time the conflict between love and marriage and a writing career intensified. Beginning in the spring of 1895, Nellie confided this turmoil to her private journal with greater force and intimacy than she would record it in her public autobiography some years later. On the one hand she recognized "the greatest gift on God's earth: a happy and requited love," and she prayed: "May God spare my darling to me! Surely the sun will never go down in the sky while it is yet in the East. I have gained by my love. I have gained a reverent and a thankful heart toward the God who gave it, and a great yearning love for . . . Humanity."[26] Wes had supported Nellie in her goals and had assured her that she need not lay aside her ambition if she married him: "He would not want me to devote my whole life to him, and he often said so." But by New Year's Eve, in 1895, just eight months before her wedding and only a few days before Wes came to meet her family, Nellie evidently still felt that by marrying Wes she was necessarily killing off the writer she wanted to be.

> She saw herself so full of ambition and the desire to excel that everything is made subservient to that; and O, the high hopes, the day dreams of greatness and fame, never, never to be realized . . . I was to have been a great author and send my tho'ts to the millions and sway the minds of many and hear the whole world ring with my praise . . . O angels who pity us in our frailties, why did you not take me then as I lay on that green bank and dreamed that my dreams had come true?[27]

Nellie Letitia Mooney McClung never became the great author that in her youth she aspired to be, though she did become well-known in Canada as a writer and as the author of at least one Canadian best seller.[28] And when, eventually, she did "sway the minds of many," it was through her role as a social reformer. By the time this occurred, Nellie would have acquired a more mature attitude toward both her goals and her accomplishments. It was much as Letitia Mooney had prophesied: "The world will smooth you down, Nellie. It's a great teacher." It is doubtful, though, if Letitia's youngest child would have achieved all that she did, had she not been the very kind of child that Letitia felt she must suppress.

In January of 1896, Wes made the obligatory visit to meet his fiancée's family. There had been a fear in Nellie's mind that this college graduate with a more sophisticated family background might be disdainful of eating in a farm kitchen, or else look down upon her brothers in their farm clothes. Uneasily she wondered, too, whether he would see the kind heart beneath her mother's blunt simplicity and her lack of education.[29] But when Wes arrived "looking so smart and handsome in a rough brown tweed suit," Letitia Mooney liked him immediately and Wes fitted right into the family like the last piece of a puzzle. Watching him closely with these—her "clear thinking independent people" who were "more ready to give a favor than ask for one"—Nellie saw no sign of condescension or patronage in his manner. She was content. At one point Letitia took her headstrong youngest daughter aside to tell her: "Nellie, you have more sense than I ever gave you credit for," and Letitia was so taken by Wes that she monopolized his time for the whole weekend to Nellie's amused, if rueful, delight.

On 25 August 1896, Nellie and Wes were married. The whole community had been invited, and this meant that the wedding had to be held in the Presbyterian church because the Methodist church was too small. To suit the train schedule, the wedding was set for 7:30 in the morning, for right after the ceremony the newly married couple had to board the train. It was a "dark and stormy sky," as Nellie remembered it, "poor omens for a wedding day!" But as they stood on the back platform travelling eastward on their honeymoon and from there to their new home together above the drug store in Manitou, they "looked up, and saw the clouds were parting, and a bit of blue sky was showing over the shoulder of a black cloud." It was, symbolically, with this in mind that Nellie McClung called the first volume of her autobiography *Clearing in the West*. The second chapter of her life had begun.

4

Living in Manitou: 1896–1911

❖

Manitou in 1896 was a small town of eight or nine hundred inhabitants, five grain elevators—which declared its importance as a rural centre—a creamery, a pump factory, and a flour mill. The wide main street was on a slope, distinguishing it from most flat prairie towns, but it had the same establishments: general store, butcher shop, hardware store, drug store, and three hotels. On Saturday it was crowded with farmers from many miles around, their horses tied to hitching posts from one end of Front Street to the other. The days of barter were not entirely past and eggs and butter, bacon and chickens were traded for sugar, tea, and other necessities. On Sundays the four churches drew many farmers back to town. All of the town's business and social activities were recorded in the two weekly newspapers. It was here, in Manitou, that Nellie and Wes McClung would live the first fifteen years of their married life.[1]

Returning to Manitou Nellie had the advantage of beginning married life in a community in which she already had many friends. Her status, however, had changed. Now she was the wife of the town druggist, who, as one of the few professional men in a small town, held a position of some prestige. In addition, Wes was a popular young man and played a prominent part in Manitou's athletic, social, and municipal life. Their apartment over the drug store was far from luxurious but to the young bride it was delightful. Her first home, as she later described it, was

> four rooms up a long stairway at the south side of a grim grey
> building. They were hot in summer and cold in winter, but we did
> not know that ... I loved every dish and every pan and thought

70

nothing could be more beautiful than the satin-striped wallpaper on the parlor and dining rooms, one stripe plain and one flowered . . . A hanging lamp was suspended from the high ceiling and was raised and lowered by manipulation of two chains ending in gold acorns; the shade, of frosted glass, was patterned in wild roses and morning glories and was finished with glass fringe which jingled when Adam McBeth's dray passed below on the street.

In these rooms, clean and shining, not a speck of dust showing despite the constant sifting in from the unpaved main street, "Mrs. R.W. McClung was at home on the first and second Tuesday from three to five" and—in the proper late Victorian manner—she had cards engraved with that information.

There was no question that both Nellie and Wes were not only accepted but were natural leaders in their community. They were young and enthusiastic. Anyone who thinks that life was dull in a small town in 1900 is not aware that the inhabitants of every town thought they must have a branch of every existing organization and, since there were very few people, everyone had to belong to every organization. Where there was not much variety in personnel, there were few idle moments. Nellie was soon a member of the WCTU, the Methodist Ladies' Aid, a teacher in the Sunday School, a leader in the Epworth Leagues (junior and senior), a leader of the Band of Hope (the WCTU children's group), and a member of the Home Economics Association, a forerunner of the Women's Institute.[2] As a church member Nellie served on the parsonage committee and helped organize Sunday School picnics and Christmas concerts. One night she might address the Epworth League on the topic of "Glorifying God in our Recreation," particularly in athletics; on other nights she might take part in debates. On one occasion she entertained ninety young Epworth Leaguers in her home. Somehow Nellie still found time to manage her growing household, to bake, to entertain guests, to fill in occasionally at the local school as a substitute teacher, and to make up stories to tell to her own and the neighbours' children.[3] Obviously, anyone this active had to be energetic, well-organized, and possess an equable good temper and dependable domestic help.

Wes, too, was keeping busy. He was a Mason, a member of the "Dog and Duck" hunting club, a Royal Templar when that temperance organization formed a Manitou branch, a member of the lacrosse association (both locally and provincially), a keen curler, an active member of the hockey club, an organizer of boys' baseball, a town councillor, and, when he was a little older, he offered his services as mayor.[4] If these organized activities were not sufficient there were sleigh rides and skating in the winter, and picnics and bicycling in the summer. Bicycling, in fact, was very popular, and Wes—who was "sole agent for the celebrated Cleveland Bicycle" in Manitou[5]—made a number of long-distance trips, although roads around Manitou were not designed to make it an easy sport. Judging by Nellie's unpublished story "The Bicycle Belle," the young women of Manitou accompanied the young men in less strenuous, but athletic, bicycle jaunts.

Activities in Manitou, at that time, also included village picnics and the local fair in which everyone took part, as well as private parties and community entertainment in the Manitou Opera House. Nellie had not lost her interest in dramatics and elocution. When Wes joined the Royal Templars in 1908, Nellie became the organization's "Superintendant of Elocution for Southern Manitoba" and, throughout their fifteen years in Manitou, she was in charge of literary events for the Sunday School concerts.[6] On one occasion Nellie took part in a "Selection—'Nearer my God to Thee' with Delsarte movements,"[7] though it is difficult to understand how she could have been drawn in by these stylized presentations, which she obviously disapproved of. In Chapter IV of her novel *The Second Chance*—"Something More than Gestures"—she wrote an amusing spoof of Delsarte mannerisms, which, in her opinion, were unnatural and detracted from the meaning to be conveyed by recitations. It is through the innocent eye of the heroine, Pearlie Watson, that the extravagances of Delsarte foolery are ironically unmasked. In that chapter Maudie Ducker is being trained in "gestures" that are to accompany a temperance verse typical of those of the time. To evoke "the devil's winding stair," which the drunkard inevitably followed, "Maudie did a long, waving sweep with three notches in it, and then she "scalloped the air three times evenly to indicate the down grade." When the drunkard of the old woman's tale is likened to a ship without anchor tossing at the mercy of the sea, Maudie "gave the ships a rough time of it with her willowy left arm." As the drunken ship is lost to view, "Maudie rose on the ball of her left foot and indicated 'distance' with the proper Delsarte stretch." Using Pearlie as her mouthpiece, Nellie sums the whole tomfoolery up:

"Well," Pearlie said, unconvinced, "them kind of carrin's-on may do fine for some pieces, but old women wid their hearts just breakin' don't cut the figger eight up in the air, and do the Dutch-roll, and kneel down and get up just for show—they're too stiff, for one thing. Ye can't listen to the story the way Maudie carries on, she's that full of twists and turnin's. Maudie and Miss Morrison don't care a cent for the poor owld woman."[8]

More than one elocutionist of the time must have quailed at these satiric lines! Nellie was too down-to-earth to have patience with foolish pretensions where naturalness and a genuine feeling for the meaning of a passage should predominate. It is the latter that she practised with such success in her own recitation tours of Manitoba and Ontario during her Manitou years. Newspaper accounts of the day speak of the refreshing "realistic way" in which she presented her characters, and they agree in describing the "freedom from artificiality" of her style, one with "no exaggeration of gesture or reflection, just a consummate naturalness."[9]

Debates were a popular form of entertainment as well, and here Mrs. R.W. McClung—according to the Manitou papers—was a frequent participant. No doubt she also worked behind the scenes coaching on other occasions. Certainly her training in Normal School, joined with her provocatively thoughtful mind and her enjoyment in entertaining others, prepared her well for playing a central role in such community activities. Some of the debates, though sponsored by the Methodist Church Epworth League, were open to the public and here Nellie evidently outshone all others.[10] Her ability to bring theoretical matters down to the common, daily experience of the ordinary people in her immediate environment would eventually prove to be a major strength both in her writing and her public addresses. It would also be the source of her pervasive good humour.[11]

But the small town in this era was not entirely dependent on its own resources for entertainment. There were individual stage artists and travelling companies on the circuit, and Manitou was a popular stop for many of them because the hall was always filled with an appreciative audience. Programmes ran the gamut from a company of Shakespearean players through Swiss Bell Ringers. The "Fiske Jubilee Singers" from Newark, New Jersey, sang negro spirituals, and occasionally Manitou might get a complete comic opera like "The

Little Tycoon" with a chorus of twenty-six and an eleven-member orchestra.[12] The Manitou hall, Nellie said,

> may have been a drab little place, with nothing but a raised platform and coal oil footlights, but when the blinds were drawn and all the lamps lighted . . . no opera house that I have ever been in gave out a greater feeling of high expectancy. We dressed in our best for these great occasions . . . Brides wore their wedding dresses . . . There were opera wraps which closely resembled piano drapes but no remarks were made. We were too happy to be catty.

Most of the performances, however, were a combination "Literary and Musical Recital" with songs and prose or verse recitations.[13] On at least three occasions E. Pauline Johnson made a dramatic appearance.[14] Writing forty years later of one of these occasions, Nellie vividly recalled the impression made by this beautiful young Indian woman who appeared, at first, in a startling white satin evening dress and told them of her home, "Chiefswood," near Brantford, and of her recent visit to England. In the second part of her programme Pauline appeared as a simple Indian girl in her "beaded chamois . . . and feather headdress" and told stories of her people and their battle for existence: the two costumes, perhaps, evoked the image of a poet wandering uncertainly between two worlds. Nellie would always remember the haunting rhythm of Johnson's verse: it was "languorous, picture-making poetry," she recalled, at times with "not much meaning in it, but it was surely pure music on her lips." Johnson filled the Methodist church for two successive nights and Nellie and her sister-in-law called on the Canadian poet at her hotel the next day where Johnson accepted an invitation to dinner. Nellie was enchanted by her stories and her charm: "We were living in another world, touching the hem of our own romantic past." No doubt a contact like this rekindled Nellie's desire to be an interpreter of her own people and win recognition as a writer.

Pauline Johnson and Nellie McClung never met again, but exchanged letters until Johnson's untimely death in 1913. The final bequest recorded in Pauline's will is evocative of the deep and supportive friendship between the two women.

> I bequeath to Mrs. Nellie McClung of Winnipeg, author of *Sowing Seeds in Danny*, three toilet pieces mounted in sterling silver, videlicct: clothes brush engraved with my name, my hat brush, and my comb. I wish to have her written to by either one of my executors and

told how much I valued her loyal friendship, and that I wish her to keep these little things and prize them just because they were mine.[15]

The personal nature of Pauline's gifts, and the unique request she made of her executors, clearly reflect a remarkable affinity between two women authors especially considering they met only once. No doubt Nellie would have remembered Pauline without such keepsakes, but she would have been deeply moved by Pauline's simple personal gifts and her special words.

It was not long before Nellie took on another role—that of mother. In the fall of 1896, during her first pregnancy, she was ill and disgruntled. On her twenty-third birthday she had to forego a trip to Winnipeg with Wes, and a much-anticipated visit to the Bijou Theatre there, because of severe nausea. Writing of this, some forty years later, Nellie recalled how she had raged within herself, but certainly not because she was pregnant.

> Why had not something been found to save women from this infernal nausea? What good was it? If it had been a man's disease, it would have been made the subject of scientific research and relieved long ago. But women could suffer; it kept them humble! . . . Life at the moment looked like a black conspiracy against women. If God ordained that the race was to be perpetuated this way, why had he thrown in this ugly extra, to spoil the occasion.

Feeling depressed and miserable the day Wes had to go to Winnipeg without her, Nellie walked the three miles from Manitou out to her old Hazel school district and sat on "the moss-grown stone in the coulee" where she often used to sit and think, and dream her dreams of becoming a writer. "The day was so beautiful," she later recalled, that "it hurt like an old tune. I could hear the geese going south, with that keening cry that always tore at my heart even when I was a child." She sat there for hours "huddled in misery," feeling sorry for herself, and increasingly "resentful." As the hours passed, she began to realize that "many bewildered women have gone down this same dark road and suddenly I found myself crying, not for myself but for all the overburdened inarticulate women of the world." Nellie did some long, hard thinking, alone there, in the coulee, and arrived at a conclusion that reads like a clarion call to battle: "Women had endured too much and said nothing. I certainly was not going to be meek and mild and resigned. Women should change conditions, not merely endure them, and I was positive something should be done . . . Tears were not the remedy. Women had cried too much already."

Fortunately for Nellie's peace of mind she had an understanding doctor and, after the first few weeks, her nausea disappeared and she felt much better. The McClungs' first son, Jack, was born on 16 June 1897, in the rooms over the drug store. Thereafter the family increased fairly rapidly: Florence arrived in January 1899; Paul in November 1900; and then there was a pause until Horace was born in June of 1906. Mark, the last child, was not born until 1911, after their move to Winnipeg. Nellie firmly believed, and always would believe, that being a mother was a woman's highest task. "The very best work that any woman can do in the world, is to bring up her children in the nurture and admonition of the Lord. This is her greatest, her first work. But," she continued, "that is not all."

> The woman that is only interested in her own home and her own children is a selfish woman . . . The woman who really loves her own children . . . is the woman that wants to see other peoples' children get their chance too . . . It is for this reason that many of the greatest problems of the world today are stirring the hearts of the women and arousing them to action . . . We want to help each other to build up, not scorning anyone's work, even though it be far different from our own, but each one sympathizing with and helping the other.

This maternal attitude was also held by many other women in the women's movement, and adhered to by the National Council of Women of Canada as early as 1915, twenty years before McClung wrote the first volume of her autobiography in 1935.[16]

Motherhood, therefore, did not keep Nellie McClung from leading an active life outside her home. Carrying out her resolve would have been difficult in those days before labour-saving devices in the home if Nellie had had to do all her housework by herself, but Alice Foster, a young girl from a nearby farm who came to work for the McClungs after Jack was born, remained with them for twelve years until she left to train as a nurse in Winnipeg.[17] She was capable and patient with the children, looked after the entire household when Nellie was ill, and was, in Nellie's words, "a strong right arm." There were to be many domestics who worked in the McClung household through the years and a great deal was expected of them, especially after Nellie became involved in activities that drew her away from the merely local, but the relationship between Nellie and her domestic help was very good. She practised what she preached; that was, that women who worked in private homes should be treated with consideration and fairness. Hours, at that time, would be long and pay minimal but the work, Nellie insisted, should not be degrading. Household employees should have regular hours and regular time off. If they lived in, they should use the front door and be able to entertain their own friends in the parlour at certain times. In addition, she always encouraged "her girls" to further their education. Several of her helpers were immigrants who worked for only a couple of years until they learned English, often with Nellie's assistance, and were able to go on to get a higher education, or got married—at times, much like family, in the McClung living room. In her autobiography Nellie pays tribute to many maids and housekeepers who, over the years, made it possible for her to lead the active life she did.

With four children so close in age, the McClung home was a lively place during the Manitou years. A woman who used to visit as a child remembers: "Her home was a place like a three-ring circus—everybody was witty and good-natured. They could take it, or they could dish it out to each other, and it was a joy to go there."[18] Another recalls: "It was an open house for kids—no need to worry about the furniture." In the summer there was camping at Hughes' Lake and in the evening "all the kids would gather around the campfire on the beach and Nellie would tell stories." In fact, as this woman recalls, Nellie "was the centre of attention during their stay there."[19] On Sundays she arranged an outdoor Sunday School for all the children and their visitors. At home the children progressed from nursery rhymes to Dickens, and also heard a lot of their mother's own stories. And Nellie read poetry to her children, a lot of poetry, "believing they would get the rhythm of it, even if they did not understand it."

As is the case with most mothers, Nellie liked to reminisce about these years and remember the happy times and the clever things the children did and said, choosing to ignore the frustration and minor tragedies that strike any household. In September of 1906, for example, a nearby housefire—in which a child was burned to death—came close to engulfing the McClung home too. In the spring of 1908, young Horace, who was not yet two years old, suffered a serious attack of pneumonia, and in mid-summer of the same year Nellie was stricken with typhoid fever.[20] Nevertheless, McClung, in her writing, tended to select the amusing events. She recorded, for example, how, after Jack had been rewarded for finding his lost sister, the family noted that Florence seemed to be getting lost frequently and that Jack seemed to find her with remarkable ease. Enquiry soon revealed that Jack, recognizing a good proposition, was bribing his sister to "get lost." Then there was the occasion of Horace's arrival when Paul—"with his head of thick brown curls, and dressed in a badly crumpled Buster Brown suit"—went on his own initiative to every house in the neighbourhood announcing the birth. All but one of the neighbours, a childless couple who found three McClung children more than enough, joined Paul in his pleasure at the arrival of a new brother. As Nellie watched her children grow, and observed their childlike ways and thoughts and curious turns of speech she was, once more, storing up material for fiction based on the realities of life about her. Paul, she recorded, expressed the opinion that "when a string is broken—you can glue it together," and one of the children's friends named Ray, "wanted a scab on his pudding."[21] Such sayings reflect the characteristic imagination of children and would eventually find their place in the *Danny* stories where they confer a quaint and charming touch of reality.

Years later while reminiscing about the development of the McClung family life, Nellie would observe that people generally talked "about the influence parents have on children," but failed to notice "the way children change their parents." And Nellie, having rejected the autocratic spirit of the Victorian parent, was open to an adult understanding of that influence. She knew that she had been for long assailed by attacks of "the crusading spirit" and that now, with children of her own, she wanted "to raise a family who would . . . scatter the darkness of humanity, and light the candles of freedom in the dark places of the world." But the voice of her own experience told her that she must first "give them sound bodies and sound minds and cheerful memories, not rolling the sins of the world on them at too early an age" as, at times, her own dour mother had done. She resolved to let her children "have all the fun in life" that she could reasonably give them. This was to be their inalienable "heritage." At the same time, however, Nellie claimed that the sense of "a new responsibility" came to her with the arrival of her own children.

> All children now were my children . . . Women must be made to feel their responsibility. All this protective love, this instinctive mother love, must be organized some way, and made effective. There was

enough of it in the world to do away with all the evils that war upon children, undernourishment, slum conditions, child labor, drunkenness. Women could abolish these if they wanted to.

To accomplish these things women had to present a unified voice. Nellie decided that the best organization to work through was the Women's Christian Temperance Union. She considered the WCTU "the most progressive organization" of all the women's groups at that time, and she felt that by means of it she could "stir the deep waters of complacency" and hope to establish a better world for all children.

In Canada the WCTU had been organized in Ontario in 1874 and had spread rapidly throughout the West where the abuse of alcohol had become a serious problem—just as it had been in the pioneer days of Ontario.[22] In those days, however, the WCTU was far more than a prohibition society; it supported reforms of many kinds, including women's suffrage as one means of controlling the liquor traffic.[23] The WCTU was a central part of small town social and cultural life "and people travelled long distances to attend" the events they sponsored. Even if Nellie had had no strong convictions about prohibition she would have been drawn into the Manitou WCTU, but she adhered firmly to the belief that alcohol was the source of most of the social problems in the world about her and she concluded, therefore, that the liquor business was evil.

WCTU workers have sometimes been portrayed as middle-class women trying to impose their narrow-minded standards of morality on new Canadians of the labouring class.[24] In those early days, however, Nellie McClung saw the abuse of alcohol as the curse of everyone it touched. "It is easy," she would later recall, "to see why we concentrated on the liquor traffic. It was corporeal and always present; it walked our streets; it threw its challenge in our faces!" All Nellie had to do in a little town where "the currents run deeply and we knew each other's sins and sorrows" was to look about her. She saw the potentially successful farmer who spent his limited supply of cash at the bar instead of on seed grain; the clever doctor who gradually became medically incompetent and a danger to the well-being of his patients as he drank more and more; the beloved and respected high school principal who lost his position and eventually his life as the result of alcohol; and she saw the terror of Jenny Gills, a local WCTU member who "was 'expecting' again, and her husband had celebrated the last occasion by getting roaring drunk and coming home with the avowed intention of killing Jenny and the new baby." These were examples of alcohol abuse Nellie knew of from first-hand experience and which she recorded in her speeches, in her autobiography, and, at times, in her fiction. She was not talking about a class of people set apart from herself. At no time did she consider alcohol to be the exclusive problem of the poor. And she both spoke and behaved with sympathy toward these people, whom she looked upon as victims of the liquor interests who grew rich, as she saw it, at the expense of so many whose personality and behaviour had been adversely influenced by alcohol. But most of her sympathy was for the wives and children of alcoholics, the ones she saw as innocent victims of the liquor trade. In an age when most women did not drink, it was easy to conclude "that women and children were the sufferers from the liquor traffic; any fun that came from drinking belonged to men exclusively, and the men themselves would be the first to admit that."

Nellie's first temperance lessons came from her mother. Letitia Mooney had recounted with bitterness the loss of a child because a drunken doctor had misdiagnosed his illness. In early childhood, both in Grey County and in southern Manitoba, Nellie had seen community barn raisings and picnics marred by alcohol. As a pupil she took part in the school presentation of temperance dramas, and later as a teacher she taught temperance lessons with material provided by the school board. As a member of the Methodist church, she had the evils of alcohol and the need for personal abstinence strongly impressed upon her and there was, too, the influence of her mother-in-law, Mrs. J.A. McClung, who was one of the provincial leaders of the WCTU in Manitoba.[25] And so, by 1901, Nellie was invited to deliver the address of welcome at the fifteenth annual convention of the WCTU in Manitoba. It was being held, on this occasion, in her home town of Manitou.[26]

Nellie knew from experience that she must not bore her audience with age-old statistics or the traditional gimmick of calculating "how many loaves of bread a man could buy if he never drank beer." She knew that some who drank to excess were comfortably well-off and had no use for such figures. On the other hand, Nellie also realized that she needed to understand why people drank to excess but, given the era's lack of knowledge and her own inexperience, she had only the vaguest of ideas. She could, however, arrive at some understanding of the problem through her personal knowledge of those people in her prairie environment whose lives were intolerably drab.

> I knew the lives of these country people, with their disappointments, long hours, and grey monotony; and I felt we must give them something rather than take something away . . . Prohibition is a hard sounding word, worthless as a rallying cry, hard as a locked door or going to bed without your supper. It could never fire the heather . . . People had to have something which would take them out of themselves, the Church has given many a real vision . . . but even the Church often presents a dour face, with its locked door and musty smells . . . we, the temperance women, would have to make our cause attractive. We must fight fire with fire . . . I saw in my easily stirred imagination, that life for both men and women could be made much more attractive with recreation grounds, games, handicrafts, orchestras, folk dances, better houses, better farms; new hopes for a new world.

Nellie returned again and again in her writing to her consciousness of this unfulfilled need for hope in the life and "the mind of my people."

It was typical of McClung to search out the positive, constructive approach to a problem with a freshness of insight that might provide stimulus for reform, rather than to fall back on conventional ideas that were trusted merely because they were old and established. She had wanted, in her speech, to fire the minds of her audience to action, but in doing this she discovered something about herself: "For the first time I knew I had the power of speech. I saw faces brighten, eyes glisten, and felt the atmosphere crackle with a new power. I knew what could be done with words . . . " This knowledge of the power of words was put to work, in subsequent years, in her addresses, in her reading tours, and in her writing: whether essays or fiction. And from this day forward, Nellie Letitia Mooney McClung felt committed to use the power of words in those causes that, to the best of her knowledge, might "shape the world nearer to our heart's desire."

Nellie McClung was, both by nature and by discipline, an activist, a doer. She insisted upon hope for social ills, and upon optimism in the face of despair, for that was, to her, the only constructive path to take. But the high ideals of the WCTU women of Nellie's era would necessarily be tempered in time, and there is something sadly touching in her account as she looks back, in *The Stream Runs Fast*, to report their failure. If only the women had the vote, ran their argument, they would secure prohibition and a better world. "We did not believe that women would ever become drinkers. We argued, subconsciously, that women have more resources within themselves, more outlets for their energies, and so did not need this false exhilaration." But Nellie and her group were, at this time, almost as subject to the Victorian idealization of women as were the men who fabricated the myth, and she would never forget the first time she saw a woman intoxicated. The woman came from "one of Winnipeg's best known families" and "her lapse from sobriety rather upset my theory that people drink to relieve the monotony of a drab life."

Veronica Strong-Boag has argued that there was a fundamental contradiction in the thought patterns of social activists like McClung. "Their campaign was justified at two philosophical levels. One was egalitarian, the demand for rights natural to all human beings. The other was essentially inegalitarian, based on presumptions of feminine superiority: only women had the spiritual and moral resources to reform society." The latter also emphasized the more traditional view of women as wives and mothers. While Nellie believed women had acquired different sensibilities and priorities than men, and that these peculiarly fitted them for social reform, the claim to women's spiritual superiority could scarcely be hers. With a father-in-law like the Reverend J.A. McClung, who actively supported the woman suffrage issue, and with a husband like Wes, who supported Nellie in all her feminist activities, it is impossible to conclude that she believed that women alone had "the spiritual and moral resources to reform society." Even had she been so naive in Manitou, by the time the McClungs moved to Winnipeg in 1911, Nellie would find many liberal-minded men as well as women in the Political Equality League, and she learned that male social reformers like J.S. Woodsworth improved the lot of immigrants through his "All People's Mission." Equally, she knew many—probably more—conservative-minded women who actively opposed women's suffrage and who threw up all the obstacles they could to block the advancement of women. This knowledge both broadened and deepened the arguments upon which McClung based her feminist activities, and while she continued, at times, to support what is now called *maternal feminism*—support for the opinion that a woman's first priority should be her family and therefore that women's involvement in the reform movement should largely revolve around family-oriented issues—increasingly she moved in the direction of egalitarian or *equal rights feminism*. She supported, for example, married women who did not need, but wished, to work outside the home, and she argued for women's economic independence from men, a condition her writing skills afforded her vis-à-vis Wes. This dualism in Nellie McClung's feminist principles made her "acceptable to both conservatives and liberals" and, in any case, as Strong-Boag indicates, the "distinction was never fully clarified, and suffragist arguments fluctuated erratically between the two philosophical poles, the confusion [if indeed it was] hidden for the short term by the overriding goal of enfranchisement."[27]

While Nellie was still living in Manitou, an event occurred that fired the Manitou WCTU "like a prairie fire before a high wind." The nearby town of Carman was faced with a vote on local option to determine whether the town wanted a bar, and "the liquor interests were afraid they would be defeated, for at that time women who had property in their own name could vote in municipal matters." The Manitoba government, evidently lobbied by representatives of the liquor business, decided on a particularly shameful course of action: by an Order in Council "they would quietly and without any flourish of trumpets, disfranchise the women." This flagrant injustice would eventually serve to unite the socially activist women of Manitoba in a common cause. They too would decide on a course of action. If the government of the day would not give women the vote, then the women of Manitoba would work to secure the defeat of the party in power, and "that is what we did, though it took a little time." It was "a bonny fight," Nellie later recalled with zest, "a knock-down and drag-out fight" that Nellie and her friends—"a resolute band of women"—waged with great enthusiasm. But this battle for the right of women to vote in Manitoba would find its focus in Winnipeg several years later, following Nellie's move to that city with Wes and the children. By that time the women involved in the fight went well beyond the boundaries of the WCTU. Alarmed by the problems resulting from mass immigration, rapid urban growth, and an expanding wheat economy, they advocated not only prohibition and women's suffrage but a general reform of society.[28]

In the midst of the Second World War, as Nellie completed the second volume of her autobiography, she had this to say about the WCTU in Manitou: "We really believed we were about to achieve a new

world. War had no place in our thoughts then. We were too civilized
for war we thought. We believed the enemies we had to fight were
ignorance, greed, intolerance and boredom." And so, Nellie sadly
records from the perspective of age and greater wisdom, "so ran my
dream." Nellie and the WCTU women of Manitou were full of high,
if somewhat naive, ideals. Eventually they would learn that
mankind's devils were of a darker hue, far more complex, and more
difficult to fight. Nellie would never be quite so full of illusions as she
was in the early days of the women's rights movement in Manitou.
But near the end of her days she would still affirm the vision of a
better world ahead, one that "has never faded . . . though the way
may be long and hard and dangerous." This, she always knew, was
the better course, and it "has fired man's imagination since time
began" and always—somewhere, somehow—someone would have,
like her, the courage to fight that good fight no matter what the odds.
In 1901 in Manitou, however, when Nellie gave what she hoped was
a stirring address to the annual convention of the Manitoba WCTU,
the battle, for her, was just beginning: "My head was lighter than my
heart when it was all over, for I knew that I was committed to a long
fight and a hard one."

Nellie's schedule in Manitou was a hectic one. In addition to the
busy life she led as a member of a variety of organizations, such as the
WCTU, she frequently entertained visitors: Wes's father and mother,
his sister Nellie (now usually called Eleanor), his brothers, Nellie's
sister Hannah, and many of Nellie's nieces and nephews. On at least
one occasion, after Nellie had become well known as a writer, Cora
Hind, from Winnipeg, came to visit for several days. While teaching
at the Hazel school Nellie had seen Cora Hind when the latter came
to Manitou as a guest of Mrs. Ruttan. Hind, by that time, was famous
as an agricultural journalist, and Manitobans were very proud of her.
In addition, she represented something of a role model for young
Nellie, who, in her youth, "often thought enviously of this clever
newspaper woman who was doing with great success the very thing
that I aspired to do."[29] At the time, however, Nellie was so much in
awe of this woman who had made a name for herself in the newspaper
world that she could not step forward so that Mrs. Ruttan would
notice and introduce her.

Nellie may have met Cora Hind, for the first time, at the *Winnipeg
Free Press* shortly after the mid-summer of 1905 when the Methodist

Book and Publishing House suggested that Nellie work up material submitted to them as a novel. She had already met *Free Press* columnist "Mary Markwell," the journalist's pseudonym for Kate Simpson Hayes, and had confided her tentative plans for the development of *Sowing Seeds in Danny*. Immediately Markwell said: "I'll have a tea for you in my office, and ask a few writing friends to meet you. It will do them good and you too." Two of Markwell's more likely guests, at that time, were E. Cora Hind and Lillian (Beynon) Thomas, who also worked at the *Free Press*. And Markwell's column for that week, following her writer's tea for Nellie McClung, predicted that "a new interpreter of Canadian life had arrived, and would be heard from."[30] By October of 1908, following the mid-summer publication of *Danny*, Cora Hind invited Nellie McClung to be the guest of honour—along with Agnes Laut—at the Winnipeg branch of the Canadian Women's Press Club so the members could get to know this new and unknown Manitoba novelist. Thereafter Nellie was a frequent guest of that group—"one of the brightest guests the members have ever met"[31]— and she and Cora soon became friends. Now, Nellie L. McClung, author, could invite Cora Hind to visit her in Manitou. It was the autumn of 1909, and Cora, who had a good sense of humour, fitted right in to the McClung family and subsequently wrote an interesting account of her stay. Before her arrival she wired the following instruction: "Marcel Jasper's tail. A visitor is coming." Jasper was the McClungs' horse and Nellie had told Cora that his straggly "rat tail" was a source of amusement in Manitou. To the delight of the McClungs, their local telegraph agent "could not understand the message, and spelled 'Jasper's tail' as one word and I think he thought I was receiving a code message, for he delivered the telegram to Wes in the Drug store to see if he could make head or tail of it."[32]

From the time that they first met, Cora said, like so many others, she had found Nellie "irresistible," and on this occasion she was somewhat apprehensive that a closer, more intimate acquaintance might be disillusioning. Instead, her original opinion was reinforced. Cora was accepted as a member of the family, helping out with the gardening and bargaining to mend the family stockings if Nellie would agree to read the early manuscript chapters of her second novel in her "pleasant well-modulated voice." During her week with the McClungs, Cora had marvelled that Nellie could do any writing in such a busy household. On the first morning of Cora's visit Nellie was baking a cake for a party that evening. In the midst of her preparation the minister arrived unexpectedly at the door to ask Nellie to preside at a meeting that afternoon. With only a moment's hesitation Nellie agreed. On another busy morning Cora counted at least twenty interruptions:

> long distance telephone calls, a visit from the President of the Ladies' Aid who "must see her for a moment"; a committee from the Christian Endeavor that wanted advice; "Please mother I can go out to Taylor's if I can be ready in five minutes" from her second boy Paul. He was made ready and dispatched; a lengthy consultation with her little daughter Florence because the girls of her class at school wanted to get up a millinery opening and could they do it all in the tent in the garden; numerous visits from her youngest boy, a dear little golden-haired chap, who called himself "Hor-Barrie-Clung" being a new and original rendering for "Horace Barrie McClung." These were a few of the things that interrupted the reading that morning.[33]

On another afternoon Cora and Nellie had resolved to take a scenic autumn drive along the Pembina Valley without any of the children. But, as it turned out, looking after Horace would interfere with the maid's music lessons, "so the small man was tucked in between us" in the McClung car and off they went. This trip gave Cora another chance to observe a woman who, from the first, "had attracted me wonderfully." She saw

> the sweetness of the woman who cheerfully answered all the child's questions and who, in the various calls that we made in the valley, found something cheerful and pleasant to discuss with the members of each household. I could see that her visits were highly prized and I did not wonder at it, for she has, in a pre-eminent degree, that rare virtue, forgetfulness of self and power to enter the lives and interests of others.[34]

The young Nellie Mooney—whose energetic, outgoing personality had seemed merely egotistical and self-centred under the repressive sway of her mother—was freed now, from constrictive admonition. The result was that in maturity Nellie McClung directed her strong ego outward toward the benefit of others. It is clear, too, that her emotional and intellectual attentiveness to her children was Nellie's considered reply to the Victorian oppressiveness she had experienced from Letitia Mooney. Nellie had learned to recognize "a child's need for security" as well as a child's need to feel free to question and be answered, and to be encouraged to try its wings, and to grow in its own direction. Cora Hind described the McClung children at this time as "bright, fun-loving, and mischievous" but added: "Mother's word is law. There are not too many rules, but, when a rule is laid down, it has to be adhered to." In sum, she stated, "the greatest camaraderie exists between mother and children."[35]

Cora also observed the quality of Nellie's relationship with her husband and, of course, Wes's response to his wife. "I have rarely seen more perfect sympathy between husband and wife," she recorded. "R.W. McClung is a big, silent man, but it is only necessary to see his eyes follow his wife about their home to realize that theirs is, in very truth, a marriage."[36] Nellie was amused at the word "silent." That just proved, she quipped, that when she and E. Cora began talking, no one else had a chance except Horace B. "who can *make room*."[37] Cora accounted, in part, for the closeness she saw between Nellie and Wes by their habit of going away together whenever it was possible.

> One of the dear delights of the year, and what is in reality a repetition of their honeymoon, is to go together, leaving the children behind, to a little hunting camp, where, for a week, they see no one but each other. He shoots ducks, for he is an ardent sportsman, and she cooks the meals and the intervals are filled with long walks and talks.[38]

Nellie was careful not to let four children and her busy schedule of activities lead to neglect of her husband. Indeed, in 1909 an idea she recorded for a short story indicated her awareness that "a man's affection for his wife is apt to go cold if not kept properly nourished, just like a tub left dry will fall to staves."[39] But the closeness of communion between husband and wife, as Nellie herself has pointed out, was not won at the expense of differences of opinion that might lead to arguments. Certainly Wes's red hair bespoke the quick temper of his personality, a temper, his son Mark recalls, that generally arose over only unimportant matters and dissipated as quickly as it appeared, partly because Nellie had acquired constructive methods of easing it.[40]

> I am not going to say that we never had a cross word. Two people of strong character are bound to have a clash once in a while, and there is no harm done by a plain straight-spoken word, but I can truthfully say this—there never was a bitter word said or one that rankled . . . [Wes] was a good straight debater, with a sense of justice and fair play that has always held my admiration.[41]

A marriage entirely without tension, Nellie believed, meant that one party was being totally submissive to the other. The Victorian concept that a wife was more an adjunct of her husband than a person in her own right, and that the wife must passively and obediently reflect her husband's opinions rather than cultivate her own, was the recipe for an unhealthy relationship, and both Nellie and Wes rejected it. Yet Nellie asserted, and all outside opinion seems to confirm, that Wes was the strongest supporter of all her endeavours. A female interviewer for the Winnipeg *Grain Growers' Guide* (11 January 1911) pointed out that "Mrs. McClung is happily mated with a husband who is progressive enough to have assimilated the modernism of 'equality of the sexes' and supports her in her literary ambitions with unfailing sympathy and encouragement." Of course, the young Nellie Mooney had made this something of a condition for their marriage and, in any case, Wes had been raised in a family whose mother was independent-minded, and who raised both her male and female children to share the same household responsibilities and, where it was logical, the same privileges. It is difficult to believe that Nellie could have accomplished all that she did—especially in the early days of this century— without her husband's full encouragement.

Nellie McClung possessed a remarkable ability to keep her priorities straight. The family came first, and each member of that family— from their maid, through the children and their father—was made to feel that each was listened to and responded to and had his proper place. But Nellie's public role was vital to her also. Only a woman of great resourcefulness and adaptability, order and calm efficiency, could balance so effectively the needs of her active family with such a vigorous schedule of public interests, obligations, and accomplishments without creating the negative sense of feeling burdened or of making others feel she was doing them a favour. It is not surprising that Cora Hind saw Nellie McClung as a "beautiful ideal," and this kind of unstinting praise is repeated again and again from those who knew her well.

Still, Nellie was far more aware than Cora might think that marriage and a family were not always the proverbial bed of roses. "Raising a family brings great joy," she confided to her journal many years later, "but certainly does not bring peace. I found that out in the turbulent years that followed that August morning when the two young people, just married, stood on the rear platform of the Northern Pacific train, and saw the clearing in the west, which betokened a fine day tomorrow. And tomorrow," she added firmly, "was fine." On the whole there had been "health and happiness . . . and a reasonable amount of harmony." But very sagely she added: "When I hear married people say they never had a quarrel or a harsh word, I look at them with great interest and some suspicion." Nellie was a realist who knew that people could not "live through all the changing scenes of life with its manifold irritations" and never show anger or marked differences of opinion.[42] In fact, in an unfinished verse manuscript, written in the early days of her married life in Manitou and evidently addressed to Wes, Nellie refers to "the strain of life when life is ill" and frankly acknowledges "there's one Above, who tempers life/With sweet and bitter, good and ill." The poem's overall theme is the gentle admonition that she and Wes should be careful each day in the present to create "a shining link/In memory's golden chain . . . " so that, near the close of their lives, they might both look back upon their marriage with contentment.[43] Perfect bliss, to someone as wise and down-to-earth as Nellie McClung, was mere fantasy. Yet, during an interview with Nellie McClung in 1947—just four years before her death—Margaret Ecker Francis observed that at one point "a tall, slightly-stooped man, with unruly hair and a twinkle in his eye" came into the room and the two "grinned affectionately at each other."

> Wes McClung crossed to his wife's chair and put his hand protectingly on her arm for a moment . . . and the two smiled at each other again, their smiles full of youthfulness and of some private joke. Together, somehow, they seemed much younger than they did separately . . .
> As they sat together, the last rays of the setting sun caught their faces in its glow. It was almost too much. It was the happy ending straight out of a McClung novel . . . [44]

Throughout the first ten years of their married life in Manitou the McClung business appears to have prospered. In 1899 Wes enlarged his store and expanded his stock so that he possessed "one of the largest and best assorted stocks of Drugs, Druggist's Sundries, Stationery, Wallpaper, Holiday and Fancy Goods, etc., to be found in Southern Manitoba." In the same year he was selling the Parmalee Library and, as he was also a "Graduate Optician," he gave free eye examinations and sold glasses at "standard prices." The expansion may have been Wes's response to competition from a second drug store established in Manitou that year.[45] In a small town of less than one thousand people, two drug stores may have been one store too many, but one would hardly expect the McClung business to suffer. His was the older, more established of the two stores, and Wes was personally very popular in the town. In 1900 Wes was selling the McIntosh Library of books at "10¢ a book and 150 books to choose from," he bought a house for his growing family, installed a "national cash register" in his Manitou store, sold a farm that he owned jointly with a business associate for a total of $2880.00, and bought a third "Drug and Stationery" business in nearby Crystal City evidently with a younger brother, Herbie, in mind. In June of that year Herb would graduate from the College of Pharmacy in Winnipeg, winning the silver medal for his year, and by September "the Crystal City Drug Emporium"—refurbished into a "handsome new store"—was being operated by "H.S. McClung and Co." Probably Herb was repaying Wes, who appears to have set his brother up in business. By the spring of 1901 Wes had a new store sign in gold letters, and by the fall of that year "had built a new brick building across the street with a hall above where the Foresters and Masons met, and sometimes socials were held."[46] The rent from this building would increase his regular income.

It is surprising, then, to discover in the 28 December 1905 issue of the Manitou *Sun*, that Wes had sold his business to Messrs. W.A. and Charles Parker. The actual transfer was scheduled to take place on 15 March 1906.[47] Nellie's explanation for this unexpected decision, as published in her autobiography, was that Wes suffered from "a primitive Methodist conscience" and had become abnormally anxious from the strain and responsibility of his work. Though he had "two good assistants," according to Nellie, Wes was "the only licensed pharmacist" in his drug store "and he was always afraid there might be a mistake" with possibly fatal consequences. Wes's "usual good disposition began to cloud over," as Nellie recalled many years later, and he developed what appears to be a neurotic habit of getting up from bed at all hours of the night "to see if the [drug store] doors were locked": surely a curious concern since Wes advertised that a "Night Clerk"—who slept in the back of the store—"will cheerfully leave his downy couch . . . at any hour of the night" to fill prescriptions, stamp letters, or tell the time, "and he will do it all with a glad and winsome smile." Nellie began to feel that Wes would recover from "nervous exhaustion" if he no longer had to worry about prescriptions. Certainly strain that was severe enough to alter one's personality and normal behaviour patterns would be a sufficient reason for changing one's occupation, but the fact of such anxiety—Methodist-induced or not—hardly seems an adequate explanation why a prosperous professional man with a growing family should dispose of a successful business: especially when he had no alternative occupation in mind. Still, no other explanation has been discovered.[48]

For the next several years Nellie, Wes, and the children lived primarily on income from the rent of two farms bought with money from the sale of the drug business, and Wes "built telephone lines . . . for one season, and the years fell away from him, and the whole family was happy," according to Nellie.

The life of Nellie McClung in Manitou, as described to this point, could be—to a large extent—that of many wives and mothers living in a small western town. Women with an income adequate enough to hire domestic help were usually active outside the home in a number of organizations. And in every town there were one or two women who stood out as leaders in their community. But during these years Nellie's life took on another dimension, one that set her apart from such women. She became a writer and a public speaker of national— and international—renown, for marriage and a family had not changed Nellie's ambition to become an author. During this early period of her married life in Manitou, Nellie began writing children's literature, moved on to short stories for adults, and by 1908 had published her first novel, *Sowing Seeds in Danny,* a Canadian best seller. The resulting acclaim brought a number of advantages: not only to Nellie, but to Wes and the children. Not the least was financial gain that, by this time, was sorely needed. Although by 1908 Nellie had been receiving sporadic income from her writing and her reading tours, helping supplement their limited income, for much of the time between March 1906, when Wes sold the drug business, and mid-1911, when he secured a position as city salesman for a large Winnipeg company, there was considerable financial worry that must have rivalled the strain that Wes apparently felt in filling, correctly, prescriptions in a pharmacy. By late 1907, for example, Nellie was urgently trying to solicit "any sort of literary work" such as "book reviews and criticisms" from H. Nicols, editor of the Winnipeg *Telegram*:

> My reason for wanting such work is because I have to do it and because I need the money. I would be content with a modest remuneration tho, for work of this kind comes easy to me. I write quite a few short stories for magazines. The *Woman's Home Companion* paid me $500 for 20,000 words this year [1907] and the *Delineator* paid me $75 for 2,500 words. I mention these not to give the impression that I expect a high rate, but to give you confidence in my ability to turn out stuff that people might want to read. What I want is a settled sum which will come in every week or month that I can depend on.[49]

In October of 1908 Nellie was still seeking regular payment for journalistic work, this time from A. Dennis of the Winnipeg *Tribune* who indicated that he had papers at Elmwood and Kenora—though both were printed in Winnipeg—and he suggested that Nellie could do newspaper work for either one.[50] As early as January 1907, however, Nellie and Wes were toying with the idea of moving to Vancouver,[51] evidently to make a new start, but they finally settled on Winnipeg in the spring of 1911 when Wes became a salesman for the Manufacturers' Life Insurance Company. Although one Manitou paper referred to Wes as about to become the Winnipeg salesman for a large drug firm—which would have been a logical step for a nonpractising druggist—if he did so, it must have been for only a very brief period.[52] By mid-summer they had bought a comfortable house at 97 Chestnut Street in Winnipeg, and the next day Nellie recorded in her journal: "We like it—especially me! Now I'm busy writing. I need the money. Don't talk to me." At this time the McClungs must have been optimistic that their financial problems would soon end for, in the next few days, they also bought a lake shore cottage at Matlock Beach on Lake Winnipeg. Sometime prior to leaving Manitou, perhaps with Nellie's earnings, they had also purchased part ownership in a cottage that—with a fine disregard for financial worries—they had named "Pleasure Bent." Nellie's oldest sister, Lizzie Rae, whose husband had been killed by lightning in 1901, had the cottage next door, and many members of both families must have visited over the summer months, particularly Wes's mother and father, as the Reverend J.A. McClung had retired and moved to Winnipeg in the fall of 1901. It appears that Nellie and Wes had joint ownership of the first cottage with Wes's sister Eleanor and her husband, Percy Anderson, for it was Eleanor who conceived the idea that they "simply had to have a beach front" to hear the waves and watch the children boating and swimming. Although the foursome were able to trade the old cottage on the new one, they still had to pay the difference, and Nellie confessed to her journal: "I need it [money] now worse than ever." Still, they planned to christen the new cottage "Heart's Desire or Heartsease," perhaps as a symbol of their new-found sense of release from the monetary burdens of the past five years.[53]

There is no doubt that the financial pressures of these years had spurred Nellie's desire to earn income from her pen, and she searched diligently for every possible source of publication. One periodical that accepted pieces from her at this time was *Canada-West Magazine*, which began publication in Winnipeg in 1906 under the editorship of Walter E. Gunn, a well-known figure in the Canadian newspaper and publishing world. This publication was "under the editorial direction" of the Western Canadian Immigration Association, founded in 1904 in Minneapolis by "about eighty gentlemen interested in various ways in the development of Western Canada." They sought literary and other material on the Canadian west both to inform and stimulate American interest, and published authors like Agnes Deans Cameron and Emerson Hough, who was a notable contributor to the *Saturday Evening Post*: "Few men have a livelier interest in Western Canada . . . or know it better."[54] Nellie began submitting material in the fall of 1906 when Herbert Vanderhoof of Chicago was secretary for the Immigration Association. He accepted a McClung verse, "The Lay of Mary's Land," for the January 1907 issue of *Canada-West*, and a story entitled "Babette" appeared in the November issue of the same year. Another poem was accepted for the December 1908 issue.[55]

At this time, probably to Nellie's dismay, the magazine was unable to pay for submissions, and much of their material was republished from other periodicals. By 1908, however, Vanderhoof had "an editorial appropriation from which we can pay for stories." He had also secured a free pass for Nellie on the Canadian Northern Railway from Winnipeg to Edmonton and return, and also free passage on the Canadian Pacific line from Strathcona, near Winnipeg, to Vancouver via Calgary and return "as a guest" of his magazine. This, he said, "gives you an option of returning to Winnipeg in two ways." The idea was that Nellie—by this time, well known as a Canadian writer—would gather material for "a series of articles on the west" that Vanderhoof hoped to publish in *Canada-West* as a means of promoting interest in that part of the continent. Though he generously agreed to the prior publication of these articles elsewhere, which was, of course, to Nellie's financial advantage, he declared categorically: "I want copies of everything you write." Nellie had requested a pass for Wes, too, though it is not clear from the Vanderhoof correspondence whether one was obtained. At any rate, both Nellie and Wes left Manitou in early June for a tour that would take two months: from Winnipeg through Saskatoon to Edmonton on the Canadian Northern, and from there via Calgary, Revelstoke, and Kamloops, to Vancouver on the Canadian Pacific.[56] Few issues of *Canada-West* are extant, and no publication arising from this trip has been found; however, there must have been some. Those manuscript notes that do exist, though incomplete, show Nellie's interest in the varied topography of the land, the quality of the soil and kinds of crops grown, the development of towns and cities, the quality of the hotels, economic and other signs of progress: the sort of information that Vanderhoof would have wanted for his magazine. The notes are sometimes detailed, sometimes sketchy.

> *Verigin:* "the sportsman's paradise—little lakes, park lands, ducks innumerable . . . leaving long rippling paths behind them, fat and saucy."
>
> *Rama:* "a small clearing in the wood shows a little group of sod-roofed houses . . . and a pile of lumber and shingles gives promise of what is to come."
>
> *Dalmeny:* "a large billboard calls the attention of the passersby to get off and invest their money in a real sure thing. The billboard is about the biggest thing in the town, but the land around it is excellent."
>
> *Rocky Mountains:* "They are too magnificent to be grasped . . . Some places attract with a strange fascination. They call you back again and again . . . The natural bridge at Field is the place that calls to me . . . It's the mighty, slappity dash bang of the torrent that laid hold upon me. It is mighty strong! But you won't understand . . . unless you see it!"

Evidently Nellie and Wes managed a side trip through the Okanagan Valley as far as Kelowna via the spur line south to the

Landing and the comfortable CPR steamboat. The Okanagan Valley was "paradise valley" to Nellie.

The McClungs must have returned to the main railway line and evidently continued on through Kamloops, Mission Junction, and Harrison on to Vancouver, although the existing portion of Nellie's journal excerpts make no mention of the Pacific coast. Returning as far as Revelstoke, the McClungs took a spur line south to Arrow Head Landing where they boarded the *S.S. Kootenay* through the upper and lower Arrow Lakes to their southern extreme at Robson; and always the eye of the author was alert:

> The sunset on Arrowhead is a sight to remember . . . The mountains were as blue as a blue pigeon's wing and behind them the sky was dyed cerise. The lake was calm and glassy and on its edges the mountains stood up and down; every mark, every stone, every uprooted tree was given back faithfully in the quiet waters.

From West Robson, Nellie and Wes took the train the twenty-seven miles east to Nelson, and then went on to Cranbrook where they stayed, and later caught the overnight Soo-Spokane Flyer—on the CPR line—back to the prairie flatlands.

> When we got up in the morning the scene was changed. Just one long treeless stretch of country, nothing more exciting than a snow fence and a sandpile. Bunch grass grows on this apparently almost arid soil, and on it herds of cattle and horses roam and thrive. It has a beauty of its own too, and this great, sun-burnt plain—it rolls into great, flat broad-backed knolls . . . Maple Creek is a city of the plain . . .

At times the reader is conscious that Nellie was a prairie dweller: "Nothing friendly about these mountains. You can't make a pet of them." Interspersed among the travel notes are native Indian tales and anecdotes, such as: "Wasakajack-Indian Santa Clause." Such observations, over the years, interested Nellie very much, perhaps as a result of her friendship with Pauline Johnson. As a Canadian author who had, by this time, one novel and several published short stories to her credit, Nellie L. McClung had a strong sense of the immediacy of her environment, and it was with both foresight and confidence that she prophesied: "some day some writer will come who can write of the marvels of this land."[57]

From Nellie's success as an author sprang another aspect of her career: that of recitalist and public speaker. As the fame of *Sowing*

Seeds in Danny spread she was increasingly in demand as an entertainer-recitalist—at first in Manitoba—and later in Ontario. Nellie's first venture into this field was in Winnipeg at the request of her mother-in-law, who invited her to give readings from *Danny* at Grace Church to benefit the WCTU home for friendless girls. This was a new and exciting experience for Nellie. She believed that her first performance sounded like "Friday afternoon at the country school," but westerners were anxious to hear this new author in their midst who wrote about their own country, and soon she received numerous invitations from small, rural, southern Manitoba towns where she filled Methodist and Presbyterian churches and, on at least one occasion, the Roland Anglican Church. Sometimes the churches in these communities, or young peoples' groups, or the YMCA or WCTU organizations acted as her sponsor. Between 1908 and 1911 she was invited to at least a dozen small towns in southern Manitoba—several asking for repeat performances—and invitations came also from Moose Jaw and Regina, in Saskatchewan, as well as across the border in St. Vincent, Minnesota. The Ladies' Aid in Elkhorn—with commendable foresight—stated: "We would prefer to have you come before the rink opens, if at all." And on one of the occasions when she performed at Grace Church in Winnipeg, a newspaper account, referring to a bouquet of flowers presented to Nellie at the end of her recital, added: "Very few in the large audience . . . were aware that the bouquet was a token of appreciation of both book [*Sowing Seeds in Danny*] and writer [*Nellie McClung*] from Sir Daniel and Lady McMillan"—the lieutenant-governor of Manitoba and his wife.[58]

In 1910 she was reading not only from *Danny* but from its sequel, not yet published, *The Second Chance*, and brought out an advertising flyer offering her services as "Elocutionist, Entertainer, and Reader." Prospective sponsors were encouraged by quotations from several newspapers declaring Mrs. McClung to be like her book, "bright, vivacious and optimistic"; "her easy grace, her clear enunciation, and the sparkle of her eyes, all combine with a naturally strong and attractive personality to hold her audience simply spell-bound. Those who met her will never forget her genial good-humour . . . " On the one hand, she "provoked her audience to bursts of laughter," yet on the other hand, "her sublime pathos brought tears to the eyes of many." She was commonly declared "one of the best entertainments ever held" where "every word is heard, every gesture graceful, and her face is full of expression."[59] From the time of Nellie's first venture into the entertainment field newspaper accounts mention her attractive voice—gentle, yet clear and heard in every part of the hall—her flashing eyes, her vitality and compelling presence on the stage. Later, when she became both nationally and internationally prominent as a public speaker—particularly on the women's suffrage issue—such qualities did much to win sceptics in her audience to her cause. Meantime, E.W. Walker, head of the wholesale department at the Methodist Book and Publishing House in Toronto wrote Nellie in the spring of 1910: "You must have a regular picnic, a continuous picnic, going to these small burgs being lionized in the way you are, and since you are not the kind who is apt to get a swelled head you must sit back sometimes and revel in it all."[60] Indeed, Nellie must have enjoyed to the full this heady new experience, though one suspects that her mother, the dour Letitia Mooney, might not have been amused by what she usually thought of as her headstrong daughter's exhibitionism.

Soon Nellie was drawn even further afield as an entertainer-recitalist. E.S. Caswell—her editor at the Methodist Book and Publishing House—and others had been urging her for some time to come to Toronto as news of her touring success in the West spread. F.S. Ewens at the Toronto publishing house promised to introduce Nellie "to the various literary societies around town," and he added that Marjorie MacMurchy, president of the Canadian Women's Press Club, "stated that if we could induce you to come down, the Press Club and other sister organizations would give you a good time here in Toronto." He assured Nellie that if she came east she "would be well received." Caswell laughingly advised her that "a few lessons to 'Wes' in the interval on 'The Care of Children' and 'How to Run a Wifeless Home' would put him in trim for the hiatus in the home," and he assured her "I've lots of friends among the ministers throughout Ontario and Quebec, and I will do all I can to make your trip a Triumphal Progress." Meanwhile, a Presbyterian minister in Waterloo, and "the pastor of the largest Congregational Church in the city" were both eager to engage Nellie even before she had decided on the tour, and Ewens also promised that in Toronto "you are almost sure of an evening at Elm Street Methodist Church . . . and no doubt you would be sure of one at Broadway Tabernacle." He expressed "no doubt but that you would be able to fill your programme very quickly, erstwhile taking in oyster suppers etc. supplied by press clubs and other organizations of like nature."[61]

As pressure mounted for an Ontario tour, Nellie finally agreed to go down in mid-November for about a month, but not without considerable apprehension. She feared that her readings, so well received by western audiences, might not suit what she believed to be a more sophisticated Ontario audience. Then, too, she dreaded—although with some degree of excitement and curiosity—visiting so large a city as Toronto. In the event, however, Nellie's recital tour of Ontario brought nothing but mutual pleasure, and must have been a thrilling experience for a young writer who was now fulfilling her childhood dreams of fame and authorial success. In Toronto she was royally treated by her publisher, by the Canadian Women's Press Club, and by the various church groups fortunate enough to obtain a booking. Marjorie MacMurchy met her at the railway station in Toronto and made her feel like a celebrity, and a very welcome one. Soon Nellie had a new hairdo, Toronto style, and a new dress—which always gave her confidence—and she was ready to face the world. Everywhere she went audiences were enthusiastic and newspaper reports flattering: "she convulses her audiences with the life-like presentations she gives of her own characters"; "she is like a clear fresh air from the westlands."[62] She was entertained and interviewed wherever she went. She met "Toronto society" and the "literary elite" at luncheons and receptions. On one occasion she was guest of honour along with Mrs. Snowden, a noted British advocate of women's suffrage.[63] The Methodist Book and Publishing House had a luncheon in her honour—the menu humorously illustrated with quotes from *Danny*. Back home the Manitou and Winnipeg papers gloated over the success of *their* author.

In Toronto Nellie gave at least five recitals, and also spoke in towns like Whitby, Hamilton, Peterborough, Kingston, and Waterloo—all asked for "return engagements." The Peterborough *Review* (8 December 1910) observed: "Mrs. McClung has only been in Ontario for a few weeks on this visit, but in that time there have been so many requests for her lectures that it was with difficulty that she could be persuaded to come to this city . . . In Toronto Mrs. McClung has been greeted with crowded houses at each lecture engagement." The Hamilton *Herald* (10 December 1910) anticipated a large and cordial welcome for Nellie since Toronto reports indicated she "took her audiences by storm." By the 17th of the month the same paper announced that Nellie "has quite decided to come back to Ontario next year." All of her audiences were very much aware of the fresh and natural vitality of her style: "Mrs. McClung has fascinating tricks of expression and gestures all her own, and lacks the less fascinating mannerisms of the average elocutionist . . . she makes the scenes seem to be taken from somewhere around one's own home, and the characters are very real . . . "[64]

On her return home, Nellie stopped off in Port Arthur where the Women's Canadian Club and the Canadian Women's Press Club greeted her with tremendous warmth. The Fort William *Daily Times-Journal* (20 December 1910) described with evident relish Nellie's "strong, winsome and womanly personality," which, they said, "makes her beloved wherever she goes"—just like her novel. In the same issue the newspaper published a poetic eulogy a local citizen had written in tribute to Nellie and read to her as a preliminary greeting to this novelist and woman whom so many had come to love and admire. One of the stanzas sums up the gist of the whole verse:

> You have given us Danny, Nellie McClung,
> And Danny has given us you,
> And we clearly trace in his winsome grace,
> The "Lady of Manitou."

The general claim was that "never in the history of Port Arthur has a more enjoyable entertainment been given." Unless she stopped off in Winnipeg, this was the last recital Nellie gave on this particular tour, until her triumphant return to Manitou where the local papers had already enthusiastically likened *their* Nell to "Dickens and his marvellous receptions as a reader of his own works." In an act of appreciation for home-town support, Nellie began the new year in Manitou with a recital, at lowered rates, for an entirely local audience. The Manitou *Western Canadian* reported on this recital "to a large audience" in her home town: "There was scarcely a house in Manitou not represented while many came from outlying points to pay tribute to the talented woman whom they knew, for twenty long years, and whose name is fast becoming a household one on account of her charming pictures of prairie life."[65]

At this time, before she became a controversial figure, there were no criticisms, no suggestion that as a wife and mother she should be at home instead of going on a month's tour as recitalist and speaker. These kinds of criticisms appeared only when she dared to speak about women's suffrage, and appeared on political platforms instead of the entertainment circuit.

As a celebrity Nellie began to get invitations to deliver public addresses, not just to give readings. Even in 1910 any well-known person was considered an instant authority, even if her real expertise was in writing fiction. Nellie McClung, however, did not stray far from topics she was familiar with. In early 1911 the University of Saskatchewan Agricultural Societies' Convention was meeting in Regina under the auspices of the Saskatchewan Agricultural College, and Nellie had been requested to entertain with readings on both the first and last evenings of this meeting. The same occasion marked the first annual Convention of Saskatchewan Homemaker Clubs, and Nellie had been invited to address the women to help mark this memorable event.[66] Her speech, variously entitled "The Importance of Social Life in Country Homes" or, as some newspapers labelled it, "The Right of a Child to a Good Start in Life," was a topic that Nellie felt strongly about and was more than qualified to give after thirty years' experience of rural life in the West. The same address was delivered later in the same month to a joint meeting of men and women at the Agricultural College in Winnipeg. Her address had a marked impact on both audiences. "It is rarely that either man or woman has spoken on a Winnipeg platform and made the profound impression" that Mrs. McClung did, said one columnist, "the address was one that should appear in every newspaper in the Canadian west . . . " Perhaps with the view of reaching that wider western audience *The Nor'-West Farmer* published Nellie's address in its entirety (5 July 1911).[67]

Nellie's speech centred on how rural living might be improved, especially for women and children. "There is a strong desire for social intercourse, happiness and good times in every young heart, and there is no place where boys and girls enjoy a good time as much as in their own home." Unfortunately, she added, in rural Manitoba a "bitter cry" arises from the children in "hundreds of gloomy homes . . . where life is a serious, weary, dreary, dull grey existence," where life is dominated by excessive hard work that simply made a child's days a burden of drudgery. One farmer, she recalled, would not let his sons even go skating for fear they would get into bad habits. In an environment where parents expect all work and no play, it was inevitable that some children were driven away from home and from farm life. Yet in later years, she observed, the memory of a happy childhood brings "its cheering influence . . . to many burdened men and women . . . and helps them to bear their weight of worries." On the other hand, "the opposite of this is unfortunately true, too, and there are more people defeated in life by what is behind them than by what is before them." She concluded, therefore, that children did not need expensive toys and city-type entertainment, for the greatest "inheritance" that parents can give is "the memory of a happy childhood."

Many farm women, too, suffered from this kind of excessively restrictive attitude in an environment that could be unendurably lonely. Some years after Nellie's marriage she was watching "a demonstration of Electrical cooking and Electrical refrigeration with about three hundred other women: 'well-dressed, alert, and happy looking women . . . modern [and] sophisticated.'" On this occasion, Nellie recalled a city-bred bride whom she had called on after school. The woman stood aimlessly staring out the window, "sad and pale." "'Look at that,' she said to me. I looked and saw nothing. 'The wind,' she said bitterly, 'tearing wildly at the branches, at the clothes on the line, at the straw in the yard.'" She also pointed out that gallons of water ran by in the nearby river—useless and unharnessed as the wind. The bride had to haul water from a well outside. "She held up her hands burned by the rope." It was near six o'clock, the men would soon be back from the fields wanting a hot dinner, but the last meal's dishes were still on the table and the wood stove was "dead and black." The bride could not get it to burn.

> I had never heard talk like that, and I had never seen anyone so hopeless. Her big eyes were bottomless pools of misery and defeat. They had a festering look that frightened me. I am glad to remember that I lit the fire and helped her get the meal ready, but I was glad to get away for she talked to herself—in broken sentences.[68]

Already half-mad from the incessant wind and the harsh prairie life, the woman simply fled one day, never to return.

Writing in the forties, about prairie life in the dustbowl of the Depression years, Sinclair Ross in "The Lamp at Noon" would also expose something of that prairie loneliness that ends as prairie madness. Although Nellie McClung, as a writer, almost always gave her stories happy endings, it was not because she lacked first-hand knowledge of tragic—even brutal—endings to the stories of some people she found in her harsh prairie environment in those early pioneering days. And when she spoke to rural groups, she believed that her job was not to emphasize the negative side of prairie farming life, but rather to quickly recognize the problems, then show how they might be alleviated.

In this first of the major speeches that Nellie McClung would be called upon to give throughout her life, she advocated both private and organized activities. These people, the terribly lonely ones, she said,

> need human companionship and good fellowship—not a strong talk
> on the need of controlling their nerves. They are like the little girl
> who was afraid of the dark, and refused to be comforted when told
> that the angels were with her in the dark . . . she wanted something
> with a skin face.[69]

Nellie quarrelled with the self-righteous attitude of those who believe it their duty "to make other people good." In her opinion "it is a higher conception of our duty when we endeavour to make ourselves good and other people happy—if we may." To this end she urged that hospitality be given to the "left-out people . . . whom in our short-sightedness [we] call uninteresting" for "everybody can tell us something or give us a new point of view." We can glean, from Nellie's wisdom, some idea of what she sought to provide for her own children within their family circle; and we can see in Nellie's words a portrait of the speaker herself: the woman whom Cora Hind observed was immediately made welcome in every rural home where they stopped.

Nellie also launched a strong attack against snobbery in this address, for she found it to be part of the social problem in the new West. She condemned the woman who, remembering a more comfortable life in another place, decided she could not entertain because her present home held none of the finer amenities. Even in the towns, Nellie said, true hospitality was disappearing in the face of superficial social taboos: the woman who had no silver spoons felt she could not ask anyone in for tea. "The trouble with our hospitality now is that we make of it a burden—we smother it with frills . . . Someone else cuts the crust off the sandwiches, and so must we." This, Nellie argued, was not the original spirit of the frontier where the visitor was welcomed even though the dining table was a packing box and the teaspoon made of tin. Nellie also stressed that on lonely prairie farms men should cooperate to see that their wives were not unendurably isolated.[70] Perhaps, as she spoke, she remembered how—during the Mooneys' first cold prairie winter—Frank Burnett had brought his wife over for a visit with Letitia Mooney even though the severe cold made it easier for him not to trouble with such a trip. And Nellie often told the anecdote of the man who brought his wife in to an insane asylum, saying: "I don't see how she can be crazy . . . Where would she get it? She hasn't been off the farm for twelve years!"[71]

This address was typical of hundreds that Nellie would give in the years to come: practical down-to-earth advice based on eyes that clearly saw the realities about her, yet leavened with humour, and presented with a vivacity of manner that never failed to win both audience attention and sympathy.

In 1911 when the McClung family moved to Winnipeg, Nellie regretted leaving her friends and activities in Manitou, yet this move must have been a very attractive prospect for her. In the years between 1908 and 1911 she had been growing more and more a part of a very energetic and enthusiastic group of women in Winnipeg, members of the Canadian Women's Press Club, who were interested in both writing and reform. In Manitou Nellie's efforts toward temperance and women's suffrage were necessarily limited, but these women with their newspaper contacts—Cora Hind, Francis Beynon, Lillian (Beynon) Thomas—were at the centre of things and wielded considerable influence at a time when Nellie had become "a firm believer in women—in their ability to do things and in their influence and power." These women journalists held meetings of the "jolliest" kind, and declared that their professed aim was to meet women who were prominent in journalistic or writing careers, to lend support to members of the women's press club, and to be interested "in any woman who is doing something for the uplift of the sex."[72]

But Nellie also came in contact with aspiring Winnipeg authors and journalists—both men and women—through her several invitations to the Winnipeg Quill Club beginning in February 1909. This group included serious students of writing and of the writer's market. Their aim was not only to "talk shop" (as they called their analyses of literature), "but to get into print, and be paid for being there." They discussed such matters as the distinction between "hack work" and more serious forms of literature; what "the essentials for the success of the western Canadian novelist" were; and whether, in fact, "distinctively western novels" existed. To this end they argued about such matters as "interest of plot, strength of mental conflict, descriptions of scenery, local colour, slang or dialect," and any other points that suggested themselves.[73] Nellie must have been flattered by the attention they paid her as a successful first novel writer, and after one visit her friendly manner, her wit, her willingness to share any secrets of "the way to get published" had won her a place in this eager group. Unfortunately the club survived for only a single year, and was well buried by the time Nellie took up permanent residence in Winnipeg. It was the kind of literary stimulus she needed and would have thrived upon, for it would have freed her from the authorial isolation she suffered in Manitou. Still, many members of the Quill Club were also members of the CWPC, and no doubt such literary discussions continued on a less formal basis.

Having made these stimulating contacts it is not unlikely that Manitou social circles became a little dull. Although in her autobiography Nellie does not admit to any responsibility for the McClung family move to Winnipeg, it is likely that she initiated and promoted the idea. Urban life offered physical amenities as well as intellectual opportunities not found in a small town in those days. In a discarded rough draft for *The Stream Runs Fast,* Nellie recalled the dual attraction:

> The dream of my heart was to have running water in the house but there was no prospect then of any such state of bliss in Manitou. When I visited my relatives in Winnipeg, the luxury of hot water, which came to me by the turn of your hand, constituted one of the great pleasures of the visit. I went once a year at least—taking one child with me—and that gave me a lift for the whole year. I saw plays, heard music, and went to the Library.[74]

The McClungs left Manitou in June of 1911 after many farewell parties. The Home Economics Society farewell, for example, brought together "almost one hundred women . . . from town and country" and, as one Winnipeg paper reported, it was "the first afternoon of its kind where women of all creeds and of all conditions of life met as one." "Manitou's loss," the same article commented, "is Winnipeg's gain."[75] It would, indeed, be quite a blow to a small town to lose such an active family, and the formal address "From the Citizens of Manitou" to Nellie and Wes makes this very clear. In an illuminated manuscript the Manitou townspeople expressed their appreciation for Wes's numerous services to the town "in civic, commercial, charitable, social, athletic and fraternal matters." But to his "illustrious wife," they said, "we are even more deeply indebted." They felt honoured by her literary achievements, but were more deeply moved by her personal impact on Manitou life. Part of the address stated:

> As a social worker your labours have been carried on in an earnest and intelligent manner, destitute of ostentation. Humanity in its diverse ways has found in you a thoughtful and generous friend whose grace and charm will long be remembered by those who have been fortunate enough to know you. Your removal will leave a void very difficult to fill.[76]

The McClungs spent a quiet summer at Matlock Beach before moving to their new Winnipeg home at 97 Chestnut Street. Faced with new expenses connected with their move, Nellie knew she must devote herself even more to the task of writing, but as she became more and more absorbed in Winnipeg life there was increasingly less free time for her to do so.

5

The Winnipeg Years:
The Growing Spirit of Reform

❖

During the first two decades of the twentieth century no Canadian city could challenge Winnipeg as a place where exciting, even momentous developments were taking place. James Gray sums it up as "a lusty, gutsy, bawdy frontier boom-town roaring through an unequalled economic debauch on its way to the grand-daddy of all economic hangovers." By 1911 it was a city of 151,000, making it the third largest city in Canada: a bustling business centre through which was funnelled all the commerce of the burgeoning West. The city fathers, "obsessed with need for growth," paid little attention to the social problems this expansion was causing: the sweatshops and unsanitary factories near the city centre, and the overcrowded housing conditions surrounding the railway works and heavier industry of the North End. After the boom ended in 1912, racial and class tensions would come to the fore, but in 1911 Winnipegers saw no clouds on the horizon.[1] The McClungs quickly adjusted to their new surroundings. In October there was a new baby, Mark. But this did not prevent Nellie from continuing her activities in the church, the WCTU, and the CWPC. She also continued to be in demand as a speaker and, in her spare moments, carried on with her writing. In 1912 a volume of short stories appeared, *The Black Creek Stopping-House*, the last of her fiction until the 1920s. *In Times Like These*, published in 1915, was a collection of suffrage and prohibition speeches, and *The Next of Kin* (1917) was a semi-autobiographical collection of essays and fictional sketches. Her articles, which appeared widely in western publications, dealt with the same issues. In addition, she continued to give recitals throughout the West and often combined attendance at a WCTU or a church Woman's Missionary Society (WMS) conference with recitals in nearby places.

Perhaps the most satisfying contact for Nellie at this time was the Winnipeg branch of the Canadian Women's Press Club. This organization was formed in 1904 with a Toronto chapter, but it quickly spread across the country at this time when journalism provided an employment opportunity for many outstanding women. In Winnipeg there was a particularly active group of women journalists headed by E. Cora Hind, the internationally noted commercial and agricultural editor of the *Winnipeg Free Press*. Hind was definitely the dean of Winnipeg women journalists, but there were other busy members of the profession, such as Mrs. Lillian Beynon Thomas, and her sister Francis Beynon, Mrs. Genevieve Lipsett-Skinner, and Kennethe Haig. "By definition women journalists were literate, articulate, opinionated individuals closely attuned to the currents of thought swirling around them." They were "leaders in the women's movement both regionally and nationally . . . In their pooling of information, support and tactical expertise, [these] Winnipeg women were clearly laying the necessary foundations for effective political action."[2] Once McClung became one of the network, she was firmly launched on both her political and writing career. In the fall of 1911 there were thirty-one members who eagerly welcomed Nellie McClung as a successful novelist: she had published a Canadian best seller and had already proved, on earlier visits to the club, that she was ready to share her publishing experience.

Before coming to Winnipeg Nellie McClung had looked at reform needs from a rural and small town viewpoint. Through the WCTU she had already been a proponent of prohibition and women's suffrage. In Winnipeg, work for these and other reforms was to become a much more important part of her life. As she talked with Cora Hind, Lillian Thomas, and Francis Beynon, she learned more about the inequities of the law where women were concerned. They stressed the need for a Dower Law to protect married women from loss of the homestead that they had worked to improve along with their husbands; the need for an amendment to the *Homestead Act* to permit women, like men, to be granted free land; the need to change the laws of guardianship, which now recognized the father as sole guardian; and the need for laws to protect working women. All of these reforms were advocated by the WCTU, and Nellie would already have been acquainted with them. The Winnipeg women journalists, however, were in close touch with both rural and city areas, and now Nellie heard many more personal stories.

Nellie was also seeing city poverty for the first time: the slum housing in which immigrants were forced to live, and the sweatshops and factories where women and young girls worked long, hard hours in unhealthy and unsafe conditions for a pittance. She also saw bars on every corner and liquor in every grocery store. As well, many workers squandered much of their small income in the bars before the paycheque ever reached home. In spite of repeated union demands that workmen be paid by the week or at least every two weeks, and paid in cash, the impractical custom of monthly paycheques persisted. When workmen got off work at six or seven at night, the banks and stores that would have cashed their cheques were closed. "The one place that was always open and always had cash on hand to accommodate the workers was the boozery, and there was always a handy saloon en route home from work." Once in the bar, the men were subject to the universal custom of the time to stand a round of drinks for everyone present. On payday, as a result, too many working men came home drunk and penniless.[3] They and their families suffered.

When Nellie became aware of this problem, she was more keen for prohibition than ever, though she realized that prohibition would not solve all the problems. Through her church, for example, she learned of the social work performed at All People's Mission, which was under the direction of the Reverend J.S. Woodsworth. In fact, in 1912 she was invited to write an introduction to the mission's annual report in which she described the work of the mission as seen "through the eyes of a visitor." In it she declared her belief that this mission exemplified the new missionary spirit in the church, and she commented, with irony:

> Not so very long ago old clothes were considered the most acceptable offering to place upon the missionary altar . . . By this plan many an attic was kept tidier . . . In like manner ugly but durable garments bestowed on orphans may be a little hard on the orphan, but are wonderfully soothing to the conscience of the giver.

Now, she said, the churches were recognizing that old clothes charity and long distance mission work were not enough. Since All People's Mission was in the immigrant area, most of its work was devoted to teaching the newcomers the language and customs of their new country and providing healthy recreation for children and young people. She described in some detail the kindergartens, night classes, mothers' circles, girls and boys clubs, gymnasium classes, factory girls' teas, and fresh air camps. "All People's Mission," she concluded, "is not a charity—it is an institution which aims at making charity unnecessary, it teaches the people to help and respect themselves."[4] One of the lessons Nellie learned from the mission was that Manitoba needed a compulsory education law, for many of the children who attended the mission's kindergarten did not go on to public school. She recognized that decent living wages would have to be paid so that the children did not have to work, but she also argued that as long as there were liquor outlets better wages would be no solution. Like most reformers of her day Nellie McClung believed in Canadianizing the immigrant—primarily through citizenship training in the public school system. She did not, however, share in the prevalent Protestant, English-Canadian bigotry toward foreigners, especially toward those central Europeans who were often seen as "degenerate."[5] Nellie was convinced that immigrants should be on farms, not in the city, and she urged that this should be made possible for them; but for those who remained in the city, regulations should be passed to improve their housing. These new insights into urban poverty did not change Nellie's primary convictions. Prohibition and woman suffrage, she thought, were still the best solutions, but in the meantime she worked actively for other reforms.

The women of Winnipeg had been agitating for changes to a number of laws but the Conservative government of Manitoba, led by Sir Rodmond Roblin, had not been receptive to their approaches. In 1911 a delegation of women representing a number of women's organizations had approached the Law Amendments Committee seeking protection for widows; that is, a law that would prevent a man from willing his property away from his wife. The women were treated patronizingly and almost with contempt. They were told that 99 percent of men were just, and that women could trust the judges to be fair in settling any such case. The attorney general reminded them that "a husband is never far wrong, and is better capable than anyone else of judging what he should leave to his wife. If he leaves her penniless there is a good reason." When they raised the matter of a Dower Law they were sarcastically asked, "Do you want us to set up divorce courts too?"[6] The government had also been uncooperative with the women's attempts to achieve stricter controls of liquor sales, and although they had passed factory safety laws and had appointed factory inspectors, visits to a few sweatshops in the city made it clear that enforcement of the laws was not effective. When Mrs. Claud Nash urged the local Council of Women, made up of members from the various women's organizations, to bring pressure on the government to appoint a woman inspector, the council named Mrs. Nash and Mrs. McClung to look into the matter and approach Roblin. Nash thought that the best way to prove their point would be to take Roblin to see a factory or two. She must have had a persuasive manner for shortly the two women set out with the premier. They were driven in Sir Rodmond's car with its cut-glass vase ostentatiously holding a carnation. Roblin—whom Nellie described as "a florid, rather good-looking man in his early sixties, somewhat pompous in manner"—was comfortable in an expensive beaver coat, and complacently rested his plump hands on a gold-headed cane. All was in stark contrast with the disheartening sight the two women were about to reveal.

As they drove along Sir Rodmond assured the two reformers that they were making a big fuss about nothing: work was, he told them, good for young people. As a boy he had worked from dawn to dusk on the farm. Indeed, he intoned, these girls they were so concerned about were working merely for pin money. Furthermore, they likely lived at home and didn't need men's wages. Many of the women were foreigners, he argued, and what they had here was better than what they left behind.[7] According to Nellie the two women let him run on, offering no arguments because they believed that the factories they were to visit would be a better argument than any they could raise. Nellie tells the story in a memorably understated way:

> We conducted the Premier down dark, slippery stairs to an airless basement where light in mid-day came from gaunt light bulbs hanging from smoky ceilings. The floor was littered with refuse of apple peelings and discarded clothing. There was no ventilation and no heat. The room was full of untidy women, operating sewing machines and equally unattractive men cutting out garments on long tables . . . We led the Premier through a side door into the foul passage where a queue had formed before a door marked "Toilet" . . . We drew his attention to the fact that there was no separate accommodation for the women, and we did not need to mention that the plumbing had evidently gone wrong.

Roblin, choking from the fetid air, was anxious to get away. They left hurriedly but the women persuaded him to visit one more factory. The building was in a little better shape, but some of the girls working there were obviously in poor health. When questioned, one of them said she could not take time off because her father was out of work. She was lucky, she said, to have a job. The manager, when asked about "sick leave," replied abruptly that he was not running a charitable institution. When Mrs. Nash asked about required visits from the factory inspector, the man looked puzzled and assured her that he didn't need one: "All the girls are glad of the work. I have no trouble with them." The conditions of the factory and the manager's ignorance regarding the purpose of factory inspectors underlined the need for the enforcement of inspection.

As the car headed back for Roblin's office, Nash and McClung tried to convince the premier that a trained social worker, a woman, should be appointed as a factory inspector. Roblin was shocked by what he had seen but, with a curious lack of logic, he stated that he was all the more positive that "it's no job for a woman. I have too much respect for women to give any of them a job like this." All he would promise was that he would talk with the cabinet minister responsible.

Nellie and Mrs. Nash reported back to their Council of Women local with the story of their interview and with information they had gathered about many such sweatshops operating in the city. To their distress they found that their recommendation for a strong protest from the council was not acceptable. They were accused of treading on toes—becoming controversial—and the council, it was argued, could not become involved in "politics." The CWPC, too, although it had many members who were sympathetic, felt that they were not the proper vehicle for such reform efforts. The more seriously concerned women decided that a new organization was needed, and so the Political Equality League (PEL)—a nonparty organization—was formed.[8] Although the primary purpose of this society, which included both men and women, was to obtain the vote for women, it was also interested in social reform. The two subjects were intertwined as far as the PEL was concerned.

Although the Political Equality League was formed in Winnipeg, it was constituted as a provincial organization so that locals could be formed in any area. Anyone who was interested but could not yet form a local could be a member at large. Both Cora Hind and Francis Beynon were able, through their columns, to reach a large number of the country women, as were others who edited pages in farm journals and received troubled letters from farm women. While the WCTU was probably the chief voice for women's suffrage in rural areas, most of the Winnipeg women had, like Nellie, country backgrounds themselves, and still had family members and friends on the farm so that they were in close touch with rural problems, such as those engendered by the lack of Dower laws. In addition, a great number of Nellie McClung's popular speaking engagements took place in rural Manitoba. Perhaps it is for these reasons that there appears to have been no conflict, in Manitoba, between those middle-class city women who were instrumental in founding the Political Equality League and the women on the farms.[9]

During 1912 and 1913 Nellie McClung's platform appearances were commonly sponsored by rural WCTU, WMS, Young People's, or Home Economics Societies who invited her to give recitals as a fund-raising project. Nellie usually spoke for a set fee, the surplus to go to the sponsoring society. After the formation of the PEL she began to combine recitals with suffrage talks. On occasion she would give her suffrage talk at the end of the recital, but more often she gave a separate speech on another night. Gradually she began to get invitations to speak exclusively on suffrage, often from groups of women who wished to stimulate interest in a PEL local. On other occasions she was specifically instructed to avoid controversial topics. No matter what her subject, however, Nellie was always able to attract a large audience. Every newspaper account of her meetings speaks of the largest hall available being filled, and describes how people were often turned away because the hall was full. When she was scheduled to speak at a convention the numbers present suddenly increased.

It is clear, too, that from the moment Nellie McClung walked on to a platform she carried the audience with her. Her description of Pearlie Watson—"There was a smile in her eyes that was contagious. The whole roomful of people smiled back at her, and in that moment she established friendly relations with her audience,"[10]—could equally well apply to Nellie McClung herself. Even when the roomful of people became five thousand in Winnipeg's Industrial Bureau the magic still worked. Her well-modulated, very pleasant voice reached every corner of whatever hall she was in. She moved on the stage—using arm and body gestures—gracefully and naturally. While she made people laugh with witty quips and funny stories, she was no stand-up comic for there was no doubt of her seriousness and sincerity as she expressed her concern about the ravages of the liquor trade or other social abuses. Her illustrations might be slightly rewritten Bible stories or incidents from her own life but they were all familiar to the people in her audience. Sometimes an audience hostile to her views was won over for the duration of her talk. Even when she became a political campaigner, and had to face hecklers, she did not seem to encounter an audience that remained hostile.

Contemporary theorists of first-wave feminism and the suffrage movement argue the dichotomy that has arisen in the recent past between the terms "maternal" or "social" feminist as opposed to "true" feminists, that is, "equal rights" or "equity" feminists is a false one. It has been noted, for example, that "while the arguments used by the women can be labelled, the women themselves cannot. Most accepted both feminist arguments, emphasizing one or the other as seemed most useful and appropriate, apparently without feeling any contradiction."[11] Nellie McClung was no exception for she shared both views. The so-called "maternal" feminists wanted the vote for women to reinforce the position of women in the home and because they thought that women had different priorities and sensibilities than men. Women, they argued, would use their votes merely to change the laws to protect women's property rights and to eliminate liquor—thus protecting the home. They would work for better medical care for country areas only so that women could have children more safely and so children would be healthier. They would press for legislation that provided more severe penalties for crimes against women: such as wife-beating, abduction for purposes of prostitution, and rape. The "maternal" feminists did not expect women to do anything to radically change the status quo.[12]

All of these maternal goals were indeed supported by Nellie McClung. She believed that when women got the vote the world would be improved because women paid more heed to social needs and less to material gain. Women, she said, would use their ballots "to protect the weak and innocent, and make the world a safer place for the young feet."[13] While casting ridicule on the argument that giving women the vote would destroy the home, Nellie also makes clear her belief that the home and family, as they then existed, would and should be strengthened rather than weakened. She could laughingly assert that "women's sphere is anything that men don't want to do,"[14] but she believed that women did have a natural sphere "to guide and sustain life, to care for the race," and that "deeply rooted in almost every woman's heart is the love of home and children."[15]

There was never any question in her mind that the family was the mainstay of the country's life, but she also thought that married women needed to be stirred up, to take an interest in things other than their homes. In this way home life would be improved, not threatened. "The most deadly, uninteresting person and the one who has the greatest temptation not to think at all, is the comfortable and happily married woman—the woman who has a good man between her and the world, who has not the saving privilege of having to work."[16] She scoffed at the picture she had seen in a women's magazine showing a pretty young wife pouting because her husband sat reading the paper at the breakfast table. "Personally," Nellie commented, "I sympathize with the young man and believe it would be a happier home if she were as interested in the paper as he and were reading the other half of it instead of sitting around feeling hurt."[17] In her own home she went one better than this and read the paper aloud to the family providing commentary and interpretation.[18] "Ideas," she insisted, "do not break up homes, but lack of ideas."[19] Nellie criticized "the sweet and pliable type" of woman who "has made life harder for other women" by always giving in to her husband.[20] As well, she had little use for the women she called "Gentle Ladies" who still believed in the masculine terror of tears and the judicial use of fainting to get their own way; yet she was realistic enough to sympathize with, rather than scoff at, the woman whose husband would not allow her to attend WCTU meetings. When questioned about her own position, however, she replied that Wes gave her every support in her activities, but that she honestly could not say what she would have done if he had strongly disapproved.[21]

There is, then, ample reason to classify Nellie McClung as a "maternal" feminist. It is in the rhetoric of every speech she made. But this is not the whole story. On many other occasions Nellie clearly used the arguments of "equal rights" feminists. When she appeared before the legislature of Alberta in 1915, for example, she asked for the vote, not as a privilege, but as a right.[22] Women, she said, should not have to present any other argument than that they are persons. Indeed, this was the first premise of the Winnipeg PEL.

In Nellie McClung's opinion there was no valid reason why women should not have the vote. Despite all the antisuffragist arguments presented, Nellie asserted the equal rights argument that what men truly feared was that they would lose their exclusive hold on power and position. It reminded her of the old grace: "Six potatoes among the four of us,/Thank the Lord there ain't no more of us."[23] She could not believe that men's real motive was to protect women. When men started talking about "the fair sex" and "women's influence" and "the hand that rocks the cradle," she said, they were handing out "dope." She warned women, therefore, to beware of being lulled into acquiescence by such tactics and to look more carefully at the real situation.

> These tender-hearted and chivalrous gentlemen who tell you of their adoration for women, cannot bear to think of women occupying public positions. Their tender hearts shrink from the idea of women lawyers or women policemen, or even women preachers . . . They cannot bear . . . to see women leaving the sacred precincts of home—and yet their offices are scrubbed by women who do their work while other women sleep—poor women who leave the sacred precincts of home to earn enough to keep the breath of life in them . . . is there any pity felt for them? Not that we have heard of. The tender-hearted ones can bear this with equanimity. It is the thought of women getting into comfortable and well-paid positions which wrings their manly hearts.[24]

At least one contemporary feminist sees the "equal rights" argument, such as that put forth by Nellie McClung, as "potentially radical" in its "powerful threat to male supremacy" both in the home and in the world at large.[25]

Nellie knew that many women were wage earners because they had to be. Why should they not have a vote? "Is it any comfort to the woman who feels the sting of social injustice to reflect that she, at least, had no part in making such a law?" According to Nellie, all careers should be equally available to women and men. She even went beyond this. Although the work force contained many single women—some in sweatshops and some, like Cora Hind, in good career positions—Nellie argued that married women, as well, should be free to choose to work outside the home, not because they have to but because they wish to. While she believed that all women had maternal instincts, she also affirmed that all women were not meant to be housekeepers, and she illustrated this in one of her short stories in which she portrayed a woman with two children who served inedible meals in an untidy house and was frustrated by her failure. When the opportunity arose for her to take a teaching job she was highly successful and her house was kept in beautiful order by a frustrated school teacher who had all the qualifications of a teacher except the imagination to arouse her pupils' interest.[26] This was not, of course, an attack on family life. It was simply another way of organizing family life.

On occasion Nellie McClung took a more radical feminist stand. The greatest drawback to marriage, she said, was the economic dependence of the woman: "Independence is sweet and when marriage means the loss of independence, there are women brave enough and strong enough to turn away from it."[27] Like most reform-minded women of her day she was influenced by Olive Schreiner's *Women and Labour*. In a lengthy passage in *In Times Like These* she uses material from Schreiner to prove that "wherever women have become parasites on the race, it has heralded the decay of that race."[28] She did not see an immediate solution but wrote:

> The time will come, we hope, when women will be economically free, and mentally and spiritually independent enough to refuse to have their food paid for by men; when women will receive equal pay for equal work, and have all avenues of activity open to them; and will be free to choose their own mates, without shame, or indelicacy; when men will not be afraid of marriage because of the financial burden, but free men and free women will marry for love, and together work for the sustenance of their families. It is not too ideal a thought. It is coming, and the new movement among women who are crying out for a larger humanity, is going to bring it about.[29]

McClung had also read Charlotte Perkins Gilman and on several occasions advocated, as did Gilman, the centralization of what were considered home activities. She argued that woman power, particularly in the country home, was inefficient. The age of specialization should point the way to specialization in household chores. She visualized the country village under this new scheme:

> There would be a central station, municipally owned and operated, one large building fitted out with machinery that would be run by

gasoline, electricity, or natural gas. This building would contain in addition to the school-rooms, a laundry room, a bake-shop, a cream-ery, a dressmaking establishment, and perhaps a butcher shop.[30]

Not only would this central agency free the housewife from many chores, it would provide work for many young people who now went to the city. Although Nellie did not picture all the meals being centrally prepared as Bellamy does in *Looking Backward,* which she had thoroughly digested, these opinions did take her well beyond the views commonly expressed by her fellow suffragists. They also took her well beyond the more traditional, less radical opinions she held as a young woman in Manitou. These feminists' views, how-ever, were not Nellie's most common arguments, perhaps because she believed her audiences were not ready for them, or perhaps she was not quite convinced herself.

Medical care was another area in which she believed radical change was necessary. No one, she argued, should be deprived of proper health care because of location or lack of money. The prob-lem of the isolated farm home, in her opinion, could be solved by the work of large numbers of specially trained nurses and a few well-equipped country hospitals. They should be paid for by taxes on land held by speculators and by the large companies who prospered through the development of the West. As usual she made her point more graphic by telling the story of a woman on a lonely farm going into labour with no one present but her husband and a small child. He has been to the closest neighbour but there is no woman home there, so he has sent the hired hand to seek help. Then a "pioneer nurse" arrives at the door after learning that her services are needed. The young couple are grateful and relieved when the baby arrives safely, but wonder how they will pay the bill. Then they find that the nurse is paid by the government. This, Nellie told her audience, could be the scene all across the West and would be if women had the vote.[31] But she would have liked to carry state medicine even further. Medical protection should be provided, she argued, just as police and fire protection were, and an emphasis should be placed on preventive medicine.[32] Such views on medical care certainly took her beyond the conventional outlook attributed to the "maternal" feminist.

Nellie also believed that women should not be restricted by their womanhood. Perhaps this is best illustrated by a later event. When bars reopened in Alberta in the 1920s after prohibition, women were

117

not admitted, and Nellie took part in a campaign to end this discrimination. "We protested the action of the Alberta Hotelman's Association when they decided that women should not enter their beer parlors. Not but what we knew it was much better to be out than in, but we believe in equality."[33] Given her strong and lasting prohibition views, the incident reveals Nellie as a true "equal rights" advocate.

It seemed to Nellie McClung, too, that women's clothing epitomized the restrictions placed on females. Although she had always been very clothes conscious, and dressed as attractively as possible for her public appearances, she disliked clothes that inhibited the normal movement of the body. Therefore, just as she had resented, as a child, the voluminous skirts that prevented her from playing active games, she resented the man-inspired styles of the prewar era that, in her opinion, were accepted only by those women who couldn't face the idea of equality.

> The hideous mincing gait of the tightly-skirted woman seems to speak. It says: "I am not a useful human being—see! I cannot walk—I dare not run, but I am a woman. I still have my sex to commend me. I am not of use, I am made to be supported."[34]

Understandably, she resented the fact that activist women were always portrayed as unattractive with the implication that if a woman had beauty she would not need to be out seeking votes, or homesteads for women, or dower rights. "When a newspaper wishes to disprove a woman's contention, or demolish her theories, it draws ugly pictures of her. If it can show that she has big feet or red hands, or wears unbecoming clothes, that certainly settles the case—and puts her where she belongs."[35]

It is difficult to fit Nellie McClung's views entirely into either feminist category. Undoubtedly many, perhaps most, of her arguments place her in the "maternal" feminist group, and yet she breaks out of this on occasion to dream of a more equitable world. Her beliefs might best be summed up in these words: "Men and women have two different spheres when considered as men and women, but as human beings there is a great field of activity which they may and do occupy in common. Now it is in this common field of activity that women ask for equal privileges."[36]

On the whole, the Manitoba suffragists depended on their own resources, with few outside speakers. In 1911 the English suffragette Mrs. Pankhurst visited Winnipeg and to the amazement of the antisuffragists, and perhaps some of the suffragists, she gave a reasoned, calm address with none of the militancy they had expected. Nellie entertained the English militant in her home. Later in the same year Miss Barbara Wylie gave a more spirited address to a large audience and apparently, in private at least, tried to stir the Canadian women to more militant action.[37] Although the members of the PEL hoped that their goals could be achieved in Canada without such drastic action, they sympathized with the English women. As Nellie said, on one occasion: "I regret lawlessness. Whether all the militants have done was right God only knows but I would rather take my place with them in the last day than with the women who sit at home babbling of indirect influence and womanly charm but never doing anything for the betterment of humanity."[38]

There appears, too, to have been little contact with suffragists from other Canadian provinces although Nellie spoke in Saskatchewan, Alberta, and British Columbia, and in fact attended the inaugural meeting of the Edmonton Equal Franchise League.[39] The Toronto suffragists had tried to form a national organization but by 1912, due to differences in ideology and personality clashes, Canada had two so-called national groups: the Canadian Suffrage Association and the National Union of Women Suffrage Societies of Canada. In June of 1912 the Manitoba PEL decided not to affiliate with the Canadian Suffrage Association. This decision was reaffirmed in 1914.[40] Although the National Union named Winnipeg's Dr. Mary Crawford a vice-president and Nellie McClung a convenor of organization,[41] they do not seem to have played an active part. At this time the vote was a provincial matter and its proponents in Manitoba saw little value in outside contacts, particularly with Ontario. In Canada there never was a truly national suffrage organization.

Throughout 1913 the suffragists kept up their efforts, trying to create support for suffrage in Manitoba that the premier would not be able to ignore. To this end the PEL published and distributed a number of pamphlets: a statement of their reasons for wanting the vote for women; *The Legal Status of Women in Manitoba* by Dr. Mary Crawford; and *The New Citizenship* by Nellie L. McClung. PEL members spoke wherever they had an opportunity and they circulated petitions at every public function from stampedes to church bazaars.

Finally in January 1914, the PEL executive decided that it was time once again to approach the Manitoba Legislature. The activities of the PEL had stirred up a great deal of attention, one result being ten thousand signatures on petitions. Other organizations, most of whom had supported suffrage for years, were prepared to join the PEL in a deputation to present the petitions and their case. Crawford, designated to approach the premier and arrange the meeting,[42] secured Roblin's permission to present their case to the legislature. One account described the delegation as:

> probably one of the most cosmopolitan companies that has ever approached a government in the interests of a single reform. It represented many nationalities: Anglo-Saxon, Icelandic, Hebrew, African, Polish, and it is difficult to say how many more. High browed professors were there shoulder to shoulder with plain working girls. Nurses, lawyers, businessmen, journalists, doctors and quiet little housewives whom the census describes as having no occupation.[43]

The delegation were all in "deadly earnest," but Roblin's response to "logic" and "the avalanche of argument" that was put to him was "decidedly ineffective." The delegation was presented to the premier by Harvey Simpson, the member for Virden, and Dr. Mary Crawford, as president of the PEL, introduced the speakers.

Nellie McClung, representing the Political Equality League, was the last and most effective speaker. Although she was gracious, she stated unequivocally: "We are not here to ask for a reform, or a gift, or a favor, but for a right—not for mercy, but for justice." She pointed out that some men argued that politics was too corrupt for women: "I have never heard a satisfactory explanation of why politics should be corrupt. There is nothing inherently vicious about politics and the politician who says politics are corrupt is admitting one of two things—that he is a party to that corruption or that he is unable to prevent it. In either case . . . he is flying the white signal of distress and we are . . . anxious to come over and help him." Current laws, she also argued, were not satisfactory since one boy in every five families becomes a drunkard because liquor traffic is not controlled by legislation. Thousands of girls are poor and hungry and thousands of women are driven by poverty to a life of shame. She pointed out that white slavery (prostitution) was rampant because the punishment for such crimes against women "is two years imprisonment, the same punishment that is meted out to the man who steals a tree or shrub valued at twenty-five dollars." It was time, she insisted, that the woman's point of view be applied to such legislative and legal issues. Nellie then went on to argue the logic of reversed conditions. "How would you, Sir Rodmond, like to be governed by a parliament of women?" The premier bantered: "I have a good wife." "Like a flash Mrs. McClung turned to the delegation. 'Ladies and gentlemen, we have another reason for encouragement. The premier has a good wife, so, surely, he at least will not be afraid to trust the women with the franchise.'" Turning again to Roblin she prodded, some people say "'that your government is afraid to grant the franchise to women.' 'They say a good many things about us,' Sir Rodmond interjected. 'But,' Mrs. McClung continued, leaning towards him earnestly, 'We don't believe it, Sir Rodmond.'" This quip was met with "uproarious applause." Finally Nellie concluded: "Sir Rodmond, we have come to the last ditch in our onward march towards freedom and usefulness and we are stretching our hands to you to help us over. Sir Rodmond, it is your move."

Sir Rodmond rose, and in his pompous manner proceeded to utter every cliché ever offered as reasons for refusing the franchise to women. First he assured them that if their cause was just then they would eventually succeed, though he neglected to guess in which century. But just now, he added, looking at the extreme measures taken by suffragettes in England when faced with what he blandly called "a few short days of disappointment," Roblin queried: "Is there not cause for the authorities to hesitate in extending the franchise to women?" Though he recognized that the delegation before him was "large," "respectable," "intellectual," and the women members "lady-like," he worried whether they might become incendiaries like their European counterparts. "As you know," he pontificated, "we all draw our inspiration in legislation, theology, art, science and other subjects from the Motherland. Now, that being a fact that none will dispute, can you, can anyone, in confidence say that the manifestations that have been made by the women there constitute a guarantee that if the franchise is extended, what we have today will be preserved and not destroyed?" Female "hysteria," in this view, heralded the downfall of the traditions of the British Empire, and Roblin's servile colonial mentality prevented the assessment of an issue on its own merits.

Next, he brought up the destruction-of-the-home argument. National greatness depended on the home. "Does the franchise for women make that home better?" he worried. Not surprisingly, his

question brought cries of "yes" from the gallery, but Roblin was ready
for that.

> The facts are against you. It has been said by your president today that
> you want the suffrage because it has been beneficial over the line. But
> for every marriage in the United States there is a divorce. Will you tell
> me that that is in the interests of society? The divorce rate in the
> United States is caused by the fact that woman has left that sphere
> which as wife and mother she occupied for fifty or a hundred years.

This time the cries of dissent from the gallery annoyed the premier,
and he said petulantly: "I say so. I did not dispute you when you
were speaking. You will be good enough to listen to my reply." He
had not yet finished with the old chestnuts. He wanted, he said, to
protect women from themselves. They believed they were right, but
he knew that suffrage was not in their best interests.

> My wife is bitterly opposed to woman suffrage. I have respect for my
> wife; more than that, I love her: I am not ashamed to say so. Will
> anyone say that she would be better as a wife and mother because she
> could go and talk on the streets about local or dominion politics? I
> disagree. The mother that is worthy of the name and of the good
> affection of a good man has a hundredfold more influence in
> molding and shaping public opinion round her dinner table than she
> would have in the market place, hurling her eloquent phrases to the
> multitude. It is in the home that her influence is exercised and felt.

Furthermore, he added, women didn't use the vote when they had
it. He was told that "in Colorado they shrank away from the polls as
from a pestilence." Again "no's" from the women annoyed the
premier. "I tell you that is what I have read. Your no's have no effect
on me." He was not, however, going to admit that politics was
corrupt. "I have been in politics for many years and I do not know
of anything corrupt." A ripple of incredulous laughter brought forth
the next question. "If you know that politics is corrupt," he queried,
"why do you want to interfere with it?" But he reiterated that he had
no knowledge of corruption. No one in his government had ever had
a suggestion made to him that was corrupt or improper.

He even made an appeal to class prejudice. "I believe woman
suffrage would be a retrograde movement, that it will break up the
home, that it will throw the children into the arms of the servant girls.
Indeed, I am afraid my friend Mr. Rigg [a noted western labour
leader] might shortly come to us for the extension of the franchise to

servant girls, on the plea that servant girls have as good a right to vote as any other class of women." This statement must have been greeted with some astonishment by the delegation who had asked for the vote for women on the same basis as men, with no intention of excluding any woman who was a citizen of voting age.

Roblin concluded with the chivalry argument, which Nellie and other speakers had ridiculed for years. He "referred to the early training he had received from his mother and how she had instilled into him a great respect for women that placed them on a much higher plane than man"—a height from which women, apparently, could only sully themselves should they descend to earth to vote. The obvious culture and intelligence of "Mrs. McClung and other eloquent speakers" proved that men have made "great sacrifices that the idol of his heart might have that culture and accomplishment such as we see here today." Where, he intoned, "can you get better evidence of women's superiority and the high place that she occupies than has been given here?" He thought how delighted Lloyd George and Asquith would be if they had been approached "in the same ladylike manner." Nevertheless, Roblin declared himself "unequivocally opposed" to the vote for women in Manitoba. He held that the extension of the franchise would be a "backward step" and that he could not see what women would gain.[44] Apparently if women were not placid, and complacent but cultured "idols" of inactivity and nonintelligence, the whole fabric of society would crumble. In fact, Nellie had captured Sir Rodmond's brand of chivalry in a clever little ironic verse, "A Toast to the Ladies," ostensibly written "by an old fashioned Country Gentleman." The last stanza reads:

> The ladies—God bless them,
> Our troubles they share 'em
> So lock 'em away
> In the parlour or harem.
> We give them ideas,
> We pay for their chains,
> And what is more sweet
> Than a wife without brains?
> So here's to the angels
> We foster with elegance,
> Bless their sweet eyebrows,
> But d—n their intelligence.[45]

As Nellie McClung sat listening to Sir Rodmond's speech she was delighted. The suffragists had come to this meeting with little hope that their request would be granted. They had planned a mock parliament for the next night in the Walker Theatre. This was a device that had been used in other cities, and Lillian Thomas had decided to produce one in Winnipeg. Simply, it meant that roles would be reversed—a women's parliament in a world where men were voteless would listen to a request for the suffrage from a delegation of men. Nellie had been away from the city when this scheme was planned and had received little notice that she was to play the premier. There was no hesitation on her part in accepting the starring role, but she was concerned about her speech. This play had no script. What would she say? Now, here was Sir Rodmond providing her with a speech that hardly needed to be burlesqued. She had not dared to hope that he could be so pompous and insensitive; that he could leave himself so completely open to ridicule. She could not take notes as she sat at the table on the floor of the legislature but she listened intently and watched and memorized every move he made.

> I observed every gesture, the attitude he struck when he caught his thumbs in the armholes of his coat, twiddling his little fingers and teetering on his heels. That denoted a jocular mood. When he wanted to be coldly reasonable though fair withal, he held his elbows close to his body with the palms of his hands outspread. I tried to absorb every tone of his voice, from the ingratiating friendly voice, calculated to set everyone at their ease, even though they were in the presence of a great man, to the loud masterful commanding voice which brooked no opposition.

As the delegation left the chamber Nellie McClung could not resist a final jab. "We'll get you yet, Mr. Premier." The moment the meeting disbanded Nellie hurried home to practice before the mirror. Wes and Jack had been in the gallery and with their help the speech was written and rehearsed.

The next night an overflow crowd gathered at the Walker Theatre. The newspapers had carried detailed accounts of Roblin's rejection of the delegation's request, and the public sensed that they were in for a rare treat. It was rumoured that even some members of Roblin's caucus were surreptitiously buying tickets. Before the curtain went up Nellie came on stage to tell the audience that they were not presenting a fanciful picture, but one in which there was a one-sex parliament as presently existed: only this time it was a woman's parliament in a country where men were deprived of the vote. In fact, she said, they were so anxious to present an authentic play that they had visited the legislature recently to get local colour. Even this opening speech was greeted by laughter and almost continuous applause. There was no doubt that the audience were there to enjoy themselves.

The curtain rose to reveal the women members in evening gowns covered by black cloaks, seated at desks. First, two petitions were received: one protesting against men's clothing—six-inch collars and scarlet ties must be outlawed—the second asking for labour-saving devices for men. Mrs. W.C. Perry then presented a bill to confer dower rights on men. The members of the Opposition knitted, read newspapers, or taunted the speaker with remarks like, "you're just trying to get in right with men"—a clever sally greeted with ribald laughter by the audience. Kennethe Haig replied for the government and then the government members, as one, voted "no."

All of these speeches were received with delight, but the moment people had been waiting for was the arrival of a deputation of men led by Mr. R.C. Skinner with a wheelbarrow full of petitions asking for the vote for men. When his eloquent plea ended, the premier "rose and launched into her reply to the delegation, almost every sentence of which was interrupted by gales of laughter." From the moment Nellie opened her mouth the audience saw Sir Rodmond Roblin. The little girl who had been reprimanded for mimicking her aunts was in her glory now. Her voice dripped with tolerance and kindly understanding for these misled men as she complimented them on their courtesy and gentlemanly appearance. "If men were all so intelligent as these representatives of the downtrodden sex seem to be it might not do any harm to give them the vote. But all men are not intelligent." Now she adopted her serious mien: elbows close to her sides, palms outstretched. "There is no use giving men votes. They wouldn't use them. They would let them spoil and go to waste. Then again, some men would vote too much." Now her voice took on a warning note. "Good men shrink from the polls as from a pestilence." Then in a scolding tone Nellie asked how the men could have the audacity to come asking for the vote when seven-eighths of court offenders were men. "Surely you do not ask me to enfranchise an army of law breakers? Giving men the vote would unsettle the home

. . . In administrating the government we have studied economy. We have studied every dollar—to see if we could make better use of it ourselves. We have been very generous, we are paying fourteen women for every government job." Then Nellie's voice returned to the soft soap tones. She took on a pious manner.

> The modesty of our men, which we reverence, forbids us giving them the vote. Man's place is on the farm . . . It may be that I am old-fashioned. I may be wrong. After all, men may be human. Perhaps the time may come when men may vote with women—but in the meantime be of good cheer. Advocate and Educate. We will try to the best of our great abilities to conduct the affairs of the province and prove worthy standard bearers of the good old flag of our grand old party which has often gone down to disgrace but never to defeat.

As the delegation retreated, Mr. Skinner delivered his parting shot: "I venture to say that we will get you yet." After the deafening applause and the laughter of the audience had subsided, the women's parliament prorogued.

Even the Conservative Winnipeg *Telegram* admitted that the mock parliament was a great success and quite amusing. In its account, however, the audience was entirely female, Nellie McClung's speech was "somewhat overdone," and the women on stage were successful because "they actually revelled in their pretence of holding office and that secret ambition that they all shared undoubtedly accounted for the great success of the entire program." The other papers could exult in the evening's success without any qualifications. "Smiles of anticipation, ripples of merriment, gales of laughter and storms of applause punctuated every point and paragraph of what is unanimously conceded to be the best burlesque ever staged in Winnipeg." Many other centres staged mock parliaments, but it is Winnipeg's that is remembered: perhaps because no one else had a Roblin, and no one else had a Nellie McClung. Because of the success of this performance it was repeated in Winnipeg and taken to Brandon but subsequent performances, although successful, could not come up to the initial performance and the women turned down offers from other centres. The mock parliament brought many new supporters to the cause and, being a financial success, it funded the rest of the campaign. The suffrage supporters had not expected the mock parliament to endear them to the premier, and they realized that now, in order to achieve their goal, they would have to fight for the defeat of the Conservative government. It was necessary for the movement to become politically partisan.[46]

After Roblin's adamant refusal to take the suffrage petition seriously there was little doubt that women's suffrage would be an issue in the next election. When the Liberal Party convention met in March of 1914 the organizers invited the PEL to send speakers. The members chosen to attend were Lillian Thomas, Nellie McClung, and Eleanor Anderson. The convention was hailed as a first: the first time in Canada that women had addressed such a political assembly. Mrs. Thomas gave only one reason why women should vote—democracy. Nellie McClung followed with a short appeal for support, as usual using humour as well as logic. She pointed out that women were not looking for any special privilege but simply for a fair deal. Some people argued, she said, that women's voting would cause trouble in the home, that political rows would occur between husband and wife. "Well," she added, "if they agreed right along, all the time, I think a little dispute once every four years . . . " but she was unable to complete her sentence because of laughter and applause. She went on: "Others said women should not have the vote because they could not fight—'Go to war' I mean," she said amidst renewed laughter. "On these grounds many men should be disenfranchised." McClung asserted that she did not like the term "women's rights." The struggle was between men and women ruled by sense and reason against those ruled by prejudice and ignorance. She claimed to be speaking for the motherhood of Manitoba and urged the party to put into the hands of these women the weapon of votes with which to defend their children.

The speeches were, of course, well received because the party leadership had already decided to make female suffrage a part of their platform. The PEL decided to support the Liberals in the next election and it soon became apparent that for the first time women were to play an important role in a political campaign in Manitoba.

Nellie McClung was very active in this campaign, and the Liberals showed their appreciation of her skills by having her follow Roblin around the province whenever possible. Her schedule became hectic. In one week, for example, she spoke in Minto on Monday, Elgin on Tuesday, Melita on Wednesday, and Killarney on Thursday. At Melita she was met by a band, and nearly the entire population turned up at the station to escort her to her hotel.[47] Everywhere she went the largest hall in town would be packed. Of course, at this time in western Canada political speeches at election time were a popular form of entertainment. When Roblin came to town he too drew a large crowd. Nellie McClung, however, was a major drawing card for the Liberals. Every candidate was anxious to have her in his riding so that he could make his appeal to the largest possible assembly. People flocked to hear Nellie because they expected to be entertained, and they were not disappointed. In particular she ridiculed the idea of the premier presenting himself as a temperance advocate. She even provided statistics to show that the temperance cause had suffered setbacks due to the Roblin government. In Manitou, she reported, the temperance advocates had twice obtained the required number of names on a petition to force a local option vote: once the petition was declared illegal because the names were on separate sheets; the second time it was illegal because the sheets had been glued together. During Roblin's term, liquor licences had increased from 171 to 324, and private clubs allowed to serve liquor increased from 1 to 21.[48]

Addressing a crowd in Neepawa just after the premier had spoken there, Nellie quipped:

> Sir Rodmond was in splendid form on the occasion on which he spoke in Neepawa. His speech fairly scintillated with inaccuracies and glittered with mis-statements and vibrated with unintentional humor. Perhaps the funniest thing he said was that, as a temperance man, he was glad to see that so many people had made the sacrifice in time and money to attend the temperance convention in Winnipeg. Sir Rodmond has always been glad to see the temperance people sacrifice time and money. It came as a great surprise to us that he is a temperance man ... Sir Rodmond long ago divided temperance people into two categories. In the first class he placed himself, in the second class all others. Then he decided to work for the first class.[49]

When Roblin complained that the temperance people were forcing him into an unnatural position, that is, they were making him appear to oppose temperance when what he was really doing was opposing the ridiculous and socialist idea of a referendum, McClung retorted: "His halo of being a temperance man seems to be in danger of slipping, and he is holding it on with both hands while trying to pat himself on the back with another. It is an unnatural position."[50] Nellie McClung frequently referred to Sir

Rodmond mockingly, as a "safe" man; one who had his principles, *of course*, but not uncomfortable ones; who was honest, *of course*, but still had his honesty under perfect control. She scathingly portrayed the Conservative government as completely under the thumb of the premier. The unthinking members of the legislature were simply *automata* voting on command. A favourite story of hers was of the Conservative member who had not spoken for years. People in the gallery began to wonder whether he was alive. Then one day a draught blew in behind him. He sneezed, and rose to close the window—the only move on his own initiative that he had ever been seen to make.[51]

In Carman, Roblin's riding, Nellie went to Conservative head-quarters to invite the workers to her meeting.[52] She said she was going to hit the premier pretty hard and hated to do it without giving his supporters every opportunity to speak for him. The men in the headquarters were stunned and if they attended the meeting they kept quiet. This would have been a great disappointment to the audience because of Nellie's reputation for thriving on witty replies to hecklers or those who asked deliberately awkward questions. On one occasion when Nellie was explaining the benefits of having female suffrage a man called out: "In Colorado, where women vote, a woman once stuffed a ballot-box. How can the lady explain that?" "No one could expect women to live all their lives with men without picking up some of their little ways!" McClung flashed back.[53]

Although Nellie occasionally mentioned direct legislation, com-pulsory education, and national schools, she confined herself for the most part to prohibition and suffrage. She did not let her audiences forget that she was supporting the Liberals primarily because they supported these two issues. The Conservatives, nonetheless, contin-ued to oppose female suffrage. One of the many vulnerable argu-ments they used was that by giving women the vote they would be giving the franchise to "ignorant" foreign women. Nellie saw no reason why *all* women should not receive the franchise on the same basis as men. In addition, she vigorously attacked the use of the word "ignorant," which was commonly attached to the word "foreigner."

> In our blind egotism we class our foreign people as ignorant people, if they do not know our ways and our language. They may know many other languages, but if they have not yet mastered ours they are poor, ignorant foreigners. We Anglo-Saxon people have a

decided sense of our own superiority, and we feel sure that our skin is exactly the right color, and we people from Huron and Bruce feel sure that we were born in the right place, too. So we naturally look down upon those who happen to be of a different race and tongue than our own.[54]

Nellie McClung understood that newcomers to Canada should indeed learn about Canadian citizenship before they voted. But she also argued that the well-off city women who commonly employed these noninformed new Canadians could easily take the time to teach their immigrant workers both to speak English and to understand the voting process. Certainly this was an obligation she always placed upon herself. "We have no reason to be afraid of the foreign woman's vote," she concluded. "I wish we were as sure of the ladies who live on the Avenue."[55] On the other hand, when she argued that it was unfair that an educated woman should be without the vote when a "twenty-one-year-old youth just landed on our shores" is given it merely because he is a male, she was not denigrating the immigrant, but simply arguing against an injustice. Yet Nellie's picture of the immigrant woman was also a stereotype: intelligent, hardworking, thrifty, struggling to raise her family, often hindered by a drunken husband. For Nellie, all that was needed was to stop the liquor traffic and put immigrants to work on the land instead of amongst the evils of the city. This was an oversimplified solution, but more attractive than the pessimistic view of some that "these people"—as immigrants were often slightingly categorized—could not be assimilated and, in particular, that immigration from eastern Europe should cease.

The Conservative opposition to suffrage was based on the assumption that it was a fad supported by a small minority of women. If it was ignored, the Conservatives thought, it would probably go away. Liberal leader T.C. Norris's acceptance of female suffrage, according to his opponents, revealed his weakness. Roblin, on the other hand, continued to assure his audiences that his wife didn't want the vote. Naturally Nellie McClung kept up a constant ridicule of this absurd Conservative stand. As she told the Young Liberals meeting in Winnipeg:

He [Roblin] told us that he did not believe in women's suffrage personally, that he had been brought up to lift his hat to the ladies, and that he always gave up his seat in street cars to the ladies. That, of course, should help us a good deal but it was hardly an answer to our question. We were there asking for plain common justice, and an old-fashioned square deal and in reply to that we got hat lifting. I feel that when a man offers hat lifting when we ask for justice we should tell him to keep his hat right on. I will go further and say that we should tell him not only to keep his hat on, but to pull it right down on his face.[56]

Nellie's eyes must have twinkled mischievously when she added that Roblin, on this occasion, reminded her of an old ox they had had on the farm many years before, named Mike. Mike wouldn't let the rest of the cattle near the water trough even when he had had all he could possibly drink, he just "deliberately and with difficulty put his two front feet over the trough and kept all the other cattle away." When the suffrage delegation visited the legislature and Roblin spoke for the government, "he said in substance: 'You can't have it—so long as I have anything to do with the affairs of this province— you shall not have it!' . . . I said to myself: 'Where have I seen that face before?' Suddenly I remembered and in my heart I cried out: 'Mike!—old friend Mike! Dead these many years! Your bones lie buried under the fertile soil of the Souris Valley, but your soul goes marching on! Mike, old friend, I see you again—both feet in the trough!'"[57]

The Conservatives, too, tried ridicule. They portrayed Norris as a man who "will go down in history as the adopted father of political fads . . . the so-called leader of the party plays a very second fiddle to Mrs. Nellie McClung."[58] The *Telegram* ran a cartoon that depicted Norris surrounded by a horde of annoying, buzzing mosquitoes called "school question," and "referendum and recall," and insects like "the Rev. C.W." [Charles W. Gordon, "Ralph Connor"] and "Calamity Nell" were drawn carrying a votes-for-women banner. In another cartoon Norris is shown as a fisherman with too many lines. They wished to present the Liberal Party as a disorganized crowd with no real leader and Norris as a desperate man who would adopt any reform mentioned to him.[59] The amount of attention that the Conservative papers now gave to Nellie McClung indicates that she had indeed become a troublesome opponent. In Brandon she was burned in effigy.

The glowing accounts of Nellie's successes on the platform were not, of course, to be found in Conservative papers. The Brandon *Sun*, early in the campaign, pointed out that Mrs. McClung had always been well received when she gave recitals and lectures, but now she dared to speak on politics. "She made no apology for being there," the editor reported with obvious amazement at such effrontery, "and in a defiant manner seemed to glory in the shower of adverse criticism she has brought upon herself." He further acknowledged that "McClung has the power of being able to mimic splendidly and when she alluded to any cabinet minister in a sarcastic manner there were always those ready to cheer." The account, although meant to denigrate, portrays a speaker who at least partially won her audience in spite of opposition to her cause. When Nellie made an error in a speech stating that The Pas had three liquor outlets when it did not, this was seized upon as evidence of her dishonesty. The Neepawa *Register* declared that she was "entirely discredited by her statement."[60] When one notes the harsh things she was saying about Roblin and the Conservatives it is amusing to find that a small error in the number of liquor licences in The Pas was the only "lie" the opposition papers could find. They did not, for example, deny her comment that "it is said that Sir Rodmond even takes a personal interest in Manitoba brewing concerns, in fact something like principal and interest." Roblin soon learned that it was just as well not to mention Nellie McClung's name. In Winnipeg he expressed his "intense regret" that Nellie had taken the platform against him and was following him about the province, but when he said, "and I am told that she is coming here," he was stopped by a storm of applause.[61]

Nellie McClung, of course, could not resent the open attacks of a political campaign, but it was the first time she had come up against this situation and at times she was probably disturbed by them. Certainly she did feel hurt that her opponents dragged in her family. This kind of opposition does not seem to have appeared in print but was carried out by word of mouth. Her children were described as wild and unruly, running the streets neglected; and on at least one occasion it was stated that they were frequently fed by a neighbour.[62] Her husband was rumoured to be contemplating divorce. But Nellie knew that when she went out to speak she left behind her a well-run household. The children were well cared for in her absence by their father and by their two domestic helpers.[63] While the older children were interested in the campaign, Florence was at an age when it was difficult to have a mother who was in the political eye, a subject of both praise and criticism. On one occasion she expressed her wish that her mother could be like other mothers, but quickly she retracted to declare her support.[64] Even the younger children became aware of criticism. One day Horace sneaked Mark in through a hole in the back fence. Like any normal three-year-old, he was spattered with mud, one stocking at half-mast. "Quick, now," said Horace. "It's a good thing I got you before the *Telegram* got a picture of you—Nellie McClung's neglected child!"[65] To make a joke of the criticism Mark was taught, when asked his name, to reply: "I'm Mark McClung. I'm the son of a suffragette and never knew a mother's love."[66] In some towns, before Nellie's arrival, the Conservative organizers spread rumours of Nellie McClung's neglect of her family, hoping to persuade people not to go to hear this disgrace to "motherhood."[67] Nellie tried to counter such attacks by beginning her speeches with a joking reference to the fact that she had just phoned home and that her family was fine. The younger children were in bed, she announced, and the older ones doing their homework. This was always greeted with laughter and applause. Beneath the joking reply, of course, Nellie was serious. Not only would it be bad for the women's suffrage campaign to have such rumours believed but the rumours hurt her personally. She unequivocally believed that the welfare of her family and her home was her responsibility and one that she was, indeed, fulfilling. A few years after the Manitoba women's suffrage campaign was over, she recorded her strong feelings about this issue: "I cannot think of it without bitterness, and that is the fact that there are people mean enough to show hostility and spite to the children, when they differ from the mother politically . . . It is all rather pitiful to know that people can be so cruel. That is the one part of my public life that has really hurt."[68]

Newspaper coverage might have led one to believe that Nellie McClung was the only woman participating in the campaign, but this certainly was not the case. In her autobiography she is careful to pay tribute to others such as Winona and Lynn Flett, who were both effective on the platform. Lillian Thomas also spoke frequently and she too was able to handle herself well in the face of opposition. Francis Beynon both spoke and supported the cause in the *Grain Growers' Guide*. Cora Hind was too busy to take to the campaign trail but used her columns whenever possible to back the campaign. Many other women who were not public speakers worked hard behind the scenes. For the first time a significant number of women were actively involved in a political campaign. Of course, it remained a small minority of women, just as only a minority of men were actively involved. Among these women Nellie stood out, as one editor put it, "conducting herself with a dignity and ability that made her the joy of her own party and the target of the enemies' heaviest artillery."[69]

Near the end of the campaign Nellie McClung was chosen to speak at two mass rallies in Winnipeg. On the night of the first, Walker Theatre—which held twenty-five hundred—was filled by seven thirty and the doors closed. Because of the large numbers of women who usually attended Nellie's meetings, the ground floor was reserved for men only. They, after all, were the ones who could vote. A crowd almost as large waited outside. When Nellie arrived she graciously climbed on a wagon and addressed those outside. Inside, she began her formal speech by revealing that she had received an anonymous letter threatening to expose instances of her past life if she did not desist from her public utterances. She challenged the writer to print what he had to say on the front page of the morning *Telegram*. This was greeted by thunderous applause. She then spoke for one-and-a-half hours, without notes, "using all the telling force of dramatic art." The newspaper report assured those who had missed her that there would be one more opportunity on the eve of the election. The *Free Press* predicted that although the Industrial Bureau, where the rally was to be held, seated five thousand, there would be lineups two hours before the meeting. "The greatest auditorium in Winnipeg is too small for the crowds that would like to hear Mrs. McClung."[70] This prediction was correct. The hall was full and every inch of standing space was occupied. It was a hot evening and the crowded hall was stifling but the audience remained patient through many speeches. When Nellie finally rose to speak she "received an ovation such as seldom falls to the lot of any one in the public eye. It was a remarkable demonstration of affection and esteem."[71]

Not surprisingly the Liberals, and perhaps Nellie McClung in particular, believed that they would win the election. It was a disappointed Nellie who heard, that night, that the Conservatives had been returned to office. Nevertheless, the disappointment was eased by the knowledge that the Liberals had greatly increased their popular vote, and had cut the Conservative majority from sixteen to seven in a larger house.[72]

After the excitement and constant travelling and speaking, it was a relief for Nellie to retreat to the family cottage at Matlock Beach. This peaceful interlude was shattered by the news of war. Apparently the gathering clouds had been totally ignored by the cottage dwellers: "When the news of war came we did not really believe it! War! That was over! There had been war, of course, but that had been long ago, in the dark ages, before the days of free schools and peace conferences and missionary conventions and labour unions! . . . a big war— that was quite impossible! Christian nations could not go to war."[73] As they looked back at the boarded-up windows of the cottage at the end of the summer they felt that a pleasant chapter in their lives had ended. The fact of world warfare must have seemed like a loss of innocence to them. Not long after the return to Winnipeg, Wes received an offer to become Manufacturers' Life manager for the northern Alberta area. His base would be Edmonton, and they were to move at the end of the year.

In the meantime Roblin heard from Nellie McClung once more. At the beginning of the war there was considerable unemployment. The government increased this by closing down public works, according to Roblin, as a war measure. Individual companies were also cutting back on employees and even domestic workers were dismissed as an alleged economic "contribution to the war." Nellie McClung frequently criticized this kind of false war effort made at the expense of others. "Many women believe in sacrifice," she said, "but they prefer the maid to make it." With other prohibitionists she decided that the proper place to make economic cutbacks was in the liquor trade. When the Social Service Council, in September, asked the government to receive a delegation to present this opinion to the legislature, as usual Nellie McClung was to be the chief spokesperson.[74] When Sir Rodmond refused, Nellie published her speech as an "Open Letter to Sir Rodmond":

> When the first shock of the war came upon us its effect was to produce a panic. Everybody felt it. Many did foolish things. You immediately closed down the public works. Your impulse was right. You knew something should be closed, but if you will pardon this criticism from the laity you closed the wrong thing. The bars should have been closed, and the public works kept open, even expanded. However, it may be easy to criticize. People often on hearing the honk of an auto jump back, when they should jump forward.

She concluded with a warning to Roblin:

> In your petty kingdom, Sir Rodmond, you rule not wisely but too
> well. But the world moves, and independence of thought is growing.
> Some day the people of Manitoba will have democratic government.
> With our eyes turned toward Europe and its terrible conflict, the
> majority of us realize that never before has autocracy been so
> hateful, never before has democracy been so sweet.[75]

No doubt Roblin viewed with some pleasure the McClungs' im-
pending departure from Manitoba. A persistent mosquito can
cause great irritation.

Even after Nellie McClung left Manitoba she had one last involvement with Manitoba politics. Not long after the 1914 election,
scandals concerning the Conservative government began to
emerge.[76] Finally, in May 1915, Roblin resigned and T.C. Norris was
asked to form a government. The leadership of the Conservative
Party went to Sir James Aikins. Immediately Nellie received telegrams
congratulating her on her share in Roblin's downfall. Her example
and efforts had, one correspondent wrote, "changed conditions of
public sentiment in Manitoba." When an election was called for
August 1915, Nellie was urged to return to take part. It was rumoured
that she was invited by both parties. In fact, the Conservatives assured
her that they were now promising prohibition and women's suffrage
and she could support them with a clear conscience. Her reply
"quickly broke off these overtures."[77]

Because of the prohibition drive going on in Alberta that summer
Nellie was unable to come to Manitoba until the last week of the
election campaign. She spoke in many centres near Winnipeg that
week, including Manitou. In her speeches Nellie expressed doubt of
the sincerity of the Conservatives in both their suffrage and prohibition planks. They were promising to bring back the *Macdonald Act* (a
prohibition act), but Nellie suspected that if they were elected, it
would be "wrapped up in tissue paper for the next occasion. That was
known as political economy,"[78] she quipped. The support for
women's suffrage seemed an even more expedient and questionable
party plank, and Conservative leader Sir James Aikins appeared
half-hearted in his endorsement of it. He criticized the Liberal
demand for another petition before introducing legislation to give
women the vote, but he also said he "would sooner take the advice of
a few excellent women I could trust. If the principle of women's
suffrage is right—and the Conservative convention said it was right—

then there should be no delay in giving the suffrage to some women at all events." His use of the word "some," his expressed fear that some "unworthy women" might get the vote, and his strictures against enfranchising "foreign women" gave Nellie plenty of ammunition for her speeches. She said she was afraid that if the women brought Sir James a petition he would look at the names and say "No, not the right class!" She wondered what would happen if a man had to be judged "worthy" before he could vote. "If there was to be a morality test there would be a strange revision of the voters' list." In almost every speech Nellie defended the right of all citizens of voting age to cast a ballot. On the eve of the election the Liberals held a large meeting in the Walker Theatre. The hall was filled with a crowd of exuberant supporters long before the meeting was scheduled to start. When F.J. Dixon came in, he received an "enthusiastic ovation." The same was given to Mr. Johnson, who had led the disclosure of Conservative Party scandals. The entrance of Mrs. McClung, however, "was the signal for a perfect storm of cheering and applause."[79]

This time the Liberal expectations were fully justified. They won an overwhelming victory. Nellie McClung was at the *Free Press* office following the returns when the crowd outside demanded her appearance. She came to the window to be greeted by "an outburst of cheering while hats, handkerchiefs and walking sticks were waved aloft." She agreed to speak and the crowd fell quiet. If they were expecting to be amused at the expense of the defeated Tories, however, they were disappointed, for Nellie spoke in a calm, deliberate manner, and there was no gloating over a defeated opponent but rather a reminder of the great responsibility the new government now had to fulfil its promises. Graciously she concluded with an expression of great appreciation to the male voters: "On behalf of the women of Manitoba, I desire to extend our gratitude and to express the hope that you will never be sorry for the vote you have cast this day which will make it possible for the women of Manitoba to stand side by side with you in the next election."[80] The Liberals honoured their promise and on 28 January 1916 the women of Manitoba became the first Canadian women to win the right to vote in provincial elections and to hold provincial office.

There can be no doubt that in the Manitoba election campaigns Nellie McClung reached the pinnacle of her public career. Already nationally well-known as a recitalist and the author of a best seller, she now gained recognition as a formidable political fighter. "In intellectual keenness, in tenacity of purpose, in prophetic vision, and in constructive capacity, this woman has shown herself not only the equal but superior to much that has been considered in the other sex cabinet timber," wrote one admirer.[81] Not only in Manitoba but across the country her success was commented on and her congratulatory telegrams spanned the country from Montreal to Vancouver.[82] As the suffrage campaign progressed she had honed her oratorical skills, culminating in her remarkable performance on the eve of the 1914 election. The flattering tone of the letters inviting her back for the second campaign attested to the value that the Liberal leaders put on her electioneering ability. There were many predictions that she would some day be a cabinet minister, and more than one writer suggested she would make an excellent premier. Prophesying that she would one day attain this position one editor wrote: "If the lady's administrative abilities are in any degree equal to her wit, eloquence, and sound sense it will certainly be a fine thing for the Province."[83] In the future Nellie McClung would play a prominent role in many organizations, receive appointments that recognized her ability, even be elected to a legislature, but she would never again receive the attention and the outpouring of praise that was bestowed on her during and after this Manitoba campaign.

This rare old photograph of Nellie's Irish-born father, John Mooney, was taken more than one hundred years ago. John Mooney arrived in Canada from Tipperary, Ireland, in 1830 at the age of eighteen, driven from his homeland by the famines. He never lost his love for Ireland, though, and in her autobiography Nellie recalled with sadness that the family had never thought to send him back home to his beloved Ireland for a visit before his death. *Courtesy M.J.G. McMullen, author of "Recalled to Life," Souvenir Booklet of Nellie McClung*

Letitia (McCurdy) Mooney, Nellie's Scottish mother, was twenty years younger than her husband when they were married in 1858. Though as a child and young woman Nellie often thought of her mother as stern and forbidding, she later grew to respect her strength of character and blunt kindliness. *Courtesy M.J.G. McMullen*

Nellie, pictured here in 1879 at age five, spent her early childhood on the Mooney farm in Grey County, Ontario. She was the youngest of six children. The Mooney farm was small and stony, and the promise of a better life in the West made the family decide to take their chances on a homestead there. They settled near the junction of the Assiniboine and Souris rivers. *Courtesy M.J.G. McMullen*

The town of Manitou had a four-room school and a normal school. Nellie was offered her first teaching position at Hazel School, near Manitou, at the age of sixteen, though she had not attended school herself until she was ten. She taught in a number of rural and small-town southern Manitoba schools, including the one in Manitou. *Courtesy British Columbia Archives and Records Service/80003*

Above left: Nellie, shown here at the age of nineteen, enjoyed the small rural towns in Manitoba in which she taught. She described her life then as "uproariously, unreasonably happy" and claimed that anyone who felt that life was boring in a small town had never visited one. *Courtesy Glenbow-Alberta Institute/NA-5032-1*

Above right: This picture of Nellie's nephew was used on the cover of *Sowing Seeds in Danny* (1908). The book became a Canadian best seller and as the fame of the novel spread Nellie was increasingly in demand as an entertainer-recitalist. *Courtesy British Columbia Archives and Records Service/E-6028*

As an author, Nellie McClung frequently used her fiction to convey her social and reform ideas, combining her craft with her determination to improve the lives of those around her. *Courtesy British Columbia Archives and Records Service/E-5182*

Nellie and Robert Wesley McClung. From all accounts the couple had a solid, loving relationship. Her marriage to Wes in 1896 did not mean Nellie had to turn her back on her writing and the social causes so important to her, though had Wes objected, she admitted she did not know what she would have done. *Courtesy British Columbia Archives and Records Service/D-9034*

This photo, familiar to many Canadians, depicts Nellie at the height of her career as an author. She published sixteen books and countless short stories and articles. Nellie's earnings from her pen no doubt provided her with a degree of independence few women of this era were able to experience. *Courtesy National Archives of Canada/ PA-30212/Jessop*

Monday evening, Nov. 9th, a

FOWL SUPPER

will be served in WASEY'S HALL, from 6 to 8 p. m., after which a Grand **CONCERT** will be given in the BANK HALL by local talent, assisted by Rev E. J. Hopper B.A., Mrs Nellie McClung, of Manitou, the authoress, who will recite and read from her book "Sowing Seeds in Danny" declared by reviewers the equal in laughter and sympathy to anything that Ian McLaren or Ralph Connor has written, and by Mr J. Dean I.S. M., Tenor of the London and Provincial Concerts, England, and more recently of Carman.

Thanksgiving.   *Full Moon.*   *Kings Birthday.*
Come and Celebrate.

Admission to Supper and Concert.

Adults 50c.   **Children 35.**

Echo Press, Swan Lake.

Manitobans were exceedingly proud of the author in their midst. During the Manitou years Nellie had found it difficult to set aside time to write. "When no one comes to see me and the phone is not ringing, and the children are at school and there's nothing in particular to do I write." *Courtesy British Columbia Archives and Records Service/E-6022*

Friday,	WATERLOO PRESBYTERIAN CHURCH	Tickets
Dec.	## NELLIE L. McCLUNG, The popular Manitoban Novelist, — Author of —	A Limited Number
16.	"Sowing Seeds in Danny" and "The Second Chance." In her Delightful Programme of	a'
at	**Readings and Recitations.** Vocal and Instrumental Selections by Leading Amateurs.	**25**
8 p. m.	"THE MAPLE LEAF FOREVER"	Cents.

Nellie's success as an author led to a career as a recitalist and public speaker, where she was truly in her element. It was not until she dared to speak out on political and social issues rather than appear as an entertainer, however, that she was criticized for going on tour rather than remaining at home as a wife and mother. *Courtesy British Columbia Archives and Records Service/E-6012*

Portrait of Nellie at age thirty-seven. In her public appearances Nellie would often use humour and her quick wit to make her point, and halls were usually filled to overflowing when she was scheduled to speak. Nellie was also able to draw on her own life experiences to make her audience identify with her. Newspaper accounts were full of her ability to "carry" her audiences and bring them from tears to laughter and back again. *Courtesy British Columbia Archives and Records Service/39858*

HE SEES THE POINT OF THESE JOKES

This cartoon, published in a Conservative Winnipeg newspaper in June 1914, portrayed Nellie as a pesky mosquito troubling Manitoba Liberal leader T.C. Norris. Norris's acceptance of female suffrage, according to his opponents, meant he had buckled under the pressure, thereby revealing his weakness as a leader. *Courtesy British Columbia Archives and Records Service/E-6029*

Nellie reached the pinnacle of her public career in the Manitoba election campaign of 1914, in which she played a prominent role. Though she was not an official member of any political party, the amount of attention paid her by the Conservative press indicates that she had become a troublesome opponent. In some towns the Conservative organizers spread rumours of Nellie's neglect of her family and asked that people not go to hear this "disgrace to motherhood." "Calamity Nell" was even burnt in effigy in one community. *Courtesy British Columbia Archives and Records Service/E-6013*

Fathers! Mothers!

The Liquor Traffic takes one boy out of every fifth home. HAVE YOU ONE TO SPARE?

IF NOT

Make Alberta Dry, Twenty-First July

Vote FOR the "Liquor Act"

Vote $\boxed{\text{X}}$ Yes

You vote at Poll No............which is located

at...

Nellie continued to fight for prohibition once she moved to Edmonton. In the summer of 1915 the Alberta government presented a prohibition bill to the people for a direct vote, and Nellie, of course, participated in the campaign by touring the province for six weeks speaking in defence of a ban on alcohol. On 21 July the "drys" won, outnumbering the "wets" 58,295 to 37,509. *Courtesy McClung Papers, Volume 2, British Columbia Archives and Records Service*

Francis Marion Beynon was a journalist and a friend of Nellie McClung. She was the women's editor of the *Grain Growers' Guide*, an active member of the Canadian Women's Press Club, and helped to organize the Political Equality League of Manitoba, the province's main women's suffrage organization. *Courtesy Provincial Archives of Manitoba/N13687*

Lillian (Beynon) Thomas, like her sister Francis Marion Beynon, was a Winnipeg journalist and a close friend of Nellie McClung. She was one of the women who organized the "mock parliament," in which the Political Equality League staged the play "How the Vote Was Won." She was also a member of the Canadian Women's Press Club. *Courtesy Provincial Archives of Manitoba*

Visit of leading British suffragette Emmeline Pankhurst to Edmonton in 1916. Nellie McClung is front row, centre; to her right are Emmeline Pankhurst and Emily Murphy. The child in the photo is Mark McClung. *Courtesy British Columbia Archives and Records Service/39849*

Left to right: Nellie McClung, Alice Jamieson, and Emily Murphy. This photo was taken in Edmonton on 19 April 1916 when women in Alberta succeeded in their long struggle to gain the vote. In celebration, Nellie and her companions bought new hats and had their photo taken. *Courtesy British Columbia Archives and Records Service/B-6791*

Lord Chancellor Sankey on his way to deliver judgement in the "Persons Case," 18 October 1929. The case had been appealed to the Judicial Committee of the Privy Council in England. The JCPC declared that women were "persons" within the meaning of the 1867 *BNA Act* and therefore eligible to sit in the Senate. The implications of this judgement were felt throughout the British Empire. *Courtesy British Columbia Archives and Records Service/F-5316*

Photo taken in the Ante Chamber of the Senate on the occasion of the unveiling of the plaque honouring the "famous five" women involved in the "Persons Case": Emily Murphy, Henrietta Muir Edwards, Louise McKinney, Irene Parlby, and (at right) Nellie McClung, next to William Lyon Mackenzie King. *Courtesy British Columbia Archives and Records Service/39860*

This photo of Nellie McClung was likely taken in the late 1920s before the move to Lantern Lane, when the McClungs were living in Calgary. Nellie served as a Liberal member of the Alberta Legislature from 1921 to 1926, at which time the United Farmers of Alberta were in office. As an MLA she would often criticize or support policies on the basis of what she thought was right for the public, rather than towing the party line. *Courtesy British Columbia Archives and Records Service/D–9033*

Left to right: Hugh Atkinson (son-in-law), Wes McClung, Horace McClung, Mark McClung, and Florence (McClung) Atkinson. *British Columbia Archives and Records Service/C–8524*

Lantern Lane, 1861 Ferndale Road, Gordon Head, Victoria, B.C. The McClungs "retired" to Victoria in 1933, and moved into Lantern Lane in 1935, where they lived until the end of their lives. Here Wes could indulge in his passion for gardening and Nellie could continue her writing. *Courtesy M.J.G. McMullen*

The McClung family, taken at Lantern Lane, 1942. *Left to right:* Horace, Paul, Florence, Jack, and Mark. *Seated:* Nellie and Wes McClung. *Courtesy M.J.G. McMullen*

Nellie McClung and grandchild. Visits by members of the family to Lantern Lane were frequent and it became a favourite spot for the grandchildren. *Courtesy British Columbia Archives and Records Service/39855*

Even before the move to Victoria, Nellie began to suffer from arthritis, but it did not seem to slow her down. In addition to writing, speaking engagements, travelling, and entertaining friends, she concerned herself with the plight of Japanese Canadians during World War Two and of Jewish refugees, among other causes. She also persisted in her fight to improve the status of women in society. *British Columbia Archives and Records Service/39857*

In 1936 Mackenzie King asked Nellie to accept an appointment to the board of governors of the newly reorganized Canadian Broadcasting Corporation. This photo of the First Board of Broadcast Governors was taken on 3 November 1936. Other board members were: Leonard W. Brockington, Chairman; Rene Morin, Vice-chairman; Wilfred Bovey; J. Wilfred Godfrey; N.L. Nathanson; Victor Odlum; Rev. Alexander Vachon; and Alan Plaunt. Nellie fought for new stations and better frequencies in the West, and was a vigorous participant in discussions concerning programming. She remained a member until she was forced to resign in 1942 due to failing health. *Courtesy British Columbia Archives and Records Service/F–2083*

Golden Wedding Anniversary of Wes and Nellie McClung, 1946. *Front row, seated:* 3 grandchildren—Nellie McClung, John McClung, Maxine McClung; *seated, centre:* Nellie and Wes McClung; *back row:* J. Turnbull (family friend), Mrs. H.B. McClung with Barry, Horace McClung (son), Mrs. Jack McClung (daughter-in-law), Mrs. Florence Atkinson (daughter), Miss Jane Atkinson (granddaughter), Mrs. C.P. Anderson (sister of Wes McClung), Paul McClung (son), Mrs. Paul McClung, Mr. Hugh Atkinson (son-in-law). Missing are Mr. and Mrs. Mark McClung of Ottawa, Robert McClung (grandson), Jack McClung (son), deceased. *Courtesy British Columbia Archives and Records Service/39853*

Nellie McClung in her seventies. Nellie died in 1951 at the age of seventy-seven. In 1973, her centennial year, Nellie was honoured by the issuing of a Commemorative Nellie McClung Stamp. Some people felt the honour was marred by the unattractive way Nellie was portrayed on the stamp. The likeness was more suggestive of the stereotypical repressive, tight-lipped temperance worker than of the serene, outgoing, and attractive woman we see here. *Courtesy Florence (McClung) Atkinson*

This commemorative monument, dedicated to Nellie McClung, can be found nestled in a wooded area in Grey County, Ontario, Nellie's birthplace. The plaque reads: "Nellie Mooney McClung, Lecturer, Legislator, Teacher and Writer, Ardent Advocate of Women's Rights in Canada, Author of 'Sowing Seeds in Danny' and other works. Born near Chatsworth, 20th October 1873. Died in Victoria, B.C., 1st September, 1951." *Collection of the author*

6

The War Years: 1914–1919

❖

When the news of war reached the McClungs in the summer of 1914 while they were still at Matlock Beach north of Winnipeg, it caused no immediate change in their lives. But the war did cast its inevitable shadow. The children began to play battle games, while the adults gathered anxiously on the porch to discuss the war and raise questions that none of them could answer. Even Wes's father could shed little light on the situation and the McClungs searched the newspapers for explanations. Perhaps because of her ignorance of world events at this time Nellie became much more aware of current events in future years, and conducted several "current events" clubs. On 24 August the McClungs closed the cottage to return to town. There they would prepare for their move to Edmonton in December.

Among Nellie's friends, news of the McClungs' proposed move to Edmonton was greeted with dismay. Francis Beynon wrote: "To have one's departure mourned by a whole province, with the possible exception of a small group of legislators, is an honor which falls to the lot of but a few people but ... [Nellie McClung] may enjoy that enviable distinction." Beynon also went on to praise McClung as a private person:

> Meeting her day by day she compels respect by proving herself to be a high-minded, generous-spirited woman with never an evil word for anyone. Her thoughts are so fully occupied with the great issues of the day that she has no leisure for small bickerings and little jealousies, and the same bigness of outlook has saved her from having her head turned by the adulation of the public. As it is she comes back from her most conspicuous successes just as jolly and natural and comfortable as ever. Her gracious platform manners are

in daily use in her own home and her beguiling Irish smile is far more often brought into play for her "ain folk" than for her admiring public. All the West knows that Mrs. McClung is a brilliant woman, but only those who have seen her with her husband and children in her own home know what an altogether lovable person she is in her private life.[1]

The PEL, in their farewell address, described Nellie as "the universal woman who cannot be localized," and said it was only fair that they should share her with another province.[2]

Leaving Manitoba was very difficult for Nellie McClung. Not only had it been her home for thirty-three years but it had been the scene of her recent successes. Telegrams had arrived from all over the province and beyond, attributing much of the Liberal gain in the election to her. Many people had suggested that her success as a campaigner would lead to a cabinet post, probably as minister of education. This must have had a tremendous appeal to a person as innovative and ambitious as Nellie. "In my moments of exaltation," she wrote many years later, "I had great dreams of what I could do for rural education, especially among the foreign born." But she also recalls that along with her disappointment at departure came a modicum of relief:

> When the McCurdy strain in my blood dominated I grew cautious because of my inexperience . . . I knew I could make a good speech. I knew I could persuade people, and I knew I had a real hold on the people of Manitoba, especially the women, but I also knew that . . . I could easily undo all I had done for I knew the world would be critical of women for a long time. If a woman succeeded, her success would belong to her as an individual. People would say she was an exceptional woman. She had a "masculine" mind. Her success belonged to her alone, but if she failed, she failed for all women everywhere. With this in mind, . . . I said nothing to anyone, but it reconciled me to the move. I felt I was being let down over the wall in a basket.[3]

These thoughts may well have gone through her head at the time, but it is difficult to believe that had she been given the opportunity of a cabinet post she would have turned it down. She would have accepted the challenge as she did every other challenge that came her way. Chances are, however, that she would never have been asked, despite the predictions. There were many capable women in

Manitoba but when Norris gained office he did not see fit to call any of them into his cabinet.

Despite Nellie McClung's regret at leaving Winnipeg, she was keenly interested in her new home and found the city of Edmonton exciting and different. She felt as though she was living on the northern frontier. "Edmonton was a city of glamour. To the north lay the great white world of mystery, the land of dog teams, northern lights and undiscovered treasures." In the stores she saw prospectors buying supplies and "stately Indians in moccasins and beaded coats." As usual Nellie welcomed novelty and to her "the whole atmosphere of the city was young, hopeful, and full of surprises." Even the climate was a pleasant surprise—brisk and clear and more invigorating than Winnipeg. "I never felt better or more keenly alive. I could work all day and all night and in addition to the duties of a home and a family of five, I wrote the book *In Times Like These* and several short stories that first winter."[4]

Nellie was not allowed to remain at home with family and writing, though, nor would she have been content with that life for long. As soon as she arrived in the city she was welcomed into the Edmonton Equal Franchise League, the Edmonton Women's Press Club, the WCTU and, of course, the Methodist Woman's Missionary Society. One of her first callers was Emily Murphy—Mrs. Arthur Murphy—a well-known author as "Janey Canuck" and president of the Canadian Women's Press Club. Although McClung and Murphy had very different backgrounds—Murphy came from a well-to-do Ontario family, her brothers were lawyers and judges, she was married to an Anglican clergyman—their similarities in personality and ideals were stronger than the differences. They shared a love of writing, the energy and ability to tackle almost any job they believed would help improve society, and, perhaps the greatest cement of friendship, a similar sense of humour. The acquaintance soon developed into close friendship that survived any differences of opinion over the years. "Having known and loved her for years," Mrs. Murphy once wrote, she could assure the public that "those most severely critical of Mrs. McClung are strangers to her or [persons] who, for some reason or other fear her influence." Emily declared unequivocally, however, that Nellie McClung had no "cannibalistic tendencies," and that "in her personality there is a geniality and open frankness that almost invariably disarm your hostility and . . . win you to her cause . . . We may not agree with her viewpoint . . . but nevertheless, we all turn out to hear her, for her gift for interpreting public situations has almost become a public function." In sum, she added, "there is no doubt that Carlyle was wholly correct when he said that 'the right good fighter was oftenest also the right good improver, discerner, doer, and worker of every kind.'"[5] As in Winnipeg, Nellie found a core of active, enthusiastic women like Emily Murphy working for suffrage and prohibition—some with more emphasis on one than on the other, some like Nellie seeing them as equally important.

Nellie McClung had not been long in Edmonton when she addressed the provincial legislature. In February of 1915 the Edmonton Equal Franchise League organized a large delegation to present their case for female suffrage. There were twelve speakers, men and women, and Nellie was chosen to speak last—perhaps because they knew her speech would be the most eloquent. The Edmonton *Bulletin* described her address as "remarkable, not only for the many clever things that she said, but also for what she did not say." Her approach to Sifton was very different from her approach to Premier Roblin because she knew that Sifton was basically sympathetic to the cause. "Premier Sifton," she said, "when you reply to this demonstration I don't think you will tell us that politics are too corrupt for women." Sifton shook his head in acknowledgement, and Nellie continued: "I don't think you will tell us either that women don't want the vote." Again Sifton shook his head. "That's good," said Mrs. McClung. "The men tell us with a fine air of chivalry that women should not be given the vote because women don't want the vote, the inference being that women get nothing unless they want. Women get a lot of things they don't want—the war, the liquor traffic, and lower pay for equal work. Surely you would not want the irresponsible women to set the pace for the rest of us?"

Ignoring the usual arguments for women's franchise, Nellie "gave many reasons for, as she said, 'the hope that is in us.'" She asserted that many members of the cabinet recognized the great contribution that pioneer women had made in the West and that they therefore accepted the justice of the women's claim to a vote. "If they recognize the justice of it," she concluded, "there was no more to be said." Sifton did not commit himself at this time, but he promised that the matter would come before the legislature at its sitting early next year. The delegation left in a far more optimistic mood than the Manitoba delegation had left its legislature the year before.[6]

Although Nellie McClung also made several speeches to church and other groups, she was devoting much of her time to the polishing and rewriting of lectures to bring out in book form—the volume appeared in the spring of 1915 under the title *In Times Like These.* While she worked on this her thoughts dwelt on the war. It was very difficult for her to formulate her views on this particular conflict. She certainly did not join in the "outburst of enthusiastic patriotism" with which, we are told, most Canadians responded,[7] perhaps because some of her friends were committed pacifists, among them her closest Winnipeg friend Lillian Thomas, her sister, Francis Beynon, and Lillian's husband, Vernon. From them she heard the view that this war was no different from others in the age-old European feuds. British peers, they told her, held stock in the Krupp works in Germany and one of the first captured German guns was found to have been made in England. "Was this good enough to fight for?" they asked. "War was a game, a plot against humanity and would go on as long as the common people could be depended on to do the fighting." On the other hand another close friend, Cora Hind, a woman Nellie had admired for many years, was totally committed to the Empire. "We were British and must follow the tradition of our fathers," Hind declared. Nellie almost envied Hind's uncomplicated faith in comparison to her own nagging doubts, and she resented Hind's attacks on those, like the Thomases and J.S. Woodsworth, who thought otherwise.[8]

Nellie's speeches at this time and her books, *In Times Like These* and *The Next of Kin* (1917), reveal much of this mental struggle. Her strictures against war were so strong at the beginning of the conflict that it is surprising she escaped criticism: "History, romance, legend and tradition having been written by men, have shown the masculine aspect of war and have surrounded it with a false glory . . . If I go to my neighbour's house, and break her furniture, and smash her pictures, and bind her children captive, it does not prove that I am fitter to live than she—yet according to the ethics of nations it does."[9] She saw war as a disease: "the withering, blighting, wasting malady of hatred, which has its roots in the narrow patriotism which teaches people to love their own country and despise all others." She recognized, too, that war hardened people to grief and misery, and "twisted the whole moral fabric." In addition, war weakened a nation physically. The fittest go to fight and "the epileptic, the consumptive,

143

the inebriate . . . stay at home, and perpetuate the race!"[10]

To Nellie McClung, then, war was a fault of civilization as a whole, and she made no attempt to justify individual nations or occasions. And although she agreed with those who said that Christian nations could not go to war, she pointed out that there were no truly Christian nations. "Once a year, of course, we hold a Peace Sunday and on that day we pray mightily that God will give us peace in our time and that war shall be no more . . . But the next day we show God that he need not take us too literally, for we go on with the military training, and the building of the battleships, and our orators say that in time of peace we must prepare for war."[11] At this time Nellie McClung seemed to be close to pacifism, but she diverged from her true pacifist friends because, while still abhorring war, she came to accept the present conflict as a battle between good and evil. She became convinced of Germany's guilt, and believed that this was indeed a war fought to uphold democracy. Historian Thomas P. Socknat has pointed out that "while the pre-war peace movement more or less disintegrated with the shock of war, the immediate reaction of most peace advocates was temperate. On the whole they agreed with the majority of their fellow Canadians that the war was unfortunate but necessary to rid the world of European militarism, and they supported the British cause . . . [but] some pacifists attempted to maintain a moderately realistic position by combining support for the war with a continuing struggle against militarism and its brutalization of society."[12] McClung was one of these.

Nellie's change of attitude was due partly to the propaganda stories of atrocities committed by the Germans in Belgium. She, like most Canadians, accepted as factual the grossly exaggerated accounts reported by the British. She wrote frequently of these horrors. "We know that in the invasion of Belgium, the German soldiers made a shield of Belgian women and children in front of their army; no child was too young, no woman too old, to escape their cruelty; no mother's prayers, no child's appeal could stay their fury!" She struggled to understand how such a situation could come about, and with an almost total lack of knowledge of the causes, concluded it was the result of too much masculinity in the world. If there had been women of influence in the Reichstag, she naively suggested, they would have blocked the Kaiser's war plans[13]—a statement that provoked many amused or incensed criticisms from the reviewers of *In Times Like*

These.[14] The sinking of the *Lusitania,* another tragedy fully exploited for propaganda purposes, was also instrumental in driving Nellie to the conclusion that while war was evil, this particular war must be fought with an all-out effort or the world would be destroyed spiritually if not physically. This reasoning made it possible for her to accept Jack's enlistment and his departure for overseas—not without great sorrow but sustained by the belief that he was fighting for a just cause and against evil.

> When I saw the first troops going away, I wondered how their mothers let them go, and I made up my mind that I would not let my boy go . . . It was the Lusitania that brought me to see the whole truth. Then I saw that we were waging war on the very Prince of Darkness, and I knew that morning when I read the papers, I knew that it would be better—a thousand times better—to be dead than to live under the rule of people whose hearts are so utterly black and whose process of reasoning is so oxlike—they are so stupidly brutal. I knew that no man could die better than in defending civilization from this ghastly thing which threatened her![15]

Vernon Thomas was sorry to see Nellie move so far from the pacifist position, but as a friend he could understand. After seeing her in New York, in 1917, where he and his wife had sought asylum from jingoistic Winnipeg, he wrote to Woodsworth: "I believe that she is a good woman, earnestly anxious to do good. She has her eldest boy at the front in the trenches, a mere boy, and so there you are. It is difficult for her to think it is all wrong. Yet in her heart she hates war and well knows that it is wrong." The context of the letter suggests that Woodsworth had expressed disappointment at Nellie McClung's support for the war effort. A letter from Nellie to Lillian (Beynon) Thomas written just a few months prior to this shows McClung attempting to heal a similar breach in friendship over the war issue.[16]

Jack's departure for overseas on a cold winter morning, 4 December 1915, is poignantly described in *The Next of Kin.* The early morning departure time only added to the gloom. "The morning is a dismal time anyway, and teeth will chatter, no matter how brave you feel! It is a squeamish, sickly, choky time—a winter morning before the sun is up." The whole family accompanied Jack to the station. Nellie and the mothers of his friends who were also leaving had vowed that there would be no tears so there was a false gaiety about the occasion with smiles and laughter concealing sorrow. The situation was eased by the large number of young people who came to see the boys off—caught up in the romance and glamour of the occasion. The true feelings came through when Jack came to say goodbye to his father and could only say, "Oh Dad! Good old dad!" What he said to his mother she does not record. When the train had pulled out they walked home through the quiet streets and Nellie noted the crystal frost on trees, poles, and wires. "It seemed like a beautiful white decoration for the occasion, a beautiful, heavy, elaborate mourning—for those who had gone—and white, of course—all white—because they were so young!" The tears came when she tidied up his room, tears for her son and for all the youths who were being deprived of their boyhood. Pondering on the curse of war she wrote:

> The saddest places of all the world to-day are not the battle fields, or the hospitals, or the cross-marked hillsides where the brave ones are buried; the saddest places are the deserted campus and playgrounds where they should be playing; the empty seats in colleges, where they should be sitting; the spaces in the ranks of happy, boisterous schoolboys, from which the brave boys have gone—these boys whose boyhood has been cut so pitifully short.[17]

In her diary she expressed a more personal sense of loss.

> When we came home I felt strangely tired and old though I am only forty-two. But I know that my youth has departed from me. It has gone with Jack, our beloved, our first born, the pride of our hearts. Strange fate surely for a boy who never has had a gun in his hands, whose ways are gentle, and full of peace; who loves his fellow men, pities their sorrows, and would gladly help them to solve their problems. What have I done to you, in letting you go into this inferno of war? And how could I hold you back without breaking your heart?[18]

From this time on her thoughts of the war began with her son in the trenches. If he were just gun fodder for the munition makers then the sorrow would be too great to bear. She had to believe that the cause was just and that good would come from evil.

The most obvious and positive benefit of war, in Nellie's mind, was the success of the prohibition movement. The war provided the prohibitionists with an additional, highly persuasive argument—patriotism. For the sake of the war effort liquor sales must cease. The liquor traffic, the prohibitionists argued, hindered the war effort because grain needed for food was used to make spirits; men, whose best skills and strength were needed in industry and in the army, were weakened physically and mentally by indulgence in alcohol; money, needed for war purposes, was spent in bars. The soldiers were fighting this war in order to create a better world, they said, and postwar Canada would be better only if the liquor trade had been eliminated. The antiprohibitionist argument that prohibition was a restriction on personal liberty was hard to maintain in the face of all the wartime restrictions. Considering that soldiers were sacrificing their lives for their country, the prohibitionists argued, surely the civilians could give up an indulgence that harmed both their country and themselves. Nellie McClung liked to point out that the Kaiser was a perfect example of a man who believed in personal liberty for himself. Prohibition was presented, then, as an integral part of the war: to vote against prohibition was to vote for the Kaiser, for Germany. Under wartime conditions this appeal was hard to resist without finding yourself labelled a traitor. The opposition argument used before the war—that ending the liquor trade would put men out of work—was also ineffective after 1915 when there was a need for manpower in the army, in industry, and in the fields.

The war actually stimulated the reform movement, in the West especially, by producing a "transformation in public attitudes to reformism, changing them to the point that 'men who scoffed a few years ago are the foremost now to demand reform.'" People were more ready to accept government intervention and saw it as a necessary part of the war effort. Reform goals such as prohibition and changes in taxation, previously objected to as "an unacceptable degree of state intervention in the lives of its citizens," were now viewed by many as worthwhile causes in the effort to win the war and redeem Canadian society. The climate had changed.[19]

In the summer of 1915 the Alberta government presented a prohibition bill to the people for a direct vote. Nellie, of course, enthusiastically participated in the campaign to persuade Albertans to vote for the bill. For six weeks she toured the province. Seventy-five thousand copies of the act were distributed. The campaign ended with a giant parade of fifteen thousand Alberta citizens through downtown Edmonton. Later, recalling that impressive sight, Nellie observed that farmers walked with lawyers and doctors, college girls and others.

I am proud that no politician stood between the people and the right to decide. I couldn't help thinking when I marched down Jasper avenue of all the talk we heard last summer in the campaign about the referendum being unconstitutional and un-British and unfair, and about it trampling on the rights of the people. They told us the referendum was the rule of the rabble. Thank God I belong to the rabble.

Some women, she recalled, were timid about demonstrating in this manner. It was all right to ride in a car, they argued, but marching in a public street was undignified. At this point an old lady with crutches drove up to the parade site and Nellie, assuming that the woman planned to drive the parade route, asked if she would take others with her. The old woman said that anyone was welcome to ride in her car, but she was going to walk. "Do you know what a tree looks like that's been winter-killed?" Nellie asked her audience, looking back on this incident:

> . . . a little tree that's tried to leaf, and been frostbitten, and tried again and been frostbitten. By and by it gives up. This woman's face was like that. She had suffered so long and so intolerably that now she was winter-killed.
>
> She came to us on crutches and she asked if she might march. It was three miles, mind you, and she was old. But she did it. And every time her crutch came down on the pavement and every time she took a step she whispered, "Dry-dry-dry!" Do you wonder that the women who lacked courage before got down from their autos and went with her?[20]

On 21 July 1915, the vote was held; the support for prohibition was decisive. Only thirteen of fifty-five ridings voted "wet" and in the popular vote the "drys" outnumbered the "wets" 58,295 to 37,509.[21] Editorials praised Nellie McClung's efforts in the fight: "The most untiring devotion, the greatest energy, the highest talent and the most abounding enthusiasm made her an inspiration wherever she appeared."[22] The Manitoba referendum was held the next year with similar results. Again Nellie returned to Manitoba to contribute to the cause. Unable to get to Winnipeg until a few days before the referendum, she spoke as often as she could, ending with the tremendous effort of six speeches on Sunday, the day before the vote. According to one women's editor, she spoke to twelve thousand people and still there were some who went away disappointed that they did not get into her meetings.[23]

The first province to introduce prohibition (not including Prince Edward Island, where prohibition was enacted as early as 1901) was Saskatchewan in December 1916, and the other provinces soon followed, with the exception of Québec, which prohibited retail sale of liquor for a brief period in 1919. The federal Unionist government, elected in December 1917, imposed total prohibition of the manufacture, importation, and transportation of any beverage containing more than 2.5 percent alcohol for the duration of the war. The prohibitionists were at last successful—for the time being. Nellie believed that once tried there would be no turning back from the experiment and that the good resulting from this change in society would balance the evils of the war. After four years of prohibition she was able to record that crime in Alberta was reduced, the prison farm had been sold, jails were being emptied, bank savings had increased, and business had benefited from the increase in food and clothing sales. She must have thought the millennium was near.[24]

In apparent contradiction of her earlier statement that war "twisted the whole moral fabric of a nation" and "hardened us to human grief and misery," Nellie now believed that war could force people to realize they had been worshipping the wrong gods. The shock of the casualty lists, she argued, made people "recast their table of values." They realized that "it is not wealth or cleverness or skill or power which makes a nation or an individual great. It is goodness, gentleness, kindliness, the sense of brotherhood, which alone maketh rich and addeth no sorrow." Canadians had, Nellie believed, become more aware of the sufferings of others and less self-centred, and were now prepared to make Canada, after the war, "The land of the Fair Deal."[25]

The war also aided the cause of female suffrage, although in western Canada it would probably have come very shortly in any case. The Norris government in Manitoba acted promptly after receiving a petition on 23 December 1915, and on 27 January 1916, the bill enfranchising the women of Manitoba and enabling them to be elected to the legislature received third reading. The galleries were crowded—chiefly with women; many carried the suffrage colours, purple and yellow, others held banners. There was an atmosphere of great excitement. The executive members of the Political Equality League of Manitoba were given seats on the floor of the house. The bill was read by Mr. Johnston, a long-time suffragist, an Icelander, and son of one of Manitoba's early suffragists. There were a number of speakers eager to express their approval of the measure and then the question was put.

> A deep silence, a solemn silence, fell on the whole assembly as the speaker put the question. A deep chorus of assent rang through the Chambers, and not a sound of dissent . . .
>
> The bill was passed, the women were people, persons, voters. It seemed too good to be true. From the gallery rose a clear, sweet voice, singing "Oh Canada" and soon it was joined by a great chorus of voices all filled with emotion. Quickly following that came "For they are jolly good fellows."[26]

Few people knew that it was only due to last-minute pressure from Francis Beynon and Lillian Thomas that the legislation contained the clause permitting women to sit in the legislature.[27]

Suffrage societies across the country celebrated this first victory. Others followed quickly. Alberta's turn came in April. On the day that women got the vote in that province, Alice Jamieson (Canada's first woman magistrate) linked arms with a jubilant Emily Murphy and Nellie McClung as they walked down Jasper Avenue seeking some way to celebrate the occasion. As they could not drop into a bar for a drink, they bought new hats and had their photo taken. Saskatchewan women had won the right to vote on 14 March; British Columbia and Ontario the next year. Now that they had the provincial vote, western Canadian suffragists turned their attention to the federal vote as well as continuing to agitate for women's suffrage in the remaining provinces. When the issue was raised in the House of Commons during the 1916 session it was clear that there was still opposition to women's suffrage, particularly from the Maritimes and Québec. However, during a speech in London, Ontario, opposition leader Sir Wilfrid Laurier stated he had been won over to the women's cause. Prime Minister Borden was slower to capitulate. When he visited Winnipeg in 1916, Nellie McClung brought the matter to his attention. "We feel that we should have the franchise given to us without any further agitation, for we are too busy to fight for it, and we will greatly begrudge the time if we have to do so." Borden's noncommittal reply was that "certainly, the women of Canada have earned the right to consideration."

The matter was raised twice during the 1917 session, and by now most members supported it in principle. The main obstacle now was the method of determining the federal franchise. Liberals wished to retain provincial control of the voters' lists with the result that the federal vote would go only to women who had received it provincially. The Conservatives tended to think that the federal franchise should be separate. Much to the women's surprise, Borden, on his return from England in 1917, declared himself in favour of female franchise not because of their war service but because they had made clear "their right to a voice in the government of the country in which they live." But he seemed in no hurry to introduce the necessary legislation.[28]

With the probability of a wartime election, concerns arose over the large numbers of naturalized Canadians from enemy countries whose votes might be opposed to the war effort. The "alien" or "foreign" voters, as they were misnamed, were expected to vote Liberal—against conscription—and so demands arose for their disfranchisement. Although Nellie McClung believed that conscription was necessary, she did not think the answer lay in taking votes away from naturalized Canadians. In 1916, however, she spoke to Borden urging that British and Canadian-born women be enfranchised to provide a more balanced electorate. This proposal was not well received by most suffrage workers. Francis Beynon condemned the idea in her column in the *Grain Growers' Guide* and Nellie quickly withdrew her proposal, although she defended her reasons for making it in a letter to the same publication. She emphasized that she viewed this limited enfranchisement of women as a war measure only; she was not committed to it and certainly did not wish to divide the suffrage forces in any way "for the cause we stand for has in it the whole well being of humanity and as such cannot be jeopardized by a difference of opinion over the method of procedure. Because I place woman suffrage above all personal consideration and because I know that any one person's judgement is quite liable to be faulty I will withdraw the suggestion of a partial franchise." Beynon expressed her pleasure in receiving the letter and knowing that she and Nellie McClung could still work together. She was sure that Nellie had not given sufficient thought to the difficulty foreign women would have in getting the vote if all Canadian women were not enfranchised at the same time.[29]

The Conservative government of Prime Minister Borden, bedeviled by scandal, financial and political problems with the railways, and opposition to its conscription measure was anxious to achieve a coalition with the Liberals. Borden had decided to introduce conscription to support the Canadian war effort but did not want to see his government defeated over the issue in a federal election. He therefore proposed a nonpartisan Union government of Conservatives and Liberals whose primary purpose was the prosecution of the war effort. Wilfrid Laurier, the Liberal opposition leader, was invited to join the coalition but declined the offer, fearing the consequences in Québec, especially over conscription. The idea of a nonpartisan government appealed, however, to western Canadians and consequently many western Liberals bolted ranks and agreed to run as Union candidates. To ensure either a Conservative or a Unionist victory, the government introduced two measures guaranteed to provide votes for the government. Both affected the position of women. By the *Military Voters' Act* all army personnel overseas were enfranchised. This gave the vote to youths under twenty-one and to the nurses, the only women in the services at this time. The more controversial measure was the *Wartime Elections Act*, which disfranchised conscientious objectors and all those born in enemy countries and naturalized since 1902, and enfranchised all women who were British subjects and had close relatives overseas. It was a partisan move on the part of the Conservatives, as those being disfranchised had traditionally supported the Liberals. Some of the suffragists approved because it would help ensure the return of the government. The stories of men in the trenches who could not have leave, and the wounded men sent back without a proper convalescence because of lack of reinforcements, guaranteed that most women with men overseas would vote for the party that promised those reinforcements. Nellie McClung certainly desired the return of a government pledged to an all-out war effort, but she did not approve of the *Wartime Elections Act*. She wrote to the Calgary Next of Kin Association to congratulate them on their resolution asking for the vote for all women.

> I heartily agree with this, and hope that a similar expression of opinion will come from all the Next of Kin Associations. It is a matter for deep regret that any act should be passed which will make a cleavage in the ranks of our women citizens who are today bearing their full share of the burdens of life whether they happen to have relatives at the front or not. I hold firm to the belief that I would have been quite as good a citizen if my eldest child had been a girl, and

quite as much interested in my country's welfare, but that fact would have put me outside the pale.[30]

Nellie did not approve, either, of the disfranchisement of natural-ized citizens. During the 1917 Alberta election when this idea was being proposed she had expressed her disapproval of any such measure, arguing that these people had been invited to settle in Canada and when they were naturalized had been accepted as full citizens. While travelling in northern Alberta for the Red Cross after the *Wartime Elections Act* was passed, she wrote of a meeting in Edward "at which men spoke rather sadly and bitterly of their cancelled franchise." These Austrian-Canadians were the real Cana-dians, in Nellie's opinion, "by choice and not birth," and their wholehearted support of the Red Cross work proved their loyalty. By disfranchisement, the government had foolishly and unjustly "made them men without a country."[31] She sought, also, to explain the Ukrainian objection to compulsory military service in an article, "The Ukrainians in Canada." "For long bitter years they have had to submit to its exaction, and have had to fight for a country for which they had no love. For them conscription is another name for tyranny." Austria, she pointed out, had treated them better than Russia had so it was not surprising that they hesitated to enlist to fight with Russia against Austria. She deplored the fact that some people called Ukrainians cowards. "When people have watered their liberty 'with blood for rain' for centuries, they are not likely to be wanting in courage . . . " Yet "we have that type of mind in Canada," she complained, "who are convinced that the proper way to deal with our 'alien born' citizens now is to disfranchise them. History does not mean anything to people like that."[32]

Shortly after the passing of these acts a Unionist government was formed and an election called for December 1917—an election that turned out to be the bitterest ever fought in Canada. To be a Liberal was to be disloyal. Those who failed to support the government were traitors. At the time of this election Nellie McClung was in the United States on a lecture tour in support of American women's suffrage so she took no part in the campaign, nor was she home in time to vote in the first federal election for which she was eligible. Despite her disapproval of much that the Conservatives had done and had not done she undoubtedly would have voted Unionist. She admired Laurier but she feared that his strong Québec support would weaken

Canada's war effort. Besides, the formation of a Unionist government in 1917 meant more to reformers like Nellie McClung than just an all-out war effort. They saw it as the culmination of the reform efforts: the promise of an end to "petty politics, materialism and corruption."[33] Nellie described it as "an indication of better things. It is a confession, too, of the failure of the party system, which will no doubt die hard, and the wriggling of its tail will be seen in the sulphuric utterances of the party press for many a day. But its hour has come and it might better depart gracefully."[34] Nellie McClung, then, saw the war as bringing about not only prohibition and women's suffrage but also an end to party strife. Looking back this seems naive and ridiculously unrealistic but Nellie was by no means alone. There can be little doubt that the majority of the five hundred thousand women voting in a federal election for the first time in December 1917 cast their votes in favour of the Unionists, even though many of the women disapproved of the limited nature of the women's franchise. They were sure that by the next election all women would be entitled to vote.

Throughout the fight for prohibition and suffrage Nellie's speaking engagements took her beyond the Prairie Provinces. In 1915, after the Alberta prohibition referendum and the Manitoba election, she went to Vancouver to deliver a series of lectures. As always, the crowds were considerable, the largest was a gathering of four thousand in the Georgia St. Arena. In the autumn of 1915 McClung accepted an invitation to tour Ontario. Although she had given a reading tour there in 1910 this was her first venture into Ontario as a lecturer. The talks she gave—which had been given on earlier occasions—were soon to be published in *In Times Like These*, although she seldom adhered strictly to the text. According to almost every reporter, it was her flashing eyes, her smile, and her attractive voice that immediately caught the attention of anyone meeting her for the first time. "Her eyes glow and her conversation sparkles with enthusiasm for [her message]," wrote one interviewer.[35] Jean Graham of *Saturday Night* told her readers that even if they were, like herself, opposed to women's suffrage they would like Nellie McClung "who is the sunniest-natured Westerner who ever kept an audience amused and interested."[36] To Ontarians, in fact, she was the embodiment of the West. "Nellie is some Chinook," said one reporter.[37] And another somewhat patronizing account of her Massey Hall speech said that her voice "has not a trace left in it of the East. Her vernacular is also Western," and "she has the almost childlike straightforwardness of the prairies."[38] One cannot help but notice that McClung was often praised more for her style than the content of her speeches. This would never have disturbed her. She knew that her chief method of communication was logic wrapped in humour, for she felt that this more readily gained audience attention and ensured that her points remained with her audience long after she had left the stage. A typical McClung strategy was to reduce her opponents' arguments to the absurd: a stylistically effective, and very memorable, technique.

As usual her meetings were enthusiastically attended although one observer suggested that she was speaking only to the converted.[39] On 14 October, at her first lecture sponsored by the Ontario Equal Franchise League, she spoke to a large gathering delivering what one paper called "one of the most brilliant speeches ever delivered within the walls of Massey Hall."[40] Perhaps it was the success of that speech that brought the crowds out to Timothy Eaton Memorial Church a few days later. "Scores of people, recognizing the futility of getting within hearing distance, reluctantly gave up the effort and returned homeward, while others more aggressive remained in the vestibule and pushed their way forward among the dense mass as best they could. The passages were all chocked, eager listeners leant over the railings of the stairways."[41] In Ottawa, the Russell Theatre was filled to overflowing and the doors closed. The police were called out to move the crowd away.[42] In Toronto she spoke to the Canadian Women's Press Club, urging women journalists to make women's pages something more than recipes and social tidbits. Speaking to this group of Toronto's middle-class society matrons Nellie cautioned them against trying to "appeal to our best women," a term she had heard used in connection with suffrage goals. "God only knows," she said, "who are our best women. I don't." They must try to appeal to every woman. On this and several other occasions during her trip she urged Ontario to catch up with the West.[43]

In the spring of 1916 Nellie McClung accepted an invitation to speak at the Mississippi Valley Suffrage Conference in Minneapolis. Here she met, probably for the first time, some of the leading American suffragists. She shared the platform with Mrs. Carrie Chapman Catt, president of the National American Woman Suffrage Association (NAWSA); Clara Ueland of Minnesota, as well as the presidents from many of the state associations; Dr. Effie McCullom Jones of Iowa, and other leading American suffragists. Her contact with American suffragists here probably led to the publication of a McClung article in *The Suffragist* (9 September 1916), at that time the "Weekly Organ of the Congressional Union for Woman Suffrage." By October they solicited a second article from her.[44] There were representatives from twenty-one states at the Minneapolis conference. It was a well-attended and highly successful convention at which Nellie McClung "made a real hit, delivering her remarks with a 'punch' that struck home to the audience." Her chief speech was at a mass banquet. The next day the *Minneapolis Journal* reported:

> Somebody seemed not to have opened the door but to have taken the side off the house and a west Canadian breeze blew in . . . Everyone knew instinctively that here was a suffrage advocate of a type different from any ever seen here before and soon the audience had waked [*sic*] up and if it had been Harry Lauder on the stage instead of the Canadian woman with her Scotch-Irish burr there could not have been more enthusiasm. Humorously and in direct appeal to the men Mrs. McClung told of the campaign in Canada that finally brought victory.[45]

Thomas Johnson, the Manitoba legislator who had introduced the suffrage bill, was in the audience and wrote home to Percy Anderson: "Mrs. McClung was there 'up against' the leading women of the U.S. and I tell you honestly there were only one or two in her class. Everybody was raving about her. She is certainly doing Canada *some* good. I don't know of any better advertising that Canada could get than she is giving us."[46]

Before the convention was over tentative arrangements were made for Nellie McClung to carry out a speaking tour in the fall of 1916, sponsored and arranged by the NAWSA. Organizers considered this a very critical period, and it seems Nellie McClung was generally hailed as someone who could put life into the campaign. The NAWSA offered her two hundred dollars per week for four weeks, and expenses. When Nellie suggested that she would like to tour for two months Catt said that she would do her best to place her.[47] In the end, the tour lasted for more than two months, and there were few days without at least one speech.

Nellie began her tour by speaking at a luncheon in New York City on 3 November, where she was Catt's guest. From there she went to

Buffalo for an evening meeting and over to Toronto for a speech at Deer Park Presbyterian Church. From 8–10 November she was in Wisconsin speaking at Racine, Milwaukee, and Superior. Next came Indiana with talks in Elkhart and Muncie, followed by Louisville, Kentucky; Nashville, Tennessee; Birmingham, Alabama; and New Orleans, all in six days! That was followed by a week in Texas where she joined a group who were touring by automobile. She spoke in Galveston, Houston, Waxahachie, Fort Worth, and Dallas. After visits to Springfield and Kansas City, Missouri, and one stop in Nebraska she may have taken several days off over the Thanksgiving holiday before heading home with stops, along the way, in Minneapolis, Grand Forks, Bismarck, and Fargo. Although her typed schedule from headquarters does not mention West Virginia and Maryland, she also visited these states, perhaps before her New York engagement. The West Virginia report for 1916 reads: "A flying squadron of West Virginia men and women speakers was sent in groups to thirty points . . . and Mrs. Nellie McClung of Canada joined the squadron and spoke at several points."[48]

Nellie's American tour must have been a gruelling trip but one which she thoroughly enjoyed, although strangely she does not mention it in her autobiography. Her daughter Florence, age seventeen, travelled with her, and everywhere they went mother and daughter made new friends. The presence of an attractive daughter and the photograph Nellie carried of her whole family did much to increase her appeal to those who feared "unfeminine" suffragists. According to one reporter: "The audience knew that it was not hearing some hair-brained enthusiast but a real woman who had done and was doing a real woman's part in life impelled by a desire to serve her nation, her people, and even extend her influence for good into other spheres."[49] In most centres Nellie and Florence were billeted in private homes, and correspondence over the next few years shows that after even one night in a home Nellie McClung had made a warm friend of the hostess and her family. She later sent them Christmas cards, photos, or even in some cases a copy of her next book when it came out. American suffragists, in fact, were very interested in both *In Times Like These* and *The Next of Kin*. They enthusiastically passed copies around from friend to friend, the National Association publicized her most recent book in their newsletter, and some state groups sold her books at their meetings. On at least one occasion, Nellie turned over her royalties on books sold at a Boston suffrage meeting to that municipal organization. Later, during her 1917 tour for NAWSA, she evidently permitted both the Texas and Iowa Equal Suffrage associations to print her satiric feminist poem "Jane Brown" in pamphlet form and keep the net proceeds for their cause.[50]

Everywhere Nellie McClung appeared she was enthusiastically received. The newspaper reports all stress that she was different. In Corsicana, Texas, "'it was so different,' was heard a hundred times after Mrs. Nellie McClung of Canada had finished her address on suffrage at the Carnegie library. It was acknowledged that the speaker was by far the ablest woman who has ever spoken here on the subject of equal suffrage."[51] At the Wisconsin Women's Suffrage convention her talk was "one of the most rousing speeches of the entire convention."[52] As in Canada the audiences roared with laughter but often "tears were not far behind."[53] The speeches seem to have been variations on those she had already used in Canada, and frequently she threw in a plea for prohibition although these two issues were not so closely tied together in the United States as they were in Canada. Nellie McClung could make an audience laugh at a simple funny story or cry at a sad one. It was this gift, her ability to carry an audience with her, that made her "different," for the arguments she used varied little from those the American suffragists were using.[54]

McClung had hardly arrived home in November 1916 when she began to get urgent invitations to return to the United States. Pennsylvania wanted her for two weeks or more in January or March.[55] Minnesota pressed her to come to a gathering of suffrage workers in Duluth because "the women in the northern part of the state are very much in need of rousing and we feel that you are just the person to do it." When Nellie turned down this request they invited her to their convention in the fall.[56] Massachusetts was in the midst of a Constitutional Convention and the state suffrage association asked Nellie to come to speak to the Suffrage Committee of that body.[57] The executive of NAWSA was also well pleased with Nellie's 1916 tour and the secretary, Nettie R. Shuler, reported that "Mrs. Catt and I are crazy to bring you on here again."[58] They invited her to speak at their December 1917 convention and suggested that another tour be planned around that date. McClung spent about a month in the U.S. starting at the suffrage conventions in Wisconsin (14–15 November) and Minnesota (16–17 November), but the rest of the tour is not clear as many of the engagements were arranged while she was en route.

No doubt the National Convention of American suffragists in Washington, from 12-16 December, was the highlight of this tour, for Nellie would have met again many of the women with whom she had made friends during her two tours. There was also a spirit of exuberant celebration at the convention because of the great victory that had just been won in New York: an amendment to the state constitution giving full suffrage to women. There was, of course, a more sombre note too because of the war. Perhaps for this reason Nellie's two addresses reflected the two themes of the conference: women's suffrage, and women and the war effort. At a Sunday afternoon mass meeting she described how suffrage came to Canada and on the final evening, on a platform with representatives from England and France, she explained what war had meant to the women of Canada. The NAWSA newspaper said of the latter speech: "She kept her hearers wavering between laughter and tears as she hid her own emotion behind a veil of stoicism and humour."[59] The executive of the NAWSA were so pleased with her contribution that they gave her a cheque for $100.00, despite their earlier stated policy that there could be no remuneration.[60] There is no doubt that at this time Nellie was the best-known Canadian suffragist in the United States, as was probably the case in Canada. This was Nellie McClung's last American tour, although she received urgent requests to return in 1918. She did, however, return to Wisconsin in 1919 to speak at their annual local state convention of suffragists.

During the spring of 1918 Nellie was deluged with invitations to speak at church anniversaries, WCTU meetings, Red Cross meetings, and a variety of conventions, from Ontario to British Columbia. Her publisher, Thomas Allen, proposed an Ontario tour with an offer of one thousand dollars for ten lectures. Invitations also came from farther afield: from New Zealand to take part in prohibition campaigns, and from Scotland for an educational campaign prior "to the first Poll under the Temperance Act."[61] She does not seem to have considered these offers from afar and of those closer to home she accepted very few for at this time she was busy working on a book with a young man who had been a prisoner of war. One day he had simply appeared at her door in Edmonton to ask her to write his story for him. At first she said no but "then he mentioned that he was a returned soldier and had been for sixteen months a prisoner in Germany and had made his escape—That changed everything."[62] Private Simmons moved in with the McClungs and Nellie devoted as much time as she possibly could to listening, guiding, and writing.[63] The book, *Three Times and Out*, was published in November 1918, unfortunately just at the end of the conflict when people did not want to hear any more about war.

Despite the outstanding war effort of the women of Canada, many of them felt they could contribute even more effectively. Nellie believed that many women who were just sitting around knitting could be doing much more vital work. During the latter part of the war she became concerned about the effect the war was having on the education of Canadian children, particularly in Saskatchewan and Alberta. In Alberta, in 1918, there were nine hundred teaching vacancies—most of them in one-room rural schools. Nellie raised this issue on every possible occasion, urging women to fill these vacancies as their contribution to the war effort. She made two recruiting trips to British Columbia during 1918 because this province had a teacher surplus. In her speeches she attempted to make her audiences realize that this was a national issue. Illiteracy, she argued, would be detrimental to the whole country not just to the province in which it occurred. The problem seemed to her especially serious because in many cases it was the communities of the most recent immigrants who were without teachers.[64] Speaking in Alberta she advocated higher salaries as one means of filling these vacancies since, although the minimum had been raised to $840.00 per year,[65] some school boards were still advertising a salary lower than this. Women were also needed in the farm kitchens. Therefore it was suggested that city women, many of them with farm backgrounds, could go out to help during harvest so that the daughters of farmers, familiar with the new farm machinery, could help out on the land. There were, of course, women working in jobs that only men had held before the war, but it seemed probable that more use could be made of woman power in this war if the women and the jobs could be brought together through some coordinating agency. In response, a Canadian Women's War League was proposed, and the idea advertised widely, but nothing seems to have materialized.[66] Subsequently, Nellie McClung and Emily Murphy proposed to Prime Minister Borden the mobilizing of Alberta women through a "plan of registration, conducted by some

The War Years: 1914-1919

provincial organization of women" to meet that province's farm and teacher needs. Borden replied that the federal "scheme of registration which the Government is considering is very comprehensive, and I should think that it would fulfil the purpose which you mention."[67] Both parties were anxious to avoid duplicating each other's efforts, so Borden passed the McClung–Murphy letter on to Newton Rowell, vice-chairman of the War Committee, for consideration. All of these efforts seemed haphazard and uncoordinated, so Borden's plan to hold a Women's War Conference was welcomed.

Nellie McClung received an invitation to attend the conference of women to be held in Ottawa, 28 February–3 March.[68] The delegates were all chosen by the federal government.[69] First they selected a representative from each national women's association, and rather surprisingly, because neither was a truly national organization, the National Equal Franchise League and the Canadian Suffrage Association. The Hon. N.W. Rowell, organizer and initial chairman of the conference, explained that in addition the government "sought to secure, as far as was practicable, women who have particular knowledge of women's work in their own provinces, in connection with agriculture, industry and the many varied forms of women's particular work." There did not appear to be any representatives of women working in factories, but there was an attempt to have a fair distribution from across Canada. Nellie McClung and her fellow western delegates travelled by train to Ottawa in late February. They were, for the most part, women well known to one another. Altogether there were nineteen delegates from west of Ontario. These western delegates did not waste their time on the train but discussed the issues they expected would arise and prepared resolutions.[70]

Judging from the brief published report of the three-day conference, the federal government seems to have carefully orchestrated the affair. Nellie McClung, a member of the coordinating committee, reported later that this committee "had their duties assigned for them; we had typewritten sheets put in our hands telling us what each of our duties were on each committee."[71] On the second day the different sections—National Health and Child Welfare, Agriculture and Production, National Registration and Industrial Activity, and Thrift and Economy—met to draw up resolutions. These were presented to and discussed by the whole conference that evening and on Saturday the cabinet members were again present to hear the final

161

resolutions and make comments on them. The report is by no means a complete transcript of the conference, but it does reveal that Nellie McClung spoke up for equality for women entering the work force and made a plea for teachers for rural areas. Her main concern was a resolution urging that all grain going to England should be milled in Canada to insure that it not be used for liquor. The western women had drawn up this resolution on the train and were eager to put it before the conference. After very little discussion—because it was introduced of necessity very near the end of the conference—the measure passed 34–12 with many members abstaining.

On the whole, resolutions that passed were very general and meaningless. They called for greater cooperation among women's organizations. They pledged themselves to help persuade the nation to give up luxuries, although they found it difficult to define "luxury," which, according to the discussion, could include everything from hats to fashionable weddings. The section on Thrift and Economy introduced the astonishing proposal that municipalities should be "enabled to order the inspection of garbage cans and to inflict fines for any waste discovered." The report does not indicate whether or not this proposed intrusion into the garbage pails of the nation aroused controversy. In fact, most of the discussion on the report of this committee centred on whether or not daylight saving was a real thrift measure. The conference declared its wholehearted support for the full-scale registration of citizens planned by the government and gave assurance that women's organizations would provide volunteers to look after the registration centres.

Although Nellie did not play a particularly prominent part in the conference, as far as one can judge from the printed report, at least one newspaper suggested she was more of a force than the official report conveys. The reporter for *The Toronto Star* described her as "the outstanding person among the many prominent women assembled from coast to coast . . . Her ability, her influence, and her charm is [*sic*] felt at every gathering." Such a description would not likely endear the reporter to the other "prominent women," although the same report suggests that Nellie McClung received a particularly warm welcome from those leading Canadian women who were present. "On her arrival, although she had but stepped from the train to the lunch room affair, after a trip across the continent, and was travel weary, yet [she was] not too tired to respond to the enthusiastic greeting of the assembly, by a short inspiring address in which she warned against the soporific effect of knitting—it makes a woman think she is doing something."[72]

Certainly McClung's grain resolution seems to have received more publicity than the others, but in this case not favourable. Critics ridiculed the idea of Canadian mills trying to handle all the wheat now shipped to England. The newspapers said that "the precious wheat would moulder in granaries in Canada while the poor war-worn women and children in Europe would perish for lack of bread." Newspapers that carried liquor advertisements yet expressed sympathy for women and children reminded Nellie of the boy who murdered his mother and father and then appealed to the court to have mercy on him because he was a poor orphan. The resolution, she pointed out, referred only to grains that would be used for beer because whiskey was no longer being manufactured in Britain. Wheat could not be used for beer so only barley and rye would be affected.[73]

The conference accomplished very little and most of the resolutions were never implemented, but it does indicate an attempt on the government's part to pay some attention to the new segment of voters. It seems the conference aimed to inspire women to greater war efforts without actually making any change in the nature of those efforts. They did not intend, as Nellie McClung and Emily Murphy and probably some of the other women wished, to mobilize women and direct them into more useful and less traditional fields. Cora Hind resented Senator Robertson's assertion that women could not replace many factory workers because the men were "skilled." Hind reflected that most of these skilled men had been farm workers a few months before, that women could be trained just as easily, but that the unions would not allow it to happen.[74] Nellie McClung was incensed at one speaker's frivolous remark suggesting that the women were merely eager for a holiday in Ottawa. She retorted: "It is not a very easy thing for busy women to give up their work and take a long, tiresome journey to Ottawa. I do not know that we regarded it so much as a privilege . . . as a duty, and I believe the women who answered that invitation went with an honest desire to do anything they could, and did not regard it as a pleasure excursion at all."[75] Perhaps the women of 1918 were not as sensitive to the patronizing tone that today's reader finds in almost every one of the ministers' speeches. Yet surely Nellie McClung and others must have snorted in disgust at the Honourable F.B. Carvell's belittling remark that "we all have some experience of the organizing ability of women within the last few months, and *it is a great surprise to most of us*." Evidently he felt he was reassuring a group of anxious women when he went on to inform them that the government did not intend to put women to work in the fields. He seemed ignorant of the fact that the Women's Conference had advocated that measure, at some length. In fact, Carvell appeared unable to conceive of significant, nontraditional jobs for women. Most of the other speakers in their efforts to make the women realize that the government appreciated them resorted to what Nellie had, on other occasions, called "soft soap" and "dope."

Neither Nellie McClung nor Cora Hind actually criticized the Women's War Conference, but their reports of it are decidedly lukewarm. For them, its major contribution was in bringing together a network of women from all across the country. The conference, however, had failed to make any progress toward a more effective use of woman power in the war effort. The government, on the other hand, probably saw it as a success: the women had passed the resolutions the government wanted passed and had assured the War Committee of the support of a large number of women for the stricter controls put on food and fuel during 1918.

When the war ended in November Nellie was in bed with the flu—apparently not the virulent type that claimed so many lives that year. She wondered if the right decisions would be made to ensure that there would be a lasting peace. She was afraid that women would "settle down after the war and slip right back into our old ways—our old peaceful ways—and let men go on ruling the world, and war will come again and again." She also feared that there would be a spirit of revenge that would start the trouble all over again. There must, she believed, be an effort for peace as great as for war. "The trumpets are calling for healers and binders who will not be appalled by the task of nursing back to health a wounded world, shot to pieces by injustice, greed, cruelty, and wrong thinking."[76] The worst danger was that "we should defeat the Germans but enthrone militarism in our own hearts and therefore defeat ourselves worst of all."[77] As early as 1915 she spoke of the need to put an end to narrow patriotism, to create world citizenship. "Our neighbour will be every man of whatever race or creed or colour. There will be no trade barriers between nations to breed distrust and jealousy or suspicion between men."[78]

According to Nellie, women needed to be present at the peace conference if these ideals were to be realized. She argued that in four years a greater change had taken place in the lives of women than in the last four hundred years. "Women who for years, battled sometimes gently, sometimes stormily, for their proper place in the world, only to be repulsed, have been invited, coaxed, bribed to come in and take it." They have been told: "Come out of the kitchen. Your King and country need you." If women were needed to fight the war, Nellie asserted, there was an even greater need for them to make the peace.[79] Indeed, many individuals and women's organizations urged Borden to include women in Canada's delegation to the peace conference, but he saw no "possible advantage" in selecting representatives from societies such as the National Council of Women or the Red Cross Society for he did "not know of any work they could do if they came." He said, too, that if he wished to have women in the delegation there were plenty of Canadian women already in England whom he could select, but "I should prefer, however, not to take any action"—and he took none.[80] Despite Nellie's strictures against revenge and her call for healers and binders she advocated an unspecified punishment for the men who had raped women and children in Europe. There should be women at the peace conference because men would be thinking only of "territory and re-building cities and levying war taxes." They would give little thought to the "women of France, Belgium, Serbia and Poland who had suffered what we call, for lack of a better word, the loss of honor. That is not what we mean, but it serves." In 1918 even Nellie McClung could not use the word *rape*. She hoped that the German women would be at the peace settlement because "they should know first hand what brutish things their men have done . . . Part of the punishment that should come to the German military commanders and German soldiers should be the scorn of their own women." She concluded this article with the words, "we want women representatives at the peace conference for the proper settlement of what is past and for a guarantee of the future."[81] There is no hint as to what she believed should happen at the peace conference. Somehow the presence of women would insure a just settlement.

The war was really over for Nellie McClung, however, the day Jack returned in March 1919, physically unharmed after four long years. It was a day of great rejoicing for the family. Their returned soldier was twenty-two, matured beyond his years by his war experience. Mark followed him around in hero worship wearing his tin hat until the family declared it too heavy for a little boy. The older boys were proud but found it difficult suddenly having an older brother who thought them immature and undisciplined so they nicknamed him "the Iron Duke." Like many returned soldiers, Jack wanted to put the war behind him and would not talk of his experiences. He gave his wartime diary to his mother with instructions that he never wanted to see it again. In 1944 while writing *The Stream Runs Fast*, Nellie spoke of the shock it was to him to find life going on almost as if nothing had happened. When a man asked him in a jocular tone, "Well, young fellow, how does it feel to win a war?" he quietly replied, "I did not know that wars were ever won. Certainly not by the people who do the fighting." Inevitably he had lost many friends: one of his Edmonton friends, Freeman Kelly, was killed on Armistice Day, and after his return, another close friend died in an English hospital. Jack tried hard to adapt but Nellie writes:

> I knew there was a wound in his heart—a sore place. That hurt look in his clear blue eyes tore at my heart strings and I did not know what to do. When a boy who has never had a gun in his hands, never desired anything but the good of his fellow men, is sent out to kill other boys like himself, even at the call of his country, something snaps in him, something which may not mend . . . but all I could see then was the miracle of Jack's safe return, and to us he was a glorious being clothed in the shining raiment of one who has come back from the dead.

That fall Jack returned to university. Soon he was prominent on campus as manager of the rugby team and premier of the student court and the committee of student officers. The house once more filled with his friends. When, at times, he grew discouraged and thought he was too old for college his mother and father urged him to continue. In 1923 he graduated as class valedictorian, and won an IODE scholarship that took him to Oxford for three years to study international law and constitutional history.[82]

As for Nellie, Jack's involvement in the war had changed her from a near pacifist to one who believed that *this* war at least was a battle against the forces of evil and, perhaps, a war to end all wars, though she never became an enthusiastic patriot. The enormity of world-wide conflict had shaken her faith, if not in humanity, at least in national leaders, and her own internal struggle to understand the state of civilization at this time was immense. She was always to fight against narrow-minded patriotism and what she saw as masculine-conditioned militarism, and she held that if women were more publicly involved in world affairs at the international level, wars would not occur. Women, she felt, were more inclined toward peace, and for this reason she thought that leading women should have a prominent place at the peace conference. To her mind, the main positive decision to arise from the war was the prohibition of alcohol. She had fought for this all her life and would be bitterly disappointed when it ended. The war years were a turbulent and troubling time for Nellie McClung, both privately and publicly, and she felt these years had prematurely aged her.

7

Alberta Politics: 1917–1926

❖

Although Nellie McClung was extremely busy with war work and public speaking in the years 1916–18, she did not neglect the important issue of women's role in politics. She was afraid women might see the achievement of the vote as a goal in itself and fail to take advantage of the power that had been placed in their hands. Only a minority of women had participated in the suffrage campaign and Nellie worried that just as apathetic women had made the achievement of women's suffrage more difficult, so continued apathy might negate the victory. On the other hand, she knew there was a danger women might jump on a bandwagon and waste their newly acquired strength on an unworthy cause. If women were to be a useful force in politics their interest must be aroused and they must be organized for the purpose of political education. Nellie did not see the old Liberal and Conservative parties as suitable organizations to perform this task. As Lillian Beynon Thomas indignantly pointed out men and women who had taken no part in the struggle for women's suffrage were now eager to organize Liberal and Conservative women's leagues. She urged women to remain independent and reminded them that "it is the non-committed vote that swings the election."[1] Nellie heartily agreed with this view. A questionnaire circulated by the Saskatoon Political Equality League asked "Should women join a political party?" to which Nellie replied:

> I do not think that women should identify themselves with political parties, for the reason that they will work against instead of with each other . . . Dividing the women into two hostile camps will leave the

situation very much as we found it, with all its old bitterness, squabbling and waste of energy . . . I like to think of women forming their own opinions, uncontaminated by party hypotheses.[2]

By remaining independent in thought, she believed, women could exercise a purifying influence on the old parties, encouraging them to choose candidates wisely. Women could, for example, use their influence to bring an end to the patronage system, "the basic evil of all our public life."[3] Nellie, like many western reformers, believed that the old established parties had become corrupt but were not beyond redemption.

In warning women against the danger of joining the Liberal or Conservative parties, Nellie was not advocating a separate Women's Party. In 1918 some Ontario women under the leadership of Constance Hamilton, president of the National Equal Franchise Union, tried to establish such a party. This movement won little support in the West. Irene Parlby and Violet McNaughton led the attack against the proposed platform and against the very idea of such an organization.[4] They agreed with Nellie that women would compromise their independence almost as much by joining a women's party as by belonging to one of the old parties. Women should remain free to vote for any candidate who supported women's interests. To Nellie this meant that first and foremost the candidate must be a prohibitionist. After that came espousal of the many other reforms that she believed the majority of women supported: improved health care, better working conditions on the farm and in industry, equal homestead rights, and equality under the law in marriage, divorce, and child custody.

Although Nellie McClung disapproved of formal party association, she realized that there had to be some kind of organization or women's concerns would not be brought to the attention of the politicians. On the very day that the suffrage bill passed the Alberta Legislature, Nellie and Emily Murphy met to discuss how this might best be achieved. They decided that the National Council of Women, which already had law committees in its local councils, could provide a central gathering point for the proposals of many women's groups and at the same time could disseminate to its members information on women's issues and advice on methods of procedure. Although they believed that the National Council was not the ideal organization for this purpose, their chief concern was to act quickly before the enthusiasm engendered by the newly won franchise could wear off.[5] Women must be made aware of the existing problems before they could be counted upon to form a wise political force. "The reason for the apparent indifference of so many women on questions of social welfare," Nellie wrote, "is that they do not know, and do not think, and are not able to imagine."[6]

When the war ended Nellie was deeply disturbed by the unrest and discontent she saw around her. Strikes erupted everywhere, and deep-felt discontent resulted in radical proposals at union conventions and farm gatherings. "War," Nellie observed, "has shown how defective and unjust and inadequate our present system is—honest men and women are not able to get enough to maintain them in the humblest form of life."[7] Nellie appeared totally disillusioned with the Union Government. She and other reformers, of course, had hoped for so much from this administration; perhaps it was more than any government could produce. Now they saw evidence of corruption and patronage and lack of response to problems the reformers considered paramount.

In the postwar period, Nellie McClung thought that the federal government was taking the wrong measures to deal with the social unrest, which it perceived as Communist inspired. Harsh measures, such as "the deporting of agitators, the banning of books, the suppression of papers, cannot effect a remedy," she warned.[8] Her ideas of what could be done appear in an incomplete manuscript in her papers, probably written in Winnipeg during the General Strike of 1919—the height of labour unrest. Her feelings were mixed. The strike appeared to her to be a takeover of municipal government by the strikers, because the only activities she saw taking place in the city were, according to the placards, "By permission of the Strike Committee." No doubt she was in contact with friends like Cora Hind, who would be unsympathetic to the strike. She might also have spoken to her former reform colleagues Woodsworth and Dixon, who would express a different opinion. She must have recalled, too, at this time, her previous experience with Premier Roblin and the unjust and unhealthy conditions of the Winnipeg sweatshops. In an attempt to understand the point of view of the strikers, she talked to some of them on the street and sought detailed information from one of the strike leaders whom she does not name. As he quoted Marx, and she quoted Mackenzie King, there was no real communication. Nellie had just read King's *Industry and Humanity* and was much impressed by his idealism and his belief that industrial peace could be achieved through cooperation instead of confrontation. Through most of the manuscript Nellie appears to take the side of the antistrike Citizens' Committee. Toward the end, however, she points out that workers have gained most of the privileges they enjoy through the use of the strike; that working men have been driven to desperate measures by low wages and the high cost of living; that the solution lies not in crushing the strike, but in government measures to impose high taxes on profits, fix prices, provide better and cheaper housing, as well as state care for the sick and old age pensions. In other words, she proposed what would seem to many a radical solution: government involvement in business and welfare far beyond what was acceptable to the majority of people at that time. She thought these proposals were necessary to avoid the "cyclone" that was sure to arrive if wealth was not distributed more equitably. In spite of her radical proposals she tended to see compromise as at least a temporary solution to extremists in both capital and labour.

Like Mackenzie King, Nellie believed that the old system could be improved. The radical leaders, she warned, "seemed to feel that to destroy the old system is sure proof that a better one will come."[9] She did not agree. In a Christmas message in 1920 Nellie expressed the belief that the only solution was to effect a change in spirit, which could only be brought about by religion—"the only power that can save a dying world and kindle the fading fires into warmth and radiance." The greatest evil in the world, she declared, was

> hoggishness—the hoggishness of the inner financial circle, of those who seek unreasonable profits, of those who corner markets and drive up prices ... and farther down the scale we come to the hoggishness of the man who refuses to work ... and allows mines and factories to remain idle while people suffer from cold and hunger ... [but] I cannot get quite so indignant with them ... for though their spirit is bitter we must remember that they have had a great many things to make them bitter.

It was very popular at this time, Nellie observed, to denounce Bolshevism, and she joined in that denunciation. But while most people thought of Bolshevists as low-class foreign agitators, Nellie defined a Bolshevist in her own inimitable way: "any man, who for his own gain, hurts his fellow men by imposing on their rights, and sets aside for his own pleasure or profit constituted authority, no matter how regularly he visits the barber!" Certainly an unorthodox definition of Bolshevism, but intended as a criticism of those smug businessmen who wanted to place the blame for unrest anywhere but on themselves, and used "bolshevist" as a general term for anyone they felt was a "troublemaker."[10]

With Nellie's deep concern for the problems of society, and because of her confidence in the abilities of women, it is not surprising that she continued to participate in politics even once the immediate goals of suffrage and prohibition had been achieved. Despite her insistence on the need for women to maintain their political independence, she played an active part in the Alberta election of 1917 on behalf of the Liberal Party. Nellie insisted that this was not a contradiction since she was not a Liberal but an independent who was supporting the Liberal Party because they had passed suffrage and prohibition legislation. When Sifton invited her to speak in Calgary at the opening meeting of his campaign, the opposition paper there scoffed at him for having to hire a professional speaker. He knew, it said, that he couldn't draw a crowd himself: "So far as the crowd is concerned Mrs. McClung will be the attraction at the Grand tonight. Premier Sifton and the rest will be merely fillers."[11] McClung was, of course, not paid for her appearance and made this quite clear to her audience. "My political opinions are my own," she declared, "and my political services cannot be bought. So long as I am a citizen I will give my services to any party or any man I deem worthy of my support."[12] When Nellie McClung demonstrated her independence by appearing on a platform for a Conservative candidate, she received criticism from both parties.

During the campaign it became clear that prejudice against women in politics had not been removed by the legal attainment of the right to vote. The *Albertan* quoted Conservative candidate S.B. Hillocks as saying at his nomination meeting at Emro that "the coming here of Mrs. McClung and her trotting around the country with Mrs. Davidson in the entourage of Premier Sifton is the most brazen piece of effrontery ever perpetrated in the province." He and Tweedie, another Conservative candidate, carried their attack on McClung into many ridings and made what the *Albertan*'s editor described as "insinuations of the meanest personal nature."[13] It seemed, at times, as though the Conservatives were trying to make an election issue out of Nellie McClung's participation in it. It is difficult to understand this attack because Nellie was not carrying on a bitter campaign. In fact she did not attack the Conservatives either as a party or as individuals. She confined herself to supporting the Liberals for what they had done, urging women to get out to vote, and expressing her support for many reforms, only some of which were in the Liberal platform. The Conservatives' attitude would seem to indicate that Nellie McClung was seen as a formidable weapon for the Liberals.

The election was not a particularly controversial one and the Liberals were returned to power with a majority of ten. The new administration had the first two women to be elected to a Canadian legislature: Mrs. L.M. McKinney of Claresholm, a member of the Non-Partisan League, and Miss Roberta MacAdams, a nurse overseas, elected by the soldier vote.

Four years later, in June 1921, Nellie McClung was chosen as a Liberal candidate for the Edmonton riding. There is no indication in her papers or her autobiography how she reached her decision to stand for the Liberal Party. At the lengthy nomination meeting on a hot June evening, women were present in large numbers and played a major role in nominating and supporting nominations. Nellie, however, was not nominated by a woman but by Bickerton Pratt, a fellow member of the Canadian Authors Association. As Edmonton was a five-member constituency at the time, McClung was one of five chosen from among sixteen nominated. The Liberal leader in this campaign was Charles Stewart, who had been premier since Sifton left in 1917 to become a member of the Unionist cabinet. The Liberals faced the campaign with considerable confidence. They realized that there was discontent in the province because of low farm prices, drought, and the operation of the *Liquor Act*, but they believed that their legislative record would return them to office. At the beginning of the campaign they paid little attention to the newly formed political arm of the United Farmers of Alberta that was fighting its first campaign with accusations against the Liberals of mismanagement and possible corruption in public financing. Gradually as the campaign progressed the Liberals came to realize that the UFA and not the Conservatives were the real opponents.

The United Farmers of Alberta "asserted that a new world order was just around the corner: individual and social perfectibility could

be achieved when, as appeared likely, the growing hostility of industries, classes, and nations finally drove the competitors to acknowl-
edge that 'co-operation' alone would save them from extinction." If
this social principle were recognized as superior to the principle of
competition, their argument ran, then the inevitable bickering engendered by the party system would end, and government by consensus
would evolve.[14] Nellie was familiar with these issues from her rural
Manitoba days, and it is curious that although the UFA addressed
almost all the matters that she had spent her life fighting for, she
consistently remained loyal to the Liberal Party, probably because
they were the first, in Manitoba, to bring in female suffrage. In spite
of this loyalty, though, she occasionally broke party ranks and sided
with the more reformist UFA on issues she supported.

In her campaign speeches Nellie McClung did not confine
herself to the liquor question, but strongly defended many aspects
of the government's record. It was always much easier, she admitted, to attack than to defend. She knew that crowds liked to hear
her rake her opponents over the coals, but in this case the opponents had no record to attack. The Stewart government, she
argued, deserved the votes of the people because they had admin-
istered the province responsibly. Faced by depression and drought
in the postwar period, they had managed to supply millions of
dollars in drought relief, and fostered irrigation projects where
they were feasible. They had proved themselves a reform party by
providing a compensation plan for injured workers and the best
programme of public health in the Dominion. Women should
remember that they brought in widows' pensions, a dower law,
improved factory acts, rural nurses and rural hospitals. The opposition parties, she said, were trying to blame the government "for
the many plagues of the last few years from flu to drought,"
ignoring the sincere efforts they had made to cope with these
problems. In her appeal to the women she stressed that people
expected women to use their votes foolishly, to be easily led astray
by promises, or a good-looking candidate, or the one with the
smoothest tongue who flattered them or kissed the baby. She
argued that women must prove their detractors wrong by exercis-
ing the vote wisely. Recognizing the threat presented by the UFA,
she reminded women that the Stewart government was a known
quantity and they should not be tricked into turning the Liberals

out in favour of an unknown quantity that promised much. "The party out of power," she said, "are like the seed catalogues with their glossy pictures of things to come."[15]

On behalf of her own candidature McClung did not stress the fact that she was a woman but did, on occasion, point out the desirability of having women legislators. Women, she argued, favoured progressive legislation and would work in the legislature for measures that advanced education and health. She emphasized her position as a reformer and particularly as a prohibitionist. In the government, she said, she would continue to work for all the reforms with which she was already associated: prohibition, mothers' pensions, health care (particularly in rural areas), minimum wage, half-day holiday so store clerks could have some time off from work each week, and a widening of educational opportunities for all. "If your observations of me have led you to think that you would like me to sit down in the legislature—a place where I will have more influence, more power—if that is what you think, you will know what to do. I would try always to represent the women's viewpoint and I will try to be a healing force."[16]

The election results on 18 July 1921 were a great disappointment to Nellie. The Liberals were decisively swept from office. The UFA had a clear majority with thirty-eight seats. The Liberals had fifteen, Labour had four, and there were four Independents. The Conservatives were wiped out. Edmonton withstood the tide electing all five Liberals—McClung was third behind McClennon and Bowen. In her victory speech she expressed her thanks for her election but added: "Too many good men and women have gone down to defeat today for me to be bubbling over with joy at this time." She believed the results indicated that the public had a "short lived memory for services rendered."[17]

Among the defeated were Louise McKinney and all the other women candidates except Irene Parlby of the UFA. Even before McClung's move to Alberta she had been associated with Parlby in reform efforts. Now they would be sitting on opposite sides of the House and Parlby would be in the position of greater power. No doubt McClung had had hopes of a cabinet post but that honour went to Parlby. Irene Parlby was a minister without portfolio, but judging by her role in the House she might easily have been called minister for women. Since McClung was a member of a small and rather weak opposition, and Parlby was in a position to push for legislation that they both approved, Nellie would have to vote against her caucus to support what she believed in. The Liberals were further weakened by Stewart's departure for Ottawa and a post in King's cabinet.

Personal congratulations for her victory poured in from across the country. The family must have had a good laugh at a telegram from Percy Anderson that read:

> Congratulations you old skunk. Mamie, Eleanor and myself want good soft jobs inspecting or expecting something. We are all *molto simpatica* in this connection. Ask Wes for interpretation. Wire answer. Waiting.

There were wires from personal friends, many from women who saw her victory as a gain for women, from others who thought it was a prohibitionist victory, and even from one who believed it to be a gain for the literary community. R.J. Stead wrote: "I think that generally speaking, we may claim to go up a step in our national life with every literary person who is absorbed into its machinery."[18]

The first session of the fifth Legislative Assembly of Alberta began on 2 February 1922. Nellie took her seat on the opposition benches facing a government that had very few experienced members; a party that in theory was opposed to party politics and that had promised that all the evils of that system would be eliminated. After the election they had had to find a premier because the leader of the UFA, Henry Wise Wood, had not run and had no desire to be premier. The job went to a somewhat reluctant Herbert Greenfield.

When Nellie was assigned a seat in the chambers she was somewhat surprised by the eagerness of the assistant clerk, Mr. Andison, to extol the merits of her seatmate, Dr. J.S. State. He was one of the oldest members in the legislature and had come to Alberta twenty years before to homestead. He had been unable to deny the sick who called upon him and had soon been drawn back into an active practice with all the hardships that faced a frontier doctor. This story, of course, appealed to Nellie. Dr. State, Andison added, was very fond of puzzles. Nellie learned later that State had objected to having Nellie McClung seated beside him, but Andison had persuaded him to give it a try. Unaware of his objections, Nellie was her usual friendly self, and before long they were working on matchstick puzzles and became good friends.[19] We do not know whether his objections to Nellie were because she was a woman or because he had a preconceived notion of a militant suffragist and prohibitionist, but there were few people who could remain unfriendly to Nellie McClung when they met her face to face.

In her maiden speech, during the debate on the speech from the throne, Nellie took up the theme she was to repeat frequently during her years in the legislature: members should forget party bickering and work together to do their best for the province. On later occasions she tried to ignore the fact that each party had the next election in mind at all times and she admonished both sides for posturings that she felt were insincere; for example, when the UFA presented a surplus budget in 1926, after years of deficits, she thought that "the boyish enthusiasm" with which the UFA members cheered the finance minister was an act. On the other hand she saw no reason why her own party members should not be pleased about the surplus or about any other achievement of the government. Of course she could not resist adding that she was delighted because now the government could initiate the old age pension, which earlier they had said they could not afford. Nellie missed no opportunity to push for the reforms she supported, but petty arguing and "jabbering" seemed to her a waste of time. "We should get together and give the very best that is in us to formulate policies whereby we can handle the big problems before us. That is our business in the legislature."[20] This view of the legislature was much closer to the philosophy of the UFA than to that of the Liberals, for in theory the UFA saw the House as a kind of forum where various interests were, or ought to be, represented. After discussion a consensus should be reached.

Nellie's intention to support any measures she personally approved of meant that on several occasions she voted with the government and against her own caucus. Many years later Nellie described herself as not a very good party member,[21] but since none of the votes were crucial in a legislature with a clear government majority, her voting pattern did not become an issue although it roused some resentment among fellow Liberals.

Nellie McClung had campaigned first and foremost as a prohibitionist, and much of her first speech was an appeal to the UFA to stand fast on this matter, both as a government and as individuals. Although she acknowledged that the *Liquor Act* was difficult to enforce she saw this as no excuse for abandoning it. Nellie lost her sense of humour when it came to the liquor question. She asserted that contempt of the law was being encouraged by comedians and actors and she seemed to imply that such performances should be censored. "It is a strange thing that we allow almost anyone to come along, stranger, vaudeville performers, and insult prohibition on the stage, insult our doctors, and the whole system." She urged every member of the legislature to uphold the law by personal example. Her remarks were greeted with applause and the *Albertan* jokingly commented: "Had Mrs. McClung spoken much longer she would have had all the members there pledged to observe the prohibition without hesitation or equivocation which may be proof of the oratorical ability of Mrs. McClung."[22] This comment in itself says something about the attitude toward prohibition, since one would ordinarily assume that members of the legislature should be expected to obey the law.

At first it seemed as though Nellie and the government would be in total agreement on the liquor issue. Early in the first session the UFA introduced amendments designed to tighten up enforcement of the *Liquor Act*. The dispensing of medicinal alcohol was taken out of the hands of druggists and placed in government dispensaries.[23] Penalties for breaking the law were increased. A triumvirate was established to supervise the act. When R.C. Edwards, an independent member for Calgary, introduced an amendment to the act to permit the sale of 7 percent beer, it was decisively defeated. Bob Edwards, colourful editor of the *Calgary Eye Opener*, was a notorious drinker who had supported the prohibition referendum in 1916. The story was told that he offered to print certain material for the "dry" committee free of charge, but when the women took him the copy they found him dead drunk. Since 1916 Edwards had decided that prohibition did not work. He argued that people were drinking poison supplied by the bootleggers, and if good beer were provided, they would drink that instead, putting the bootleggers out of business. He thought that the present law profited only the bootleggers and referred to one very successful still in a church basement.[24]

Nellie, of course, vigorously opposed Edwards's amendment. After praising him for his prohibition stand in 1916, she argued that he was totally mistaken in his belief that legal beer would be an improvement. Edwards, however, was far from alone in his wish to have beer reintroduced in the province. During the 1923 session a "monstrous" beer petition asking for a referendum on beer sales was presented to the legislature. Under Alberta's direct legislation act such a petition had to be granted, but Nellie was confident that the petition would be found invalid. The WCTU immediately appointed a committee to investigate it. They found that many of the petitioners were not Albertans, some were dead, some had signed more than once, and that whole pages of names were in a single handwriting. When they checked in the localities where the petition had been circulated, they heard that it had been misrepresented and signatures obtained under false pretences.[25] Nellie was sure that what, to her, was overwhelming evidence of an irregular petition would mean it would be turned down, but to her dismay the legislature accepted it 49-7.[26] The so-called moderationists fought a hard campaign and the province voted for the return of liquor sales, this time under government control. To Nellie's great regret she was not able to play a personal role in the fight. In the spring of 1923 Wes became critically ill, and Nellie went with him to the Banff sanitarium. She would say later: "It was a case where duties conflicted, and I chose the one which is nearest and highest."[27] But she did manage to make a speech to the Women's Institute Convention on 31 May that was published in pamphlet form by the Prohibition Committee. Wes made a slow recovery, and by November they were able to travel to Victoria. They were there when Nellie heard the news that Alberta was no longer dry. It must have been a bitter blow. Just before Wes's illness, his company had transferred him to Calgary. They bought a home there in early May but did not move until their return from the coast in December. Now Nellie had to travel to Edmonton to attend the legislative sessions. She spent the week in that city, returning to Calgary on weekends. The affable alcoholic Bob Edwards of the *Calgary Eye Opener* welcomed McClung in his own unique way—probably three sheets to the wind—when he recorded in the "Society News" section of his paper: "It is rumored that Mrs. Nellie McClung may shortly move down to Calgary. None more welcome than she. But we shall all have to be on our good behaviour. Even 'Trainrobber Bassoff is going to be hung/For flouting the precepts of Nellie McClung.'"[28]

When the legislature opened in 1924 Nellie made a bitter attack on the UFA. She said she had been disappointed when they accepted a petition full of irregularities and had felt even worse when she saw this supposedly prohibition government produce a referendum that she felt was almost certain to split the vote of those who had previously supported prohibition. Even then she had expected that when the fight was on, the government members would be out in their constituencies trying to bring about a prohibition result. Instead, they decided to remain silent. These men who had, at every convention, pledged their support for prohibition had turned their backs. Nellie found this incomprehensible.

> I confess I do not understand the mentality of people who will wave a flag and shout their loyalty in the time of peace and then go way back out of sight when the battle is on, leaving the fight for other people to carry on and expect to get away with it . . . As fair weather advocates of prohibition you were a spectacular success . . . With the exception of the lady member of the cabinet you took refuge in silence.

She went on to accuse the government of deceiving prohibition people. "You got their votes and at the first opportunity you deserted to the enemy. Your pledge was a scrap of paper." She concluded: "I wish I could honestly say that I hope the new law will be a success. That statement would be as absurd as if I said I hope the man who threw the gasoline on a fire would be successful in putting it out."[29]

Probably to McClung's surprise, Parlby did not appreciate being singled out as the one cabinet member who had campaigned in the referendum. Although Parlby regretted the result of the vote, she was ready to accept the will of the people. Obviously stung by the attack from a Liberal who had always been sympathetic to the UFA, she accused Nellie of flaying her opponents instead of using the conciliatory methods she always espoused, and of attacking men she knew were too chivalrous to reply to her as they would to a man who made such a speech. McClung, who had reason to know that chivalry seldom protected her from political attacks, assured the legislature that "we are in exact equality here, and if I spoke unfairly, or made a criticism which the members of the government can answer, I beg of them not to suffer in silence. Remember Job and speak out!" None took up her challenge although one member did remark that "the lady member from Edmonton, like some other prohibitionists, is a poor loser." Many years later Kennethe Haig recorded an amusing anecdote related to the prohibition issue: "Mrs. Parlby, Mrs. McClung and Mrs. Murphy, were having a little get-together in Mrs. Parlby's room at the Macdonald [hotel] one night. As they came down the elevator into the rotunda, they were laughing and talking like a group of teenagers. Mrs. Murphy did not giggle—she laughed—and so did the other Irish woman, Nellie McClung. Next day it was all over town that these three women came rolling out of the Macdonald drunk as lords which, of course, was funny to those who knew they were all teetotalers."[30]

What the public didn't know, however, was that drink was a problem in the McClung family itself. Perhaps it was to be expected that with a mother who was such an ardent prohibitionist and so vocal about it her boys reacted against her temperance stand. Probably they felt they had to "prove" themselves to their youthful friends, sometimes to Nellie's acute embarrassment. Paul, for example, once smashed the family car when drunk, and his mother was extremely upset for fear this would become public knowledge and undermine her position. Wes calmed Nellie down and somehow managed to keep this catastrophe out of the newspapers. Certainly by the time her sons became adults, according to Mark, all four boys had drinking problems. There is no doubt that this situation would have caused Nellie much distress. Some years later when she and Mark were in Interlaken, Switzerland, on their way to a United Nations meeting, Mark suggested they have a mild liqueur after dinner. Nellie let him order her one but, when it arrived, she told Mark she was too old and set in her ways to start changing her temperance habit, and she refused to take so much as a sip.[31]

At most times the two women MLAs, McClung and Parlby, agreed on legislation in the House. They were both interested in the welfare of the family and equality for women. When the government introduced a bill to establish a minimum wage for women workers, J.S. Stewart, UFA member for Lethbridge, proposed an amendment that would have prevented married women whose husbands earned more than $150.00 a month from holding a job. McClung and Parlby reacted as one. Parlby called it an infringement on equality. McClung said that most men thought women should be kept at home to do housework. While 90 percent of women who could afford to stay home probably would, Nellie argued, the other 10 percent had as much right as any man to work. She had already argued with Premier Roblin, in her Manitoba days, that most women were working to support their families and not just for pin money. Under the double barrage Stewart quickly withdrew his motion.[32] As an opposition member McClung was free to urge increased mothers' pensions, more help for unemployed women, prison reforms, and homes for delinquent girls. Parlby, on the other hand, had to adhere to the government's programme, arguing that there were insufficient funds to provide all the services that Nellie supported. Of course Nellie was not reluctant to advise on new sources of revenue—income tax, tax on luxuries, lowering of legislators' salaries—none of which the UFA was ready to accept.[33] In 1924 the two women joined forces to introduce a resolution that supported equality between men and women in divorce proceedings. Clearly women in the legislature were having some impact on women's issues. This, along with a resolution by Davidson and McClung, that women's citizenship should not be affected by marriage, received unanimous consent because they were simply resolutions to the federal government on issues over which the provincial government had no authority.[34]

Nellie McClung was a very active member of the legislature. She attended regularly and spoke frequently. Her sense of humour was usually evident. On one occasion "the entire House was convulsed" with her retort to a young member from Vegreville. He was noted for his constant interruptions and outbursts during opposition speeches. When he interrupted Nellie's attempt to bring a motion to a vote with the protest that he had not had a chance to speak, Nellie expressed her surprise "that the member for Vegreville remained silent, for if he had any thoughts on the matter it is the first time since this house opened that he has had an unuttered thought."[35] When Nellie was scheduled to speak, the gallery was usually full. The *Bulletin* claimed: She "is the only legislator who brings her own audience with her and when 'Our Nellie' finishes speaking the exodus from the public gallery is very marked."[36] Nellie would attack vigorously when she believed in her cause, but she would not attack simply to win points for the party. In November 1925 when Premier Herbert Greenfield was replaced by J.E. Brownlee, some Liberals chose to make insinuations as to the reason for the change, trying to make political gains for the Liberal Party in the upcoming election. Nellie would not join in. Instead, in an interview, she reported that Premier Greenfield was "conducting himself with quiet dignity in the face of the bitter remarks. He seems to be like a man who is glad to be released from the burden of responsibility—a burden which he did not seek, but which was forced upon him. He has stepped down gracefully and without regret."[37]

During the 1926 session there was speculation as to whether McClung would run again. As a Calgary resident her chances of winning a Liberal seat would be slim. Calgary had returned only one Liberal in 1921, and in the recent federal election there had been a large Conservative majority. There were predictions that she would run as an independent. When the Calgary Liberal nomination meeting was held in June, however, she was chosen as one of three Liberal candidates. Although Calgary would elect five members, the convention decided that under the proportional representative system, used for the first time in Alberta in this election, the party would stand a better chance if they ran only three candidates.[38] The Conservative paper, the Calgary *Bulletin*, took the rather puzzling stand that McClung should have refused the nomination because she had been a resident of Calgary for only a short time. The editor believed that "modesty" should have compelled her to decline.[39] He argued also that she was falsely claiming to be a women's representative and that there was something underhanded about the Liberals urging Calgarians to vote for her. Apparently the *Bulletin* feared that McClung would do well because, while they continually attacked the Liberal Party and its new leader, Joseph Shaw, McClung was the only Calgary Liberal consistently criticized.

As well as presenting herself as a women's representative, Nellie McClung defended her status as a Liberal. There were murmurs that she was not a good party member—perhaps prompted by her opponents but perhaps also whispered by disgruntled Liberals who disliked her independent stands in the legislature. She frankly admitted that she had voted in opposition to her party on several occasions and might do so again because she thought that "the very essence of liberalism is freedom of conscience."[40] This, in fact, was her stand from now on. She no longer spoke of herself as an independent—she was a Liberal, but she never allowed that to prevent her from criticizing Liberal governments or Liberal politicians if she thought they were wrong.

McClung's attack on the UFA was quite vehement in this campaign. Although she could not express disapproval of most of their legislation because she was in sympathy with it, she attacked them for the *Liquor Act*. Prohibition was, supposedly, not on the political agenda in this campaign and other speakers barely mentioned it, but Nellie could not ignore what she still considered a vital issue. She could not say that the Liberals, if returned, would reinstate prohibition but she argued that the UFA had betrayed prohibitionists and should not have their votes. This betrayal angered her. She also attacked the UFA as a class government that encouraged sectionalism, narrowness, and bitterness, and had driven a wedge between city and country. The Liberals, she promised, would provide progressive government that was fair to all classes.[41] Her own legislative record, she pointed out, showed that she always put human interest ahead of property interest.[42] As usual Nellie was in demand as a speaker throughout the province on behalf of Liberal candidates, but in this election she felt the need to devote more time to her own riding and throughout the campaign she was on the defensive: defending her right to run, her credentials as a Liberal and a women's representative, and her continuing stand as a prohibitionist.

On election day, 28 June 1926, McClung was defeated in a very close contest for the last two of the five available positions. Had the electoral system used in 1921 still been in place in the 1926 election, McClung might well have won again. But, in the interval, a system of proportional representation (or preferential voting) had been introduced in Alberta's two largest cities. In 1921 all McClung needed to take one of the five available seats was to win enough votes to put her among the top five contenders. Now it was not so simple, for preferential voting not only measures support for a candidate but (through ranking) the strength of support as well. To succeed candidates had to win enough first preference votes to meet a quota (determined by dividing the total votes cast by the number of seats to be filled). In Calgary in 1926, the quota needed for election was 3,290 votes. On the first count, only the Conservative A.A. McGillivray achieved this figure, and then some. Under preferential voting, these excess or surplus votes were redistributed to the number two choice. This redistribution of choices was made over several counts until all seats were filled.

The virtue of the system, according to its defenders, is that all the voters' preferences are given weight in a series of counts and that, in the final analysis, the candidates most favoured are selected. If that claim is true, then McClung, narrowly beaten out of the fourth and then the fifth spots by two Labour candidates, who were also aldermen, could take little satisfaction in the result. She was the second choice of few voters. On each count, therefore, her support waned.

The Mayor of Calgary, G.H. Webster, a Liberal, made it in the fifth count. McClung's support, in the meantime, gradually sank as the counts progressed.

Even now, as the *Bulletin* editor analysed the results, he could not resist a dig at Nellie with his comment that "Mrs. McClung's insistence on No. 1 votes for herself detracted from the showing of the other Liberal candidates."⁴³ The counting was long and tedious, but Nellie remained in the Liberal committee rooms as the results came in. By 11 PM it was clear that one Liberal had been elected, one defeated, and that her fate hung by a thread. She went home to bed. The next morning she learned that the final count, completed at 6 AM, had declared her unsuccessful in her bid for a second term. In seeking election, a woman like Irene Parlby had concentrated backing from the United Farm Women of Alberta, an organization she had founded. On the other hand, McClung's "female sympathizers . . . were scattered throughout a multitude of associations, none so closely tied to the government as the women's farm organization."⁴⁴

Nellie's family, she reported, "behaved admirably at breakfast, even the youngest one, who is at the age when it is rather embarrassing to have a mother of any sort, and particularly so to have one that goes out and gets herself defeated." She herself tried to "make a fine show of cheerfulness," but inside was bitterness and regret. No matter how much she might tell herself that she didn't mind, that now she could go back to her own work with a clear conscience, there remained the sore thought that she had been rejected. For five years she had tried very hard to do a good job and now had been turned down. Her immediate antidote to defeat was activity. She was, she said,

> seized with a desire to cook, and I wanted the kitchen all to myself. No woman can be utterly cast down who has a nice, bright blue and white kitchen facing the west . . . I set off at once on a perfect debauch of cooking. I grated cheese, stoned dates, blanched almonds, whipped cream, set jelly—and let the phone ring. It could tear itself out by the roots for all I cared. I was in another world—the pleasant, landlocked, stormless haven of double boilers, jelly moulds, flour sifters, and other honest friends who make no promise they cannot carry through . . . I am ashamed to tell it, but I got more comfort out of my cooking orgy that day than I did from either my philosophy or religion.

The next day, still smarting from defeat, she headed for the out-of-doors—to the Earl Grey Golf Course. At first she was "too conscious of the Elbow Park houses below me; some of them vaguely resentful; some overbearingly exultant; and others leering at me with their drawn blinds, like half-closed Conservative eyes." Then she decided to name the balls "and was able by that means to give one or two of them a pretty powerful poke."

After a few such days she acquired the composure needed to analyse her defeat. She believed that she had been unrealistically optimistic. Her chances in Calgary had simply not been as high as her friends had encouraged her to believe. There is bitterness in her account of the people "who sought me out and entreated me to step out and save my country and then, having nobly performed their duty as citizens, one by one they sought the solace of the cool, sweet, far-distant places, where birds' voices call, and waters idly lap the shore." As Nellie thought about the campaign she realized that she had allowed a few friends, full of enthusiasm, to make her overly optimistic: "Looking back on it now I see I went through the campaign with a sort of courageous imbecility! So many people told me I was sure to be elected, I seemed to forget that I had deep-seated relentless antagonism from several sections of the community." First among these she placed the liquor interests. These were opponents she knew she could depend on, however, "and there are no hard feelings between us." Far more difficult to forgive were those conservative-minded voters who resented "the invasion of women." Public offices, particularly "those that carry emolument, they believe to belong by the ancient right of possession to men. They are quite willing to let women work on boards, or committees, or indeed anywhere if the work is done gratuitously—but if there is a salary they know at once that women are not fitted by nature for that!" Some women, she admitted, were in this category. She resented particularly the women who did not think for themselves. "One told me quite sweetly—'I don't know anything about this, but Charley is frightfully keen and told me to give out these cards and say I hope you will vote our ticket.' I thought of Mrs. Pankhurst and her heroic followers going to jail, and suffering the agonies of social ostracism as well as physical torture, to win for women like these the right to vote." After deciding why she had been defeated, she said she could put it behind her and put a new ribbon in her typewriter.[45] Indeed, the defeat was not a complete disaster because it gave us her amusing sketch, "How It Feels To Be A Defeated Candidate," which soon appeared in several publications.

The reasons for Nellie McClung's defeat are difficult to assess, and the complications of the preferential voting system increase the difficulty. Her own emphasis on the importance of the liquor interest is probably inaccurate. Although those in the trade would be unlikely to vote for her they were not much worried about her efforts in 1926. They knew they had won and would probably not actively oppose her candidature. On the other hand, her inclusion of prohibition in almost every speech may have antagonized many people who did not want to see prohibition reinstated and thought that the UFA had produced a good *Liquor Act.* Although McClung scoffed at the idea that she was a newcomer to Calgary this, too, may have been a factor. While she was well known in that city, she had not, because of her legislative commitments, played nearly as prominent a role in Calgary women's associations as she had in Edmonton. Many of the leading women in Calgary were Conservatives who would not have voted for her and may have influenced other women. In addition, those candidates who were successful in the election were all prominent Calgarians. Among these Nellie McClung was indeed an outsider. Perhaps it is fair to say that under the circumstances her large number of first votes indicated a fairly successful campaign.

Although chagrined at defeat Nellie probably felt some relief at being out of a legislature that once again would be under the UFA government, this time with an even stronger mandate. On the whole, the legislature must have been a frustrating experience for her. She was not temperamentally suited to the political manoeuvrings of party politics and, as a member of the Opposition, she was able to have only a minor influence on legislation. She had the satisfaction of voting for many measures of which she approved, but they were government measures that would have passed without her vote. Later, she wrote: "I enjoyed the five years I served as a member of the Legislative Assembly, but looking back at it now I cannot see that much remains of all our strivings."[46] She never ran again for public office.

8

Women's Role in the Church

❖

In June of 1920 Nellie McClung learned that she had been named a member of the Canadian delegation to the Ecumenical Methodist Conference to be held in London, England, in September 1921.[1] The nomination both surprised and thrilled her. In today's terms she was a token woman—the only female of the twenty-four-member delegation. She learned later that as delegates were being appointed one man had proposed that they choose one woman. His remark was followed by silence until he suggested that if they named Nellie McClung she could at least be counted on to bring back a lively report. The committee then approved the nomination.[2] Although Nellie was the only official woman delegate, Mrs. W.E. Sanford, of Hamilton—founding member and later president (1918-22) of the National Council of Women of Canada[3]—was named as an alternate and apparently attended the conference too. Nellie welcomed the opportunity, both as a chance to visit the British Isles and as a step forward for women in the church.

The church had been a central part of Nellie McClung's life from her childhood on, and wherever she had lived she had sought fellowship and activity within church organizations. In Winnipeg and Edmonton in particular, until they moved to Calgary in 1923, her whole family were involved in the life of their church.[4] But it was not just the church as an organization that was central to Nellie McClung's life. She believed strongly in the power of the spirit; this was the source of her optimism. If a true Christian spirit could be achieved, she thought, then social evils would disappear and God's Kingdom on earth would come about. Despite the discouraging results of most of her reform efforts, she retained this belief to the end of her life. In 1922 she wrote:

> There is no greater falsehood than the belief that human nature
> cannot be changed. Christ knew that the evils of human nature could
> be cast out—the stony heart exchanged for the heart of flesh, and that
> fear, which is another name for hatred, could be cast out by the
> perfect love. Christ not only knew this—he lived it, and demonstrated
> it . . . Everytime that we say that human nature, meaning the evils of
> human nature, cannot be changed we deny the success of Christ's
> mission.[5]

But the world, she said, suffered from "Spiritual Anaemia."[6]

In 1926 Nellie wrote the article "My Religion." It was republished
in 1942, and appeared once again in the United Church publication
Onward, in 1951, just before her death. Her fundamental beliefs had
remained unchanged and in the article she affirmed that they were
established in her childhood when she accepted the promise "that
God would make it up to everyone who suffered here." She claimed
that "doctrinal discussions have a mouldy taste and are dusty to the
palate . . . It is not so much spiritual food we need as spiritual
exercise." She loved the Bible and particularly Christ's words. Of
these she thought that the most important were "'feed my lambs'; that
was a slogan for all of us to take from his lips. If we love Him, He tells
us in these three words how to show it. It is not 'Chant my praises';
'Defend my theories'; 'Kill my enemies.' No, no—but a greater, better,
lovelier task, 'Feed my lambs.'" To Nellie this meant fighting the evils
that harmed the lambs. "God demands our love, not just our amiabil-
ity . . . if we love humanity we must hate humanity's enemies . . .
Toleration when applied to weeds, germs, dirt, mad dogs, and racial
poisons, ceases to be Christian virtue. It becomes indifference and
cowardice." On the other hand, she warned that intolerance should
not be applied to the religious beliefs of others. "God reveals himself
in many ways. Religion is a bridge and as such must have two
qualifications. It must carry our weight, and it must endure in the tide
of great waters. If it has these two qualifications then it is a good bridge
irrespective of size, color, or shape. It is a deadly sin, I believe, to lay
our axe to the arch of another man's bridge."[7] Her unwavering faith,
however, did not mean that she accepted unquestioningly the decisions of the institutional church. One of the ways in which she believed
it had gone astray was in its attitude toward women, for McClung was
convinced that women should be on an equal footing with men within
the church. She was impatient with the dry theological arguments and

the endless citing of traditions that were used to oppose women's attempts to reach this goal. Women, she felt, had the right to a voice in the administration of the church and to hold any office including that of ordained minister. For her there was no valid argument against this fundamental right. She did not blame God for women's inferior place in the church.

> God created man in his *own* image . . . male and female created he *them* . . . It would seem from this, that men and women got away to a fair start. There was no inequality to begin with . . . there were no favours, no special privileges. Whatever inequality has crept in since, has come without God's sanction . . . The inequality has arisen from men's superior strength . . . It is easy for bigger and stronger people to arrogate to themselves a general superiority. Christ came to rebuke the belief that brute strength is the dominant force in life. It is no wonder that the teachings of Christ make a special appeal to women, for Christ was a true democrat.[8]

In a book sarcastically dedicated "to those Superior Persons, men and women, who are inhospitable to new ideas . . . ," a book that sets forth the firm belief "that the woman's claim to a common humanity is not . . . unreasonable," Nellie McClung outlined her ideas on "Women And The Church" in very forceful language. In this essay she claimed that the male-dominated church held women "in mild contempt," always spoke of women "in bulk" as if they were not individuals, claimed to "understand women far better than women understand themselves," and gave a "masculine interpretation" of religion. "I believe the Protestant religion has lost much," Nellie argued, "when it lost the idea of the motherhood of God." Throughout history, she claimed, "the church has contributed a share . . . in the subjection of women" from the marriage service through the masculine refusal to let women hold positions of power within the church. "Women," she said ironically, "may lift mortgages, or build churches, or any other light work, but the real heavy work of the church, such as moving resolutions in the general conference or assemblies, must be done by strong, hardy men!" But "sex prejudice," Nellie knew, "is a hard thing to break down" and while "the best and ablest men in all the churches are fighting the woman's battle now," there were still a large number of small-minded, narrow-souled men and women to contend with.

But when all is over, the battle fought and won, and women are regarded everywhere as human beings and citizens, many women will remember with bitterness that in the day of our struggle, the church stood off, aloof and dignified, and let us fight alone.[9]

After careful deliberation, Nellie claimed that the cause for the churches' "antagonism" to women ministers lay in "sex jealousy," and that gentlemen "of the old school" believed that "women should all be housekeepers whether they want to be or not." This, in turn, reflected the churches' opinion that women were merely "assistants" or "helpmates" for men, with no right to a "life of [their] own." To Nellie, the belief that women must cherish no hope or ambition of their own was both cruel and unjust. She also condemned the churches' adulation for "the self-sacrificing mother, who never had a thought apart from her children, and who became a willing slave to her family." Children, she said, did not "always" need a mother's care, and the church failed to see the damage that the slave-mother inflicted both on herself and her family. "The church," Nellie criticized, "folds its plump hands over its broadcloth waistcoat and makes no protest" against such abuses. The churches' "comfortable respectable pews" simply encouraged a "narrow-gauge religion," and she would, on occasion, quote—or delightfully misquote—the Bible to defend her position. While Nellie stressed the practical need for women ministers, her fundamental argument was that of equality between men and women.[10]

During the war Methodist women were seeking the right to be voting members at all levels of church government and the right to be elected to all administrative bodies of the church. One argument advanced by the men who opposed women's entry into the full fellowship of the church was that women would then ask for the right to be ordained. Nellie agreed that this would indeed follow, but she saw this as a natural and inevitable outcome of the women's movement, and she, and others, both male and female, believed that the time had arrived when that forward step should be taken.[11] In 1914 at the Manitoba Methodist Conference, Nellie's father-in-law, the Reverend J.A. McClung, fought aggressively for the right of women to sit on the church courts. "He had made up his mind that if the conference turned the motion down, he would canvas every woman he met to go on strike for one year and do no [church] work."[12] The motion passed. At the Canadian Methodist Assembly in 1918 another resolution was introduced to the effect that women should have equal rights with men in regard to all the privileges of church membership. Surprisingly, this resolution passed unanimously. Perhaps the delegates were influenced by the surge of women's gains in the political world at this time. The *Christian Guardian* reported that "No one voted against it, and only a very few extra brave refused to vote for it."[13] But a second resolution, that the ministry be opened to women, met a different fate. A heated debate took place. Finally, it was decided to refer the whole matter to the local Quarterly Official boards, and the *Christian Guardian* blandly suggested that "the whole discussion was largely academic, as we have yet to hear of any sister who is desirous of entering the Methodist ministry."[14]

While the matter was under discussion at the boards level there was no attempt to organize the proponents of ordination, and Nellie McClung had little contact with others on the issue. Therefore, when she received the appointment as a delegate to the London conference she was pleased to have the opportunity to express her views on the role of women in the church before an international audience.

The Atlantic crossing, being part of an international gathering, and meeting in historic Westminster Hall were exciting experiences, but the conference itself did not provide the spiritual uplift Nellie had expected. Her first shock came at the opening banquet when some southern American delegates refused to sit beside black delegates. Nellie and a man from Wichita, Kansas, quickly moved to take the rejected chairs. The dinner speaker, Sir Robert Pearkes, was a disappointment too. With wry humour Nellie recorded in her diary: "The brightest spot of the evening was Lady Pearkes' diamonds." The sessions, too, seemed cold and mechanical. The speakers were "eloquent, easy to listen to, polished and prepared. The programmes rolled off the assembly line according to plan. It was a great gathering, well planned and executed, but my heart was not warmed."[15]

On the eighth day of the conference the first session was entitled "Women's Work." Although one speaker said that women's work should not be limited, she gave no suggestions for changes. Another speaker must have made Nellie shudder as he pulled out every cliché available. He even dared the patronizing phrase, "The hand that rocks the cradle still may rule the world." While he thought that women were important to the church, their role, as he described it, was the narrow one they had been playing for many years.

The second session was entitled "The Awakening of Women."

The speaker's view of women's work, and indeed of the work of the church, was a little broader than that of the previous speakers but there was no hint of a real change in women's position—no suggestion of equality but simply one more call to service and a greater opportunity to influence rather than to lead.[16] Following this essay Nellie McClung gave the first response to "The Awakening of Women." According to the newspaper accounts it was the conference that awoke. One reporter said: "Mrs. McClung carried the conference by storm with her unconventional and daring sayings,"[17] and another called her "racy, delightfully frank, and above all reasonable."[18] All accounts of her speech mention that it was punctuated by applause and laughter. Today, reading the speech, it is hard to understand that her remarks were "racy," "unconventional," or "daring," but there is still a breath of fresh air, a wit, a liveliness that jumps out even from the printed page in contrast with the stodgy speeches that came before and after hers.

She began by expressing her distaste for the title, "The Awakening of Women," which suggested that women had been asleep. "Women," she said,

> have always been awake. The woman of fifty years ago who carded the wool, spun it, wove the cloth to clothe her family, made the clothes without any help from Mr. Butterick or the Ladies' Pictorial, brewed her own cordial, baked her own bread, washed, scrubbed, ironed without any labour-saving devices and besides this, always had dinner on time, and incidentally raised a family and a few chickens in her spare time, may be excused if she did not take much interest in politics. But her lack of interest was not any proof that she was asleep—she was only busy.

Women now, she pointed out, had more spare time. "Therefore, they have turned to new activities. It is too late to discuss whether they are happier, or better, or the world safer. The clock will not turn back." Some women, she argued, had not taken advantage of their new opportunities and for them leisure simply meant time to be lazy, but this group was small. Nellie went on to scold the church because it had missed the opportunity to provide guidance for women in these new times. Instead, it tried "to herd them back to safety." To illustrate, she told the anecdote of a young girl who went to her pastor "with her soul on fire to do something for humanity and he asked her to keep fresh flowers on the altar." When the war came the nation had been forced to ask for women's help and women won a new place in the world's esteem, but many of the bravest, cleverest, most patriotic women have chosen to work outside the church. They had done this, Nellie warned, because the church had not supported women's causes.

> It should have led all the reform forces in bringing liberty of soul and freedom of action to women. It has not done so. I mean officially. Individual members and ministers have done so, and to them we are very grateful, but the church has been slow to move—stiff and cold. It preached resignation when it should have sounded the note of rebellion. Many of the brightest women grew impatient and indignant and went out of the church figuratively slamming the door. Slamming an innocent door has always seemed to me a misdirection of energy. It is better to linger after the sermon and interview the minister.

The church, she emphasized, had not afforded women the means of self-expression. "On special occasions," she said,

> womanhood has been garlanded with roses and smothered with praises. The motives in all this have been the highest and best, but it does not appeal to the average woman to hear womanhood spoken of in such condescending terms of sickly sentiment [as if it were] a sort of glorified disease.

"It is no use blaming it on Paul," she admonished her large and mainly clerical audience, "just because he once told a chattering group of women to stop their noise and give him a chance to settle the dispute among the men. None of us blames Paul for this. Look at the handsome way he came back with his great declaration regarding the Kingdom, 'There is neither Jew nor Greek, male or female, bond or free—for all are free.' This text has not been given so much publicity as the other one." The church needed women in the pulpit, she advised, and "if the ministers who oppose the ordination of women had a real vision of the ministry they would welcome women to the pulpit."

McClung went on to plead for more emphasis on service and less on abstract theology. She had, she said, "listened to a lot of theology in the last eight days—more than I ever knew existed in all the world." Canada needed teachers and workers who "were not so strong on fine points of doctrine" as on the "spirit of service." She described the hospitals and boarding schools of western Canada where "our workers are not so intent on making Methodists out of these people" as on interpreting God's love. She told them the story of a medical Methodist missionary who came to the bedside of a dying Russian woman. She was fearful and troubled so he asked the nurse to bring a candle. "The candle was brought and lighted, and then the Methodist doctor, who forgets he is a Methodist and only remembers that he is the servant of the living Christ, kneeling by the bed, began to repeat the prayer for the passing soul in the language the dying woman understood—the language of her own country and her own church, the strong words that had comforted many in days gone by in her distant home." If that theology seemed strange, Nellie said, she could tell them that it got results. "The Russian boy who used to drive the doctor on his rounds caught the gleam, and is now an ordained minister of the Methodist Church." She ended her address with a plea for teachers and missionaries for western Canada.[19]

The discussion that followed "The Awakening of Women" session was limited. One American delegate spoke in favour of the ordination of women but others simply emphasized the work that women were already doing.

On the whole the conference was a disappointment to Nellie. There was too much form and not enough substance. She did not sense the strong spirit of service she had expected, the majority of delegates were obviously not ready to support the ordination of women, she was disturbed by the emphasis on doctrine, and the differences between the various branches of the Methodist Church made unanimity impossible on even a resolution of support for the League of Nations.

When the conference ended on 16 September, Nellie did not leave for home but remained for another two months to visit London and travel to Scotland on a speaking tour for the Women's Guild of Empire. While in London, Nellie also made contacts in the publishing world in hopes of arranging for the publication of an English edition of *Purple Springs*. In particular Lady Rhondda, owner and publisher of *Time and Tide*, became a friend. Lady Rhondda was attempting to gain the right to sit in the House of Lords and was interested in Nellie's achievements in Canada. After this visit Nellie received *Time and Tide* and occasionally published in it.[20]

At the end of September Nellie travelled to France. Her visit to the cemeteries was a poignant reminder of the terrible cost of war. As she looked at the "acres, and acres, and acres" of white crosses, the horror of the war came back to her, and those questions that she had wrestled with a few years before returned. "Surely it was not for this that these brave young fellows were born. I tried to think of them as lying at peace in the land they fought to save; I tried to pray that it might lie lightly to their bones and that God's richest treasures in heaven might be their inheritance, but I knew it was all wrong and my heart was hot with rebellion." This feeling was intensified when she visited Vimy Ridge. The great rolls of rusting barbed wire, wheels, shafts, and other bits of wreckage were still lying around, but below they could see men ploughing and flowers were growing up under their feet. She wrote: "There was something about all this placidity and composure which seemed wrong. I don't know what I expected to find, but certainly it seemed that we had forgotten too soon the wanton destruction of human life. How cheaply blood had flowed into this unheeding soil!" Of course, when Nellie was writing this for *The Stream Runs Fast* in the 1940s, the world was once again in the midst of a bloody war and no doubt she was expressing current feelings as well as those she experienced in 1921.

Back in England Nellie prepared for her speaking tour under the auspices of the Women's Guild of Empire. Her travelling companion was Mrs. Flora Drummond who, along with a Miss Ayrton, impressed Nellie very much with their vigorous speeches against strikes and communist socialism, and their urging workers to increase production.[21] Having little knowledge of working conditions in the British Isles, Nellie seems to have been easily convinced that the workers were making unrealistic demands and holding up production with frivolous strikes. This is in sharp contrast with her opinion that in Canada low salaries and unsatisfactory working and living conditions were the chief causes of strikes. Although Nellie was a strong-minded woman she could, at times, be easily swayed by a strongly put position presented by individuals she admired.

Nellie McClung's speeches for the Guild were Canadian immigration talks. She particularly urged British women to emigrate to Canada. Admitting that all British immigrants to her country had not succeeded, she argued that failure could be avoided if the country the immigrants were going to was described honestly, so she set forth the difficulties that immigrants faced in Canada. Apparently she did not recognize that people who are warned of the hardships they will face often overestimate their ability to cope, and that the vast and lonely stretches of the prairies are hardly comprehensible to someone who has lived all her life in England, no matter how honest a description is given.[22]

On this trip, of course, Nellie McClung welcomed the opportunity to see something of her mother's native Scotland.[23] After the Scottish tour Nellie returned to London where she spoke to the Forum Club[24] and was entertained at a luncheon by the Society of Woman Journalists.[25] Early in November she boarded ship to return to Canada, probably spending most of her time en route writing up her experiences, because she began almost immediately after her return to lecture on her trip. A note in her papers indicates that she gave her talk "Up to London" twenty-five times.[26] On her way home she was entertained by the Toronto branch of the newly formed Canadian Authors Association[27] whose president had been corresponding with her about an Alberta branch.

In the years following the conference Nellie continued her struggle to win the right for women to be ordained. Perhaps because of her new duties as an MLA she was not one of the delegates to the Canadian Methodist Assembly of 1922, the first assembly for which women were eligible. This gathering received a summary of the reports from the Quarterly Official boards on the question of the ordination of women. The committee that examined these reports recommended to the assembly that the proposal for the ordination of women be turned down. Women delegates, led by Mrs. Keeton and Louise McKinney, moved for the appointment of a committee of twelve, including three women, to examine the question and report to the next General Assembly. Although McKinney was, according to the *Christian Guardian*, one of the ablest debaters at the Methodist Assembly, the proponents of women's ordination were not able to win even this limited victory. Women faced many of the same attitudes, foes, and arguments in the women's ordination question as they had encountered in the women's suffrage question. Those opposed to creation of a committee argued that it could accomplish nothing, the facts were clear and indisputable: women could not stand the hardships of the ministry, women's first Christian duty was motherhood and the family, and, finally, ordination for women at this point might interfere with the negotiations for church union with the Presbyterians. This latter argument was convincing to many who might, in principle, have supported ordination for women in the church. The *Christian Guardian* editor, however, did not stress this point, but ended his editorial with these words:

> The debate was interesting, but back in the minds of most of the delegates was the unmistakable conviction, that we could not afford to allow our young women to face the hardships of our ordinary work upon terms of equality with men, and the problem of a married woman preaching while her husband cared for the family and provided the meals, is one that cannot be dismissed with a joke.[28]

For the next three years the question of church union overshadowed the matter of ordination. Nellie McClung favoured union and had advocated it for some years because of the need for churches in western Canada and the fact that one small town might have several Protestant denominations and another town have none. She was amazed to discover that these practical considerations were not enough to overcome what she considered to be the minor doctrinal objections of many apparently reasonable people. She had, she said, been brought up on the stories of the Scottish Convenanters and "had thrilled to their brave words of defiance and the courage of the people who gathered in caves to sing their psalms and worship God as free men in their own way," but now she saw this opposition to church union as narrow-minded and senseless. The practical needs of the people should outweigh any doctrinal differences, which she saw as relatively unimportant. Wittily she dismissed the problem as "spiritual strabismus."[29]

When church union was accomplished, in 1925, women returned eagerly to the issue of the ordination of women. In 1922 the Presbyterian Church, like the Methodist, had turned down a proposal for their ordination. The Congregationalists had always permitted the ordination of women, but none had been ordained in Canada.[30] Now the women had renewed hope that a new United Church (comprised of the Presbyterian, Methodist, and Congregational churches, as well as the General Council of Local Union Churches) would be ready to respond to new ideas. And this time there was a candidate. That created an entirely new situation, as Nellie saw it: "Whenever the matter of ordination was raised the answer came back: 'There is no woman asking for ordination. Hold your tongues. Let well enough alone. When we get a request for ordination we will deal with it.'" She went on to say that now there is an overture from the Saskatchewan Conference [to the General Council] requesting ordination for Miss Lydia Gruchy. Here now we have what you have always desired to see, a woman graduate in theology asking for ordination. She has been two years preaching and carrying on very acceptably. What are you going to do with her? Dear, dear. This is most embarrassing.[31]

No embarrassment could equal the inconvenience of nonordination for Lydia Gruchy who, despite the fact that she served a three-point charge like any male clergyman, was unable to perform marriages or serve communion to the members of her three congregations, but had to call on her overworked male colleagues to assist her. A committee was established to prepare a statement for the information and guidance of the presbyteries—this statement to be circulated to all ministers with the remit asking the presbyteries for their opinion on the ordination of women. The committee was all male, all ministerial, and the one westerner appointed, Dr. E.H. Oliver of St. Andrew's College, Saskatoon—who had encouraged Lydia Gruchy—was apparently unable to attend the committee meetings, which were held in Toronto. The statement circulated as required and the presbyteries made their replies. Few women were involved because few were members of presbytery. They obtained an indication of how the matter was being handled, however, from an article written by the chairman of the committee, Dr. Ernest Thomas, and published in the church magazine, *The New Outlook*. The article entitled "Shall We Ordain Women?" had a very definite answer—"No."[32] Instead, a new order of the diaconate should be established so that women could be ordained to this lower order and, according to Thomas, would thus be satisfied. He argued, as did the document circulated to the presbyteries, that:

(a) the history of the church revealed that women had never been ordained,

(b) the ordained women would not be accepted by congregations, particularly by the women of the congregations, and

(c) ordination would provide an obstacle to further church union.[33]

To supporters of the ordination of women the arguments appeared trivial and one clergyman emphasized this by a parody of Dr. Thomas's list:

(a) we never heard of such a thing,
(b) your sisters might not be pleased, and
(c) whatever would the Jones's say.[34]

Furthermore, the arguments completely ignored the need that the Saskatchewan Conference had clearly expressed for a fully ordained minister. As a deaconess, Lydia Gruchy would be unable to do anything more than she was already doing.[35]

Others, too, had been very critical of the education, the wages, and the living conditions of church deaconesses. Methodist Church deaconess Alice A. Chown, for one, argued that "a little smattering of everything" was "hayforked" into the deaconess course of education. In addition, their remuneration was pitiful. "In ignoring the plight of the deaconesses, the church was guilty by implication of the same exploitation of women as other employers who refused to pay women a living wage." Chown went on to criticize the very existence of a deaconess order. "Perhaps the purpose [of a deaconess society] is to furnish nice little satellites for Methodist ministers . . . women who will clasp their hands with admiration at the greater knowledge of the pastor . . . It seemed to me that the course of study was aptly framed to fill Ruskin's ideal education for women, the ability to appreciate other people's learning, not to be competent oneself." The antidote, of course, was John Stuart Mill on *The Subjection of Women*, full theological education, and the ordination of women.[36]

In the two years between General Council meetings, the debate was carried on in the church paper, magazines, and on the platform.[37] Nellie McClung played an active part in this ongoing controversy and no doubt her forceful speech to the 1928 Alberta Conference helped produce the result headlined by *The New Outlook* as "Edmonton Presbytery Approves."[38] Not surprisingly Nellie was one of the delegates from Calgary to the General Council held in Winnipeg in September 1928. She was made a member of a committee to consider the replies from presbyteries on the ordination of women and to bring a recommendation to council. Within that committee a very heated debate took place. There was basic disagreement as to the meaning of the responses from the presbyteries. According to Nellie only twelve presbyteries returned a definite "no," thirty-three said "let's do it right away," and forty-three said "we believe in the principle." She interpreted this as seventy-six in favour and twelve opposed. Dr. Ernest Thomas interpreted the returns as fifty-five opposed, thirty-three in favour, and twenty-one who did not return the remit probably opposed.[39] Even he had to admit that his idea of a diaconate had been completely turned down. The committee finally arrived at a compromise resolution, and they agreed that Nellie McClung, as committee secretary, would present the report and speak to it. The recommendation stated that "the General Council takes no action in the matter of the ordination of women to the ministry, but puts itself on record as holding that there is no bar in religion or reason to such ordination."[40]

According to a Winnipeg paper Nellie's speech on the report "brought excitement to its peak." She began by describing it as not a very heroic resolution, but indicated that women could be encouraged by the admission that there was no rational or religious bar to the ordination of women. She said that a member of the committee from an Ontario city had assured her that women of his church had come to him opposing the ordination of women. Knowing the problems in the West, Nellie was incensed: "What difference will it make to these women . . . ? They would never have to listen to a woman preacher. But in some places it would make a difference." She told of the work being done by Lydia Gruchy and scoffed at the idea that women who could labour on homesteads could not stand the work of the pastorate. But, she assured her audience, even if ordination was granted it would be a long time before many women would be ready. "Some men," she said, "seem to be afraid that immediately they grant ordination the women will wash their hands at the kitchen sink and rush to them pleading 'Ordain me.' People," she added "can be too careful. I heard of a man who would not buy a calendar because he was afraid he would not live the year. I thought it was only a story until I sat on this committee. Now I am ready to believe anything." Despite her disappointment, however, Nellie urged the council to support the resolution.[41]

Dr. Sclater, a brilliant preacher and minister of a large Toronto congregation, followed with a speech also urging council's support for the resolution. He tried to minimize the significance of the resolution, though, by pointing out that there is no bar in religion or reason to republicanism in this country, but that nobody would think of taking steps to set it up. He urged council to show the country that the United Church was truly united.[42] It was with considerable relief, one imagines, that the executive of General Council saw this resolution pass without amendment.

This, of course, was not the end of the controversy. As a member of the committee Nellie felt that she should not speak in public or in print against the resolution, but when Dr. Thomas published an article in *Chatelaine* in which he attacked Nellie McClung's speech to Council,[43] she felt freed from any restraint and replied to him on the platform and in letters to *Chatelaine* and *The New Outlook*.[44] A few years later Nellie still had to remind church members that Home Missions had reported a shortage of fifty-two men.

> The church's attitude is brutally clear. It is this. "We can't supply men for all the districts of western Canada. Children are growing up in ignorance—and it is just too bad. But even that is easier for us to bear than to have to lay aside our prejudices against women. We won't say that of course. We'll say that women could not stand the hard work. We'll say it might disrupt the church. We'll say there is no demand for women preachers. We'll be scriptural and quote Saint Paul."

Nellie dismissed with apt sarcasm the pedantic forty-one-page statement circulated by Thomas's committee to the presbyteries.

> It raked the past and explained the future. It gave the presbyteries a peep into the Canon of Hippolytus and the Ignation Epistles. It mentioned Pentadià, Silvina, Sabiniana, Olympias, and Philip's four daughters (excellent ladies, no doubt, but quite dead), yet not once did it ask the brethren what they thought should be done in the matter of ordination for Miss Lydia Gruchy.

The document, she argued, did not provide information to help the presbyteries make an informed judgement. Instead it tried to influence the decision with biased information about the committee's views. Moreover, by introducing the diaconate they clouded the issue, which should have been clearly and simply: "Are you in favour of ordaining women, yes or no?"[45] She particularly resented Dr. Thomas's reference to the woman preacher's sex appeal.

> He sees in the woman preacher not the theologian, not the exhorter, nor the prophetess. No, no, he sees only this—the "Woman Temptress" . . . Dr. Thomas, the great expositer of doctrine, the encyclopedia of church history, who can dash off a brilliant essay while another

man would be thinking of the opening sentence. Dr. Thomas whom we think of as a great mind, not subject to human frailties, thinks of even a woman preacher as a "temptress" stirring up mixed emotions in her audience. Dear me. How surprising.[46]

In December 1928, two months after General Council, a public debate was held in Central Church, Calgary, and later repeated in Macdougall Church, Edmonton, on this subject: "Resolved that the United Church of Canada should grant ordination to women on the same basis as men." The affirmative was upheld by Nellie McClung and the negative by the Reverend W.A. Lewis, of Calgary. On both occasions large crowds attended. Mark McClung remembers this debate as the first time he really saw his mother in action on the platform. He vividly recalls how she dominated the debate and captivated the audience—speaking with her hands, her body, her eyes moving up and down the platform—pointing an accusing finger at her innocent opponent. "I knew she'd prepared herself as she prepared me for debates. But not a note, not a hesitation in speech, and the flow of words and the gestures and her eyes going around all the time. She really was a magnetic speaker."[47] As usual there was wit and humour in such remarks as: "It is about time we got rid of this old-fashioned idea that we are a sort of glorified Ladies Aid with the great work in life of pushing some man up the ladder." Lewis brought forth the well-worn argument of women's inability to face the hardships and difficulties of a rural charge with an attempt at a humorous picture of a woman preacher in her Sunday best trying to free her horse from a slough. Nellie demolished this picture with the observation that a woman would have sense enough to be carrying her "Sunday best" in a bag and be wearing suitable clothes for a dirty ride across the prairies. Lewis was no match for Nellie McClung in argument or witty rebuttal. The judge awarded her victory on both occasions.[48]

When the Judicial Committee of the Privy Council declared, in 1929, that women were eligible for Senate seats, Nellie used the occasion in a radio speech to remind listeners of the hurdles still to be overcome, including, among others, the right to be ordained. "It is a matter of humiliation," she stated,

> that the church has been the last to yield to women full rights and I believe the women themselves are to blame for that. One of the leaders in the women's work of the church defended her position

that women must not be ordained by saying that women must first "prove their place in the church." That shows how poverty-stricken she was for an argument.[49]

Throughout the controversy Nellie was more indignant with those women who opposed ordination than she was with the men. She was particularly disappointed with the lack of support from the Woman's Missionary Society, whose president had betrayed the women with her comment at the 1928 Council: "You have not asked us what we [the WMS] think of the ordination of women—and it is just as well. You will find us very conservative." On hearing these words, Nellie looked with consternation at one of the older ministers who supported ordination. Eloquently, he drew his finger across his throat. "How the men who opposed ordination loved her for her few words," Nellie McClung wrote later. "The man who reported that day's proceedings for *The New Outlook* spoke glowingly of her—how feminine and attractive she was, and how becomingly dressed." Her idle words, Nellie believed, set ordination back ten years.[50]

The controversy continued. In the years after the disappointing 1928 resolution Nellie never missed an opportunity to criticize the United Church for failure to act. In an article in *The Country Guide* after women's right to sit in the Senate had been confirmed, Nellie wrote:

> We cannot understand the mentality of men who dare to set the boundaries of women's work. We object to barriers, just as the range horses despise fences . . . now with the Senate doors open there are only the two great institutions that will not accept women on equal terms—the church and the beer parlours.[51]

Despite continued efforts by many in the church and particularly by the Saskatchewan Conference, the years passed and no further steps were taken. Finally, the secretary of the Saskatchewan Conference was instructed to notify the General Council that it intended to ordain Lydia Gruchy at its next conference, in 1935, "unless at its meeting in September 1934 objection thereto is made by the General Council." This bold stand was strengthened by an assertion of the conference's "rights of determining whom it should ordain" and a request that "no obstacle" be placed in the way of her ordination.[52] As a result of this a new attempt was made by council to obtain the opinion of the church as a whole, this time using the method Nellie McClung had suggested in 1926. The presbyteries were simply asked whether they approved of the ordination of women, and were instructed to answer "yes" or "no" without qualification. Significantly, the resolution that the question be remitted to presbyteries was moved by the Reverend H.E. Oliver of St. Andrew's College, who had encouraged Lydia Gruchy to study theology, to accept a parish, and to seek ordination.[53]

The economic picture had changed substantially since 1928. Many of the old charges in western Canada were now unable to support themselves, to establish new ones seemed almost impossible. The employment of women as ministers was perceived as a threat to men's jobs. While recognizing the economic difficulties faced by the church, Nellie McClung felt that this should not affect the equality of men and women.[54] The majority of presbyteries agreed with her. When the remits came back, the vote was seventy-nine for ordination of women, twenty-six against.[55] Appropriately, in 1936 Lydia Gruchy became the first ordained woman minister in the United Church of Canada.[56] Sadly, Dr. Oliver had died the previous year, not living to see the outcome of this long battle.

Dr. Ernest Thomas took to print again in an article smugly entitled "Ladies—We Give You the Pulpit!" He grudgingly accepted the accomplished fact but still saw difficulties. With a certain condescension he pointed out the areas of the ministry that would be best suited to women: "the guiding power in training schools for women workers in the church, in Christian education, missionary work, or girls' home work, home visitations and the care and oversight of children." He found it sarcastically amusing to contemplate that the Pension Fund might have to be amended to read "minister's widower" instead of "minister's widow," and he facetiously wondered whether the woman minister would give the wedding fees to her husband.[57]

Nellie McClung, by this time a resident of Victoria, summed up her feelings on the matter in an article entitled "The Long Road to Freedom."

> It is a long time since Erasmus in a burst of enthusiasm said he would wish that even women might read the gospels, but it has taken the full 500 years to convince the brethren and fathers of the church that women have the same ability to understand the scripture as men,

and the end is not yet. The United Church of Canada took ten years to make up its mind whether or not it could allow a woman to be ordained in its ministry. Only one application for ordination has been before the Council all these ten years. Miss Lydia Gruchy has a perfect record of eleven years in country service. Now she is to be ordained. So the United Church has at last endorsed what Saint Paul said more than eighteen hundred years ago, that there is no male or female, bond or free, but all are one in the service of God.[58]

Like the fight for women's suffrage, the battle for the ordination of women, especially in the United Church of Canada, was a long and difficult battle. As usual, Nellie McClung was one of the most active leaders in this fight against the oppression of women and their legitimate ambitions. She used her speeches, public debates, and her writing to argue her case. Though the institutional church played a central role in her life and thinking, she found it narrow-minded in its opposition to female clergy. The church, which ought to have been a leader in the struggle to empower women, lagged behind the political arena, where women had the right to vote and sit in the Senate. In Nellie's mind, the ordination of women was not only an egalitarian step forward in the battle for the rights of women, it was a rational move against the patriarchal view that only men knew what women wanted and what their limited capabilities were, and, of course, what was best for them. The opponents of women ministers rigorously adhered to the traditional notion that only men had the right, the intelligence, and the stamina to be ordained clergy, in spite of the fact that qualified women like Lydia Gruchy successfully served a three-point rural charge. Nellie accused those who opposed female ordination of sex prejudice, and in her usual rational, witty, and down-to-earth manner demolished the elaborate and irrelevant theological arguments of the traditionalists with practical common sense and a claim for the justice of the cause. Frequently she reduced the arguments of her opponents to the level of the absurd in her inimitable satiric style. Over the years the issue raised much heated debate, and no doubt Nellie could say, as she did of the suffrage fight, that it was a "bonny, knock-down fight," and one that for at least ten years exhilarated her.

9

Living in Alberta: 1914–1932

❖

Before Union, while the fight for the rights of women in the Methodist Church was in progress, another major battle over the equality of women had commenced, this time in the sphere of the federal government. Many of the women who had sought the vote believed that women's political equality should be recognized by the appointment of a woman to the Senate. There was, of course, a question as to whether women were eligible for Senate seats, but the newly enfranchised group chose at first to assume that no such question existed. Emily Murphy was, from the first, the leader of this campaign but Nellie McClung was a willing and enthusiastic participant. When a Women's Institute was established in Edmonton, Nellie was its first president and worked with Murphy and Maude McIsaac to form the Federated Women's Institutes of Canada, of which Murphy became president in 1919. Nellie was put in charge of publicity. That body, at its first conference, unanimously endorsed a resolution requesting that Prime Minister Borden appoint a woman senator.

Borden took the stand that women were not eligible for Senate seats because the authors of the *British North America Act* had clearly intended to refer to men only when speaking of calling "persons" to be senators.[1] Not to be deterred, Nellie McClung and others made the same request of Meighen when he replaced Borden but he, too, expressed the view that women were not eligible. The *British North America Act,* he said, would have to be amended in order to appoint a woman senator. Many women, including Nellie, believed not only that a woman should be appointed, but that that woman should be Judge Emily Murphy. By pressing for a specific appointment they

207

could stress her obvious qualifications for the position and ignore, at least on paper, any constitutional barrier.

When Mackenzie King became prime minister in 1921, Nellie wasted no time in letting him know her views on the Senate issue. She wrote to him on 30 December 1921: "I want to send you my good wishes and sincere congratulations and I also wish to respectfully draw your attention to the fact that there are no women in the Upper House and that I think it is about time there were." She went on to recommend Emily Murphy and assure King that this would be a popular appointment. Since this letter received no response other than formal acknowledgement from a secretary, she wrote again in February. Again her letter went unanswered until, over a year later, King replied along the same lines as Meighen, that no appointment could be made until the *British North America Act* was amended. The resolution to begin this process should, he believed, originate in the Senate.

In November of 1925 Nellie McClung again wrote to King. Though it was a very critical period for King and the Liberal Party, having just survived an election many Canadians felt should have been accepted as a defeat, Nellie could not resist repeating her plea:

> We regret the passing of Senator Sir James Lougheed. He was well respected in his own city. Rumors are floating about as to who shall be his successor. It would be a wonderful triumph for the belief that we have held in Liberal fairness to women if Mrs. Murphy should be appointed. Forty thousand women have, thro' their Societies, asked for her. Don't ignore them.

King did not delay in replying to this letter, but he made no commitment.[2] In fact there was no chance that King would take such a controversial step at this time. The Progressives, on whom he had to depend for support if he was to govern at all, were opposed to the Senate in principle. The Senate "reform" they advocated was to transform it into an elected body or to abolish it entirely. Emily Murphy found it encouraging that King did not mention the need for constitutional amendment this time but, in fact, he had no intention of doing anything.

Meanwhile, the women of Canada continued to raise the issue at every opportunity. In 1926 Nellie McClung was angered by the Senate's rejection of the old age pension legislation. Speaking to a group of women in Alberta she said:

It is high time to get new blood into the moribund body, the
Canadian Senate . . . The old men lack imagination. They are well
fed, well cared for old men, secure in their positions, and cannot
imagine that some others are haunted every day by the grim spectre
of want . . . If we have a woman there, like our Mrs. Murphy, I doubt
if the care of our old people would have been so summarily dismissed. And we *can* have women there if we stand together.[3]

Nellie, of course, knew that the presence of one woman in the
Senate would make little difference to the voting pattern of that
body. The first appointment, however, was important both to prove
that a woman could be appointed, and to begin a reform process in
the Senate through the appointment of persons—male or female—
who sought to serve their country rather than be provided with a
comfortable sinecure for their old age.

It became increasingly clear that the government intended to take
no action. A constitutional conference, which discussed various
proposals to reform the upper house, did not mention the issue of
women's eligibility. Even if someone could be persuaded to begin the
amending process it was probable that it would soon bog down for
there was no agreed upon method of amendment and the question
of provincial rights would certainly be raised. The premier of Ontario, the Honourable H. Ferguson, declared that he wanted no
tampering with the *BNA Act* and "if such drastic action must be taken
before the Red Chamber opens its gilded doors to women, he would
favour them [the doors] being reserved as at present for a men's
own."[4] Since women in Québec still did not have the provincial
franchise, it was clear that Québec politicians would be unlikely to
support any move toward such an amendment.

Fortunately for Emily Murphy's peace of mind, her brother recommended another route. A clause in the *Supreme Court Act* stated that
"five interested persons" could ask for an interpretation of any part of
the *BNA Act*. If such a petition was accepted, all expenses would be
paid by the government. Murphy decided to take this action, and
Nellie McClung was more than willing to add her name to the petition.
Three other prominent Alberta women were approached, enthusiastically approved of the idea, and added their names: Irene Parlby,
Louise McKinney, and Henrietta Muir Edwards.[5]

The government accepted the petition but did not accept the
complicated set of questions Murphy had drawn up to accompany it.

She wished to cover all bases by having the Supreme Court declare what steps could be taken to amend the *BNA Act* if there were a negative answer to the first question: "Is power vested in the Governor General of Canada, or the Parliament of Canada, or either of them to appoint a female to the Senate of Canada?" Even this question was unacceptable because the Parliament of Canada had no part in Senate appointments. The other questions, they argued, were irrelevant and incorrectly worded. As the Department of Justice wisely pointed out, there was only one question at issue, and it was simply: "Does the word 'Person' in section 24 of the British North America Act, 1867, include female persons?" Murphy was unhappy with this simplified version of the petition but after some protest, agreed.[6] The petitioners chose Newton Rowell, a well-known Toronto lawyer and former leader of the Ontario Liberal government who had supported women's suffrage, to plead the case before the Supreme Court. He was supported by the attorney general of Alberta, and opposed by the solicitor general of Canada, the Honourable Lucien Caron, and by Charles Lanctot, representing the provincial government of Québec.

There was some dismay in the ranks of national women's organizations that Emily Murphy had gone ahead without consulting anyone. Murphy wrote to McClung: "I hear . . . that it has been a terrible shock to the Eastern women that five coal heavers and plough pushers from Alberta went over their heads to the Supreme Court without even saying: 'Please ma'am can we do it?'"[7]

The case was heard by the Supreme Court in March 1928. Rowell argued that the word "persons" was inclusive of women as well as men, that the only word defining "persons" in the clause was the word "qualified," and that the qualifications listed could apply to women as well as to men. This simple argument was, of course, fully supported by lengthy explanations and precedents. The argument presented by the Crown was six times as long. They had many precedents to quote, for the question had risen many times in England—including Viscountess Rhondda's unsuccessful attempt in 1922 to be admitted to the House of Lords. Their final argument, however, rested upon the claim that the men who drew up the *BNA Act* did not intend women to sit in the Senate. The solicitor general even suggested that if they had so intended, they would have referred to senators and senatresses![8]

On 24 April 1928, Chief Justice Anglin handed down his opinion. He concluded that the *BNA Act* must be interpreted precisely as it was intended in the period when the act was passed, and since women held no public office of any kind in Canada in 1867, the Fathers of Confederation could have had no intention of including women among the persons to be summoned to the Senate.[9] This decision had more to do with the Supreme Court's desire to protect the *BNA Act* from liberal interpretation than it did with any decision about women's rights. The negative reply was a great disappointment to the petitioners, and the Honourable Ernest Lapointe's statement that the government would take steps to have the *BNA Act* amended did little to impress them.

Murphy decided, and the other four petitioners agreed, that the next step should be to appeal the decision of the Supreme Court to the Judicial Committee of the Privy Council in England. Again, the government paid the expenses and Newton Rowell agreed to plead the case. Counsel for the Crown was Eugene Lafleur.[10] The case was heard at No. 1 Downing Street for four days, from 22 July to 25 July 1929. The arguments did not differ greatly from those presented to the Supreme Court of Canada the previous year. On 18 October 1929, the lord chancellor, Lord Sankey, read his judgement in full, although it had become customary to read only a summary of JCPC decisions.

The *BNA Act*, he said, was "planted in Canada, a living tree capable of growth and expansion within its natural limits." The JCPC did not wish to take a narrow, technical view of the act but to give it a liberal interpretation. He pointed out that they were not deciding any questions as to the rights of women, but only their eligibility for a certain position. After reviewing the wording of various sections of the act, their lordships had noted: that the word "member" is not in ordinary English confined to male persons, and if Parliament had intended to limit the word in section 21 referring to members of the Senate, it would surely have made this clear; that the word "person" is ambiguous and may refer to members of either sex; that there are sections of the act that use the word "person" to include female persons—for example, in section 133, which says that any "person" may use English or French in the courts of Canada; that in some clauses the adjective "male" is used to modify "person." Lord Sankey concluded:

> Having regard finally to the provisions of the Interpretation Act of 1889 their lordships have come to the conclusion that the word "persons" includes members of the male and female sex and that therefore the questions propounded by the governor-general must be answered in the affirmative and that women are eligible to be summoned and become members of the Senate of Canada.[11]

The implications of this remarkably objective decision would exert tremendous force on the public position of women throughout the British Empire.[12]

The women who had worked so long for this result were exuberant. Nellie McClung, speaking to a women's group shortly after, declared: "Ladies, hang Lord Sankey's picture on the wall of the Community Rest Room with Newton Wesley Rowell's beside it, and let these names and the names of the other Lords of the Judicial Committee of the Privy Council be kept in perpetual and grateful rememberance, Lord Darling, Lord Merrivale, Lord Tomlin, and Sir Lancelot Sanderson."[13] There was a tendency to ignore Lord Sankey's statement that the court was deciding only whether the government of Canada had the right to summon women to the Senate. They were making no comment on women's rights or on whether the government should summon women. Perhaps with some frivolous intent newspapers carried headlines reading "Women Declared Persons," but Canadian women were amused by the headlines for, as one said, "we've known we were persons all along."[14] Agnes Macphail, member of the House of Commons and with the Progressives' contempt for the Senate, remarked drily that she was glad the women had won, but she did not know why any woman would want to sit in that out-of-date institution.[15]

There was little disapproval of the decision in Canada's newspapers, but there were the usual warnings to women not to expect too much—the fact that women were declared eligible did not mean that the appointments to the Senate would follow. The editor of the Vegreville *Observer*, in fact, thought it was a hollow victory.[16] Nellie McClung had high hopes that Murphy would be appointed. Murphy worried for fear some limit would be placed on the number of appointments—perhaps only one woman for each region. Both were overly optimistic. A woman was appointed to the Senate in 1930 but she was not one of those who had fought for women's rights. Cairine Wilson, the first woman senator, was a staunch Liberal who was unlikely to cause any ripple on the placid waters of the Senate. While King was probably wary of Murphy's Conservative family background, he was undoubtedly much more concerned that she would be a controversial and disturbing presence in the Senate. Nellie McClung had the necessary Liberal association but she, too, would be prepared to rock the Senate boat if she thought it necessary. Also, her independence of party, established in her years as an MLA, would not have helped. One editor expressed his approval of Wilson's appointment in words that read, unintentionally, like a scathing indictment:

> A lady of retiring disposition, of refinement and culture, Senator Wilson's interest in public affairs has never been tinged with the desire for personal recognition or advancement: it had little appeal for a lady of her station, and she took no part in the agitation for the recognition of women's right to sit in the Senate. That right having been conceded it is eminently fitting that she should be the first appointee rather than one of the very industrious women politicians, spinsters, and others, who have talked incessantly of their rights as women without discharging any of their responsibilities as such.

This editor had curious ideas about the qualifications of women senators, ones he did not extend to their male counterparts.

> She has never permitted her political interests to interfere with those other, and perhaps greater, responsibilities of citizenship, her duties as a wife and mother. Her eight children have been carefully reared and guided; their home life has been sheltered and secure, and in their upbringing the new Senator has rendered a real and substantial service to the state to whose councils she has now been called.[17]

Although disappointed and annoyed at the appointment, Emily Murphy was amused at the editor's obvious satisfaction that the appointment had not gone to one of the petitioners: "Ah well," she wrote to Nellie McClung, "no one loves us now. It's nothing for us but the 'garden' and 'worms.'"[18] Nellie was amused, too, at an anonymous letter she received: "Read your article re Argument of Persons. Admire your pluck but not your spirit. In thought, action and view you belong to the species of men closer than you do to women. The whole five of you. I seen your pictures." "The gentleman," Nellie quipped, "is probably no beauty either ... but that did not prevent him from passing judgement on us and reproving us for what he considers lack of feminine charm. To say that a woman is not beautiful has been considered damaging evidence against her and quite sufficient to offset her arguments." While she believed that the right reply was that they scarcely cared whether he liked their looks, she felt obliged to point out that when the Women's Canadian Club of Calgary entertained the Alberta five: "I was quite proud of my four associates . . . and I think from the enthusiastic reception given them they found favour in the eyes of the 300 women who were there to do them honor."[19]

The hope remained that Emily Murphy would get the first Alberta Senate vacancy especially considering it occurred in 1931 with a Conservative administration in Ottawa and a prime minister, R.B. Bennett, from Alberta. This time the excuse was that a Roman Catholic must be appointed to replace a Catholic.[20] Murphy resigned herself to the fact that she was not to be a senator. Over the years individuals and societies continued to put forward Nellie McClung's name, but in vain. Only one more woman was appointed during Nellie's lifetime.

As well as fighting, in the 1920s, for major recognition for women in church and state Nellie McClung was also concerned that women should recognize and try to combat less obvious inequalities. Women, for example, could take any degree at university but there were still some courses considered a male preserve. There was a general belief that women went to college to get a man, not an education, and in 1926, a man could still find a publisher willing to print his views on women attending university. In one male writer's opinion, women kept men out by taking up the young men's rightful place. If women married their education was wasted, and if they did not then the country lost good breeders: "All these girls are somewhat above the average in brains and ability. How many of these hundreds who have not married are lost to the improvement of the Canadian stock as a result of their education?"[21] When jobs became scarce in the early twenties, and when severe depression struck after 1929, women were expected to give up their work. Women, it was thought, didn't have to work—it was an indulgence, a whim. Nellie was anxious that women should not accept this argument, and she spoke frequently on every woman's right to work. She dealt ironically with attitudes toward women in an article "I'll Never Tell My Age Again!" It was a crime, she declared, for women to age. This was evidence that women in business were still thought of as a decoration. "It is no wonder that women both matrimonially and industrially look upon age as an incurable disease." As usual she was optimistic, though, and thought that the atmosphere was changing. Heroines in current books were not always beautiful, she pointed out, and female athletics had made durability and strength desirable qualities in women.[22] In another article, "Our Present Discontents," Nellie discussed what women still had to achieve. In it she collected a number of negative pronouncements about women written by men who ranged from the author of *The Apocalypse*, Rousseau, and Dr. Gregory (author of the obnoxious *A Father's Legacy to His Daughter*), to modern novelists such as Dickens, W.D. Howells, and Henry James, to show that the old prejudices were still alive and that "our literature is loaded so heavily against us."[23] Even on the local Calgary scene, she pointed out, women who successfully operated their own businesses were not eligible to be members of the Board of Trade.[24]

While Nellie perceived the 1920s as a period of transition, she saw the move toward real equality as necessarily slow: "Sex prejudice and the male superiority complex, built up since time began, will not go out in one generation."[25] On the other hand, she also argued that women themselves were partly to blame for they still did not consider themselves equals and did not act as equals. "The world (meaning the men of the world)," she chided, "are disposed to accept us at our own rating . . . " She still longed for the day when a woman was accepted as a person so that if she failed, it was a personal failure, not a failure of women in general. Nellie McClung summed up her feelings and her hopes in 1929 in these words: "We may yet live to see the day when women will be no longer news. And it cannot come too soon. I want to be a peaceful, happy, normal human being pursuing my unimpeded way through life, never having to stop to explain, defend or apologize for my sex."[26]

By the time the McClungs moved to Calgary only the two youngest boys were at home. Jack, having finished his degree at the University of Alberta, had gone to Oxford to pursue graduate work. Florence had married Hugh Atkinson and was living in Regina. Paul, who was never much interested in school subjects and apparently found it difficult to settle down to school routine, left home as soon as he was old enough to be on his own. He went to Texas where, after a few years, he married and became established as a car salesman. He did not, like many boys who leave home young and go far away, lose touch with his family. In 1925 and again in 1934, Wes and Nellie had happy visits to his home in Tyler, Texas, and got to know their grandchildren, Robert and Maxine. In 1924 Horace and Mark were still in school. Horace was not a scholar and found school work difficult, but Mark was following in brother Jack's footsteps with a brilliant scholastic record. He was a keen debater, well-coached by his mother.[27]

The Calgary home—at 1501 7th Street West—was a centre for activities of all kinds. The living room was large enough to accommodate meetings of the various societies to which Nellie belonged, and it seems that almost every visiting celebrity—churchman, author, politician, lecturer—was given a reception at the McClung home. On several occasions it also provided the setting for a wedding: of relatives, at least one of the McClung maids, and a young Calgary friend who was far from home. The McClung dinner table had frequent guests ranging from famous persons to shy girls from the country whom Nellie had met at the Good Cheer Club. Nellie had the knack of making everyone feel at ease. She had the same effect on guest speakers whom she introduced. Agnes Macphail reported after her visit to Calgary in 1931: "Often when someone has been greatly praised all our expectations are not fulfilled. But Nellie McClung was just what I expected her to be. Her presence . . . made speaking easier. Her warm sympathy could not but help. I liked her immensely and oddly enough felt that I had known her always." Macphail was also impressed with Wes and glad of the opportunity to talk to him in his home. "We do not hear so much about him," she said, "but he is worth hearing a good deal about . . . He is a man of substance financially, mentally and physically . . . he is very proud of his wife's achievements."[28]

Nellie McClung could not have entertained so often if she had not had loyal and efficient help in the house. She did very little, if any, housework or cooking in these years. Reading, writing, entertaining, and participating in many organizations provided full-time occupation. The so-called servant problem was a subject of much discussion in the 1920s, but Nellie experienced few problems due to her wisdom in choosing, and the fair treatment of, her domestic help.[29] Nellie and others argued that the problem resulted from the way maids were treated. Often they were made to feel inferior. They were always expected to use the back door and if allowed to entertain at all had only the kitchen in which to receive friends. Free time was only grudgingly allowed, like a favour conferred, and maids were expected to be on duty all the time—idle moments during the day were considered by the mistress a waste of time. If domestics were treated well, Nellie thought, some would prefer domestic work over factory work.

Dating back to the time Nellie lived in Winnipeg at the turn of the century, those feminists with whom she associated concentrated on the conditions of domestic service in various periodical articles they wrote. "The grievances of Manitoba domestics received greatest newspaper publicity in the years immediately before World War I as Winnipeg journalists active in the women's movement welcomed to their columns correspondence discussing women's issues and problems . . . Information came from letters written to the women's page editors by both domestics and their employers." In 1909 some of the most animated discussions were found in Lillian Beynon Thomas's correspondence section of the *Free Press*. The writings revealed cases of "mistreatment," of "inadequate accommodation," and "overwork."[30] McClung, along with her fellow reformists, sought to alleviate these abuses, and they looked to their own households first.

Many of the maids who worked for the McClungs in Calgary were immigrants. Today this raises the spectre of exploitation, and even in the 1920s Nellie knew that many domestics were taken advantage of by unscrupulous employers. She tells of one maid who, dismissed with pay owing, was unable to collect until a woman Nellie describes as a fiery Scotswoman from the Clyde appeared at the employer's door with a policeman.[31] In fact the policeman was off duty, but the ruse worked and Mareska got her money. Nellie also despised the hypocrisy of those women who wanted credit for helping immigrant girls when their only interest was obtaining domestic help. She illustrated this in a long ironic verse satirically called "Standards."[32] In her short story "The Girl from God Knows Where," Nellie again condemned the treatment of an immigrant maid in an ordinary family where thoughtlessness rather than deliberate cruelty was to blame.[33] Unfortunately conditions for most domestic workers had improved very little by the 1930s.

Since Nellie did little cooking or housekeeping, her domestic help cleaned house, waited on the boys and Wes, washed and ironed, and prepared the meals. The McClungs did not pay higher wages than other employers—fifteen to twenty-five dollars a month in the early thirties. The difference, Nellie believed, was in the way her "girls" were treated in the home. She fully appreciated their services and let them know that she did. The women were not frustrated by petty restrictions and they realized that the McClungs were interested in them as persons. They were encouraged to have a private life and to further their education if they wished to do so. If their knowledge of English was weak, Nellie taught them the language herself. In addition, Nellie's motherly concern led her to take an interest in knowing "how my girls were spending their leisure time." Some women might have resented an employer's interest in their private lives, might have felt that it was patronizing and interfering, but the general concern for their well-being that Nellie conveyed seems to have appealed to the young women who worked for her. Nellie made sure her "girls" never felt demeaned by their domestic work. She

> made their friends welcome and did not expect that the friends should be entertained in the kitchen either. It is good for a girl's morale to have the use of a den or some other pleasant room where she can forget the washing of dishes or the peeling of potatoes; and I would not expect my girls to go around by the back door when a young man brought them home. They had their own key to the front door and there was always a verandah light burning for them when they were out and they knew they were always welcome to bring their friend in for a cup of coffee. Little privileges like this help a girl to know that she is a person of importance with the protection and dignity of a family and a home.[34]

At least once a year Nellie's domestics were encouraged to give a party for their friends in the McClung home. The living-room rugs were rolled up for the young people to dance, and many of their national dishes were prepared for the occasion. Nellie particularly remembered the Swedish parties: "How the house rang with laughter and song and the dining-room table was replete with braided cardamon bread, pineapple cake, pickled fish, which was eaten with rye bread"—a typical Scandinavian "smorgasbord." On such occasions Nellie and Wes "were on hand to welcome the guests, but when that duty was performed we faded away and left them to their fun. And never once was this privilege abused."[35]

Two of the McClungs' maids in Calgary were sisters from Norway—Randi and Astrid. Randi remembers her life with the McClungs as a very happy experience. She had been living in Canada for several years when a Swedish girl who was leaving the McClungs in order to try factory work suggested that Randi apply. Because of an unfortunate experience with her previous employer Randi had no letter of recommendation, but Nellie talked with her and then said: "Well, I will take you on your face." Her "association with the girls from Europe," Nellie once recorded, "gave me a chance to know something of the minds of their employers and some of this knowledge was painful, but revealing."[36] Randi says that being hired by Nellie McClung was her lucky day. After a few months, Randi's sister decided to come to Canada and Nellie employed her too. In those Depression days, Randi explains, a girl felt lucky to have a job at all, but she still feels that "no one else had it so good—we could feel so at home." In many ways they felt like members of the family. They did not eat with the family but did not resent this—it seemed natural. That was the McClungs time to be together and, Randi says, "It suited us. It was handy." They did not wear uniforms, or have to use the back door, or eat food different from the family. They could help themselves and offer their friends a snack when they came to visit. Nellie called them "her girls," a term they saw as loving, not patronizing. "Lots of times," Randi remembers, "Mrs. McClung would bring some of her guests out into the kitchen and she would say 'I want you to meet my girls, and some of them were so friendly and nice and other ones you could just see were thinking 'My goodness. Taking us out to the kitchen to say hello to the girl!' But that was the way Mrs. McClung was."

The McClung household Randi describes was a busy, happy place. "Mr. McClung," she says, "had a quick temper. He had to have it out and then it was so nice. She had her own ways of handling her husband. I guess she had a great understanding of her family." Wes was just as kind to the maids as Nellie was. "We had such fun with him—my sister and I. He was like a kid as well as a grown person." Horace, too, was fun and considerate—having difficulty finding a job during the Depression, but working sometimes for the Hudson's Bay Company. Mark was by then a senior high school student whom Randi remembers as quiet and "busy studying." During the Depression, Randi recalls there was a steady stream of men at the door looking for a meal for there was always a pot of soup on the stove or meat and potatoes. No one was turned away. Nellie, with her interest in people and always alert to the possibility of a story, would talk to the men while Randi got a plate of food ready. Wes, meantime, came to believe that Nellie was being too soft. Why should the McClungs feed everyone? The next time the doorbell rang, he said he would answer. "And he did," Randi chuckles, "and you could hear him say, 'Why do you all come to Calgary? We have hard times here too.' But after a while 'Come on in' and they got the soup just the same." Randi remembers most vividly that she felt loved and appreciated and trusted by the McClungs.[37]

Nellie McClung was also fortunate, while in Calgary, to obtain the services of a young woman who chose to combine the work of secretary with any other jobs that needed to be done. Winnie Fudger was a Newfoundlander who had come to Alberta a few years before and taken a business course. On graduation she obtained a position with Laura Salverson—author of *The Viking Heart* (1923) and the autobiographical *Confessions of an Immigrant's Daughter* (1939)—who was a frequent visitor to the McClung home, often accompanied by Winnie. When the Salversons decided to move to Toronto, Nellie asked Winnie to come work for her. Winnie found the McClung household very different, and she missed the close friendship that she and Laura Salverson had developed. She felt that she worked *with* Salverson but *for* McClung. Typically her days were long. There was a great deal of typing—of short stories, speeches, and letters, but she also chose to help out with preparations for visitors, sometimes took over in the kitchen on the maid's half-day off, and pitched in to do the ironing because the boys thought "she ironed their shirts just right." When Nellie went on a speaking tour, Winnie took over as a house-keeper.

Both Randi and Winnie stress that the McClung family was an exuberantly happy one, with close family ties. Winnie says:

> Her children . . . were wonderful to her, and she was marvelous to them. I can see her now when she'd hear the front door open . . . it didn't matter when those boys came in—from school or from work or wherever . . . she'd run half way down those stairs, and they'd run up: "Hello, mother dear," and they'd embrace each other. I don't think they ever failed to do that. I used to think it was so nice to see—her two sons.[38]

Randi remembers, too, that Wes would always call out "Nellie!" when he came in, and from wherever she was, would come the answering call "Wes!" When Nellie was going to be away from home, she'd tell the girls to see him off every morning and wave goodbye just as she always did.[39]

Although much of Nellie McClung's time from 1921–1926 was necessarily taken up by her legislative activities, she continued to write. While she was an MLA she wrote the novelette *When Christmas Crossed the Peace* (1923), as well as her best, and last, full-length novel, *Painted Fires* (1925), the story of a Finnish immigrant girl. The nonsocialist Finnish people in North America saw this as a very sympathetic book and welcomed it.[40] It was translated and appeared in Finnish newspapers in serial form in the United States, and in 1927 was published as a book in Finland. Because of difficulties over royalty payments from Finland, Nellie received two pictures by Finnish artists as her only compensation, but she treasured the pictures and was pleased that her book had won acceptance among the Finnish people.[41] She also wrote an editorial each month for the *Western Home Monthly*, and published short stories and articles in *Maclean's*. For Nellie, writing had always been an activity that had to be fitted in to a busy schedule, and probably she had as much free time during these years as she had in Manitou when her children were small. She could still say, quite truthfully, "When no one comes to see me and the phone is not ringing and the children are at school and there is nothing in particular to do, I write."[42]

Two organizations in which Nellie McClung was active in the Edmonton–Calgary years broadened and strengthened her literary interests. From its inception, in 1921, she was—like most members of the CWPC—vitally interested in the Canadian Authors Association and immediately worked to establish an Alberta branch. Nellie arranged for an inaugural meeting in Edmonton in April 1921, at which the president of the CAA, J.M. Gibbon, was to be present.[43] With his assistance Nellie formed an Alberta branch that, within a year, was large enough to split into Edmonton and Calgary branches. Subsequently, she was active in the Calgary branch, becoming its president in 1925.[44]

The CAA's annual national convention, which Nellie attended regularly, brought her into contact with most of Canada's writers. During these years she was an active member of the CAA, both locally and nationally, frequently serving as a regional vice-president or councillor-at-large. At the 1925 convention in Winnipeg Nellie was appointed to the Resolutions Committee. She seconded two important resolutions:

one, put forth by John Murray Gibbon, urged the Canadian government to publicize a private report on the Copyright Bill so that parliamentary debate on the issue could resume; the other, moved by Robert Watson, urged the American and British authors associations to work to remove foreign income tax imposed on Canadian authors who published in those countries. Neither British nor American writers publishing in Canada were subject to Canadian income tax. At the same convention Nellie was asked to give a brief speech at a public literary session. A sketch from the Manitoba *Free Press* reported in *The Authors' Bulletin* says:

> Nellie McClung came home. She says so and the audience believes her. Same beautiful voice, same cadences, same flavor of dramatic instinct, same rollicking wit. "Wild men of the west and wise men of the east"—the dear old soul in Ontario who "had three children living and two out west"—Mrs. McClung's audience grins with her, chuckles, agrees with her that authors who can contribute to "Canadians all" have the gift of life for Canada. Nellie McClung, born with the gift of laughter and the sense that the world is a little mad, a little kind, a little cruel—made up of human beings.[45]

At the same convention Nellie contributed briefly to Frederick Philip Grove's address on "Realism in Canadian Literature." While she could have agreed with only a few of Grove's comments, she practised as much "realism" as she could in the Sam Motherwells, the Eva St. Johns, and the Wymuths of her fiction. Unlike Grove, Nellie McClung would be constitutionally unable to "agree with all sides" in a fictionally dramatized moral conflict, and would have found Grove's sense of "tragic necessity" temperamentally and intellectually alien to her character and beliefs. Against Grove's concept of "true realism," then, Nellie McClung argued that "the greatest thing an author can do is to teach human beings self-expression—without which life is changed from a well-rivered landscape into a pestilential swamp." Her reformist, and unabashedly "didactic," impulse led McClung to emphasize man's capacity to improve himself and change his environment for the better. In 1931 she was invited to deliver one of the CAA series of talks on regional literature, dealing with Alberta authors. She decried "the visiting impressionist" who spends a brief day passing through the West but claims "to see more than we do." She suggested that themes for western Canadian writing could be found in the "miserable impulse" that some Canadians bore toward immigrants to Canada, and in the work that missionaries of all faiths were contributing to the quality of life in wilderness areas. She harshly condemned those who wrote about foreigners and native Indians from a stereotypical position merely because they were thought to be quaintly superstitious or crafty or combative. She believed that

> to exploit the weakness of any people, to paint a dark and unrelieved picture, with no hope or gleam of light, is a poor ambition for any writer. Writing is a gift, and as a gift, should be held sacred and inviolate. A writer should feel himself to be one of the forces that are shaping life toward beauty and understanding.

Lyn Harrington, historian of the CAA, has written that anything Nellie McClung said "with her native wit and forthrightness went down well with most audiences," and her "vigour proved a hard act to follow" for the next speaker. Occasionally Nellie was the literary guest at other CAA branch meetings, such as the Saskatchewan group in 1926 and 1928.[46]

The nationalism of the CAA appealed strongly to McClung. She knew from personal experience that many Canadian writers needed the support and encouragement that such an organization could provide. She resented the implication that the CAA was somehow mercenary and unworthy for she was aware of its efforts to get departments of education to include works by Canadian authors in school readers, and because one of the CAA's first and continuing endeavours was Canada Book Week. The aim of Canada Book Week, according to Professor W.T. Allison in 1926, was to draw the attention of Canadian people "to the fact that we have a national literature which must not be neglected . . . " For him, as for Nellie, it was an educational, rather than a commercial campaign, which could aid "the shaping of our national consciousness."[47] This effort to persuade Canadians to read Canadian books would, of course, if successful, help Canadian authors financially, but she sincerely believed that it would also help Canada become a nation. Within that Canadian context she used the association, whenever she had the opportunity, for regional promotion: to make Canada, and particularly those Canadians who lived in Ontario, aware that there was a healthy, if young, literary community in western Canada. She was convinced that the West had something unique and valuable to contribute to Canadian literature.

The Calgary branch of the CAA held frequent meetings. Some were public lectures given by noted members or guests with the aim of bringing "literary ideas, especially Canadian ones, to our community." Nellie McClung took part in one entitled "Calgary Authors and Their Books" along with Flos Jewell Williams and Laura Salverson. On another occasion Nellie "was greeted by a packed auditorium when she delivered for the first time her new lecture 'The Romance of Everyday Life.'"[48]

In addition to their public meetings, the Calgary branch met once or twice a month in members' homes to discuss what Nellie described as "more technical" matters pertaining to the craft of writing. Prepared papers and discussion took place on such topics as: "Romanticism versus Realism," "The Relation of Psychology to Literature," and "Colour and Sound Effects in the Short Story." With a practical eye turned to the writer's market, they analysed characteristics of "*The Saturday Evening Post* Story," studied the first and second prize-winning stories in a *Maclean's* contest—one of which had been won by Nellie's Winnipeg friend Lillian (Beynon) Thomas—and in 1928 they analysed the characters of Mazo de la Roche's award-winning novel, *Jalna*. The November 1926 *Authors' Bulletin* announced that Nellie McClung's short story "The Neutral Fuse," published in *Maclean's*, had "secured honorable mention in *O'Brien's Best Short Stories* (1925), an honor accorded only to two or three Canadian writers in the past," and perhaps this tribute led to the study of some of her work. In addition, the Calgary members worked to expand their philosophical background by studying works like Will Durant's *The Story of Philosophy*. This may have been their response to continued criticism that the CAA was the epitome of materialism, parochialism, and ignorance. On the other hand, the group immersed itself in Graham Wallas's *The Nature of Thought*, referred to at the CAA by noted Canadian journalist B.K. Sandwell in 1927 in support of his argument "that nations do develop a national way of thinking" and "that their literature will be of greater value to these nations, if they embody . . . these national modes of thought."[49]

Occasionally, topics for discussion at the local branch level were inspired by stimulating, and at times controversial, issues addressed at the annual conventions. These were reported on at length in *The Authors' Bulletin*, and sometimes roused considerable debate in the newspapers of the day. During this period, journalist and literary

reviewer William Arthur Deacon dealt with the principles and practice of literary criticism, a commonly felt gap on the Canadian literary
scene. The charge of "parochialism," however, was partly the result
of the CAA's emphasis on topics of national literary interest, such as:
"Literature and National Life," "Unexplored Fields of Canadian
Literature," and "Distinctively Canadian." Self-conscious literary
questions of these kinds were to be expected in that time and place.
Some have persisted to this day. Such queries fostered discussion—
pro and con—and must have acted as a much-needed stimulant in the
development of an indigenous Canadian literature. Writers, for
example, were encouraged to "stop trying to write like Americans or
Englishmen and for awhile be content to be Canadians, perhaps in
time developing a Canadian style that will be distinctive." Authors like
Nellie McClung, who began their writing career isolated from fellow
writers and the writer's market, must have been gripped by the
ferment of ideas. One western spokesman commented that "the
surprising thing is not that Prairie literature is limited, but rather that
it should exist at all."[50]

During the formative years of the CAA, Nellie McClung not only
worked on her last novel, but continued to write short stories,
sketches, and essays. It is possible, too, that the first, remarkable
volume of her autobiography, *Clearing in the West* (1935), was stimulated by addresses such as that by Ruth Holway Higgins at the CAA
conference in Calgary in 1928. Higgins complained that "our Canadian History text-books are DRY AS DUST! Yet Canadian History is full
of Drama, Romance, and the Human Interest that lies in every-day
life." She pleaded with Canadian writers:

> Take us all back, grown-ups and children too, back to the days when
> the *country* was young. Show *why* life was different then. Make history
> interesting and we'll like it. Enlightenment about the past will guide
> us in the interpretation of our future national development.

Interesting history, Higgins argued, dealt with "what Canadians in
their farms and in their shops were doing and thinking, instead of
what some English governor was writing to some English Colonial
Secretary." History, she said, "is the record of *all* the people—men
and women—great *and* small" including the pioneer woman, without whom there would be no Canadian history at all. Higgins
concluded with "a plea for books that will give us a more intimate
and more sympathetic contact with the past through interesting and

humanizing records of the lives of men and women who made our history."[51]

When Nellie McClung heard such words, it must have seemed to her that her old schoolteacher and friend, Frank Schultz, was tapping her on the shoulder. This, too, confirmed her personal experience that a "story" existed in the lives of the ordinary people in those small Manitoba towns where she had lived and taught: those real people, slightly disguised, that she had always written into her fiction. Perhaps this was the impetus that prodded her to record for posterity "that small legacy of truth" that told her own, and her family's part in the larger story of the opening up of the Canadian west in the 1880s. Certainly it is history, but written with the graphic vividness of fiction.

After her electoral defeat, Nellie McClung had time for another literary activity that fulfilled a long felt need—the serious study of great literature. The Calgary Women's Literary Club was an organization dedicated to such study, not a social club using literature as a flimsy excuse for meeting. Membership was limited to thirty-five women, and although the club had a waiting list, and Nellie's name does not appear on it, her application for membership was accepted by the executive in the fall of 1926—an indication of her literary and intellectual reputation in the community. Membership in this club involved commitment. A programme committee proposed the course of study for each succeeding year, and set up a course outline flexible enough to permit the leader of each topic to take as much time as necessary when they dealt with long or difficult works. The entire 1927–28 year, for example, was spent on Thomas Hardy's verse drama *The Dynasts* (1908), and the study of Robert Bridges's *The Testament of Beauty* (1929) was spread over the first five months of 1931. When the latter poem seemed to demand a student's familiarity with Plato's *Phaedrus*, Kantian ethics, or Essenian and Manichaean thought, the group valiantly pursued these related ideas. Attendance was rigidly monitored. Absence for more than three of the weekly meetings without a legitimate, written excuse to the secretary, constituted a breach of the rules and could result in lost membership. From 1926 through 1929 Nellie seems to have attended regularly, but when she began extensive lecture tours in 1929–30 she had to seek special dispensation so that she would not be expelled. Members were expected to read and be prepared to discuss the literature under study. Although they sought outside advice on book lists and occasionally had an outside speaker—usually from the University of Alberta English Department—the lectures were ordinarily given by the members themselves.[52] As was the case with any of Nellie McClung's activities, her family became involved. Mark remembers his father resting on the sofa during the lunch hour as Nellie read to him from *The Dynasts*.[53] The Calgary Women's Literary Club was a formidable organization. The members were eager, hard working, and made a point of being intelligently informed about the best material available on their subjects. There is little doubt that Nellie would have been even more appreciative of this kind of intellectual and literary stimulation in the formative writing years of her life.

By the spring of 1930 Nellie McClung began accepting speaking engagements and when, in 1931, she agreed to make an Ontario tour that kept her away from home for more than a month, she was unable to continue as a regular member. The club members, however, realizing how much Nellie had given for the good of others, and not wishing to lose the pleasure of her company when she was able to attend, broke their strict regulations and made her an honorary member. Despite the fact that she had been an avid reader all her life, Nellie had always felt that her limited formal education had deprived her of the opportunity to study literature. This organization and the Calgary branch of the Canadian Authors Association, then, must have given her great satisfaction.

In 1932, with Wes's retirement drawing near, Nellie and Wes decided to move to the west coast. They considered both the Okanagan Valley and Vancouver, but finally decided to settle in Victoria. As usual, many were sorry to see Nellie leave. One columnist wrote: "We are saying goodbye to the kindly, humorous, vigorous citizen who will leave behind a gap that cannot be filled."[54] Another pointed out that all of Canada shared Nellie through her writing and speaking, but "in the places where she has lived there is the additional tie of her lovable personality to deepen the affection for her." Though Nellie declared her intention "to retire"—except from writing—that sounded unconvincing to the reporter and did, indeed, prove to be impossible for anyone so energetic as Nellie L. McClung.[55]

10

Antiromantic Fiction
of a Feminist

❖

Nellie McClung was an extremely popular author in her time, and it was through her writing that many Canadians first came to know her. Since those days, mainstream literary critics have often dismissed her fiction as effete romanticism when, in fact, the essential thrust of her writing was antiromantic. She frequently used her fiction to convey many of her social reform ideas, thereby combining her craft with her determination to improve the lives of those around her, especially women and children. Again, the result has been that mainline critics—generally males—have written her fiction off as merely didactic and therefore unworthy. A feminist reading of her fiction does much to reverse this narrow-minded, patriarchal approach. McClung sought, through her writing, to brighten the spirits of rural people in the West—"my people," she often called them—whose lives were frequently burdened with excessive drudgery in those early days when the West was being opened. To this end she employed considerable humour, a trait that was a natural part of her disposition. Much of that humour through which she engaged her readers was satirical in spirit, an aspect of her writing that has consistently been ignored or overlooked. In fact, there has been practically no in-depth analysis of McClung's fiction. This chapter examines her fiction from these perspectives.

As an established author Nellie looked back with great amusement at her childhood endeavours to become a writer. "My earliest writing was epitaphs for dead kittens, setting forth their virtues and the sad parting from their bereaved mother, which was purely fictitious in both places, for they had no virtues, conspicuous or otherwise, and the old cat didn't care a tinker's hoot about them."[1] The writer's ambition would stay with her, however, and Nellie made clear to Wes that marriage and a family would not change that desire.

Not long after Nellie and Wes set up house over the drug store Nellie thought her opportunity had arrived when a salesman came to Manitou with the exciting news that a new magazine, *Town and Country*, "would carry each month pictures and sketches of the leading people in one of the more important country towns." Nellie was chosen to write sketches for Manitou after she paid five dollars for a subscription. Eagerly she went about town collecting information and discovered "that every house had a story." Although the magazine was a myth and the young confidence-man disappeared with her five dollars, Nellie felt her time had not been wasted. The stories she collected—some from local town "characters"—would eventually be transformed into fiction that evoked the small town prairie life she knew so well.[2]

By the early 1900s, Methodist and Presbyterian Sunday School publications began accepting brief editorials, verse, and short narrative sketches from Nellie that demonstrated a marked capacity on her part to engage the imaginative interest of her readers. Many reflected the skill she had developed from telling stories to her own children. The editorial choice of material for such publications was determined by content: the moral message and spiritual uplift. Still, McClung's pieces were notably superior to comparable material in the same pages. Where the average editorial was conventional in idea, pompously instructive in a heavy-handed style, and morally self-righteous in tone, Nellie's were freshly imaginative in insight and conveyed in a dramatized narrative form. In one, for example, a woman said she couldn't think of anything to give Myra for her birthday for Myra had everything. Myra's aunt replied: "Give her a Chinaman to teach . . . Get her to do something for someone."[3] Such a gift was unexpected, but not without practical relevance to small prairie towns, each of which had its Chinese restaurant or laundry resulting from cheap oriental labour imported for the building of the CPR. Indeed, the Manitou Woman's Missionary Society—probably at Nellie's instigation—taught English to their six Chinese residents "five nights each week."[4]

By contrast, most of her fellow authors of Sunday School stories wrote in the stiff and patronizing manner of the adult who deigned to write for children, who, in turn, were presented as miniature adults: thinking grave adult thoughts and expressing them in stilted adult language. Such writers were out of touch with the real world of children—how they think and feel, how they view the adult world around them, and how they express those views. Their characters were obnoxious cousins to *Little Lord Fauntleroy* and *Goody Two-Shoes*. In a few years time more than one book reviewer of Nellie's *Sowing Seeds in Danny* (1908) would observe that more of such natural children were needed in the world of children's fiction where the reprehensible "Elsie Books" held sway with the sentimentally "good" heroine constantly awash in tears. Nellie's fictional children, then, from the earliest days of her writing were plausibly realistic, that is to say, they were mischievously naughty. They were based on Nellie's first-hand observation of the real ways of her own children. For this reason, Nellie's tales of this time were engagingly charming: both for adults who were moved to chuckle with memories of their own children's ways, and also for those child readers who must have recognized in Nellie's fictional children something of themselves.

At times, in the early 1900s, Nellie was so prolific that she inundated Dr. W.H. Withrow, the Canadian Methodist Sunday School paper editor, who occasionally managed to send her two dollars for her voluminous efforts: "I do not know that I can use all of your articles" and, perhaps with exasperation, "I have enough on hand for some time."[5] McClung was writing too much, too easily, but she was also aware that she needed literary guidance. She appealed to Withrow for advice regarding both style and content, but he left such matters up to Nellie's "good judgment," although on one occasion he indicated a preference for stories "having some local colouring."[6] Of the many books for sale in the McClung drug store at this time, Nellie was particularly struck by the short stories of Bret Harte, noted as an author of western American local colour. "I began to pay more attention to my reading, even trying to analyze short stories, in an attempt to discover the technique. I remember how diligently I pored over Bret Harte's *Luck of Roaring Camp*, trying to see how he produced the effect on his readers." She grew more observant, carefully "watching for stories" in the lives of people around her, and keeping a record of ideas for future stories that would evoke this western Canadian mileau.[7] One, for example, which

Nellie planned to call "Winter Killed," concerned a woman whose primitive pioneer life was so harsh that her barren, marginal existence broke her heart. She had endured "too many trials and privations" so that, ironically, "when the good time came, she could not rise to the occasion."[8] Themes such as this, used by Nellie in her fiction, were notes drawn from the burned-out lives of real Manitoba people whose spirits were broken by the drabness of their existence.

In 1904 Nellie McClung began experimenting with more developed short stories aimed at an adult reading audience. It was her mother-in-law who gave Nellie a nudge to begin writing in earnest by drawing Nellie's attention to a short-fiction contest sponsored by *Colliers Weekly*, an American publication, and encouraging her to write and submit a story. The manuscript, called "Sowing Seeds in Danny"—which ultimately became the first chapter in a novel with the same title—was returned to her in early 1905 as "worthy of special attention," although it did not win the prize. In March of the same year, "on impulse," she sent the manuscript off to the Canadian Methodist Book and Publishing House where William Briggs, the book steward, suggested that she work the story up into a novel and resubmit. Briggs also suggested that Nellie submit "a few short stories such as this to the Magazines, or large weeklies, American as well as Canadian, in order to get your name known to the public. Then you would have a prepared constituency of readers" for a full book.[9] Nellie was certainly not averse to having her name known to the public, and she set about achieving this goal. It was the very stimulus she needed. Soon she was receiving requests for stories from American magazines like *The Ladies' Home Journal*, the *Delineator*,[10] the *American Magazine,* and the *Woman's Home Companion.* In Canada periodicals such as *The Canadian Magazine, Saturday Night,* and the *Canadian Home Journal* vied for her short stories. By the time *Sowing Seeds in Danny* (1908) was brought out by Doubleday in the United States and by William Briggs's Methodist Book and Publishing House in Canada, McClung's was a household name in both countries. Theodore Dreiser at the *Delineator* wrote to Doubleday: "I hope you will let me have more of her work, and would be glad if you would get a Thanksgiving or a Christmas story out of her."[11] In Canada, M.O. Hammond of the Toronto *Globe* was shrewd enough to advertise that he had secured a McClung story for his paper. "It is one of the best short stories published in recent years . . . you realize at once why publishers are so eager for control of her manuscripts."[12]

Early drafts of *Sowing Seeds in Danny* were criticized by Briggs's reader Jean Graham of the *Canadian Magazine* for "the black being too sombre and the white too dazzling,"[13] and called for her to provide one of her character's (Sam Motherwell) with some occasional sense of generosity to balance his stinginess. In essence this request was asking Nellie to depart from the harsh reality that she too often saw in the lives of some settlers in her community. It was, in fact, a characteristic sufficiently in evidence in rural Manitoba at that time and Nellie spoke out against that tendency—particularly the harm it inflicted upon the wives and children of such families—in a speech she gave to agricultural society meetings in Saskatchewan and Manitoba in 1911, variously entitled "Why Boys and Girls Leave the Farm," or "The Value of Social Life in Country Homes." As a young, inexperienced writer at the time, she gave in to Graham's demands.

Still, Nellie possessed too much of the enthusiasm and self-confidence of the aspiring author to realize that she was in need of sound literary criticism in spite of the indications of promise as a writer. As the *Danny* novel grew, however, she would not only recognize the need for greater knowledge of the craft of writing, but receive it. E.S. Caswell at the Methodist Book and Publishing House suggested "Why pass me by if you'd like me to go over your stories?" and he offered to have them typed for her free of charge. He also began criticizing the *Danny* excerpts, sometimes giving priggish advice asking Nellie to blur some of the realities she saw about her. Caswell, for example, often "felt that sacred things were treated too lightly to be agreeable," particularly when some of her characters were portrayed as "using the name of the Deity lightly." This, he assured her, "will mar the story in the eyes of seriously disposed persons." "It's so easy for you to be facetious," he chided, "that you all too frequently allow the impulse to carry you away. You need to discipline yourself along this line." Caswell also took exception when Nellie permitted one of her characters to swear. "I question that daring remark of Mrs. M[aquire's]: 'I hope she'll—give—him—hell!'" While Caswell conceded that the passage was "immensely expressive" in context, he stated bluntly that "it will give most readers a shock." Now, she was strong enough to refuse such editorial advice. Caswell also fussed anxiously about Nellie's comic portrayal of a children's temperance meeting in the Band of Hope chapter, where the children were bribed with candy into signing a pledge against consuming alcohol.

> Really, while I thought of it as humorous and clever, yet as the chapter proceeded I felt somehow that it was being treated almost too lightly—I hesitate to use the word *flippantly*, as it may seem an objectionable or an offensive word, and yet it seemed to me your love of fun had carried you almost into that region, and made rather a burlesque of the meeting.

This burlesque approach was precisely what Nellie McClung intended, and when she refused to treat the episode with the gravity that Caswell stodgily preferred, he was forced to admit that he admired her "spunk," though his final word on the matter was portentous caution: "I have given my warning."[14]

In spite of her obvious need for editorial assistance, Nellie steadily refused to trim her robust humour to satisfy Caswell's prim anxiety. She learned very quickly to have faith in her own judgement of such matters, and at times resisted with passion Caswell's pious advice. As McClung's novel developed, both Briggs and Caswell became conscious that they had a best seller on their hands. By September 1908—about two months after the initial publication of *Sowing Seeds in Danny*—William Briggs informed Nellie's father-in-law that she had as good as "struck oil."[15] Caswell, who had been editing McClung's manuscript, came to the same conclusion much earlier, and decided to profit from Nellie's anticipated royalties. He set up a secret and shabby deal that placed him in a position of conflict of interest with his own employer. He knew he was dealing with an eager, but naively inexperienced, author. From the beginning Briggs had clearly stated that the Methodist Book and Publishing House would "gladly do anything" to secure her an American publisher from whom her Methodist publisher would buy pages to put together books for the Canadian market. Now Caswell shrewdly offered his assistance at a price: "I wonder if you'd care for a partner in this story?" To sweeten the pot, he offered her two hundred dollars down, said he would try to secure an American publisher, as well as a Canadian publisher who could offer her a better deal than Briggs, and suggested they "divide the royalty between us." Later, Caswell could not come up with the cash so felt resigned to accept only 10 percent of the royalties. Subsequently he went through a multitude of suggestions for increas-

ing her/his profit, even so far as advising her to seek another
Canadian publisher, and finally telling her to secure inflated royalties
from his own employer. Caswell's letters to Nellie are filled with
words of caution: "This will be a private arrangement;" "I don't want
a soul here to know I am to get anything out of it," and so on.[16] At first
his numerous ploys must have been confusing to Nellie, but soon she
would have realized she was in a very unsavoury situation. Still, she
stuck to her original naive agreement, and consistently paid Caswell
10 percent of her royalties on *Danny*. While Caswell's readiness to
profit at Nellie's and his employer's expense was professionally
shabby, his enterprise was commendable, and he certainly taught
Nellie much about the Canadian and American book markets, as well
as how to bargain shrewdly so that her financial gain would be much
greater than it might otherwise have been. By 18 August, about a
month after *Danny* hit the American bookstores, Doubleday reported
it had sold over one thousand copies and had commenced the third
printing for a total of about sixty-five hundred copies. In Canada
Danny was well on the way to becoming a best seller. In December
1908, Caswell confidently signed a letter to McClung: "yours for the
10,000."[17] His prediction was rapidly coming true. Indeed, in 1947,
three years before her death, *Sowing Seeds in Danny* was into its
seventeenth edition and was still being reprinted in 1965.[18]

As a child Nellie McClung was fed on a diet of romance writing,
and one can only consider it to her credit that she did not fall into the
romance trap of her place and time. As an adult McClung considered
herself an antiromantic writer as she understood the term. Signs of
McClung's antiromantic bias were evident from the earliest days of
her writing career and all through that career she burlesqued such
gross romance writing as an "insidious" influence on young people.
"The Lady Gwendolyn has nothing to do but lie on a couch and eat
bon-bons and ponder whether she will say 'yes' or 'no' to Lord
Elfenstein, and when the sixteen year old gets her poor foolish head
filled with scenes like these it is hard for her to get down to washing
dishes and cleaning lamps."[19] In a short passage of antiromantic
spoofing, Camilla—the ineffectual pink lady's maid in *Danny*—records
in her diary that she likes baking and housework so much "that it
shows clearly that I am not a disguised heiress."[20] In the same novel
McClung spoofs young Pearlie Watson's sense of melodrama. In the
chapter "How Pearl Watson Wiped Out the Stain," Pearlie is working

at the hard-hearted and stingy Motherwells for three months in order to cancel the ten-dollar debt remaining on the yellow caboose that formed the core of the Watson home. At the time of her departure, Pearlie casts herself in another of those romantically melodramatic postures that her author always spoofed.

> "I will go!" she said with blazing eyes. "I will go, I will wipe the stain off me house once and forever!" waving her arm dramatically toward the caboose which formed the sleeping apartment for the boys. "To die, to die for those we love is nobler far than wear a crown!" Pearlie had attended the Queen Esther cantata the winter before. She knew how poor Esther felt.

At the time of Pearlie's departure "her small supply of clothing was washed and ironed and neatly packed in a birdcage"—the ludicrous suitcase undermining all of Pearlie's melodramatics. Such intentional bathos as a satiric device was common in McClung's fiction,[21] as the satiric reduction to the absurd was a common device in her political and social reformist speeches.

One of Nellie McClung's most amusing antiromantic passages involves young Tom Motherwell's invitation to a party at their neighbours, the Slaters. Tom knows he will have to sneak out after his parents have gone to bed since they are opposed to anyone having fun. Tom is sweet on Nellie Slater, and Pearlie's imagination is immediately fired to a high romantic pitch. For her "here was a rapturous romance." Of Nellie Slater she asks: "Has she eyes like stars, lips like cherries, neck like a swan, and a laugh like a ripple of music?"

> Pearlie knew all about frustrated love. Ma had read a story once, called "Wedded and Parted, and Wedded Again." Cruel and designing parents had parted young Edythe (pronounced Éd-ith-ee) and Egbert, and Egbert had just pined and pined and pined. How would Mrs. Motherwell like it if poor Tom began to pine and turn away from his victuals?

The homely word "victuals" undercuts the flight of Pearlie's romantic imagination. Of Nellie Slater and Tom Motherwell,

> she wondered if they ever met in the moonlight and vowed to be true till the rocks melted in the sun, and all the seas ran dry. That's what Egbert had said, and then a rift of cloud passed athwart the moon's face, and Edythe fainted dead away because it is bad luck to have a

cloud go over the moon when people are busy plighting vows, and wasn't it a good thing that Egbert was there to break her fall.

Pearlie contrives to sneak out of the house with Tom's Sunday clothes, which she leaves by a tree in the pasture. Later that night Tom would escape from his joyless parents, dress in the field, "and then, oh bliss! away to Edythe."[22] Pearlie is a twelve-year-old child whose flights of romantic imagination help her bear her poverty and the lack of time for play. Otherwise her feet are planted firmly on the ground and her mind is wholly practical.

It is interesting that in 1908, the year that *Sowing Seeds in Danny* was published, L.M. Montgomery's *Anne of Green Gables* also saw the light. Both Anne and Pearlie place a strong priority on the power of the romantic imagination. One can as easily see a Megan Follows acting the role of the engaging Pearlie Watson as she has the charming Anne with an "e." In Montgomery's book, however, romance is entirely child-oriented, whereas McClung, at such times, satirizes adult nonsense. There is a great deal of good-natured spoofing of romance in McClung's work, as well as more serious satire, but the reading of literary criticism of McClung's novels often makes one wonder whether the critics are attributing the romantic flights to Nellie McClung herself, rather than to a charming little romantic girl character in the novel.[23] McClung was essentially a satirist at heart, and irony and satire weave their way through her fiction from beginning to end. The writing of satire requires *some* degree of sophistication, a quality never accorded McClung by Canadian literary critics.

Sometimes McClung would gently spoof the romance mode; at other times she could be biting and astringent. The contrast between Mrs. Motherwell as a young girl and her adult stinginess is a case in point. As a child she had played the "tinker, tailor, soldier, sailor . . . " child's incantation and, ironically, ended up with a "rich man." "Then she had dreamed dreams of silks and satins and prancing steeds and liveried servants, and ease, and happiness—dreams which God in His mercy had let her forget long, long ago." At first she had "struggled hard against her husband's penuriousness . . . But he had held her down with a heavy hand . . . At last she grew weary of struggling, and settled down in sullen submission, a hopeless, heavy-eyed, spiritless woman, and as time went by she became greedier for money than her husband." Now she was "tired, unutterably tired, not with that day's work alone, but with the days and years that had passed away in grey dreariness; the past barren and bleak, the future bringing only visions of heavier burdens." Her childish dreams and her adult reality were bitterly opposed.[24] Mrs. Motherwell's cynical disillusionment marked another of McClung's "winter-killed" souls. She is typical of some of those pioneers in the West that Nellie McClung occasionally observed, whose personalities suffered from a too arid life marked by deprivation.

The bare granite house of the Motherwells is a reality and a symbol: "an outward manifestation of wealth and power"; "a symbol of spiritual" dearth.[25] Going out to the Motherwell farm, Pearlie takes great pleasure in the beauties of nature, only to be brought up short by the aridity of the Motherwells' grey stone house "gloomy and bare," a symbol of their "lives of barren selfishness" in a house whose windows have never been opened. The closed windows are a metaphor for closed minds with their sense of superiority and therefore isolation from others. The hailstone that breaks Pearlie's attic window to let the fresh air in is less a sentimental passage than it is part of a "structure of significance."[26] It signifies that, unlike the Motherwells, Pearlie has an open, searching mind.

Nellie McClung would describe a good deal of such harshness and degeneracy, but it was rare for her to dwell on the darker psychological side of human nature. Her emphasis was rather on the darker side of social conditioning. Still, at the Chicken Hill School in *The Second Chance,* during a game of shinny at recess, big Tom Steadman slashes viciously at little Libby Cavers with his stick. Bud Perkins fights Tom on Libby's behalf, and McClung describes the pupils who "closed in around them and watched the fight with the stolid indifference of savages or children which is much the same thing."[27] No doubt McClung had in mind the vicious and demoralizing fights that took place at her first school-teaching job. In *Painted Fires* she depicts an even darker psychological side of the degenerate magistrate at Bannerman, where Helmi's husband, Jack Doran, goes for news of Helmi's whereabouts: "The magistrate rubbed the bristles on his chin with a distinctly soiled forefinger, then with one thumb he pressed back the cuticle on the other until it hurt. He loved to do this. When he couldn't hurt any one else he hurt himself." He tells Jack that Helmi has had an affair with the Englishman Arthur Warner, and that she is now working in a Chinese restaurant in

Edmonton. "I suppose you know what it means when a white girl goes into one of those places," he says spitefully. She becomes an opium addict and a whore. "He did not need to hurt his own thumb now—Jack Doran's face was enough. It had grown suddenly old and seamed and full of hatred."[28]

In addition to the grosser traits of the romance tradition that were typical in McClung's day, there is a more modern, more sophisticated use of the term "romance" as it is used, for example, by Dick Harrison in *Unnamed Country: The Struggle for a Canadian Prairie Fiction* (1977). Even here McClung's fiction does not conform to quite a number of the romantic characteristics described by Harrison and attributed to writers like Nellie McClung.

Harrison links the sentimental romance to the Garden-of-all-the-World myth that originated in the American west when that part of the United States was being settled.[29] The Canadian "garden," says Harrison, was "solidly British" in spite of "some light-hearted raillery at the English remittance man or the green farm pupil." Foreigners of non-British stock "can sometimes be amiable creatures, but are usually distasteful if not vicious." There is, he says, a good deal of Anglo-Saxon "bigotry" marked by little "sympathy for ethnic minorities."[30] Nothing could be further from the truth where McClung is concerned. In *The Stream Runs Fast*, for example, McClung's interest in Finns is evident:

> For years I had wanted to write an immigration story in the form of a novel. I wanted to portray the struggles of a young girl who found herself in Canada dependent upon her own resources with everything to learn, including the language.
>
> I thought first of taking a Ukrainian girl as my heroine for it was easy to get books on the Ukrainian background, but I had been greatly attracted to Finland because of its advanced attitude to women. Finnish women received the vote and sat in parliament long before any other women, and I wondered about this and what quality of mind had brought it about.[31]

Nellie McClung also had a Finnish maid at the time upon whom she could draw for information. As well, Nellie deals sympathetically with two immigrants, Helmi Milander of *Painted Fires,* and Helga, in the poem "Standards." In "Standards" McClung defends young Helga, a Finnish domestic who is badly treated by her "respectable" Anglo-Saxon mistress.[32] Another example is found in "The Black

Curse" published in *Chatelaine* in 1931. In this story Nellie sympathizes with Borska Taski in opposition to the flighty and frivolous school teacher Maizie Trent, who boards with the Taskis, but flirts with Mr. Taski. Borska puts a black curse on Maizie, who dies in a car accident when drunk.[33] McClung's sympathy for the immigrant is again evident when Mareska Balla, the Hungarian maid in the Becker household, in "The Girl From God Knows Where," is ironically described by McClung as "one of the odd pieces of human jetsam cast up by the tide of immigration 'from God knows where,' as the Bishop of London [probably Bishop Lloyd of Saskatchewan] so graphically phrased it when he chided us for our warm welcome to those 'unpreferred continentals'" from Eastern Europe. McClung's irony is strong. After four years at the Beckers, "if a survey had been taken of the foreigners who came to our shores, Mareska would have been entered in the column marked 'successful,' for had she not delivered a family of good British stock from the necessity of manual labour? Not one member of the Becker family washed a dish, made a bed, or even put a record back in its place." In this story the people of "British stock" are satirically condemned and Nellie McClung's sympathy is entirely with the foreign maid, who is valued only for her work although she longs to feel needed as a person. The religious motto on her mother's crocheted "Hazi-Alldas"—"Before they call, I will answer them"—becomes an ironic and secular commentary on her future life with a family of the "idle rich," who were "all for self . . . so bad and mean."[34] In her short story "Three Christmas Eves: 1938–1939–1940" Nellie tells the story of a German immigrant, Carl Stromberg, who opens his shiny new restaurant in Princeville, Alberta, on 24 December 1938, with a party for the orphanage children. He is perceived as a fine Canadian citizen who supports every good cause. "If all Germans were like Carl Stromberg, we said in Princeville, our minds would be easier."[35]

Far from being British-oriented and a bigot, lacking sympathy for foreigners, McClung was, in fact, the opposite. In an address to the Canadian Authors Association in 1931 she gave a talk on "Foreigners" in which she paid tribute to them, and pointed out "that in the days to come the children of these people would play a very influential part in the building up of a Canadian nation." The applause showed she had won over her audience in a plea "for greater

239

tolerance and fair play in the treatment of people from central Europe,"[36] something she practised in her fiction. Indeed, British characters like the shiftless Felix Martin in the short story "O, Canada!," who lived entirely on the bounty of women's organizations, and the two racist British magistrates in *Painted Fires*—magistrates Windsor and J. Edgerton Blackwood—were depicted as undesirable Anglo-Saxons who did nothing to help build the Canadian mosaic.

Harrison argues that writers like McClung connect the garden myth with "the spirit of empire, with its tendency to impose the dominant Ontario-British minority in the West."[37] Again this is not an accurate description of Nellie McClung's fiction. For example, one of McClung's most effective stories, "The Way of the West," is antipathetic to characters who are governed by British ways and attitudes. Here, in a satirical tale that was originally titled "The First, the Fourth, and the Twelfth"—a story about the American and Canadian national celebrations and the celebration of the pro-British Orangeman's day—Dominion Day slips past without notice. The American celebration, however, is carried out with great enthusiasm by those settlers who originally came from the States. They have a band, Stars and Stripes everywhere, games, firecrackers, a picnic, and all the trappings of exuberant good fun. The picnic is held in a grove across from the home of a fiery Irish Orangeman, Thomas Shouldice. To Shouldice, the American settlers' celebration is un-British and a blatant affront to King Edward. When he sees some Canadian families joining in he is incensed, but when the local priest, Father O'Flynn, joined them, Thomas "was sure that the Americans and Catholics were in league against the British."

Shouldice immediately decides to organize an Orangeman's "walk" on the glorious twelfth, though there are only seven Orangemen in the neighbourhood, and two Catholic families, who are described as "peaceable, friendly people." There would be a parade with fife and drum with Shouldice, in full regalia, on his "own old, spavined grey mare," as well as antipopish speeches and songs. Getting a speaker, however, poses some difficulties. To his astonishment the Methodist missionary suggests Father O'Flynn. "But he's a papist!" Thomas explodes. The Methodist missionary pooh poohs this little detail and adds, "There's no division of creed west of Winnipeg. The little priest does all my sick visiting north of the river, and I do his on the south."

News of the event spreads throughout the neighbourhood. The Americans, not knowing what an Orangeman's walk is, nevertheless arrive for the celebration—as does Father O'Flynn. When asked about the celebration O'Flynn gives "an evasive reply" but mutters under his breath, "It is an institution of the Evil One to sow discord among brothers." The "walk" begins. The Americans, "sorry to see so few in the procession," all fall in behind with their band instruments to help and Father O'Flynn joins them. Ironically the "walk" reflects "the spirit of the West . . . unifying, mellowing, harmonizing all conflict-ing emotions—the spirit of the West that calls on men everywhere to be brothers and lend a hand." At the end of the "walk," Father O'Flynn steps forward with a short speech on brotherhood, then leads in the Lord's Prayer. It must have been with a twinkle in her eye that Nellie McClung ended her comic social satire:

> Where could such a scene as this be enacted—a Twelfth of July celebration where a Roman Catholic priest was the principal speaker, where the company dispersed with the singing of "God Save the King," led by an American band.

"Nowhere," Nellie argues, "but in the Northwest of Canada" where "that illimitable land" forces man to be "kind and neighborly and brotherly."[38] In other words, traditions and attitudes formed by cultural imperialists from Britain and the East are seen as forces of alienation and disharmony. Despite what Harrison says, Nellie McClung never looked backward to central Canada or Great Britain for the roots of western culture, and in this story she supplied a Canadian answer to what Harrison refers to as "the problem of new land and old culture."[39]

Other characteristics of the "garden myth," as Harrison describes them, are that the land, to the pioneer, is "suggestive of a garden awaiting cultivation," and there is marked "optimism" regarding "a new promise of endless abundance." "Nature," Harrison says, is "regenerative," while the city is "trivial or corrupt." "The cities of Nellie McClung's stories are areas of exploitation and vice." Such romances as McClung's "are permeated with a quasi-pastoral assump-tion that the country is regenerative while the city is sinister or moribund." Further, there is "a romantic attitude to man in nature." The pioneer believes in "a beneficent natural order" for "there is something redemptive about this new beginning" which is "in some way sacred."[40]

Typical pioneers whom Nellie McClung portrays, for example, are the Cavers family, the Motherwells, the Paines, the unnamed woman trying to grow cabbages in *All We Like Sheep*, and the Bentons in "The Neutral Fuse." None of them conforms to Harrison's opinion of romantic pioneers in early Canadian fiction. To begin with, Bill Cavers in *The Second Chance* is drunk so often that he is rarely in the fields and, in fact, can't "prove up" on his parcel of land even though Mrs. Cavers and little Libbie work the fields, trying to make a go of it. In *Danny* the Motherwells work hard—indeed they do nothing but work—but only out of greed for the money they make. Mr. Paine, in *Purple Springs*, is a hard and penurious man who forces both the farm work and the housework on his helpless wife and reinforces her hopelessness with harsh verbal abuse. The unnecessarily impoverished condition he forces upon his family is shocking to those who observe it. As well, the unnamed woman who is trying to grow cabbages that dry up and blow away in the drought in *All We Like Sheep* lives in such hopeless despair that she finally wonders if farming is divinely sanctioned after all. "Isn't it right for us to plant seed and expect them to grow . . . Or are we presumptuous? . . . " In "The Neutral Fuse," the English bride Sadie Benton, and her husband live in "the drought area of the west." "The last seven years have been lean and sad ones." She keeps the East Golding community cheerful in the face of immense odds against success, but privately confides her fear and despair in her diary day after hopeless day. Human carelessness would be understandable to her, "but when God sends destruction [hail] it is terrifying . . . I am trying to keep on believing, for it is a wicked thing to sow the seeds of unbelief, and I will not say a word to anyone." Keeping her despair to herself compounds the problem psychologically. Trying to keep her hopes alive, Sadie plants a flower garden on the protected side of the house away from the endless prairie wind. All the hope she has left is that they will bloom and bring beauty to her arid world. Finally, that night, the wind comes "fierce and without mercy" destroying all her flowers. Again she records her hopeless despair in her diary: "I know it isn't the flowers alone/That the wind has murdered in roaring glee;/It isn't the flowers that are lying dead/With blackened body and bleeding head—/It's me!" When the neighbours next see her she is "serene and calm, but queer" in the mind. Prairie madness has started its insidious invasion of her brain.[41]

Furthermore, Harrison's dichotomy between the evil city and the idyllic countryside is not posited by Nellie McClung's fiction. In fact, nature is seen as "regenerative" in only one of McClung's short stories, "Red and White," where an Indian family goes into the wilderness to get away from the white man's unpleasant civilization. Cities occur so rarely in McClung's writing that it is hardly worth the critic's attention. In any case, if in the city of St. Paul there is the lustful and sexually exploitative Mike, of *Painted Fires*, there is simultaneously the motherly cook, Kate, who protects Helmi. If in Winnipeg there is an irresponsible and exploitative Eva St. John and a prejudiced magistrate Windsor, there are also the Miss Rogerses, and the Reverend Mr. Terrys of the world, who stand firmly for truth, justice, and human rights. In the story "Thirty Years," it is the city that acts as a regenerative force on the "poor, broken . . . unbelievably old and worn" Mrs. Branson, who finds "deliverance" in the city after thirty years of backbreaking toil on the farm.[42] In her personal life, Nellie McClung loved and valued the rural life of farm and village as well as "regenerative" trips into the wilderness, but she loved even more the vitality, the excitement, the active zest of city men and women who, for example, fought with her in the suffrage campaigns. The vitality of the city branches of the Canadian Women's Press Club as well as other city organizations animated McClung. The city provided advantages that rural life could never give her or her children. Helmi's night-time view of the city from a window in the Girls' Friendly Home, situated on a hill, could easily be McClung's: "the sleepless, restless, shifting city! She loved it; she was part of it."[43] Nellie was aware that evil existed in urban and rural settings, but it was the latter she chose to write about.

The only genuinely "Edenic" description of nature occurs in *Painted Fires* when Helmi's aunt Lili comes from America on a visit to Finland. In spite of the novel's romantic ending the story is essentially an antiromance that describes the gradual disillusionment of a romantic young emigrant from Finland. McClung says: "I tried to put myself into the character of Helmi" who saw herself "in the land of freedom, romance and easy money." Before the end of the novel Helmi is unjustly imprisoned in a women's reformatory, and she soon loses her romantic aspirations to be a "lovely lady," rich and languid like Eva St. John and the glamorous movie stars in movies Eva takes Helmi to see each week. "'*Painted Fires*' was the name I chose for the book . . . for I wanted to lay down a hard [antiromantic] foundation of truth as to conditions in Canada" that were not congruent with the literature put out by "immigration agencies in Europe" which only led to "dark tragedy . . . for the deceived ones."[44]

Every Eden in Nellie McClung's work has its evil serpent. In fact, the image of the serpent as betrayer is a continuous image throughout her writing. In *Painted Fires* the serpent is Lili's husband Mike: "He'll want you just like he wanted me. Kate, the cook, will keep you safe." Mike does see Helmi, however, and "his burning eyes" make her shudder with the lust in them. Helmi is sent to Kate's sister Maggie in Winnipeg to get her out of Mike's grasp.[45] In Winnipeg, on her Sunday afternoons off, Helmi would walk out to the beautiful countryside to enjoy nature. One day, as she dreams about romantically marrying a wealthy Finnish prospector, two men approach her. "She did not like their appearance, but she felt no fear. There was a strength in her right arm that brought assurance." When she tells them she's a Finn with no English, "the boys laughed at that and looked at each other meaningly." When Helmi runs for the safety of the city streets, the two men run after her. Helmi deliberately lets them gain on her "then, stopping and bracing herself, she gave the first one a powerful body blow which sent him rolling down the bank toward the stream below." The second man stops to help his companion.[46] In this instance, the city is a refuge from rural evils, and McClung places two serpents in an otherwise Edenic setting.

Helmi begins taking English lessons from the superficial Eva St. John. Eva is an opium addict and sends the innocent Helmi to a place above a Chinese restaurant where she is to get some "medicine." Eva instructs Helmi to tell no one. The opium den is, in its own way, a form of paradise to its users. Nellie could have learned details for the story from Judge Emily Murphy and her 1922 book on the Canadian drug traffic.[47] Here Helmi sees "a huge black glittering jar . . . and coiled around it was a red snake with its head uplifted ready to strike! . . . It held her with its cruel shining eyes, and although she knew its tongue would dart out like a red shining needle she could neither move nor scream. Then she saw that it was not a real snake at all, and that there were many of them in the room. They writhed around the great bowls that stood on the shelf above her head . . . " The Chinaman Sam hands Helmi Eva's "medicine," and at that point the house is raided and Helmi finds herself "held by a tall burly policeman" whom she throws downstairs, breaking his arm.[48] (Finnish women have been noted for their physical strength,[49] and Helmi is no exception.) She is arrested and sentenced to three months in a reformatory, for Eva, a respectable citizen in her community, will not come forward in Helmi's defence, and the loyal Helmi has promised Eva to say nothing about it. The seductive Eva and her opium serpents have betrayed Helmi's romantic dream. Like Eva, Windsor, the socially respectable magistrate, also betray's Helmi's trust. Although the arresting policeman is willing to swear that Helmi did not have enough English to know she was under arrest, Windsor refuses to hear his evidence or that of others who wish to be heard on Helmi's behalf. He shows himself to be a racist and sexist bigot who has convicted Helmi before she even appears before him. Nor does he try the case on its merits. The imprisonment of Helmi provides McClung with "an opportunity to attack Canadian guardians of law and order for their discrimination against women and foreigners."[50]

In *The Second Chance* and "Carried Forward," the funerals of Bill Cavers in the first instance, and of Hilda's mother in the second, are both likened to "a slowly crawling black snake" to indicate a post-lapsarian, or fallen, world where betrayal is strong and life has moved somewhere east of Eden.[51] The serpent image, recurring throughout McClung's books, suggests not only evil, but also a lost garden theme: Eden betrayed. When Helmi does find her "garden" it is not an Edenic, romantic garden, but a plain, earthy, vegetable one that has to be toiled in. In this sense her image of an idyllic garden is lost. This post-lapsarian theme running throughout McClung's fiction is, for the most part, undercut by the happy endings she often gives her stories. She realized she was criticized for these endings, but she had her own reasons for including them:

> By happy ending I mean that a gleam of hope must shine through the darkness some place. I see no good in a book that teaches that life is a hopeless mess . . . Error and sorrow and failure are our portion in life I know, yet no more than joy and achievement and happiness, and it is the work of the writer to portray them in true proportion, and even if the sorrowful predominates one thought must prevail, that life is . . . not wasted, not utterly wasted.[52]

Novelist and literary critic Henry Kreisel in "The Prairie: A State of Mind" argues that all discussions of literature of the Canadian west must examine "the impact of the landscape upon the mind."[53] In her writing McClung reveals the psychological impact of the prairie landscape, particularly on the minds of those who come west as adults. For them the far horizon and the eternal wind are a foreign and threatening terrain. For those born and bred on the prairie the landscape is not threatening, although at moments of crisis—such as drought or death—nature can be seen as cruelly indifferent. We have seen how drought affects the unnamed woman who lost her cabbage crop in *All We Like Sheep* and the English bride Sadie Benton in "The Neutral Fuse." In the title story of *The Black Creek Stopping-House* Reginald and Ronald Brydon, formerly of His Majesty's navy, decide to get their half-brother Fred and his bride from Toronto to come out West as their "farm pupils."

> They dwelt on the freedom of the life, the abundance of game, and the view! They made a great deal of the view, and certainly there was nothing to obstruct it, for the prairie lay a dead level for ten miles north of them, only dotted here and there with little weather-bleached warts of houses like their own, where other optimists were trying to make a dint in the monotony.[54]

Their one-sided descriptions satirize much immigration literature.[55] Soon Fred's bride, Evelyn, is negatively affected by "the dull gray monochrome which stretched before her"; "the utter loneliness of the prairie, with its monotonous sweep of frost-killed grass, the deadly sameness, and the perpetual silence of the house . . . " The prairie seems "hateful . . . cruel and menacing, and a strange fear of it seemed to possess her." She senses ominous shadows behind her and "voices, mocking and gibbering" at her.[56] Prairie madness begins to invade. Her reaction is similar to that of the maddened woman described by Mrs. Dawson in "You Never Can Tell," also contained in *The Black Creek Stopping-House*. It is a "pathetic" story

> of the lonely prairie woman—the woman who wish[es] she was back, the woman to whom the broad outlook and far horizon [are] terrible and full of fear. [Mrs. Dawson] told . . . how, at night, this lonely woman drew down the blinds and pinned them close to keep out the great outside that stared at her with wide pitiless eyes . . .

She, too, begins to hear voices "whispering, mocking, plotting" and "the awful shadow, black and terrible, that crouches behind her . . . " It is a "weird and gloomy picture" that Mrs. Dawson paints, full of "disillusionment with the romance of pioneering."[57] Another example can be found in eleven-year-old Hilda in "Carried Forward," a short story from *All We Like Sheep*. All of nature seems indifferent to Hilda's plight: "Black shadows of the drifting clouds ran over the green, like twisting, creeping giant hands which made her afraid for they all seemed to be coming to the house with some evil intention. The sickening smell of wolf willow blossoms came to her from the pasture." In this passage Hilda despairingly attempts to personalize nature, but in the end she sees nature as indifferent. The dazzling hills to the west offered no comfort: "They seemed to roll over her and crush her into a pitiful little handful of dust that the wind could drive away . . . they stood unmoving and uncaring . . . "[58] Spiritual annihilation results. McClung, then, presents Harrison's argument that in romance writing there is "a millenial harmony between man and nature" as an illusion.

It is to be expected that a feminist and social reformer like Nellie McClung would focus on female characters, though the men in her stories are authentically realistic. Being essentially oriented toward women her fiction merits special attention today as we seek to recover and understand the experiences of women.[59] We can examine her writing, for example, to see what McClung thought women should be and to define the social forces that either shape or hinder her heroines' development. McClung began writing in the late 1800s, and began publishing in the early twentieth century. It is not surprising, then, that her novels follow some nineteenth-century conventions. "There is, hence, a didactic intention, a lesson conveyed and assented to if the work succeeds. Instruction is not at cross-purposes with entertainment in this fiction, nor is entertainment the sweet-coating on a 'didactic pill.'"[60] The work succeeds in its purpose "by engaging and channeling the emotions of readers through identification with the heroine." Such novels are to be assessed in relation to their own time not by the literary standards of a later era. It is to be noted, too, that the study of women's fiction, until recently, "was carried out in a pre-feminist or antifeminist frame of mind."[61] To this day male critics such as Laurence Ricou, Dick Harrison, and Eric Callum Thompson consistently disparage McClung's fiction. On the other hand, women critics like Patricia Verkruysse and Tamara Palmer are decidedly more sympathetic.[62] Because McClung was a feminist writer, her female protagonists like Pearlie Watson and Helmi Milander are strong characters. They are women who do not—in the sentimental heroine's way—resort to tears, or pleading, or self-indulgently immerse themselves in excessive displays of emotion; McClung's heroines have as much common sense, will power, and intelligence as emotion. Like their author, "they had always been scornful of the tears of lovelorn maidens."[63] If the centre of women's fiction may be defined as "how the heroine perceives herself,"[64] then one can only conclude that McClung's heroines, such as Pearlie Watson, nurse Downey, and Helmi Milander, possess self-esteem from the beginning. Feminist writers have identified five functions literature must perform in order to be identifiably feminist. It must serve as a forum for women, help achieve cultural androgyny, promote role models, promote sisterhood, and augment consciousness-raising. McClung's Pearlie Watson trilogy achieves some of these; *Painted Fires* achieves all five.

Nina Baym, in *Women's Fiction: A Guide to Novels by and About Women in America, 1820–1970* (1978), contends that unlike late nineteenth century heroines, Pearlie Watson, from the beginning of *Sowing Seeds in Danny*, "is her own woman and requires no parent to provide identity." From the first she is a child with "force of character,"[65] a strong will, and a strong ego that knows its worth. Both Watson parents work. The result is that Pearlie has the responsibility of caring for the home and mothering the children. Even in relation to her parents Pearlie is the "director-in-chief." She represents, then, the power base in the family. She gives the orders, settles disputes, and generally keeps the family on an orderly course.[66] She is more down-to-earth, resolute, and able than the traditional sentimental heroine, who is passive, acted upon rather than active, and excessively lachrymose. Pearlie is always in command of the circumstances in which she finds herself and, in a crisis, she follows her own judgement, not that of others. Both in her strength of character and her comic romantic imagination—which Nellie spoofs—the reader can readily identify with Pearlie, whose moral autonomy is strongly evident.

Literary critic Elaine Showalter has argued that superior women novelists of McClung's day sought heroines who were "both professional role-models and fictional ideals—who could combine strength and intelligence with feminine tenderness, tact, and domestic expertise." Such heroines were "counter ideals" to the old-fashioned, Victorian heroine for they could "stand alone, reason, lead, instruct, command." They were "rebels" against the passive, self-sacrificing, and essentially self-destructive Victorian heroine, and they were marked by "growth" and "development."[67] Both Pearlie Watson and Helmi Milander, for example, were developing characters. This was, of course, more evident in the Watson trilogy, where the heroine grew from an enchantingly imaginative little twelve-year-old in *Sowing Seeds in Danny*, through the gradually more serious little thirteen- to fifteen-year-old who caused the minister's eyes to twinkle with amusement at her spiritual gravity in *The Second Chance*, to the mature eighteen-year-old who was home from Normal School in the city to take up her first teaching position in *Purple Springs* where she would be financially independent.

Like Pearlie Watson, Helmi Milander of *Painted Fires* is also a strong character, physically and mentally. At one point in the story, Mr. Wymuth, director of the girls' reformatory, grabs Helmi and begins to shake her. Helmi reacts by flinging him away from her. Later, Mrs. Wymuth comes to Helmi to tell her she has killed the director and proceeds to use this as a strategy to get at the girl's secret. They want to know who sent her to the Chinese restaurant for opium. In the middle of this, the bruised and bloody Mr. Wymuth enters the room, and Helmi speaks defiantly to Mrs. Wymuth: "'It is you who is one damn liar,' she said, in careful English. She walked past them through the open door, switching on the hall light as she passed and making no effort to walk quietly." In the dining room next day, Helmi is told to eat in the kitchen as a punishment. Helmi boldly mocks Mrs. Wymuth in front of all the girls. Staring brashly into her face Helmi says: "Your husband . . . Is he dead already yet?"[68] She will not be broken and, in a symbolic sense, she murders the situation that constrains her.[69] Although the novel is essentially about Helmi Milander, it is also about the society that assaults, constrains, and suffocates her. Part of the sensationalism in Helmi's trial for resisting arrest in an opium den results from her having been discovered in an oriental establishment. Even as late as 1937 the Canadian Federation of Business and Professional Women thought women should be excluded from certain industries on the grounds of health (e.g., underground mining) and of morals (e.g., white women working for orientals).[70] Many Anglo-Saxons tended to think there was more than a hint of white slavery and prostitution.

The series of hardships and misunderstandings in *Painted Fires* is authentically drawn in order to show the social forces that shape or hinder Helmi's development from a naive romantic to someone who has learned that chasing fabulous "painted fires" is a useless illusion. Such is the lesson of the novel, and the reader can assent to this theme because the reader can assent to Helmi, the protagonist. Her courage—which is partly rooted in her physical strength—her loyalty, her power of endurance—which overcomes her despair and thoughts of suicide—and her unflagging hope and trust that all will be well in the end are traits that the events in the novel call forth and strengthen as she matures in spite of the loss of her husband. Her ultimate refusal to give in to negative circumstance is her strongest characteristic as well as her ability to hold her familial life together in spite of its apparent break-up. At the end of the story, when Jack finally rediscovers Helmi, she has settled into her friend Arthur Warner's house, which had been willed to her after Arthur's death. Helmi lives there with two-and-a-half-year-old Lili, a female teacher who boards at the house, and old Sim, who is no longer able to work in the mine. He helps Helmi with her vegetable garden, which she uses to raise cash by selling vegetables to Mrs. McMann's Boarding House in Eagle Mines. It is a far cry from the idealistic picture labelled "Aunty's Flower Garden" given to Helmi in Finland by her Americanized aunt Lili, an Edenic picture that Helmi literally believes is Lili's garden and that she sees as a symbol of the New World in general. Helmi's Eagle Mines garden is solidly, earthily real and toiled over. It is post-lapsarian.

By the end of *Painted Fires*, Helmi Milander has moved beyond a patriarchal society of male authority figures to a matriarchal society. She has created her own security and found her own friends in her neighbours. "The hearts of the women were knitted to Helmi's because she had a way of comforting in their troubles. There was strength in the touch of her hand and healing in her presence."[71] It is assumed that Jack—when he returns from the war—will fit in to this society, but Helmi's world, as determined by her, would exist whether Jack returned to Eagle Mines or not. At no time is Helmi referred to as Helmi Doran, or Mrs. Jack Doran. She is not defined by her relationship to Jack as wife, or to little Lili as mother. She is an autonomous human being whose success marks her more the female hero of her story than the conventional term *heroine* will allow. In feminist fiction "marriage no longer strikes the same note of finality in the story of a woman's life."[72]

Whereas in earlier fiction Nellie McClung had written anti-romantic passages, *Painted Fires*, at the height of her fictive career—and in spite of its somewhat romantic ending—is from first to last *essentially* an antiromance. Unlike novelists such as Ralph Connor in *The Foreigner* "we will find not so much an overemphasis on the Canadianizing of the new-comer . . . but an emphasis on the 'Finnizing' of Canadian women." This sets McClung's heroine apart from Connor's foreigner who is shaped by the West.[73]

Quite often, in women's fiction, the term "domestic sentimental-ism" is used to imply "that the author is asking for more of an emotional response from the reader than the literary art has con-veyed; or that the wrong kind of emotion is called out; or that the author's depiction of real life is heavily slanted toward the pretty and tender and hence is not a comment on reality but an evasion of it." McClung was rarely guilty of such traits. She knew both the agrarian and metropolitan West and never idealized either. All of McClung's fiction, however, was domestic in the sense that it described events that occurred in and around a home setting, but it did not espouse a "cult of domesticity." When McClung's work is dismissed as insignif-icant or merely romantic sentimentality it is underrated.[74]

McClung, of course, was not the only writer in her time who portrayed this domestic realism. Canadian writer Sara Jeannette Duncan, in the late nineteenth century, practised—and preached—the same realism that American authors such as W.D. Howells and Henry James did. *The Imperialist* (1880) was a fine example. But while Duncan and her American counterparts wrote a brand of "genteel" realism that dealt with upper middle-class "society" in an urban setting, McClung, on the other hand, commonly dealt with im-poverished, generally lower or lower middle-class rural communities, which at times involved very ungenteel language in vicious verbal or physical abuse of women and children.[75]

McClung wrote about real life. She embraced topics that were the concern of Canadian reformists like herself and Emily Murphy—"the narcotics trade, the injustices imposed upon young aliens by the penal system, and the negative attitudes espoused by both govern-ment and society . . . "[76] While her novels cannot be classified as "great"—they lack "the esthetic, intellectual, and moral complexity and artistry that we demand of great literature"[77]— still, she had her own writer's creed and followed it to the best of her ability. Authors, she thought, can help a troubled world "by telling the truth. Unreal writing does no good, and although I am not fond of sordid ugliness, I prefer being dragged through the sewers of reality, to reading something unrelated to life." As long as there was "some purpose in the action" of such stories McClung was prepared to accept them. On the other hand, if there was no purpose discernible in the "sordid" then all one had was "cheap sensationalism," and this she always rejected.[78] As for herself, however, she said: "I think a writer should above all things portray life; because there are more decent people than the other kind, it is keeping nearer to the truth to write of those who go right, rather than of those who go wrong."[79] McClung was firmly convinced by experience that "there is drama and romance all around us . . . It lives in the hearts of the common people every-where—the man who sits beside you at the lunch counter, the woman who writes letters in the rest room, the people who stand in line buying railway tickets. They all have at least one story"—a down-to-earth story of real life. It was among such common people that Nellie would seek authentic material for her fiction. On one occasion, for example, "I helped a woman to wash her dishes one night in a country hotel, and she told me in five minutes a story which I will write some day . . . There it was—a whole story, and a sad one." But then to McClung "this world in which we find ourselves . . . is a bad world in some ways and a very sad world some times," and certain of her fictions—particularly her short stories and *Painted Fires*—convey this.[80] She objected that "in Canada we are inclined to overlook greatness in our own; we like to read of foreign parts and Spanish galleons, never observing the dramatic situations and the heroic doings right around us." Not for her the romance of far places. Indeed she deplored this taste for exotic romance and declared that "many a Canadian in shiny serge lives a more heroic life than knights of old who rode out in shiny armour."[81]

McClung saw Canada as one of the best sources of material for Canadian authors. There was material in "the story of the Indians of Canada, in the history of the Hudson's Bay Company and its fur traders, [and] in the wonderful work accomplished by airplanes in bringing succor to sick settlers in the isolated regions of the north" all of which reflected "high adventure" for those readers who wanted genuine Canadian romance. In addition, there was always material in "the battle against loneliness, isolation, discouragement, the heart hunger of the people." She pointed out that "the Canadian Broadcasting Corporation is ready to co-operate" and that it expected Canadians "to supply material." To McClung, Canada was an "endless supply . . . [which] we shall never catch up to." "Faith in the land," she strongly affirmed, "is in my blood and cannot be shaken."[82]

But, she complained, "Books about women have been written by men."

> Women have felt, have lived, have enjoyed and suffered, but few of them have expressed it in words. Men have told us what we think, what we dream, what we aspire to, what we like and dislike, what we ought to be, what we are and what we are not! What we would like to be, and never can be! All this has been done for us by men, and it was rarely that any woman objected; at least in print . . .
>
> . . . Sex-prejudice is not dead. It is still hard for some to believe that those who are physically weaker, may be equal in intelligence. But there will come, as a result of this new freedom for women, a great harvest of women writers . . . There will be books written from a new angle, and a new method of reasoning, and surprising may be the conclusions reached. A new era is upon us, in the world of literature!
>
> I would like to hear from the women themselves. I am positive that we are going to hear from them. I feel it coming.[83]

McClung's prophetic words have come true, and she would scarcely be surprised by the litany of leading Canadian authors of our day, so many of whom are women. Years later Margaret Laurence recognized that: "it is still enormously difficult for a woman to have both a marriage and a family, and a [writing] profession. I often become angry when I think of this injustice . . . " Perhaps this is why "Nellie McClung has long been a heroine of mine."[84]

There is another side to McClung's verse and fiction that has never been properly analyzed, and therefore not recognized, by literary critics, even by those who too easily dismiss her work as didactic. The range of her social reform ideas is much broader than generally admitted, and, with a few exceptions, McClung lets the story speak for itself, rather than stopping the action to moralize and sermonize. Most of her writing is issue-oriented for she uses her craft to address the social problems of her day, many of which are still with us today. McClung sensitizes her readers to social problems characteristic of a patriarchal society. As might be expected Nellie at times raises the issue of temperance, dealing with out-and-out alcoholism as opposed to social drinking, particularly as it affects the alcoholic's family and friends. McClung's novella *When Christmas Crossed the Peace,* which has been called a temperance tract, is one example. It is, however, more a romp than a tract, as the women in a northern Alberta town band together to outwit the men, who always club together to import bootleg liquor so they can celebrate Christmas as roistering drunks. McClung is aware that in feminist fiction the author must analyse the relations between women as well as between men and women. In this novella there is female solidarity against the tradition of Christmas drunkenness among the men. The opinion of the young Alberta provincial policeman is that the bootleggers "degrade the settlers—for the sake of money." He sees pioneering as "tough" enough on the women without having "to live with a drunken man—slobbering, dirty, foul-mouthed, with the subsequent ill-temper and the gradual degeneracy." "No wonder," he says, "they go crazy." Just such a woman is Mrs. Bill Lukes, "faded and anemic" with a "pathetic droop to her mouth." Her spirited red-haired daughter lashes out at her for being too easy on their father. "What right has he to hog up every cent—and blow it for his own pleasure and then get so cross when he's sobering up, that we can't live with him—you work for this money—so do I—so do the boys—but he has the spendin' of it—you've been too blamed easy, ma!" Mrs. Lukes, however, has no fight left in her, and she has gone a bit "queer" in the mind. She "began to cry with her face twisting pitifully, without a sound." McClung has skilfully caught the woman's hopeless despair in one line. In *The Second Chance* little Libby Cavers is the unhappy young daughter of the town drunk. At school, the first day, Pearlie recognizes Lib because of "her pale face" and her eternally "frightened eyes." In one glance Pearlie "read all her sad child history." McClung's attack is always against the industry itself rather than against weak human beings like Bill Cavers who succumb to its lure. She shows that a little child like Libby Cavers has been "cheated of her birthright of happiness because some men will grow rich on other men's losses and fatten on the tears of little children."[85] It was for such reasons that Nellie McClung attacked the liquor interests throughout her life.

Several of Nellie's short sketches, such as "Thirty Years" and "The Day of Deliverance," speak of freedom from varied kinds of bondage. In "The Perils of Heroism" a thirteen-year-old boy frees his family from terrible domestic bondage. "On the lonely northern farm where

[Johnny Martin] and his parents lived, a tragedy had occurred. The father, coming home drunk and raging had smashed the furniture, terrorized his wife and the younger children, and was beating the fifteen year old boy who had tried to stay his fury, when Johnny, aged thirteen, arrived on the scene. He took the shotgun from the wall, and shot his father dead."[86] The boy is permanently marred by the event.

Nellie McClung also criticized useless idle lives, whether this was self-imposed or imposed, for example, upon the elderly. She firmly believed that the aged should have independence and pursue the work of their choice. Indeed she saw work as an antidote to individual problems, such as the Calvinist conscience in "One of the McTavishes." People like Eva St. John in *Painted Fires*, the haughty Anglo-Saxon woman in the acerbic poem "Standards," and Millicent in "Bells at Evening," are uselessly indolent, self-centred, and selfish. They just "lounged and played." McClung's educative propaganda in these instances was couched tersely in an unconventional poem that ends:

> . . . Perhaps the snake was wise
> And what we call the "Fall" might well be called the "Rise."
> The only creatures that can live at ease
> Day after day and not be hurt are these:
> The long-haired Persian and the Pekinese![87]

Similarly McClung satirized unnecessary squalor. In "Babette," George Shaw, a bachelor farmer, and his Métis neighbours both live in filthy conditions. George has dirty, fly-specked windows, a rusty stove from which ashes litter the floor, a sooty pot with yesterday's blackened potatoes in it, and dirty dishes cluttering the table. It is raining and his shack leaks everywhere, he shares his soda biscuits with well-entrenched mice, and he is personally as filthy and unkempt as his hovel is. Babette, a young Métis woman who has been in school in Winnipeg for four years, returns home for a visit, and she scours out both slovenly houses. Her brother Henri brings freshly baked bread, as usual, over to George's shanty. His new appearance astonishes George, who asks if Henri's had a change of heart. "'No change heart,' said Henri. 'Change shirt, change socks, change everyt'ing. No change heart. Babette, she is home. Come on de car from de Vinnipeg. Babette wan beeg swell!'" She considers her brother "wan dirty young peeg—Bah! . . . She sweep, scrub, clean all

tam. Mais oui, you should but see Babette. She is good peopl'."
Having cleaned up her brother, Babette plans to clean up her father.
"Dad say he be dam'. Babette say we see."

As a proud Englishman, Shaw considers himself a cut above his
Métis neighbours, but Babette sees that their living conditions are
identical. While George Shaw is out in the fields she cleans his house,
cooks him a good supper, and finds his comb and old washstand. She
leaves him a telling note: "Dear Mr. Pshaw! . . . I cleaned up your
shantey to let you see how it feals to live like white folks." The note
spikes his feelings of racial superiority.[88]

By contrast, the poverty of the Paine family in *Purple Springs* is
harshly imposed on the family by Mr. Paine. He goes about the country
buying and selling cattle and is rarely home. His wife is not only in
charge of the house, but also of the farm, "and I've made it pay, too!"
Yet what little furniture they have is paid for "with my butter money" for
Mr. Paine is a "hard" man who takes all the money for himself. Peter
Neelands, a city lawyer who is stormed-in at the Paine farm, is shocked
by the living conditions. "He did not know that human beings could live
in such crude conditions, without comforts, without even necessities. It
is like a bad dream—confused, humiliating, horrible . . . " Pearlie says:
"You would never think a man with $15,000.00 in the bank would let
his wife and children live like this . . . "[89] Throughout the 1920s farm
women were repeatedly exhorted to "reduce the drudgery of their
work" by means of modern "technological improvements" such as
electric appliances. In Mrs. Paine's case—as in McClung's stinging
"Jane Brown" poem—it is unlikely that she even has a kitchen pump
but, instead, has to haul water from the well, usually situated some
distance from the house and nearer the cattle. In reality, many
feminists of the early twentieth century

> challenged the allocation of economic priorities which gave the barn
> precedence over the house . . . They argued that the greatest eco-
> nomic problem was not the absolute lack of money but rather the
> reluctance to attribute proper economic value to women's labour.
> Again and again, they lectured farm women that their labour was a
> commodity with real value and that it was not true economy to save
> everything but themselves.[90]

Mrs. Paine's unnecessarily harsh and impoverished living conditions were extreme at a time when rural living was already difficult. A
survey of rural living conditions in Manitoba in 1920 revealed that

"the heavy and unrelenting physical work demanded of the farm wife, coupled with the lack of labour-saving devices in the farm household" made for a sombre assessment. "'One of Many' said she loved work, 'but not slavery.' Another described 'too much of soul-sickening, monotonous drudgery, unbroken by recreation.'" The United Farm Women of Manitoba executive, who carried out the survey, knew that "the farm wives' work load was exorbitant" and wanted the wives to speak out and demand better conditions.[91] Even after she moved to the city McClung was in contact with farm women and their issues along with the Beynons and other Winnipeg journalists who addressed rural women's issues in the pages of newspapers and magazines.

Mrs. Paine is one more of McClung's "winter-killed" souls whose hopes are long "dead." For her, "marriage is a form of bondage—long-term slavery—for women." Men have "made the world, and they've made it to suit themselves. My husband takes his family cares as lightly as a tomcat. The children annoy him." The same holds true of young Hilda's father in "Carried Forward." One of his neighbours asks, "What's wrong with a man who can't bear the sight of his own children?"[92] The deprivations at the Paine house are not necessary. They constitute an abuse. In her fiction, McClung deals with varied forms of abuse: physical, emotional, verbal. Like some modern feminist fiction, hers are books that "radically question assumptions about the limits of women's experience" and bring into question the masculine portrayal of what they think women's experience is or ought to be.[93]

Drunkenness, as we have seen, is the cause both for physical and emotional abuse. Alcoholism, however, is not mentioned as the root for Helmi's aunt Lili being beaten by her husband in McClung's last novel, *Painted Fires*. Lili objects to her husband's frisking of drunks in his hotel bar-room. His response is to hit her "over the head with a chair." Of this McClung indicates with caustic irony that "such crude methods of dealing with women can only be safely used inside the hallowed precincts of matrimony."[94] Very few authors of this time focused on the way in which women were treated as property, in which a marriage licence essentially gave men the right to beat and otherwise control their wives.[95] Also in *Painted Fires:* "Our washerwoman's sister killed her man up at Gimli." Her employer goes to visit the convict to see if she won't repent and feel sorry. The convict says indeed she is sorry, "sorry she had not killed him long ago

. . . God had been good to her and let her find the ax just as she was getting the worst of it." The employer comes home "all shaken up" as, indeed, the passage is meant to shake the reader up. In addition, Jane Bosomworth, Mrs. Pierce's friend in "Bells at Evening," was struck by her bad-tempered husband on the occasion of an argument. It was "one awful surprise. After that I never felt the same . . . " In "Carried Forward," when young Hilda raises her voice to defend the memory of her abused and overworked mother, the housekeeper surreptitiously manages to slip a piece of leather harness into the father's hand: "Cruelly, cruelly the strap bit into Hilda's tender flesh." She is a "picture of misery" going up the stairs.[96] According to historian Veronica Strong-Boag, the WCTU "represented the organized might of women opposed to violence against women." Feminists like Louise McKinney and Nellie McClung "shared an awareness of the dangers of domestic or workplace violence that has long been central to feminist politics."[97] Another feminist has noted: "By a breach of fictional decorum, writing enacts protest as well as articulating it." The same critic observes a characteristic of McClung's fiction: "the quietly subversive power of writing, its power to destabilise the ground on which we stand"[98] and not pay tribute to the status quo.

A particular form of abuse that crops up frequently in McClung's fiction is that of the annual pregnancy thoughtlessly imposed by husbands on their wives. It is presented at its most biting in "Carried Forward" where Annie Berry "died from overwork and child-bearing. She always has one baby in her arms and another on the way." Her husband criticizes his dead wife: "Women don't seem to have the sand in them they used to have; my mother raised fifteen and lost five, and I have often heard my father say they never had a doctor in the house, and never needed one . . . " "It was quite evident," says McClung ironically, "that Luke Berry had been badly treated." Annie Berry "had a baby every year, and broke her heart when they died. To be sure Luke was a good man; he never beat her or starved her. There are other ways of killing a woman." "It's a great plan and a great world for men," says Annie's mother. Grandma Brown is shushed up so Hilda won't turn against her father. "'That's so,' she said, 'there is no use in making the child bitter. She will be that soon enough.'"[99]

Women like Annie Berry had no control over their bodies and Nellie's story forces the reader to question this. Hilda's mother is powerless within her marriage. "Her own voice has been drowned out . . . "Subversive stories like McClung's "Carried Forward" ask why women have relinquished such control to men. The story indicates a need for women's "repossession" of their bodies.[100]

Another form of abuse—verbal abuse—is at its strongest in the Paine household in *Purple Springs*. Mr. Paine has arbitrarily decided to sell the farm and buy a hotel, which his wife will have to manage along with her household chores and caring for the children. All the hard work she has put into the farm is now useless. She doesn't want to sell. In a chapter entitled "The Storm" the disturbance is both outside and inside. In the house Mr. Paine's voice "rose above the storm . . . 'I'll break you . . . and you'll not get a cent of money from me' . . . The children shrank into corners and pitifully tried to efface themselves. The dog, with drooping tail, sought shelter under the table." As Mr. Paine sees his wife "shrinking" too, he lets out "a fresh outpouring of abuse." "There's no one to help you . . . Don't you think I see it! You've no one to turn to . . . I've got you." "His last words were almost screamed at her." He threatens to take the children away from her, as was his legal right. The lawyer Peter Neelands is appealed to: "'The law . . . gives a married woman no rights. She has no claim on her home, or on her children. A man can sell or will away his property from his wife. A man can will away his unborn child—and it's a hell of a law,' he added fiercely." It is a law that McClung and others sought to change.[101]

Melody Graulich, in a study of four unusual female novelists of the American frontier, shows that "the radical conclusion of these writers—that violence against women is the result of patriarchal definitions of gender and marriage rather than of individual pathology—anticipates the analysis of the most recent feminist scholars . . . They reveal the struggles women face growing up female in a world where women are victimized and devalued." Society's attitudes toward women and marriage sanction male power and authority. Mr. Paine holds the power and controls the money in the family. His wife is neither consulted nor respected.

> When a man responds to his wife's efforts to talk about family needs and problems with only verbal aggression and violence, this *is* a mode of communication. He "teaches" the woman who controls the relationship and shows her how problems will be "solved," and tells her what to think about herself. Powerless, separated from others,

unheard, she has no way to validate her feelings. She has been successfully intimidated.

These four remarkable American authors "demonstrate women's recognition of their need of each other; most turn at some point to women friends . . ."[102] as Mrs. Paine turns to McClung's independent-minded Pearlie Watson after hearing Pearlie talk about the suffrage issue and laws against women.

It follows that much of Nellie McClung's social criticism is of gender role stereotyping, antifeminism, and women who don't speak out. Dr. Brander in *Purple Springs* has what McClung condemned as a male-chauvinist, stereotypical view of women, entirely concerned with their outward appearance. Women, he says, have "the *instinct* to dress in a way that will attract men" (italics added). They are "little frilled and powdered vixens" never to be taken seriously " . . . it is their place in life to be beautiful, and when they fail in that, they fail entirely."[103] Dr. Brander illustrates that men's image of the sexes is usually "normative and proscriptive," rather than "descriptive" and their norms are not only different from women's, but also far removed from the reality of women's lives.[104]

In *Painted Fires* Helmi, too, is conscious of gender distinctions. Although she is as strong as many men she is aware that, as a woman, she can't do all that she wants: "Men can do such wonderful things . . . but [ironically] pretty girls have a good chance." While at Eagle Mines, the narrator says: "Wasn't it provoking being a girl and not able to hit out for yourself—never able to step out and do big things, and here she was, working all day long for twenty-five dollars a month, while the poorest man in the mines had four dollars a day and only worked eight hours."[105] Equal wages for work of equal value is the implication here. Helmi's is a constant battle for self-determination, which she ultimately wins, for she refuses the feminine limitations society would impose on her. She defies the patriarchal authority system and questions the secondary nature of being female. In "Carried Forward," however, Luke complacently accepts stereotypical sex roles as he muses in the open fields about men and women. "Poor Annie, how soon she had faded and lost her looks." He fails to see the reason for this. She is overworked without any household help—though he has all the hired help he wants—and she is ill from excessive child-bearing. "Poor Annie, dragging around half dead . . . well, life was certainly hard on women. He would rather be dead than tied to a kitchen and a pack of kids; but, of course, women had always done it, and maybe they did not mind. Their brains were different from men's . . . " A free bird, and a caged bird is his complacent image for the difference between men and women. "And in that moment Luke was supremely happy in the sex allotted to him."[106] Here McClung shows how society is "sex-coded." The kitchen is insignificant for "men . . . cannot meaningfully interpret the farm wife's world." McClung has set "against one another male and female realms of meaning and activity—the barn and the kitchen . . . " "The essential crime in the story, we come to realize, has been the husband's inexorable strangulation, over the years, of [Mrs. Berry's] spirit and personality . . . "[107]

As a social critic McClung's work is saturated with satire and irony, often in opposition to antifeminist attitudes. In *Painted Fires*, for example, the board of the women's reformatory in Winnipeg is composed entirely of men, most of whom would keep it that way. "It was felt that the presence of ladies might prove embarrassing. There were certain matters [unwed mothers and prostitution] that were best discussed by men alone—besides there was always danger of women being too emotional": a stereotypical image of women as over-wrought. They did, however, permit a women's auxiliary that "in general did all those little unimportant but necessary things which women do so well," says Nellie, ironically.

The first female matron of the reformatory was a Mrs. Avery, who established controversial methods such as a "merit system," the removal of "mud-colored uniforms," education, entertainment, and happy activities. On one occasion she insisted on attending a board meeting:

> One of the members (and one of the most solid, too) began by pointing out that there should be some difference in the way well-behaved girls and fallen girls are treated. Here the matron interrupted to ask him to retract the word "fallen." She gave the Board members positive chills by the things she said about the double standard of morals which was made by men to shield men, and went on to tell them that many of the girls were innocent young things from the country who had come to work in the city to help the family at home, and had fallen victims to men's lust and hypocrisy. The very men who led them astray, fathers of families some of them, and regarded as respectable men in society, no doubt now spoke of these girls as "fallen women."

It was most embarrassing. She also hinted that there should be women on the Board and questioned the ability of men to quite understand the problems of rescue work.

Any one can see from this what sort of a woman this matron was and why the Board dismissed her.

With the firing of the enlightened and innovative Mrs. Avery, the board turned to a man, Mr. Wymuth, who "believed in hell" and firm "discipline" and an "orgy of prayers" and, for appearance's sake, Mr. Wymuth's wife who, he said, with mid-Victorian propriety, "will be guided by me entirely."[108]

Nellie McClung also criticizes passive women who do not speak out for their rights. That is why she shows Pearlie Watson, in part, blaming Mrs. Paine for not confronting her husband and demanding money to make the farm house liveable. And that is why she condemns "Jane Brown" in one of her harshest poems.[109] The strongest expression of the need for a woman to speak out is in her satire "Carried Forward." In the Berry household, eleven-year-old Hilda has never gone to school because she's the oldest child. "Ever since she could walk Hilda had had a baby dragging after her . . . and scarcely a full night's sleep had she ever had with the incessant demands of a last year's baby . . . Her little arms were so tired some nights that she could not sleep for the ache of them." It was not an uncommon experience, and one historian has pointed out that "the loss of parents, especially mothers . . . readily lead to daughters . . . aged [as young as] eleven, taking on heavy responsibilities for younger siblings . . . some regretted the time lost to play or school."[110] In young Hilda's case, long before her mother dies, this wearisome burden is imposed on her because of a harsh and penurious father who would permit no domestic help in a home with seven young children. Such men are gratified by the economic dependence of women upon them. Finally, when Annie Berry dies from overwork and constant child-bearing, Hilda knows that "she had no hope of help from anyone. This was her fight and hers alone." She recalls her mother's last words, "said hurriedly as one who is pressed for time":

> Learn to speak out, Hilda . . . when you feel something ought to be said. All your life I mean. Don't let anyone make you so frightened that you cannot speak . . . You should have been in school. I wanted you to go every day, but I was not brave enough to make a row about it . . . Your father is not a bad man—see how good he is to his

horses—but he didn't understand, and I couldn't make him . . . I sat still, too patient. It isn't patience, it's cowardice . . . It's a heavy inheritance. And I'm sorry, Hilda . . . Your father is not a poor man . . . he could hire help for us, I knew, but he wouldn't talk . . . he just went dumb . . . don't be patient. Speak out. They can only kill you—and it would be best to die fighting . . . not like me, dying because I was too dumb.[111]

Sometimes the harsh conditions lead to impaired faith. In the title story to *All We Like Sheep* a woman trying to grow cabbages is moved to despair over the severe drought. The narrator says: "She had grown older since I saw her in the spring . . . 'There's something so hard and heartless about the look of the sun that it makes me bitter,' she said . . . ; 'Tell me, because I can't think anymore . . . It seems hard to believe that God is unfriendly.'" The narrator tries to cheer her up. "I told her that good times would come again." Her response is total despair: "'It will never rain,' she said, moistening her dry lips, 'there's no rain in the clouds—there's nothing up there but more heat, and this terrible, consuming dryness . . . My heart is as dry as my cabbage plants before the wind blew them away.'" The narrator again tries to cheer the hopeless gardener: "As I looked over the parched gray land, with its burned-out grass, its wind-swept and sun-baked fields, its gaunt and eager-eyed cattle, its discouraged people, I felt the poisoned breath of unbelief coming up to attack me, and what could I do but send out a barrage of brave words?"[112]

Perhaps the most pathetic loss of faith is that of eleven-year-old Hilda in "Carried Forward." Asking where all the Berry babies come from, she is told that God sends them, which "did not increase her good opinion of the Almighty." Since Mrs. Peters, the local midwife, seems to deliver the babies, little Hilda believes that Mrs. Peters can bring her mother back to life. Though she has had too little education to be able to read, she does know the meaning of the religious motto over her bed: "Ask and it shall be given unto you." Hilda believes it literally and keeps faith in the motto through the end of her mother's funeral.

> "I am asking God, and I am asking," Hilda repeated as she saw the men preparing to screw down the coffin lid. She stood beside the coffin, wanting to be the first one to see her mother open her eyes . . . "Ask and it shall be given unto you." One screw had gone in, and the second one was being turned . . . "Ask and it shall be given unto you

... Oh, God, hear me, I am asking; do it now, God—she'll smother if you don't! ... Ask and it shall be given unto you"

Hilda keeps faith right through to the interment when the last shovelful of earth is "patted down like a hill of potatoes." Only then is she ready to go with Mrs. Peters. "Her voice was steady, but the eyes that looked into Mrs. Peters' were not the eyes of a child, but two great pools of darkness." Back at the house Hilda marches upstairs, walks to the wall, and taking the motto in her hands, she breaks it in half and puts it in the fire. "Then it was that something broke in her, and when Mrs. Peters came into the kitchen she found Hilda on the floor sobbing the dry, killing sobs of those who find themselves without hope and without God in the world."[113]

On a couple of occasions McClung deals with Métis and Indian characters. In "Babette" she presents the case of the assimilation of a Métis girl. In "Red and White" on the other hand she argues that the full-blooded Indian "pride of blood" is all the Indian has left except to pursue his own culture. Rosie Starblanket condemns white society: "'They take everything,' she muttered to herself; 'they can't let anything be ... they want to be boss of everything. Nobody is safe now—they grab everything.'" They imprison birds in cages when they ought to fly free; they live indolent, useless lives; their cottages have driven game north; they use alcohol to get drunk; they are hypocritical; and the white man's train thundering into the resort "seemed so overbearing and hostile. 'It sure don't give a damn'" Rosie muses to herself—reflecting the white attitude to Indians and Indian culture. She has a dream that her youngest son, Johnny, will go with her, "back to the life to which all Indians belonged—to the life of his father and his grandfather and the older brothers, who had fled before civilization's choking breath" to northern hunting and fishing grounds.

Johnny's girl Minnie, though she is a Métis, shares Rosie's Indian dream. In Winnipeg, where she goes to confront the magistrate who will try Johnny,

> the noise and confusion of the street traffic beat upon her mercilessly; the hurrying people, clanging streetcars, darting automobiles ... newsboys ... delivery men ... a familiar street scene on a busy morning, but to Minnie a scene of terror.
>
> A white husky dog, with wolf's ears and a collie nose, ran nervously through the throng, yelping his fear and terror—a poor lost

thing, belonging, like herself, to the kindly open spaces. She watched him, terrified, as he darted across the street only to meet a fire-engine as it came swiftly through an alley, and with an almost human shriek run blindly under its wheels! She turned away, sickened at the sight.

The dog is a half-breed, like herself, and she identifies with its terror and its death. Later when Rosie, Johnny, and Minnie are sitting on Rosie's doorstep, Minnie announces that Johnny must quit his job the next day. "Minnie's eyes commanded silence. 'Yes,' she went on, 'Johnny told me about the place down North where your other sons are, and how you would like to go, too. I know I would like it. There are too many people here, too much noise and crowds all the time, and never any quiet time any more. It's a right place for white people, but no good for Indians.'" Long after midnight the three continue to sit on Rosie's doorstep "rarely speaking, but each one happy in thinking of the big country 'down north' beckoning to them with its promise of peace and plenty and good hunting—three happy Indians about to enter into their Native heritage of open air and open sky." As a nonassimilationist tale "Red and White" is well in advance of its time.

The sense that the Indian has a culture that he wants to preserve and survive in, and has a right to, is truly remarkable for the 1920s. Nellie may have been influenced by her interest in Pauline Johnson and her Native poetry and Indian myths. The contrast between the white man's kind of "civilization" as Rosie Starblanket expresses it, and as Minnie and Johnny experience it both at the beach and in Winnipeg, is a graphically described difference. As Minnie imagines it, "they would take the two canoes and go . . . north to the big country—and live their lives as her people and his had lived theirs before all these troublesome, noisy things had come upon them." As it is, Johnny is caught between two worlds: "By day he was Jack Starblanket, in all respects a white man doing a white man's work in the throbbing avenues of trade; at night with the sound of the lake licking the gray boulders on the shore, mingling with his mother's soft voice as she told him the stories of his people, he was an Indian, descendant of Chief Starblanket, and to whom the far country called."[114]

From the earliest days of her writing career Nellie McClung satirized Anglo-Saxon class consciousness and ladylike "respectability"—

particularly where the double standard and illegitimacy were concerned. This point is strongly put in *Painted Fires* when Helmi has her baby alone in an Edmonton boarding house. Mrs. Corbett, the owner, assumes Helmi is an unwed mother and puts a ring on Helmi's finger so the doctor will not take Helmi and her baby to a reformatory. The doctor feels contempt for foreign girls. "I get so many cases where these foreign girls think they are married. Some fellow shows them a paper which he says is a license, and away they go with him . . . I tell you, Mrs. Corbett, it is disgusting how easy these girls are!" He chooses to be blind to male sexual exploitation, and Mrs. Corbett mocks his double standard. He thinks women's societies should get involved and Mrs. Corbett retorts:

> And did it ever strike you that it might be grand work for the Rotary Club and Kiwanians and such like to say a word to the men? They're doin' a fine work, buildin' Homes for these little ones, but maybe if they worked a little harder on the men they would have less need for Homes . . . I know it's a grand thing to always be able to lay all the blame on the women. You see the Lord lets her bear all the pain, and we see to it that she gets all the shame . . . [115]

In *Purple Springs* Mrs. Gray has to pretend she's an unwed mother with an illegitimate son so her dead husband's father cannot take her son from her. Mrs. Gray and Jim are treated like social outcasts in the self-righteous community. "Even if Mrs. Gray had been all they said, she had not done any wrong to them—why should they feel called upon to punish her?" It is their sense of social superiority and their self-righteousness that leads the community to place Mrs. Gray in an inferior class by herself. They condemn Pearlie Watson because she supports women's suffrage. Feelings run so high that none of the women will take her—as the new teacher—to board and, in addition, they refuse to send their children to school to Pearlie. Nellie comments, satirically:

> If she had read the crochet patterns in the paper instead of the editorials, and had spent her leisure moments making butterfly medallions for her camisoles, or in some other lady-like pursuit, instead of leaning over the well-worn railing around the gallery of the Legislative Assembly,

she would not have come across to the women of Purple Springs as too forward and too threatening. Nellie was hopeless at knitting and needlework at a time when these were female-approved pursuits, and she was often critical of women who let their minds be "entangled by trifles" as her mother-in-law put it. She supported feminist activists who were not afraid to use their minds in areas narrowly considered to be male prerogatives in her day.[116]

Too many people, Nellie McClung once said, "walk through the field with gloves on."[117] It is an accusation most critics fire right back at her own writing. Yet scan the material that crops up in her poetry and fiction: wife and child battering; verbal and emotional abuse; alcoholism; squalor; prairie madness caused by a severe sense of isolation and loneliness; vote fixing accompanied by the abduction of a voter (in "The Elusive Vote"); racial prejudice with its resultant hatred; injustice; illegitimacy and single motherhood; hopeless dependency and bondage; faithless atheism; acute Calvinist guilt (in "One of the McTavishes") accompanied by brutality to animals; the greedy hoarding of money as an end in itself; female suffrage and laws against women; lives of quiet desperation because of helpless bondage to the kitchen and constant debilitating pregnancies for want of birth control; deprivation of many kinds—mental, moral, physical; murder of abusive parents carried out by children; doubt regarding the orthodox image of God; near incest (in "Red and White"); useless and unnecessary rural death for want of medical attention; the empty, good-for-nothing lives of some of the middle class; social affectations and class consciousness (in "You Never Can Tell"); the need for day-care centres; and the nonassimilation of Indians who want to be rooted in their own culture. Yet, at least one student of McClung writes her work off partly because of its lack of relevance to our age![118] Some of the above topics were hush-hush subjects in McClung's age. Today they are more openly addressed as social problems to be dealt with by crisis hotlines, for example, or shelters for battered women and children. Given the above, it is impossible to agree with critics who argue that McClung is *merely* writing rural idylls or that her writing failed to present a realistic grasp of social issues.

Women's fiction through the history of literature in English contains much social criticism, showing that women were capable of taking a stand on social issues and of articulating their social concerns.[119] In an agrarian era when it was popular to believe that God made the country and man made the town—implying, respectively, good and evil—it is also a fact that women writers "were more ambivalent. They saw much more clearly—or at least represented more clearly—the distressing rural conditions from which city immigrants were fleeing." Authors like McClung saw drought, ruined crops and with them ruined hopes, the maddening loneliness, the drab and penurious conditions, the evils of the property laws and the child custody laws. They "recognized country vices: brutalizing labor, mean minds, vicious gossip. They saw women's lot on the farm as particularly hard . . . " even when rural life also had "peace, stillness, rest, beauty, and harmonious nature . . . "[120]

"It is a serious thing to put pen to paper," McClung said. "To have grace with words carries a responsibility. If writers are to be true to their calling, they must be prophets. They are the warders who stand on the wall. Sentries guarding the treasure house. I know this is not acceptable in some quarters. How dreadfully frightened some of our writers are of propaganda, but there is no shame in propagating an idea, if it is a good idea. It may take courage, and it may draw fire! But what of that. 'Woe unto you, when all men speak well of you!' . . . I believe a writer must have a vision of a better world if his work is to live."[121] Every one of McClung's stories propagates ideas—many as topical as today's ideas—and implicit in them is that vision of a better world where the social evils she presents are conquered.

McClung's feminism was in many ways ahead of its time, and she was concerned with issues that continue to be major items on the Canadian social agenda, yet for years her work has been buried in the dust of the past. It is the job of the feminist critic to resurrect and examine such literature. Elaine Showalter has said that:

> Before we can even begin to ask how the literature of women would be different and special, we need to reconstruct its past, to rediscover the scores of women novelists, poets and dramatists whose work has been obscured by time, and to establish the continuity of the female tradition from decade to decade, rather than from Great Woman to Great Woman. As we recreate the chain of writers in this tradition, the patterns of influence and response from one generation to the next, we can also begin to challenge the periodicity of orthodox literary history, and its enshrined canons of achievement. It is because we have studied women writers in isolation that we have never grasped the connections between them. When we go beyond Austen, the Brontës and Eliot, say, to look at a hundred and fifty or more of their sister novelists, we can see patterns and phases in the evolution of a female tradition which correspond to the developmental phases of any subcultural art.[122]

Nellie McClung's writing needs to be rediscovered, in the first place, because much of it is good literature, particularly a number of her short stories and her last, and best, novel *Painted Fires*. Second, as feminist literary critics begin to establish the canon of a *Canadian women's literature*, the work of Nellie L. McClung will have no small place in that tradition. The reeducating of the literary imagination in order to reconstruct "the social, political and cultural experiences of women"[123] is a necessary beginning to this new approach to women's literature. In taking upon herself the literary job of "voicing the voiceless,"[124] Nellie L. McClung forced the society of her day and of ours to listen to the consciousness of women. Using essentially antiromantic fiction in which she commonly presented the negative social conditioning of women, McClung articulated numerous social problems that women have in the past, and still do, experience. Implicit in all of these stories is the social reformists' fundamental answer to such negative conditioning: the rebellious, the strong-minded, self-determining woman who is not passively acted upon by the society in which she lives. Memorable female characters like Pearlie Watson, Helmi Milander, and Annie Berry, who at last vigorously speaks out against the negative conditions she experiences, all work as effective literary satires of their respective societies just by being who they are. They are not essentially unlike the feminist-activist and social reformer Nellie McClung herself. As a spokesperson for strong-minded females with admirably strong characters who fight for what they know is just, McClung has depicted realistic feminist ideals that her readers of both yesterday and today can identify with—no small feat in the early 1900s.

11

Life at Lantern Lane

❖

When the McClungs moved to Victoria in 1932 Wes was still a manager for the Manufacturers' Life Insurance, but because he was looking forward to retirement the next year they rented accommodation while they looked around for a suitable retirement home.[1] It was not until January 1935 that they found the home they wanted. "It was a rough, gray day, with razor blades in the wind," cold and disheartening. The kind of day when "no one could be enthusiastic about anything." Nevertheless, they decided to look at a vacant house they had been told about six miles out in the country at Gordon Head. Nellie remembered that as they drove up the lane between two rows of cherry trees they saw that the land sloping to the east and south was somewhat attractive. "We got out of the car . . . and then something happened which seemed like fate."

> The sun came out! A sudden, unexpected flood of light ran over the fields and down to the sea. It lingered on the bright red roof of a white house on the right, almost hidden in the trees; it caught the wings of a wind-mill on a water tower below us . . . And then it was gone, and the woolly grayness rolled back. But we had seen the beauty of Gordon Head in that one bright revealing flash.

The house itself, though, "a dark green shingled semi-bungalow, looked old and comfortless," and the first glance inside was of "desolation." Rain had soaked through the plaster and pools of water lay on the floor. In the upstairs sunroom the windows were broken. Despite these obvious drawbacks Nellie immediately fell in love with it. For her "it had the right feel." Characteristically, instead of dwelling on the faults, she noted that the floors were straight, the

270

windows were on pulleys, there were three fireplaces, and the sun-porch could be furnished as her study. "I knew I would have bright draw curtains on the windows and . . . when I looked up from my work I would see the sea!" As they explored further Nellie saw the name *John Fullerton* on the mantle of the cobblestone fireplace in the den, "and then I was sure this was the house for me, for was not my grandmother one of the Fullerton girls away back in Dundee?"[2]

Wes, too, saw the possibilities of the place although his interest was more in the surrounding land, which he visualized planted and producing a cash crop. Although Wes had earned his living at inside jobs his heart had always been in the out-of-doors, and he was happy gardening. A backyard vegetable garden had been part of every one of their city homes and here, on twenty-four acres, he would have room for all he could look after. The decision to purchase was made and the McClungs moved in as soon as possible. There were no street lights in this rural area so they hung a ship's lantern above the garage door to cast a welcoming light down the lane. From this their home got its name, "Lantern Lane." This, in turn, supplied the titles for her last two books of essays collected from her syndicated column.[3]

In April of 1935 Horace married Margaret Grace McNamara of Calgary and the couple agreed to come live at Lantern Lane. Horace could help his father run the "farm" and Margaret could assist Nellie by acting as secretary and sharing in the care of the house. In the long run this arrangement proved unsatisfactory. Nellie had, over the years, made thousands of friends in many parts of Canada and invited them all to Lantern Lane. Many came. The first year, as Margaret recalled, "it was like a hotel!" She seemed always to be cleaning and baking for company, and Horace was in constant demand to meet the visitors in Victoria, to take them on a tour, to drive them back to the boat. He was torn between his mother's need for his services and his father's dissatisfaction with his contribution to the outside work. Horace did not share his father's enthusiasm for farming and found him difficult to work for. After a couple of years Margaret and Horace wisely decided to establish their own home, but Margaret continued to do secretarial work for Nellie, and both were still drawn into the frequent rounds of entertainment. Although Wes was always agree-able, he found the number of visitors overwhelming. Fortunately, he could plead the necessity of outside work, and even the young people escaped at times. Margaret tells of occasions when Mark was home when they would wash up the dinner dishes, see that everything was ready for afternoon tea, and then all three would hurry away before the callers arrived.[4]

The McClungs never regretted the purchase of Lantern Lane, where they lived until the end of their lives. Visits by members of the family were frequent and Lantern Lane became the favourite spot for the grandchildren. Nellie writes of taking Florence's daughter Jane and Jack's Nellie down to the beach where they could play in the water while she talked to other adults who had come down for the afternoon.[5] Nellie was particularly fond of the wooded path to the beach and always took house guests for that delightful walk down Banshee Lane with its "great arbutus trees with their smooth red boles that make one want to stroke them, symmetrical maples, and evergreens so high that looking at them becomes a good exercise for the neck."[6]

Nellie felt that she was once again living in the country, but now it was not a lonely life. There were friendly neighbours, many of them former prairie dwellers. It was the kind of neighbourhood where people dropped in for a chat or brought some choice bulbs for the new garden or a jar of preserves for the pantry shelf. When the McClungs had first moved to Victoria they attended the large city churches—First and Metropolitan. They made Nellie feel she should join a smaller church more in need of workers.[7] Once they moved to the country Nellie found her ideal church just three miles from Lantern Lane: "a little white church with a wrought iron lamp above its door, on which appears the words 'St. Aidan's' . . . a more dignified name for a church than 'First' or 'Central' or 'Sixth Avenue' . . . it has an atmosphere of peace and beauty, and remoteness from this troublesome world."[8] At St. Aidan's Nellie was made an elder, one of the few woman elders in the United Church at that time.[9]

Nellie's gardening was mostly devoted to flowers. Remembering the difficulties of maintaining a flower garden on the prairies she greatly appreciated the variety of flowers and the profuse blossoms that appeared in her Lantern Lane garden with relatively little effort. Wes was not much interested in this aspect of gardening but he helped Nellie by preparing the flower beds. Nellie's interest in gardening also included onions. This apparently began as a family joke but Nellie found it good material for her syndicated column, which appeared in numerous Canadian newspapers, and the saga of her onion-growing experiences lasted for several years. At first she thought that she had chosen a fool-proof crop but she did not know then about the onion thrip. She had thought she could plant her onions and forget about them: "I had not counted on daily observation or sitting up at night with them. I had not known of this subtle enemy whose dour countenance stares out from pamphlet 36, the inexorable, insatiable thrips with . . . a hairy ridged posterior, low, beetling brow, and his braces crossed on his back."[10]

From all over Canada and the United States she received advice on how to deal with thrips. But winning this battle was not enough. Her onions had club root and were eaten by centipedes. When she entered her best samples in the Fall Fair they looked small and unhealthy beside the prize winners. The only ones that thrived were from seeds dropped accidently under the cherry tree. "Not a thrip. Not a centipede. No knotted roots," Nellie reported. " . . . that's a fine way for onions to treat me—after all I've done for them!"[11] Failure, of course, made much better copy than success.

Nellie's columns were by no means all written in this personal light-hearted manner. She frequently dealt with national or world issues and reviewed and recommended books that she had read recently. Many columns pondered the effects of the Depression and the manner in which the resulting social problems were being handled. The churches and church members, she believed, were not doing as much as they could. Only 10 percent of Christians, she wrote, take their responsibilities seriously. "If the other 90% gave as much money and time and thought to missions we would not have people living—and dying—in houses whose approach is a quagmire, in this city [Toronto] of wealth and culture."[12] There were too many unemployment experts, she decided, who did not really understand what it means to be actually unemployed: "Hunting for a job, going from place to place, getting the glassy eye from employers who point to the sign, 'No Help Required,' having doors slammed in their faces, sleeping where they can, eating at soup kitchens, or not eating at all—having that terrible, desolate feeling of not being wanted anywhere."[13] Relief camps, she was sure, were not the answer, nor was welfare. Like most Canadians of the time Nellie feared the influence of communism on unemployed workers, but her answer was much the same as it had been in 1919: "The man who has a job which pays him a living wage and gives him hope for the future does not listen to subversive doctrine. There is only one remedy for Communism and that is it. Not padlocks, prisons, deportation. These are lazy, short-sighted answers, which feed the thing they are intended to destroy."[14]

McClung became increasingly concerned about the treatment of immigrant groups in Canada. On one occasion her defence of the Doukhobors at a meeting in Toronto brought angry protests, particularly from British Columbia, suggesting that her attitude would be different if she had to live among them. Nellie also feared that the Depression was increasing nativism and she was horrified by the many demands for the deportation of immigrants. It appalled her that the federal government, to save on welfare payments, actually gave in to these demands and deported large numbers of non-Canadians who had been invited, in previous years, to settle in Canada but were now—like so many Canadian citizens during the Depression—unable to support themselves. "It is bad," she wrote, "when an individual breaks faith with his fellow-man, but a nation that betrays its trust and breaks its word invites the swift lightning of the gods."[15]

From the time that Nellie moved to British Columbia she took up the cause of the Japanese Canadians, who were denied the vote and many other rights of Canadian citizens.[16] Her support for votes for Japanese brought her into conflict with the B.C. Liberals, who were trying to assure B.C. voters that they were not "soft" on the "Japanese menace." In 1936 McClung was invited to speak on behalf of Ian Mackenzie. Mackenzie, a B.C. member of King's cabinet, was constantly urging the government to take a strong stand against Japanese immigration and to make no agreements with Japan that would guarantee better treatment of the Japanese in Canada. On this occasion, both Mackenzie and McClung "faced a hostile audience" of "mainly working men"—a number of them supporters of socialist principles—in Vancouver's Empress Theatre. Much to Ian Mackenzie's chagrin and the delight of the Conservative papers, Nellie McClung stated her belief that Japanese Canadians had the right to vote: "I believe that every human has a right to vote. I could not take the responsibility of claiming for myself a privilege I wouldn't give to anybody else." While this statement evidently "earned the cheers of one element in the audience"—perhaps those "people of progressive thought" to whom she appealed—it also roused "a storm of abuse." Halfway through Nellie's address even Mackenzie was forced to bang on the table and shout his disagreement with his

Liberal colleague above the "roar of heckling and jeering" that periodically "swept the theatre." The Vancouver *Commonwealth* happily headlined: "Noted Author Bursts Bomb at City Rally" by disassociating herself from Liberal newspaper ads that "attacked the CCF for the stand of its leaders over the Oriental franchise."[17] On this issue McClung was closer to CCF policy than to that of her own party, demonstrating her usual political independence. She continued to press for Japanese rights but found few British Columbians agreed with her. In 1936 at a Peace Meeting in Vancouver it proved impossible to put through even a resolution supporting the vote for native-born orientals.[18]

As the growing military strength of Japan stirred even greater fears, Nellie increased her pleas for kindness and understanding. In the fall of 1939 when Colonel George Drew publicly supported the demand that the Japanese should be deported in retaliation for mistreatment of British subjects in Tientsin, the sharpness in Nellie's numerous attempts at reply reveal the strength of her indignation. His "opinion . . . must make the flesh of all decent people creep," "we're not quite civilized yet," "strange to find intelligent people giving support to anything as coldly cruel as this." Her published version pointed scathingly to hypocrisy: "This statement was given out by a man who is a prominent member of one of our great churches . . . The whole idea of reprisals is definitely medieval. Christ came to establish a better way of living."[19] When it became clear that war with Japan was likely Nellie praised the intelligence and loyalty of the Canadian-born Japanese and urged that it was not only right but prudent to make them full citizens so that they would have no cause for bitterness. After Pearl Harbour she begged British Columbians to treat the local Japanese with fairness and understanding. In January 1942, she wrote:

> We have in this province of British Columbia 23,000 Japanese people, many of them natives of Canada, and some of the second generation. We have an opportunity now of showing them that we do respect human rights and that democracy has a wide enough framework to give peace and security to all people of good will, irrespective of race or colour . . .

Nellie was confident that the police force was capable of guarding against any subversive residents of Canada whatever their nationality. Bridges and factories should be guarded against sabotage, she added, but Canadians must also "guard our good name for fair dealing. We must have precautions but not persecutions."[20]

This column was published shortly before the evacuation of the Japanese from the coast. It is impossible to believe that Nellie McClung approved of either the evacuation or the way it was carried out, but there is no protest to be found in her subsequent columns. Perhaps she accepted the argument of the federal government that the evacuation was necessary to maintain order on the coast, or perhaps under war-time censorship regulations no newspaper could risk printing criticism of what the government considered "defensive" action. But Nellie did not forget the Japanese. In November of 1942 she urged that after the war there should be no further discrimination. "We should be through with racial antipathies when the war is settled, for it is not a war of race against race or colour against colour, it is a war against all racial superiorities."[21] She was worried, too, about the lack of educational opportunities for the evacuated Japanese. With the hope of persuading B.C. hospitals to accept Japanese girls for nurse's training she obtained a letter from the Lamont Clinic, a United Church Hospital (the Archer Memorial) in Alberta, telling of the successes of Japanese girls who had been accepted there.[22] She wrote to the B.C. minister of education protesting the government's refusal to accept responsibility for education in the camps.[23] Toward the end of the war as demands for postwar deportation increased, Nellie was able to add her voice to the growing protest that was beginning to surface.[24]

Nellie was deeply concerned, as well, about the plight of Jewish refugees. She was in communication with Agnes Macphail and Senator Cairine Wilson, who were trying to persuade the Canadian government to accept some of the many Jews fleeing from persecution in Europe. A letter to Mackenzie King urging him to at least admit Jewish children brought only a noncommittal reply.[25] In McClung's "New Year's Message 1938" she wrote:

> Just now the plight of the Jews in Germany is saddening everyone's heart, and furnishes the topic of conversation all around the world ... We in Canada can do something for the Jews. We have room which we will share—if we are true to the tradition of our ancestors, who never shut the door on a cold night against a homeless man.[26]

In Calgary she reminded an audience that Canadians have a square mile for every two people and "what this country really needs is more people—refugees have never harmed a country to which they have gone. They have always been an asset. If we harden our hearts against them now, our own hearts will be impoverished."[27] In 1939 she wrote to Agnes Macphail saying, "The Refugee Problem is getting me down—I mean the Gov't's sit-tight attitude . . . We have to do something or be forever disgraced."[28] It is not surprising that the few non-Jewish voices raised on behalf of Jewish refugees have been forgotten since they were unable to rouse public opinion or change government policy.[29]

It was not simply concern for minority groups that motivated McClung on these issues, it was fear of the effect of such attitudes on the Canadian way of life. "When I hear people breathing out mass hatred, condemning all Germans, all Japanese, all Italians, and advocating the deportation of all the Japanese when the war is over, I can see Hitler invading my country as truly as if the hobnailed feet of his soldiers were marching down Portage Avenue."[30]

Before Nellie moved to Victoria, she had begun to suffer from arthritis, which was to trouble her for the rest of her life. Doctors had recommended that she should live less strenuously but there is little evidence that she followed their advice despite her declaration that she intended to do so.[31] As soon as she arrived in Victoria she was called upon to speak, and she accepted many of the invitations using already prepared talks: "Romance in Everyday Life," "The Adventure of Living," and "Silver Linings," but she also prepared a new address for the Women's Canadian Club, entitled "Background of Canadian Literature," which she presented to a gathering of four hundred at the Empress Hotel.[32] In addition to writing her weekly syndicated column, she published a number of short stories, and continued working on her autobiography.

The first volume of Nellie McClung's "Own Story," *Clearing in the West*, was published in 1935. To help publicize the book and perhaps to earn some money for the many renovations at Lantern Lane, McClung went on an extensive speaking tour in the fall of 1935. She began in Calgary, where she also visited Florence, and went on to speak in Edmonton, Regina, and Winnipeg. The greater part of her tour, however, was in Ontario, interrupted by a few days in Montreal where she addressed a Women's Maritime Provinces Association meeting on the subject of "East and West" and also a combined United Church assembly. In Ontario from 4 November through 28

November she was in a different centre almost every night speaking for church groups, Women's Canadian clubs, and Business and Professional Women's clubs. Although she gave no readings from her autobiography, her tour speech did include some of the pioneer material. Nevertheless, much of her concern centred on the problems of people during the current Depression."

McClung was acutely aware of the frustration and suffering of many in the 1930s. Among western farmers "crops have failed, streams have dried, farmers have had to shoot their cattle and horses to end their sufferings." Everywhere "people have seen their children growing pale and languid." Nellie was a woman of action and saw the need for deeds as opposed to mere words. If social justice were to be achieved, she said, people could no longer impersonally leave it up to governments. "The time has come when individuals must take personal responsibility for righting a world in which there is poverty in the midst of plenty"—even to the point of self-sacrifice. Those in the middle class, like herself, who were not undergoing economic distress "must be prepared, if necessary, to accept a lower standard of living" in order to raise the living standard "of our less fortunate fellow-men."³⁴

Unlike many, Nellie McClung recognized that the unemployed suffered not only physically, but psychologically as well. Inactivity and the hopeless despair of the broken-hearted were problems that needed to be addressed. The women's clubs she spoke to were largely composed of a comfortable middle class, so Nellie urged them to use their trained minds and hands in practical ways to alleviate conditions until some social cure for economic inequities could be found. "It is not enough," she said, "that we give to unemployment relief or send vegetables to the Salvation Army." The creation of self-help projects, for example, could aid people's morale, as would greater sensitivity in the administration of welfare. One illustration was of a volunteer worker who was disgruntled to find that the eldest daughter of a family receiving welfare was taking music lessons. That volunteer, Nellie said, "did not see the heroic struggle of the other woman, her pathetic holding on to this one golden rope that bound her to better days and old ambition." Such peevish critics suffered from smallness of spirit and a lack of imagination, therefore Nellie called for a spring housecleaning in the middle-class mind so "the scales would fall from our eyes and we would see the people around us as they are; see their needs and their struggles and their failing hopes." This "seeing eye," to her, was as crucial as the "helping hand."[35]

McClung also warned against easy excuses for ignoring the unemployed. Those who had dusty "little answers for big questions"— that the poor are always with us, or the unemployed wouldn't work anyway if they had the chance—were complacently ill-informed and insulated from real social problems. Women's organizations, she suggested, could activate such people by making them "see life at close range." Although at one time she believed the discipline of work could solve many social problems, by the mid-1930s she would "withdraw that statement" with her recognition that "there is not enough work to go around [now] and there never will be again." She concluded that to save civilization we must "forge a new morality" beyond the conventionally accepted work ethic of the day.[36]

Returning from her 1935 tour Nellie made appearances in Winnipeg, Saskatoon, and Calgary, not arriving back in Victoria until mid-December, a strenuous tour for someone who was supposed to be semiretired. Her final speaking tour—from mid-February to 30 March 1937—was equally demanding.[37] On it she continued to express her concern for the poor. In Toronto she spoke to two wealthy church congregations, and as she looked around she wondered whether these people were really disturbed by the poverty she had seen in those parts of the city where the Church of All Nations and St. Christopher's House were struggling to deal with the misery that was all around them.[38] This tour by no means ended Nellie McClung's speaking engagements by invitation. She was as ready to address the local PTA and Current Events Club (which she originated) in Gordon Head, B.C., as she was to address nearly twelve hundred women in the McDougall United Church in Edmonton during a church presbyterial meeting, as well as more sophisticated audiences at the Toronto and Montreal Book fairs. She spoke on a wide range of topics including: the duties of a parent; the need for understanding and tolerance toward B.C.'s Japanese and Doukhobor communities; "Good Listening"; "The Dividends of Life"; the need to develop our distinctive Canadian humour; "Has the Church an Answer?"; and the severe drought problem in Saskatchewan. On one occasion she reviewed five recent books at the Victoria YWCA Reading Club—taking that opportunity to promote B.C. poets—while on another occasion, in Montreal, she was invited to deliver a radio address. In mid-July she led a round-table discussion on radio at the Pan-Pacific Women's Conference in Vancouver. Some retirement![39]

In 1936, a new interest and responsibility appeared in Nellie McClung's life when she was asked by Mackenzie King to accept an appointment to the board of governors of the newly reorganized Canadian Broadcasting Corporation.[40] The appointments were regional and Nellie, along with Major-General Victor Odlum, represented the West, but, as the only woman on the board she also felt responsible for making sure that women's interests and concerns were given due consideration. Nellie had always been excited by the possibilities of radio. In the 1920s she had been greatly disappointed that the United Church in Alberta did not listen to her advice on making use of radio to reach out to people.[41]

In the fall of 1936, Brooke Claxton—member of the Canadian Radio League and by 1940 federal Liberal politician—had written Alan B. Plaunt—cofounder of the Canadian Radio League, ardent supporter of public broadcasting, and appointee to the original board of governors of the CBC—regarding various notable women he thought might be asked to serve on the board of the newly reorganized CBC, though at the same time he assumed that something less than a top-notch woman would be appointed. Later, reflecting upon the make-up of the board, he suggested that René Morin, the Reverend Father Alexander Vachon, and Colonel Wilfrid Bovey "will form a clique which it will be difficult to oppose, particularly as it is possible that neither General Odlum nor Mrs. McClung will be able to attend many meetings. With wry humour he added: "I anticipate some fun and a good deal of difficulty there."[42] Clearly Nellie L. McClung was no second-class woman, nor would she permit herself to be treated like one. Her vigorous presence at all but one irregular meeting of the board—until her health failed—must have made for many a lively meeting.

At the time of her appointment to the Board of Broadcast Governors she believed that the CBC had two great purposes to fulfil: "to weave together the diverse elements of Canada's population and [to be] the means through which the Dominion could serve as an interpreter in world relations—especially between Great Britain and the U.S."[43] She believed, also, that radio could be a great educator. "Radio," she said, "is the greatest university in the world, with the lowest fees, the largest student body and the easiest manner of entrance."[44] From the beginning she was anxious that the West should perceive the CBC as national and not as something coming from the East. She urged the general manager, Gladstone Murray, to make a complete tour of the West, and at almost every meeting of the board she fought for new stations and better frequencies in western Canada. Nevertheless she was convinced by her colleagues on the board that first priority must be given to enlarging the stations in Toronto and Montreal where the population provided more money from licence fees—money, which, she was assured, could be spent to improve facilities in the West and in the Maritimes.[45]

There were meetings of the board at least twice a year, usually in Ottawa, which Nellie attended regularly.[46] Often she was able to combine these trips east with speaking engagements. The people encountered and the sights she saw as she travelled by train frequently became the subject for her syndicated column. Much of the time at the board meetings was taken up with routine discussions about frequencies and international agreements. It is not likely that Nellie was able to contribute much to this side of the work. She was, however, much concerned with programming. She listened regularly and was never hesitant to criticize when programmes she did not approve of were aired.[47] Two controversial issues, religious broadcasting and the use of the national network for political broadcasts, caused Nellie considerable concern. Unfortunately the BBG minutes contain little except final decisions and no record of the stands taken by individuals. After a running battle between individual Catholic and Presbyterian clergymen who broadcast from Toronto, the board drew up a rule stating that religious broadcasts could promote their own theology but could not denigrate others.[48] For the time being, this rather simplistic solution seemed to work. McClung was pleased because she had feared that religious broadcasting might be suspended. The controversy over use of the network for political broadcasts required more complicated rules.[49]

Another issue on which Nellie McClung made her views known to the public was liquor advertising. She had never changed her mind about the evil of liquor, and now she deplored the increase in social drinking that had occurred since prohibition ended. She was extremely disappointed when a woman MP—Martha Black—elected to the seat left vacant by the illness of her husband, told an interviewer "that she had helped to elect her husband in his campaigns—not by her speeches but by her ability to shake up a good cocktail." Women like Nellie who had struggled so hard for women's suffrage "felt betrayed . . . [since] the House of Commons needed a lot of things more than it did another cocktail shaker." She felt relieved, later on, to learn of "the mischievous delight" this member took "in shocking the complacent, which no doubt explains her first interview."[50] Having attributed the defeat of France in 1941 to a weakening of moral fibre, Nellie warned Canadians:

> Let us consider one aspect of moral laxity, the matter of social drinking . . . I think of these things in relation to young people. What chance have they to resist this evil? They see it everywhere. Moving pictures delight in drinking scenes . . . Then why is so little said about the traffic? . . . Are we so chicken-hearted that we dare not speak out?[51]

Nellie no longer believed that prohibition was the answer. "'We tried it, and it didn't work' she said. 'I'm not fighting for it now. The same result may and must be achieved by education, individual education. I have never ceased to work for that.'"[52]

With these strong feelings about liquor it is not surprising that McClung became very upset when she began to fear that the CBC, facing the financial difficulties of the Depression, was going to allow liquor advertising on its stations. This was not allowed on private stations in any province but Québec, where beer and wine could be advertised. The CBC followed the same rule, but the Board of Broadcast Governors was under constant pressure to permit liquor ads. After a meeting of the board in Regina in May 1937, at which the issue was raised and the decision reached that there should be no change in policy, editorials appeared in the Victoria *Colonist* and the Ottawa *Citizen* suggesting that Leonard Brockington, chairman of the board, was in favour of change. In an interview McClung reacted rather hastily to Brockington's alleged change of opinion by insisting that the decision reached at Regina could not be changed without full board agreement.[53] Alan B. Plaunt, a member of the board, assured McClung that there was no intention on management's part to allow liquor advertising. "The sole issue," he explained, "was whether or not stations in Québec should be allowed to continue beer and wine advertising." He chided McClung for allegedly fueling a nonissue: "I fear that the net result of the publicity I have seen so far will give the general public the impression that a part of our Board is influenced by 'the trade' and that another part has lost its sense of proportion."[54] Nellie had written to Mackenzie King asking him to intervene, and she believed that the interview he had with Brockington was influential in preventing a change of policy that would permit liquor ads.[55] As Plaunt indicated, however, it was a tempest-in-a-tea-pot. McClung's strong feelings about alcohol had interferred with her usual good judgement.

Nellie McClung also hoped she could persuade the Board of Broadcast Governors that a public system like the CBC should set an example by offering equal employment opportunities to women. She feared that the Depression was depriving women of the few gains they had made in the business world. Hard times and unemployment were being used as excuses to reiterate the old adage that women's place was in the home. In the face of this attitude, her campaign was not successful. A few women were employed to run children's shows or daytime programmes for women, but even women's groups did not support McClung's public pleas for more female announcers. When she spoke on this subject to the CWPC annual meeting, the response was lukewarm and she heard the usual lame excuse that women's voices were not suitable for radio.[56] It must have been a blow to McClung when, during the war, the "Household Counsellor" bringing women tips on how to conserve for the war effort was a man!

Nellie McClung's life, in 1938, stands out as an extremely active one—even by her standards. Early in the year she and Wes travelled by bus to California, Arizona, Texas—where they probably visited Paul and his family again—and from there took a motor trip as far as Cuernavaca in Mexico. Though Nellie once wrote that she and Wes had many different interests, one they shared was travelling.[57] During this trip Nellie observed the beauty of the California coast and the Arizona desert but, as always, her chief delight was in people: fellow travellers on the bus, the waitress in a cafe, someone she noticed from the bus window. Through contact and the novelist's imagination she made these people come to life for the readers of her syndicated column. She described, for example, her amusement at seeing a waitress in Portland "serve a whole circle of customers, wiping away the debris with one hand, making out a bill with the other, watching the toast, frying eggs, and carrying on a conversation all at one time. Only once did she stop, and that was when her wise-crack elicited no comment. Holding everything up, she reproved her public with: 'Folks, I'm talking to you!'"[58]

One highlight of this trip was attendance at a service in Aimee Semple McPherson's Angelus Temple of the Four Square Gospel in Hollywood. Nellie had first heard Aimee preach in Winnipeg in 1920, and in 1932 during a motor trip to Texas and California, she had visited the temple and written of it in an article in *Chatelaine*. At that time she had been saddened to see McPherson looking "haggard and worn . . . with hollowed cheeks and restless hands," but happy to see in the thousands who still worshipped in the Angelus Temple that "the heart of her people is loyal and true" despite the sensational accusations of fraud and misconduct that had haunted Aimee's life since the late 1920s. Nellie was being characteristically generous when she deplored the fact that Aimee was "bitterly criticized by many of the 'good' people who failed to see that she used all her talents and all her powers to spread the Gospel of the Lord." McPherson's theatrical skill, which had impressed Nellie in 1920, was still evident in 1932, and in 1938 McPherson seemed, to Nellie, "to radiate health and happiness."[59]

Once more Nellie McClung, like so many others, "felt the impact of [this] great personality" who used "dramatic and spectacular methods" to compete for the interest of young people drawn to the shallow glitter that Hollywood offered at that time. "Aimee was a great showman," Nellie said, whose beauty and success the world found "hard to forgive." But Nellie also believed that Aimee McPherson always "preached to her congregation the words of life," and she did not ever "cheapen or soft-pedal her message." On this occasion, as McPherson defended her church against the criticism in a recent pamphlet, Nellie saw her "revealed . . . at her shining best." To prove her arguments, Aimee "ran through the Gospels . . . with the speed of a race horse. Her audiences laughed and exulted with her as she covered the [other] church's criticism at every point. There was no malice in her words. Everything she said glowed with good humor."[60] This description of Aimee Semple McPherson reflects something of Nellie McClung's own sense of fulfilment when, by similar methods of humour, drama, and personality—but without the sensational props—she aroused audiences to support some worthwhile cause.

In her autobiography, McClung gives a surprising amount of space to McPherson—to the zesty joy in her worship and the practical uses to which she put her Angelus Temple. With some irony she contrasts this with the grandeur and wealth of the cathedral-shrine of Guadalupe in Mexico. Though the guide pointed out the altar "set with many a jewel and gleaming with gold" and told them proudly "how many tons of silver had been used in the church," Nellie was more deeply moved by "the poverty of the supplicants" crawling on their knees up the aisle "in their tattered rags," which made a "terrible picture." Nellie hoped that such faith would bring about "a regenerated church in Mexico, dominated by the true spirit" of Christ's ministry, which, she felt, the unorthodox McPherson had achieved. Aimee's Temple, she was told, served also as "a Bible school, a college, a settlement house and a relief centre . . . and no needy person is ever turned away from its door." Nellie observed something of Aimee's *joie de vivre* in the Mexican fiestas, however, and in her syndicated column deplored the lack of such a spirit in Canada:

> We are too staid, too settled, too much afraid of appearing ridiculous for anything like this. We say we have put away childish things forever. Sometimes we wonder if we are not too wise, too practical, too industrious, and so miss much of the joy of living. Edna St. Vincent Millay had this in mind when she wrote—
>
> "Solidly upon a rock, the ugly houses stand,
> Come and see my shining palace built upon the sand."[61]

In July of 1938 Nellie paid her first visit to the Maritimes. She was invited by the Women's Institute of Nova Scotia to speak at its Silver Jubilee convention in Halifax and to tour the province. Nellie was fascinated by Nova Scotia's history, particularly the story of the expulsion of the Acadians, which brought alive for her Longfellow's "Evangeline" read so many years before at Northfield School. What moved her most was the sight of "Evangeline's willows . . . [whose] battered trunks and twisted branches [seemed] to hold the unconquerable spirit of the men and women of that tragic time."[62] Nevertheless Nellie found it more interesting to write about the stories of Nova Scotians of the present time with whom she took every opportunity to speak: with berry pickers, fishermen, farmers, and people she met in trains and restaurants.

Although already familiar with the cooperative movement promoted by St. Francis Xavier University at Antigonish, Nellie was greatly impressed by the cooperative housing experiment in the dreary little town of Reserve Mines. The people told her "what it was going to mean to them to have their own vegetables and flowers and a decent place to live."[63] McClung saw the cooperative movement as Christianity's answer to communism. "I do not believe our people will ever take to regimentation," she wrote, "but I look forward to a time when Co-operation will prevail."[64]

While she was still in the Maritimes, Nellie received an invitation from Mackenzie King to be a member of the Canadian delegation to the League of Nations.[65] King had made a practice of including a prominent woman on most of the delegations to the League Assembly—an honour that might please the women of Canada without any of the political complications that appointments of more significance might have involved. McClung was, nevertheless, pleased at the opportunity to go to Europe again and immediately made arrangements to obtain press credentials, to continue her column with reports from Europe, and to set up a speaking tour for her return trip across Canada.[66] Despite her close attention to current events and the increasing tension in Europe, Nellie did not dream that she would be travelling during a crisis and a last minute reprieve from the outbreak of war.

McClung sailed from Québec on the Empress of Britain and landed in Cherbourg, France, on 1 September. Mark, her youngest son who was attending Oxford as a Rhodes Scholar, was able to join her, a circumstance that made the trip all the more enjoyable for her. She first went to Interlaken, Switzerland, for a ten-day gathering of the Oxford Group—recently renamed Moral Re-Armament—and then to Geneva for nineteen days from the 12th to the 30th of September. Nellie was, as Charlotte Whitton—a delegate to an earlier League Assembly—had warned her she would be, "sickeningly disillusioned with the speeches in the Assembly."[67] They were, she believed, hollow and self-serving. She could see no real commitment to peace. Nellie described the beautiful, efficient League building: designed by "architects from Rome . . . Paris and Geneva," constructed by "five hundred workmen belonging to different nationalities," and furnished with treasures "from fifty members."[68] She found it sadly ironic that these nations could together create a magnificent building, but could not cooperate to build or maintain peace. "The League lacked power . . . I mean the compelling constraining power which comes into men's hearts when they love their neighbours as themselves, and know that what concerns one concerns all . . . The sterility of the League smote my heart with a sense of helplessness . . . "[69]

As the political crisis deepened in September 1938, Mark worried for his mother's safety and she, too, felt concern. Later Nellie declared she had "seen the people of [Europe] look into the volcano of war and with them had been paralyzed with fear" but, as a writer, she continued to observe and report. She described the blackout in Geneva "like a ploughed field on a rainy night." There was, she said, "no laughter in the streets," and she wondered: "What have we done? What is the matter with us that our only defence is the blackness of night?" As they travelled from Geneva to Paris she saw all the bridges guarded, the army mobilizing, and she felt the presence of fear around her. Then came Munich. Chamberlain arrived back in Britain proclaiming peace and McClung described the effect of this news in Paris. "Paris felt like a man carried out of a burning house. Its release was too great to question the means by which it had been granted a reprieve from war [sacrifice of Czechoslovakia]. We had prayed for peace, peace even for a year. Now we have got it. Things are by no means settled and what are we going to do with that year to bring about lasting peace?"[70]

Canadian women through their educational programmes, inter-national friendships, and political lobbying in the years between the two world wars had "nourished the Canadian peace conscience." McClung, for example, objected to the insertion in school texts of poems like "The Charge of the Light Brigade," which foolishly glorified war. By 1939, however, "pacifist sentiments had to give way before Hitler's threat to the joint heritage of Christians and Jews."[71] Still, the primary question, as Nellie recognized, was how to bring about a lasting peace?

McClung had an answer to this question—Moral Re-Armament. Although the League of Nations Assembly was a disillusioning expe-rience, the Moral Re-Armament meeting at Interlaken had been a faith-raising experience. In the 1920s and 1930s this religious move-ment begun by Frank Buchman, an American, was referred to as Buchmanism or the Oxford Group movement. It based its appeal on what the group called the four absolutes: love, purity, honesty, and unselfishness. By the early 1930s it had organized evangelical teams that visited many countries, including Canada, holding house parties and larger gatherings where public confessions of lapses from the four absolutes played a prominent role. Individuals were encouraged to set aside a "quiet time" every day when God would make his purpose known. In the late 1930s they changed their name to Moral Re-Armament and became a movement for international peace. It was never a formal organization and the spokesmen for the movement encouraged people to retain their own religious affiliation. Many United Church members, including some of the leading clergy, saw the Oxford Group as a spiritual movement that would strengthen faith, but there was severe criticism as well, and the controversy received a prominent place in the columns of the United Church paper, *The New Outlook*. From the beginning, the public confessions that frequently revealed sexual indiscretions were considered to be sensationalism, helping neither the individual nor the community.[72] One woman on looking back said: "They used to say that in Vancouver after the Oxford Group had a splurge it was great for the divorce lawyers."[73]

A committee of the United Church met over a period of six weeks to study the group and its methods. They reported that on the positive side were: the appeal to seek a close relationship with God, the challenge to live by the four absolutes, the confessional opportunity which brought personal relief, the emphasis on personal conversion and personal commitment, the evangelical and missionary impulse, the stress on personal devotion and the personal experience of the Holy Spirit. On the negative side they questioned whether the movement itself lived up to absolute honesty because the stories of its origin as presented by Buchman seemed inconsistent with facts, and the movement presented as ardent supporters prominent people who had offered, at most, only qualified approval. The United Church committee also feared that Buchman's teachings had a weak Christian doctrinal basis and that God's guidance "as practised by some representatives of the movement [was] not far removed from magic and superstition." In addition they noted that the confessional seemed to overemphasize sex and tend toward spiritual self-glorification.[74] Other critics of the movement offered less balanced judgements, attacking the leaders as glory-seekers who led lives of luxury at the expense of their followers. When Buchman began to concentrate on the conversion of world leaders including those in Nazi Germany, he was accused of being a Nazi supporter, and Moral Re-Armanent was classed by many as an antidemocratic advocate of dictatorship.[75]

Nellie McClung first came in contact with the Oxford Group

when their team visited Calgary in 1933, and she attended their house party in Banff.[76] She occasionally supported the movement in her columns and speeches.[77] On one occasion she wrote: "The Oxford Group is being severely criticized but that will not hurt them. They attract criticism because they are so outrageously happy. They actually laugh at their meetings, tell jokes."[78] In 1937 she replied to columnist Beverley Baxter's criticism of the movement and received a letter from him saying that he appreciated her fair comment.[79] During an MRA meeting in Victoria some members were invited by Nellie to stay at Lantern Lane. Apparently one of them stayed about six months until one of the McClung boys told him to "get out."[80] In addition, Nellie McClung strongly supported the advent of the MRA publication, *Rising Tide.*

At this time McClung accepted the Oxford Group as a movement that "desires to help and quicken all religious thought . . . This is the basis of its great appeal to the complex world. It is simple, direct and definite. It seeks to mobilize all the forces of decency and regeneration."[81] Nellie felt that individuals in the organized churches were not attacking the problems of society in Canada and the world. "You can't save the world with bazaars and autographed quilts," she told the Woman's Missionary Society Presbyterial in Victoria. Instead, she said, the WMS must fight bigotry and prejudice, anti-Semitism and anti-Orientalism.[82] The message of the Oxford Group reinforced the belief that Nellie had always held: that individuals could be changed and the world improved by the practice of God's will.

It was at the gathering at Interlaken, however, that McClung came fully to appreciate Moral Re-Armament. This, its first world assembly, was attended by two thousand people from forty countries. The contrast with the bickering and apparent futility of the League Assembly further impressed Nellie: "The difference between Interlaken and the League of Nations, is the difference between hope and fulfillment. At Interlaken we saw the Christian message in action. We saw the effect of changed lives . . . Interlaken is in miniature what the League of Nations ought to be."[83] Nellie McClung was one of thirty press representatives who spoke at Moral Re-Armament's closing session. "There is no middle ground," she stated. "We can no longer be spectators; we must declare our allegiance to the most positive force. God is actually speaking to men and nations. This is the greatest news of the day."[84]

After her return to Canada McClung frequently mentioned the goals of MRA in her speeches and column, referring often to the movement's statement that it was necessary to bring "God control to a troubled world." She strongly advocated their method: the quiet time, the need for each individual to listen for God's instructions. She did not present these ideas as something new but equated Moral Re-Armament with the Golden Rule, the Grace of God, and the Good Neighbour policy.[85] When she addressed the Business and Professional Women's clubs in a radio speech in 1939, she stated that war had intensified the need for Moral Re-Armanent and told of "a business girl who says that business and professional life will be radically different when every stenographer takes her first dictation every morning from God . . . We used to hear about the New Woman," she continued. "Today the New Woman is out of fashion and we need a Woman who is really new because radically remade from within . . . When we are willing to accept the pain of caring unselfishly . . . we will begin to apply that radical cure which can change our business, our homes, and our country. Herein lies true patriotism—the highest national service of every Canadian Woman."[86]

In 1940 McClung attended an MRA gathering at Olympia, Washington, where once again she was much impressed with the testimonies she heard of family quarrels healed, labour disputes settled, and personal feuds ended because of the influence of MRA. Her notes written during the quiet times reveal that the conference was an intense spiritual experience for her. One day she recorded: "Christ spoke today to me by the tongue of Frank Rowell," an English participant who taught, for example, that "war begins in minds" whereas "peace begins in the heart." On another day she concluded: "Every day of my life has been pointing to this. Everyone craves guidance. We get it from others no better or wiser than ourselves." Evidently Nellie was particularly impressed by Frank Buchman, who was present and spoke frequently. "Write a letter to him," her notes record. "Send a book to his address in New York. Phone him after awhile." Some time after this gathering in 1940, Frank Buchman visited Nellie at Gordon Head and was brought around to meet her immediate neighbours, as were many other famous visitors.[87]

Nellie's sense of commitment to the "new spirit" had both national and personal implications. "God has been standing at the door of the world trying to get in. [The] only entry into world affairs is through a willing heart. I am willing." MRA members, by their example and "united action" with others of like mind, were to try to "inspire a new national mind" in this movement toward a "New World Order." "Is MRA going to be God's chance to make a new world?" she asked herself, where "a determined minority will save the world"? At the personal level, she learned, "each of us has a zone of influence," and she recorded what surely she already knew: "'I have the power to sweeten . . . [the lives of] the people I meet today . . . Show me,' she prayed, 'and I shall do it.'"

Nellie's notes also point to strong emotional self-questioning. She asked God what he would have her do and allegedly received the answer: "Carry this message far and wide." Since MRA taught that each person was to work within her own "zone of influence" and "make use of the channels" she already had, Nellie recognized, ostensibly through God's guidance, that her syndicated column was "a great sounding board," and she resolved to "study it, slave at it." She concluded that she must "follow all the old paths, but glorify them." In the past she had "tried to make people better, but now I'll try to make them new." Fortunately, Nellie's introspection and commitment did not suffocate her sense of humour. "Write about bantams, fertilizers," she told herself. "Cheerful things are God's messengers too."[88]

During the war, attacks on the MRA increased and their association with the Nazis was emphasized. McClung was much disturbed by an article by Rupert Hughes in *Liberty*, "Pacifists are Traitors" (11 October 1940), which attacked MRA in particular. Her papers contain many attempts at reply. "Mr. Hughes," she wrote, "attacks the Oxford Group in a sort of senile rage, and foolishly blames their position for America's unpreparedness. The Oxford Group have never been peace-at-any-price pacifists. Heinrich Himmler has never had any connection with them. I have had the privilege of seeing how moral re-armament works . . . I am one of thousands who are grateful to the Oxford Group for what they have brought to Canada. They are not magicians or sooth sayers. They are unselfish, earnest men and women who radiate good will."[89] Despite her strong advocacy of MRA in 1940, her columns—which were increasingly oriented to religion during the war—did not specifically advocate MRA. After the Olympia meeting there is no indication in her papers of further contact with MRA leadership except for a telegram of congratulations from Frank

Buchman and other MRA leaders on the occasion of the McClungs' fiftieth wedding anniversary in 1946.

In the late 1930s and early 1940s Nellie's health began to deteriorate seriously. Her arthritis became more of a problem, causing her to spend some time in hospital for treatment and to have an operation on her knee.[90] In spite of these handicaps she kept up, as we have seen, a very active life, but while at a Board of Broadcast Governors' meeting in Ottawa in November 1940, she suffered a heart attack. This was followed by others, which made it impossible for her to travel. She continued her work with the CBC through very extensive correspondence, however, until she resigned in September 1942.[91] She was able to meet with the board one more time when she was invited—by special request—to a meeting in Victoria in August 1943. At this time she was well enough to entertain the board at her home.[92]

Although her recovery was slow and never complete, she continued to write her syndicated column, on at least one occasion from a hospital bed,[93] but in 1943 she decided to give up the column and begin the second volume of her autobiography. In doing so, she implicitly recognized that "the hardest fact of all for women to admit and defend: that woman's selfhood, the right to her own story, depends upon her 'ability to act in the public domain.'"[94] Accordingly, *The Stream Runs Fast* largely recorded and defended her public life and explained the fame that justified this volume of her autobiography. She had been close to death in late 1942 and the doctor had told her that she could no longer drive a car, work in the garden, or travel; must avoid crowds, eat sparingly, and observe one general rule: "If you like it, avoid it." But she felt that she must write; she had a story to tell.

> I have seen my country emerge from obscurity into one of the truly great nations of the world. I have seen strange things come to pass in the short span of one lifetime, and I hasten to set it down while the light holds. People must know the past to understand the present and face the future.

Nellie had intended to begin this as soon as she settled in Victoria but her busy life and, as she saw it, the somnolent effect of the sea had intervened. Now she realized that if she was going to do it the time had come. She would have liked to call the book "Without Regret" because "there is something light and gallant about the phrase," but she concluded: "I cannot look back without regret. I can see too many places where I could have been more obedient to the heavenly vision, for a vision I surely had for the creation of a better world."[95] As she wrote she realized how quickly the years had passed and the title became "The Stream Runs Fast." In an early draft she mused that the book "has no plan. I am just going to write like the wind which bloweth where it listeth."[96] Unfortunately this is an accurate description. It is not an excellent, carefully constructed work like *Clearing in the West*. There are flashes of her wit and many vivid descriptions but it does not, as she wished it to, provide the reader with an accurate portrait of these years of rapid change as *Clearing in the West* did for the pioneer years, nor does the maturing Nellie McClung come through in the words as vividly as did the young Nellie Mooney in the first volume. She completed her task over the next two years and when *The Stream Runs Fast* was published in 1945 she was able to attend an autographing session in Vancouver.[97] She continued to write articles and provided *The Family Herald and Weekly Star* with an annual Christmas story until the year before her death.[98] Correspondence also took up a good deal of her time. She never forgot a birthday or failed to write a letter of congratulation for an achievement, or of encouragement to an aspiring author, or a kind note of condolence at a time of bereavement.

While Nellie was working on her autobiography she received what was probably the greatest blow of her life. Her eldest son, Jack, a very successful and popular prosecuting attorney for the Attorney-General's Department in Alberta, took his own life in remorse. This was a desire to make restitution for minor fraud in connection with his work by turning the pension that would come to his estate at his death over to the government as repayment for the misappropriation of funds.[99] There is no doubt that Jack's mother would have provided the money required to pay off his defalcation of government funds had he been able to face a mother of such high moral character. Still, Jack's attempt to atone for a wrong done marked him truly his mother's son, although his ultimate sacrifice would only cause her severe pain. The family, at first, hesitated to tell his mother the true circumstances of his death but, fearful that she might hear it from somewhere else, they gave her the facts. The section of her autobiography that dealt with Jack's return from the First World War had already been written when Nellie received word of his death. She had expressed her belief that the experience of war had been a terrible shock to boys like Jack—young, sensitive, idealistic. Faced now with the "tragic suddenness" of his death and the dreadful circumstances of that death, she concluded that it was the war that was responsible for his inability to cope with life despite a highly successful career. She hoped that "the boys who come back now [WWII] have a better chance: wise men [psychologists] are giving deep thought to their problems . . . and I wish—and wish—I had known more. All I could see was Jack's career—his great talent . . . " She feared that she had placed too much of a burden on him—expected too much.[100] She does not mention that her old foe alcohol had played its part in causing Jack's problems, but the memory of her joy when she had thought the battle against alcohol had been won and the disillusionment that came as prohibition ended and social drinking became a way of life in Canada, must have been in her mind. Nellie recorded that "the first few days of shock bring a merciful anesthesia," and she realized now "why people stop the clock and draw the blinds" on such occasions when their world breaks down. "It is a pathetically futile, but human, attempt to hold back the desolation which has come upon you." Horace McClung's wife Margaret remembers that for some time after Jack's death his mother was "very very silent."[101]

Nellie was able to bear the grief of Jack's death because of the strength of her family circle, the "overflowing kindness of friends," the letters from people who had known and loved Jack, and most of all because of her strong religious faith. She recalled how blind two of Christ's disciples had been, on the road to Emmaus, to the reality of His resurrection and eternal life until they recognized Him in His action of blessing and breaking the bread. "I found myself holding on to that simple sentence: 'They knew Him in the breaking of bread.' It throws a gleam of light across the desolation of this troubled world, where the whole creation is groaning under intolerable burdens." Christianity's "Great Truth" of eternal life gave her comfort. "Death is not the end. It is but the portal to a brighter, fairer world . . . The part we see with our mortal eyes does not make sense; it is like the fragment of a story you read in a torn magazine—you know there must be more of it." She resolved to see the restoration of wholeness in Jack's death and, much as she would have done years before when she was younger, she decided that "work is more than mere activity—there is healing in it."[102] Although Nellie could no longer throw herself into activity as she might have earlier, she completed the autobiography and did as much writing as she could. She told one interviewer that the doctor had told her not to write, but she was sure he meant books so she would just work on articles and short stories![103]

In 1945 she wrote the inscription for a memorial cairn to be erected at Millford, by then just a barren spot where the old town had stood. Hannah, who had become known in Manitoba as an outstanding English teacher, spoke at the unveiling of the cairn, as did Lizzie. Hannah provided Nellie with a full report of the proceedings, which, though marred by rain, were attended by a large contingent of the Mooney clan.[104] Hannah's account must have brought back many memories and no doubt Nellie would have loved to have been there, and the organizers must have regretted the absence of their most famous "pioneer." Nellie's inscription was a tribute to the pioneers who "set their resolute spirits against the many hardships of their times, and travelled hopefully in spite of everything. They had something which kept them from despair when crops failed, the cow died, the payment on the binder was due, the children were sick, and the nearest doctor was eighty miles away. They trusted in God and went on triumphantly. May we, their descendents, honour their memory by following their example."[105] Hope, this virtue essential to pioneer society, was central to Nellie McClung's life. It directed her toward the goal of social reform, and strengthened her spirit in times of personal crisis.

Throughout these years Nellie did not lose her concern for the status of women in society. In her comments on women during the war, for example, she argued that women should be in charge of food for the army, not because she wished to limit women to their traditional function, but because she believed their home experience had taught them dietary knowledge and economic skills that men, in their traditional sphere, did not acquire. She was horrified at the stories she heard of a loaf of bread per man per day. She believed women could provide soldiers with a better balanced diet—including fresh fruit and vegetables—at a lower cost. Nellie also wrote that she did not like to see women in khaki—perhaps because in her mind women stood for peace and home, whereas khaki made them seem militaristic—but she vigorously dismissed the argument that women would not accept army discipline, would sulk or cry or cheat, and be a nuisance generally.[106] Once women had been accepted in the army, she deplored the inequity in pay between men and women, and the lack of protest against this situation. Women "were declared to be persons in 1929," she said, "but now they are rated in comparison with men as nine to thirteen." She argued that women should complain, not because they were unwilling to do their part to win the war, but because "it is always a mistake to let an injustice pass unnoticed."[107] On one occasion Mark, then in the navy, was somewhat startled when his mother shot him "a straight-in-the-eye look" and asked whether women in the armed forces, like the men, received "lectures on contraception and how to look after" themselves.[108]

McClung feared that women who had entered the work force would lose their jobs when the war ended, as they had after WWI. She felt "like the old fire-horse when he hears the fire alarm" when a former Member of Parliament proposed that "it would be a good plan to remove women from their jobs in offices and factories to make places for the returned men, and to encourage marriage and births by Government subsidies." In opposition to this, Nellie argued that while shoving women out of industry would make things easier for the postwar planners, she could not imagine anything more unfair to women. "And the insulting part of it," she added, "is this loathsome idea that women would like it." The ban on married women working, she said, "should be removed forever [because] . . . neither a man nor a woman should be penalized for marrying . . . "[109] In what was, perhaps, her last letter to the *Victoria Times*, Nellie protested the closing of the Oak Bay Nursery School. Such schools, encouraged during the war to allow mothers to do war work, were being closed because now, it was felt, mothers should stay at home with their children. Nellie believed, however, that nursery schools could benefit both mothers and children, and she advised all parents and lovers of young children to read an article, published in *Maclean's*, by the popular child psychologist Dr. Blatz. The article, she hoped, would rekindle support for nursery schools. Optimistically Nellie believed that "men and women are getting to know each other better, and I can see that the hero worship of the male which was nurtured in women . . . is on its way out—unwept and unhonored by sane women everywhere. Financial dependence was one of its factors, and a grievous one too."[110]

Many of Nellie McClung's war-time columns urged women to plan for a postwar world in which things would be better, not just for women, but for all. She thought that if people had suffered enough they would try to build a world based on the Golden Rule. Noting that a recent Conservative convention denounced tariff walls, and that the Beveridge Report to the British House of Commons called for security for all, Nellie sensed a "strangely hopeful stirring of the dry bones" of the past. "The old privileges that existed for the protection of the few are passing. The pessimistic say we will achieve a classless society but all will be poor. But what do they mean by poor? Certainly there will be a levelling down. But in a world where people spend millions of dollars on luxuries and worse, while others cannot get enough for food to keep their children healthy, there must be a levelling."[111] These were somewhat radical words for her time, for "in a fundamentally middle-class peace movement only the very brave demanded an end both to armed conflict and to privilege."[112]

A happy occasion for the McClungs was their Golden Wedding Anniversary in 1946. It occurred on a Sunday, so the family attended St. Aidan's in the morning and in the afternoon received their friends at Lantern Lane. Mark was unable to attend but the rest of the family, including grandchildren, gathered to celebrate with Nellie and Wes. Jack's absence must, of course, have cast a shadow—his wife and their two children, Nellie and John, were there. Telegrams and cards came from friends far and wide and from associations both local and national. There were even letters from strangers who had loved Nellie's books or heard her speak and, learning of the Golden Anniversary, wanted to add their congratulations. Horace, who, as a child, was given to the writing of numerous "odes," supplied his verse "To Mother and Dad" to mark the occasion. Amusingly it begins: "Fifty Years ago this day/Mama wouldn't say 'obey.'" Whether this marks an unconventional fact or is merely light-hearted banter is impossible to say, but it certainly points to a marriage of equals. When asked the inevitable question, "What is the recipe for a long and happy married life?" Nellie replied, "I am sure that through husband and wife developing their individuality without impinging on each other, happiness is assured. Mr. McClung and I are fond of different activities and we have many happy times talking things over. In this way we never get under each other's feet or in each other's hair."[113] And only three years before her death Nellie wrote: "We have been married 52 years, and I still consider that the day I cut him out of the herd, was the best day of my life!"[114]

One of the most revealing accounts of Nellie's final years was written by Margaret Ecker Francis in *The Canadian Home Journal* after a visit to Lantern Lane. She described McClung sitting in her study looking over her garden. "It was a graceful picture, a sort of pastoral Whistler's mother. But the hostess shattered it in a minute. 'Have you seen this?' She produced an article from a recent periodical. 'Did you hear Matthew Halton's broadcast on Sunday?' 'Have you read this?' She dug a newly published book from among her papers. As she talked it was obvious that Lantern Lane is no quiet cloister, aloof from the world, but rather a radio set tuned to soundwaves of affairs and opinions."[115] Fortunately Nellie was able to retain this brightness of spirit and keen mind until the end of her life. The editor of *The Family Herald and Weekly Star* showed some degree of wisdom when he summed up this remarkable woman:

> Her personality was her supreme, though unconscious, achievement—not anything she wrote or did.
> For Nellie McClung developed into, and remained, a person who attracted love from all who knew her and yet inspired them with respect for her vigorous strength of character. She was an idealist . . . whose feet never left the firm and practical ground . . . the secret of her good and successful life was so simple that anyone can understand it who has not completely lost touch with reality. It was the four old-fashioned virtues of simplicity, sincerity, courage and intelligence, which combined to make Nellie McClung respected and feared as a fighter for the causes of temperance and women's rights . . . a sort of unofficial "No. 1 Woman of Canada."[116]

She had become the person whom Letitia Mooney had tried so hard to stifle.

Nellie L. McClung died on 1 September 1951, at the age of seventy-seven, after being in a coma for forty hours. Her funeral service was held in Victoria's Metropolitan Church because St. Aidan's was not large enough to hold the many who wished to attend.[117] At least twenty-one members of the Victoria and Island Branch of the Canadian Authors Association filled the seats immediately behind the family.[118] The day of Nellie's funeral, 5 September, was a beautiful sunny day. Wes, and the little grandson on his knee, sang hymns on the way to the church.[119] Ursula Jupp, a close neighbour at Lantern Lane, once said that anyone who could imagine this whole and vigorous woman "as pleasure-denying and pinched would have but to meet Nellie of the irrepressible smile and the witty tongue to know that here was a woman in whom heart and mind were vitally and humorously allied—a good woman who was FUN!"[120]—a woman with an unquenchable enthusiasm for life. Thus, though Nellie's "own familiar pastor who spoke the eulogy" was briefly "overcome by emotion," the full choral service was an impressive but joyful celebration of Nellie McClung's life; a beautiful and cheerful, rather than a sad, occasion. And Nellie would have been pleased for "that's what she was like. That's how she would have liked it."[121]

Although Nellie McClung was forced to give up the battle, still, her spirit lives on as it touches the lives of a new generation of feminist activists. Today, Canadian feminist writers—even those who criticize her for not being sufficiently radical—find her the most quotable of those energetic fighters for women's rights from an earlier age. In an increasingly secular age Nellie McClung may seem to some old-fashioned—even redundant—since her life, her point of view, and her motivation were shaped by that "Christian faith which was the ground of her being and her action." Yet one student of McClung's religious thought concluded that although "her theology is a typical product of the Social Gospel . . . trying to find a systematic theology among [her] collections of thoughts and expressions of faith could be a task to drive a classical scholar mad."[122] The religious liberalism that could encompass serious social reform, the colourful dramatics of Aimee Semple McPherson, and the emotional confessionalism of the Buchmanites was indeed a highly eclectic and pragmatic religious spirit. Not once in all of her writing did Nellie McClung ever mention the Social Gospel, yet she adhered firmly to what *she* called "a Christian socialism in the best sense of that much abused word,"[123] and she certainly fits the Social Gospel mould: "optimism about reconstructing society based on democratic Christian principles; an international outlook; an ecumenical spirit; a belief that children were born pure and not evil; [and] a conviction that people could be influenced towards good by teaching and example."[124]

Nellie McClung "believed that God required justice instead of burnt offerings and action instead of pious but empty sentiments" and, as a feminist activist, she consistently fought for justice, both social and political, particularly toward women and children and Canadian immigrants. Some modern feminists, however, do not accurately understand either Nellie McClung or her methodology.

Throughout her lifetime, for example, she used both maternal and equal rights feminist arguments as, indeed, did many of her sisters. Theological scholar Carol Hancock contends: she "demonstrated too keen an insight into the power and politics of 'woman's place' and presented too strong a challenge to be accorded the simple title of 'maternal feminist' with its attendant limitations. Her feminism, however, was so interwoven with her religious perspective and her own theological framework that the two can not be separated."[125] As for Nellie McClung's methodology she used her wit and skill as a platform speaker to win audiences rather than antagonize them. Modern feminists—particularly Christian ones—could learn from McClung that "change seems to happen best in the context of relationship. People are more likely to hear the prophetic word when it comes from someone they trust."[126] It was in this way that Nellie Letitia McClung spent a full and energetic lifetime trying to "fire the heather" in people's minds and hearts to bring about a better world.

Notes

❖

Introduction

1. Carolyn G. Heilbrun, *Writing a Woman's Life* (New York, 1988), pp. 26–27, 17–18, 52.
2. Maria Tippett, *Emily Carr: A Biography* (Toronto, 1979), p. xi.
3. Provincial Archives of British Columbia [PABC], Nellie McClung Papers, vol. 11(7), letter from Lizzie (Elizabeth Rae) to Nellie L. McClung [NLM], 29 October 1933.
4. Elaine Showalter, "Introduction" to *The New Feminist Criticism* (New York, 1985), p. 3.
5. Annette Kolodny, "Dancing Through the Minefields: Some Observations on the Theory, Practice, and Politics of a Feminist Literary Criticism," in *The New Feminist Criticism*, ed. Elaine Showalter (New York, 1985), p. 157.
6. Ibid., p. 146.
7. Adrienne Rich, "When We Dead Awaken: Writing as Re-Vision," *College English* 34 (October 1972), p. 90, quoted by Kolodny in "Dancing Through the Minefields," in *The New Feminist Criticism*, p. 148.
8. Showalter, "Introduction" to *The New Feminist Criticism*, pp. 9, 6.
9. Carolyn G. Heilbrun, "Bringing the Spirit Back to English Studies," in *The New Feminist Criticism*, p. 26.
10. Robert Craig Brown, "Biography in Canadian History," *Historical Papers* (Ottawa, 1980).
11. Carl Berger, *The Writing of Canadian History: Aspects of English-Canadian Historical Writing, 1900 to 1970* (Toronto, 1976), p. 218.

Chapter 1—Grey County and the Move West

1. Nellie L. McClung, *Clearing in the West: My Own Story* (1935; reprint, Toronto 1976), p. 18. This is the first of Nellie McClung's two volumes of autobiography. Other sources of information will be cited. For a study of the Canadian myth of the West, see Doug Owram, *Promise of Eden: The Canadian Expansionist Movement and the Idea of the West, 1856–1900* (Toronto, 1980). For the American version of the western myth of Adam conquering the virgin soil see Annette Kolodny, *The Lay of the Land: Metaphor as Experience and History in American Life and Letters* (Chapel Hill, 1975) and the same author's analysis of the American woman's frontier myth of the garden and domestic Eden in *The Land Before Her: Fantasy*

Notes

and Experience of the American Frontiers, 1630–1860 (Chapel Hill, 1984). See also *The Women's West,* eds. Susan Armitage and Elizabeth Jameson (Oklahoma, 1987). Also see Ramsay Cook, "Imagining a North American Garden: Some Parallels and Differences in Canadian and American Culture," *Canadian Literature* 103 (1984): 10–26. For the Canadian woman's perspective of life in frontier Alberta, see Eliane Leslau Silverman's, *The Last Best West: Women on the Alberta Frontier, 1880–1930* (Montreal, 1984).

2. "Townships of Sullivan," in *Illustrated Historical Atlas of Grey and Bruce Counties, Ontario,* Belden rpt. ed. (Toronto, 1975).

3. Marjorie Griffin Cohen, "The Decline of Women in Canadian Dairying," in *The Neglected Majority,* vol. II, eds. Alison Prentice and Susan Mann Trofimenkoff (Toronto, 1985), pp. 61–83, 201–203.

4. W.H. Graham, *The Tiger of Canada West* (Toronto, 1962), pp. 92–93, cited in Marjorie Griffin Cohen, *Women's Work, Markets, and Economic Development in Nineteenth-Century Ontario* (Toronto, 1988), pp. 74–75.

5. Cohen, *Women's Work,* p. 11.

6. From address delivered by Mrs. Hannah Sweet at the Dedication of the Cairn at Millford, Manitoba, Thursday, 14 June 1945, in Dr. Hugh Sanderson, *Our Pioneer Heritage* (n.d.), Souvenir Booklet for Re-Unveiling of the Millford Cairn, 12 June 1966.

7. Toronto *Globe,* 20 April 1878; 18 May 1878; 7 August 1878; 12 August 1878. Public Archives of Canada [PAC], Department of Agriculture, "Information for Intending Emigrants," n.d.

8. Toronto *Globe,* 10 April 1878.

9. Toronto *Globe,* 26 April 1878. W.L. Morton, *Manitoba, A History,* 2d ed. (Toronto, 1967) gives figures from Ontario and the British Isles as 11,500 in 1879; 18,000 in 1880; and 28,600 in 1881.

10. Hannah Sweet address.

11. Sara Brooks Sundberg, "Farm Women on the Canadian Prairie Frontier: The Helpmate Image," in *Rethinking Canada: The Promise of Women's History,* eds. Veronica Strong-Boag and Anita Clair Fellman (Toronto, 1986), p. 97.

12. Toronto *Globe,* 12 August 1878.

13. In 1881, not long after their arrival, the boundary of Manitoba was moved further west to include the area in which the Mooneys settled.

14. Hannah Sweet address.

15. Morton, *Manitoba,* p. 180. For more recent histories of the Canadian west, see *The Prairie West: Historical Readings,* eds. R. Douglas Francis and Howard Palmer (Edmonton, 1985); also *Building Beyond the Homestead,* eds. David C. Jones and Ian MacPherson (Calgary, 1985).

16. Hannah Sweet address.

17. Frank Burnett, "Memories of Struggle," *The Canadian Magazine,* January 1933, pp. 16, 40.

18. *Mortgage in Fee,* John Mooney to Canada Permanent Loan and Savings Company, 11 May 1878; *Mortgage in Fee,* John Mooney to the Canada Co., 3 April 1880; *Deed of Land,* sale of "2nd div. and 3rd div." of Lot #8, and the 1st div. of Lot #9, in Conc. 1 of Township of Sullivan, containing by measurement 150 acres or less, by John Mooney and Letitia Mooney to William Crawford. Documents registered with Land Titles Office, Owen Sound.

19. Hannah Sweet address.

20. Nellie L. McClung, *The Stream Runs Fast: My Own Story* (Toronto, 1945), p. 206. This is the second volume of NLM's autobiography.

21. Ibid., pp. 84–85.

Notes

Chapter 2—Growing Up Near Millford

1. Frank Burnett, "Memories of Struggle," *The Canadian Magazine*, January 1933, p. 40.
2. Nellie L. McClung, "An Author's Own Story," *Saturday Night*, 25 January 1913, p. 29.
3. Burnett, "Memories of Struggle," p. 40.
4. Ibid.
5. Ibid.
6. McClung, "An Author's Own Story," p. 29.
7. Gerald Friesen, *The Canadian Prairies: A History* (Toronto, 1984), p. 325.
8. W.L. Morton, *Manitoba, A History*, 2d ed. (Toronto, 1967), p. 240.
9. Peter B. Waite, *Canada 1874–1896* (Toronto, 1971), p. 125.
10. For studies on current western alienation, see Roger Gibbins, "Western Alienation," and Kenneth H. Norrie, "Some Comments on Prairie Economic Alienation," in *The Prairie West: Historical Readings*, eds. R. Douglas Francis and Howard Palmer (Edmonton, 1985). Also see Gibbins and Norrie articles in Francis and Palmer's new edition of *The Prairie West: Historical Readings* (1992).
11. Morton, *Manitoba*, pp. 211–13.
12. Ibid., p. 222.
13. McClung, "An Author's Own Story," p. 29.
14. Provincial Archives of Manitoba [PAM], Manitoba Sessional Papers, 1885, Department of Education, Inspector's Report.
15. Edward E. Best, *Memoirs of a School Inspector, 1888–1932* [197-], p. 120.
16. Provincial Archives of British Columbia [PABC], McClung Papers, vol. 1(9).
17. Ibid.
18. Best, *Memoirs*, p. 120.
19. McClung, "An Author's Own Story," p. 29.
20. PABC, McClung Papers, vol. 51.
21. Burnett, "Memories of Struggle," p. 40.
22. Violet McNaughton, "Jottings By the Way," *The Western Producer*, 20 September 1951.
23. McClung, "An Author's Own Story," p. 29. Some women, like Georgina Binnie-Clark [author of *Wheat and Women*] preferred outdoor work. Nellie was not alone in this. See Sara Brooks Sunberg, "Farm Women on the Canadian Prairie Frontier: The Helpmate Image," in *Rethinking Canada: The Promise of Women's History*, eds. Veronica Strong-Boag and Anita Clair Fellman, p. 102.
24. PABC, McClung Papers, vol. 11(7), letter from Lizzie [Elizabeth Rae] to NLM, 13 November 1933.
25. Ibid., vol. 4(2).
26. Ibid.
27. Nellie L. McClung, *The Stream Runs Fast: My Own Story* (Toronto, 1945), p. 70. Other sources of information will be cited.
28. PABC, McClung Papers, vol. 4(2).
29. Ibid., vol. 1(9).
30. Ibid., vol. 4(2); McClung, "An Author's Own Story," p. 29. In the MS version of the hanging at the Brandon court house, for example, Nellie records that a man had been hanged there a year before her visit to Brandon, and she mentions neither the crime nor the cause. In the published version, the man has yet to be hanged "the day after Christmas," for having "shot his wife, while she was ironing," after he had "come home drunk," and Nellie follows this with a brief diatribe against the "liquor business." The published version possesses far more

dramatic immediacy, and the circumstantial details create greater pathos and realism.

31. See *The Selected Journals of L.M. Montgomery, vol. I 1889–1910*, eds. Mary Rubio and Elizabeth Waterston (Toronto, 1985); also, *A Woman with a Purpose: The Diaries of Elizabeth Smith, 1872–1884*, ed. Veronica Strong-Boag (Toronto, 1980).
32. Wawanesa was a new town five miles west of the Mooney farm. Millford had almost disappeared by this time because the railway had, after all, bypassed it, and most of the residents had moved, with their houses, to other towns.

Chapter 3—Normal School and Teaching

1. W.L. Morton, *Manitoba, A History*, 2d ed. (Toronto, 1967), p. 210, notes that there was severe fall frost in 1883–85, but makes no reference to an early frost in 1889, while Alfred O. Legge, *Sunny Manitoba* (London, 1893), p. 246, records the earliest frost on record, up until 1893, as occurring on 22 August 1890, the summer *after* Nellie had completed Normal School. In addition, the Manitoba *Daily Free Press* weather and crop report for the Manitou district (15 August 1889) indicated that "harvesting operations are well under way and prospects are very good for this district. There will be more than fifty percent more wheat to market than last season."
2. Provincial Archives of Manitoba [PAM], Manitoba Sessional Paper (no. 18), 1889, Department of Education, Winnipeg Normal School, p. 30.
3. Alison L. Prentice and Susan E. Houston, *Family, School, and Society in Nineteenth-Century Canada* (Toronto, 1975), p. 4.
4. Edward Bellamy, *Looking Backward* (1887; reprint, New York, 1917), pp. 263–65, 255–57, 118–19, 150, 59–60, 53, 101, 276, 282. For suspected parallels between McClung's works and the writings of Charlotte Perkins Gilman and Olive Schreiner, see Susan Jackel, "First Days, Fighting Days: Prairie Presswomen and Suffrage Activism, 1906–1916," in *First Days, Fighting Days: Women in Manitoba History*, ed. Mary Kinnear (Regina, 1987). Georgina Taylor, who interviewed several Saskatchewan women socialists, has indicated that many of them had read and loved Bellamy's book. For a thumb-nail sketch of a CCFer who, like McClung, juggled the roles of mother, wife, teacher, and politician, see Taylor's "Gladys Strum: Farm Woman, Teacher and Politician," *Canadian Woman Studies* 7 (Winter 1986), 89–93.
5. Nellie L. McClung, *Clearing in the West: My Own Story* (1935; reprint, Toronto, 1976), pp. 251–53.
6. The need for freedom from farm and family was strong in many rural females of this era. See *Loosening the Bonds* by Joan M. Jensen (New Haven, 1896).
7. In 1887 the average salary for a female teacher was $441.31 (the lowest was $180.00; the highest, $675.00). In the same year the average salary for a male teacher was $447.17 (the lowest was $222.00; the highest, $1500.00). PAM, Manitoba Sessional Papers, Department of Education, 1887, Salaries, p. 9. The gap between female and male salaries tended to be narrower for that found in cities. See Marta Danylewycz, Beth Light, and Alison Prentice, "The Evolution of the Sexual Division of Labour in Teaching: A Nineteenth-Century Ontario and Quebec Case Study," *Histoire sociale/Social History* XVI (May 1983): 81–109. As Danylewycz and Prentice indicate in another article, women teachers "were participants in systems which, by their very structure, were designed to perpetuate and, indeed, promote unequal relations between women and men." Women teachers had "second hand status." In Toronto, for example, in the 1880s "women teachers . . . could be engaged for half the salaries required by men."

Notes

The result was a "trend towards an increasing proportion of single female teachers" as boards of education sought to economize. See "Teachers, Gender, and Bureaucratizing School Systems in Nineteenth Century Montreal and Toronto," *History of Education Quarterly* XXIV (Spring 1984): 87–96.

8. In *Clearing in the West*, Nellie indicates that Best carried with him "copies of *The Popular Educator* and the *Ontario School Journal*" and that he "always had some new books to recommend" (p. 373). She also records that by the time she moved from the Hazel school to Manitou, Best "had given me two good reports, and had said that I was one of the best disciplinarians in his Inspectorate . . . " (p. 312). For interesting and amusing accounts of prairie teaching experiences, see Max Braithwaite's *Why Shoot the Teacher* (Toronto, 1974), and John C. Charyk, *Syrup Pails and Gopher Tails* (Saskatoon, 1983).

9. Provincial Archives of British Columbia [PABC], McClung Papers, vol. 26, notebook, 31 December 1895.

10. See Prentice and Houston, *Family, School, and Society*, pp. 165–78.

11. In an interview with the authors in Ottawa (June 1974), Nellie's youngest son, Mark, expressed the personal opinion that his mother would have liked to be a minister.

12. Manitou *Mercury*, 16 January 1892.

13. PABC, McClung Papers, vol. 5(22), unfinished MS, "Six Weeks Vacation: Truth is Stranger than Fiction."

14. Ibid.

15. Ibid., vol. 22(4). See also *The Revenge of the Methodist Bicycle Company* by Christopher Armstrong and H.V. Nelles (New York, 1977). Also, for the freedom and improved health that bicycles gave to women, see Jane Lewis, *Women in England, 1870–1950* (Bloomington, Indiana, 1984), p. 119.

16. In 1890 the First Class Teaching Certificate (Grade B) entailed the study of grammar, composition, and prose literature (using Bain's text on composition, Spalding's on English literature, and Macauley's essay on Milton), poetical literature (Shakespeare's *Macbeth*), history (Green's text: chaps. I, III, VII, and VIII), algebra, geometry, chemistry, physics, and physical geography. PAM, Department of Education, Minutes of the Advisory Board, 1890.

17. Canada Department of Immigration, "Canada's Centre is Manitoba: A British Colony Open to All," n.d.

18. Manitou *Mercury*, 20 October 1894; 18 May 1895; 22 August 1896; 29 September 1894; 21 February 1895. Wes was secretary-treasurer of the Manitou Hockey Club (*Mercury*, 19 January 1895); a member of the management committee of the Manitou Curling Club (*Mercury*, 26 October 1895); and an enthusiastic cross-country bicyclist (*Mercury*, 6 July 1895).

19. "*There are days and nights that I have marked with a white stone in the burying ground of memory: September 16th, 1894, is one of the days. August 26th, 1892, is one of the nights; July 1895 is another. Put in March 7th and mark it with [undecipherable word] and April 5th.*" PABC, McClung Papers, vol. 26, notebook, 15 September 1895.

20. See Ramsay Cook, *The Regenerators: Social Criticism in Late Victorian English Canada* (Toronto, 1985) for the social reformers' questioning of traditional theological tenets.

21. Margaret Deland, *John Ward, Preacher* (Boston, 1888). References from the preceding two paragraphs can be found on pp. 251, 430, 249, 259, 166, 179, 101 and 140, 140–41, 233, 43, 85, 188, 193, 391, 405.

22. PABC, McClung Papers, vol. 26, notebook, 10 June 1896.

23. Cook, *The Regenerators*, pp. 132, 75. The beliefs of social activist and feminist Agnes Maule Machar are a case in point. She stressed "applied Christianity" as

opposed to "passive" Christianity, and she vigorously objected to rigid and "outworn formulas" or credos, "and of those who insisted on maintaining them." For her, they had "the capacity to destroy faith." See Ruth Compton Brouwer, "The 'Between-Age' Christianity of Agnes Machar," *Canadian Historical Review* LXV (September 1984): 355–67.

24. Material in the preceding paragraph is from the same journal MS, 16 September 1894.
25. Ibid.
26. PABC, McClung Papers, vol. 26, notebook [1895].
27. Ibid., 31 December 1895.
28. According to the Booksellers' and Stationers' "Canadian Summary," Nellie's first novel, *Sowing Seeds in Danny* (Toronto, 1908), shared the number one spot in Canada with *Trail of Lonesome Pine* by John Fox, Jr. PABC, McClung Papers, vol. 29, n.d.
29. Nellie's mother, Letitia McCurdy, had been raised in Dundee, Scotland, and probably had the normal schooling that girls received there at that time. It is curious, then, that on the three indentures regarding the mortgaging and sale of the Mooney farm in Grey County, she misspells her name on all three documents: (1) "Leittia Mooney," (2) "Leitita Mooney," and (3) "Leitia Mooney."

Chapter 4—Living in Manitou: 1896–1911

1. Canada Department of Immigration, "A British Colony Open to All," n.d.; Nellie L. McClung, *The Stream Runs Fast: My Own Story* (Toronto, 1945). Quotations from *The Stream Runs Fast* appear throughout this chapter. All other sources of information are cited.
2. Manitou *Sun*, 31 August 1899, 9 May 1901, 16 May 1901; Nellie V. Craig, "Remembering Nellie L. McClung," unpub. MS in possession of Mrs. Andrew Moore, Winnipeg, and Manitou *Western Canadian*, 1 June 1911; Manitou *Sun*, 7 September 1899, 14 November 1901, 19 December 1907; Manitou *Western Canadian*, 9 May 1900, 1 June 1911.
3. Manitou *Western Canadian*, 11 July 1900, 27 June 1900; Manitou *Sun*, 20 June 1901; Manitou *Western Canadian*, 10 May 1910, 20 June 1900; Manitou *Sun*, 16 May 1901, 13 April 1905, 7 September 1899.
4. Manitou *Western Canadian*, 13 June 1900, 2 April 1908, 13 June 1900, 20 April 1905; Manitou *Mercury*, 19 January 1895, 26 October 1895; Manitou *Western Canadian*, 11 April 1900, 6 December 1906.
5. Manitou *Sun*, 8 June 1899.
6. Provincial Archives of British Columbia [PABC], McClung Papers, vol. 29, from *The Canadian Royal Templar*, October 1908; Manitou *Sun*, 28 December 1899.
7. Ibid., vol. 27.
8. Nellie L. McClung, *The Second Chance* (Toronto, 1910), pp. 40–42.
9. PABC, McClung Papers, vol. 30, unidentified newspaper clipping and the Baldur *Gazette*, n.d.
10. Ibid., vol. 26, notebook (material dates 1899).
11. Manitou *Sun*, 15 March 1900, 17 August 1905; PABC, McClung Papers, vol. 26.
12. PABC, McClung Papers, vol. 27, scrapbook, "Miscellaneous clippings, 1895–1905."
13. Ibid.
14. Manitou *Mercury*, 22 December 1898; Manitou *Sun*, 27 September 1899.
15. Betty Keller, *Pauline: A Biography of Pauline Johnson* (Vancouver, 1981), p. 274.
16. Veronica Strong-Boag, *The Parliament of Women: The National Council of Women*

Notes

of Canada, 1893–1929 (Ottawa, 1976), p. 299. See also Alison Prentice et al., *Canadian Women: A History* (Toronto, 1988), pp. 169–70.

17. Manitou *Western Canadian*, 17 January 1907. On this occasion Nellie gave a farewell party in her home for Alice and her young friends.
18. Candace Savage, *Our Nell: A Scrapbook Biography of Nellie L. McClung* (Saskatoon, 1979), interview with Mrs. A.H. Rogers, p. 44.
19. Ibid., Mrs. Ascheneth Sharp, interview with Candace Savage, 10 December 1974.
20. Manitou *Western Canadian*, 25 September 1906, 19 March 1908; PABC, McClung Papers, vol. 10(2), letter from E.S. Caswell to NLM, 30 July 1908; letter from Hayden Carruth to R.W. McClung, 7 August 1908.
21. PABC, McClung Papers, vol. 26, notebook.
22. James H. Gray, *Booze: The Impact of Whiskey on the Prairie West* (Toronto, 1972); M.A. Garland and J.J. Talman, "Pioneer Drinking Habits and the Rise of the Temperance Agitation in Upper Canada Prior to 1840," *Ontario Historical Society Papers and Records* 27 (1931): 341–64.
23. Manitou *Sun*, 22 February 1900. See Alison Prentice et al., *Canadian Women*, pp. 172–74, 178. See also Nancy M. Sheehan, "Women's Organizations and Educational Issues, 1900–1930," *Canadian Woman Studies* VII (Fall 1986): 90–94.
24. For more background on the WCTU, see Nancy Sheehan, "The WCTU on the Prairies 1886–1930: An Alberta-Saskatchewan Comparison," *Prairie Forum*, vol. 6, n. 1 (Spring 1981): 17–34; and P. Voisey, "The 'Votes for Women' Movement," *Alberta History*, vol. 23, n. 3 (Summer 1975): 10–23.
25. Manitou *Mercury*, 1899 (incomplete date on newsclipping).
26. Manitou *Sun*, 20 June 1901.
27. All the quotations in this paragraph are from Veronica Strong-Boag, "Introduction" to *In Times Like These* by Nellie L. McClung (1915; reprint, Toronto, 1972), pp. viii–ix. See also Alison Prentice et al., *Canadian Women*, pp. 169–70.
28. See John Herd Thompson, *The Harvests of War: The Prairie West, 1914–1918* (Toronto, 1978), p. 95, for a discussion of the reform movement in western Canada at this time.
29. PABC, McClung Papers, vol. 23(4), 9 February 1944.
30. Ibid., vol. 23(3), Nellie L. McClung, "A Memory: Kate Simpson Hayes ('Mary Markwell')," n.d.
31. Provincial Archives of Manitoba [PAM], Canadian Women's Press Club Papers, Winnipeg Branch, Winnipeg *Telegram*, 5 March 1909. The CWPC aimed "to work together to advance journalism as a career for women." See Barbara Freeman, "'Every Stroke Upward': Women Journalists in Canada, 1880–1906," *Canadian Woman Studies* VII (Fall 1986): 43–46.
32. PABC, McClung Papers, vol. 23(4).
33. Ibid., vol. 17 [E. Cora Hind], "A Lady of Manitou," *Canadian Home Journal*, December 1910, p. 53.
34. Ibid.
35. Ibid.
36. Ibid.
37. Ibid., from a note written on the margin in NLM's hand.
38. Ibid.
39. PABC, McClung Papers, vol. 26, notebook (memos and sayings dated from 6 May 1909).
40. Mark McClung, interview with the authors, Ottawa, 25 June 1974.
41. PABC, McClung Papers, vol. 18, undated letter from NLM to F.C. Beecher of the *Western Prairie Gazette*, Glenboro, Manitoba.

Notes

42. Ibid., vol. 2(2), MS (apparently written in the 1940s when she was commencing *The Stream Runs Fast*).
43. Ibid., vol. 22(3).
44. Margaret Ecker Francis, "Nellie McClung," *Canadian Home Journal*, October 1947, p. 102.
45. Manitou *Sun*, 8 June 1899, 7 September 1899; PABC, McClung Papers, vol. 27, scrapbook, "Miscellaneous Clippings: 1895–1905"; Manitou *Western Canadian*, 21 November 1900; Manitou *Sun*, 4 May 1899.
46. Manitou *Western Canadian*, 13 March 1900, 16 May 1900, 9 May 1900, 6 June 1900, 22 August 1900, 8 August 1900, 19 September 1900, 24 April 1901; and the Manitou *Sun*, 17 October 1901.
47. Manitou *Sun*, 28 December 1905.
48. PABC, McClung Papers, vol. 27, scrapbook, "Miscellaneous Clippings: 1895–1905." According to records of the Manitoba Pharmaceutical Association, because of "failing health" Wes gave up his pharmacy licence in 1908 when he officially "retired, in good standing," private correspondence with the authors, 28 January 1987. See also *The History of Pharmacy in Manitoba* (1954) by Dr. Dougald McDougal.
49. PABC, McClung Papers, vol. 3(7), rough draft of a letter from NLM to H. Nichols, n.d.
50. Ibid., vol. 10(2).
51. Ibid., vol. 10(1), correspondence, letter from E.S. Caswell to NLM, 14 January 1907.
52. Manitou *Western Canadian*, 1 June 1911.
53. PABC, McClung Papers, vol. 26, notebook, 5 August 1911; Manitou *Western Canadian*, 1 May 1901; Manitou *Sun*, 5 September 1911.
54. "Canada's New Magazine," *The Canadian Thresherman and Farmer*, December 1906, p. 42; also "Western Canadian Immigration Association," *The Canadian Thresherman and Farmer*, April 1904. Hough was the author of popular romances of the American west. In 1909 he would publish *54–40 or Fight!* a romance of the Pacific rim concerning the British-American dispute over the northern border of the Oregon territory in the 1840s.
55. PABC, McClung Papers, vol. 10(1), letters from Herbert Vanderhoof to NLM, 10 December 1906 and 26 November 1907; also, vol. 10(2), Vanderhoof to NLM, 6 October 1908.
56. Ibid., vol. 10(1), Vanderhoof to NLM, 26 November 1907; vol. 10(2), Vanderhoof to NLM, 22 April and 22 May 1908; vol. 29, unidentified newspaper clipping, n.d.; and the Manitou *Western Canadian*, 4 June 1908.
57. PABC, McClung Papers, vol. 58 (MS begins 5 June 1908).
58. Ibid., vol. 30, a collection of newspaper clippings regarding NLM's various recital tours, 1910–1914; and vol. 10(3), letter from Mrs. G.C. Smith, Secretary, Ladies' Aid, Elkhorn.
59. Ibid., vol. 20, McClung recital flyer; vol. 80, newspaper clippings.
60. PABC, McClung Papers, vol. 10(3), 11 May 1910.
61. Ibid., letters from F.S. Ewens to NLM, 12 May 1910 and 18 August 1910; E.S. Caswell to NLM, 11 June 1910 and 21 October 1910; F.S. Ewens to NLM, 2 November 1910.
62. Ibid., vol. 30, newspaper clippings and [Fort William] *The Daily Times-Journal*, 20 December 1910.
63. Ibid., unidentified newspaper clipping, n.d.
64. Ibid.

Notes

65. Ibid.; Manitou *Western Canadian*, n.d.
66. See *Legacy: A History of Saskatchewan Homemakers' Clubs and Women's Institutes, 1911-1988* (Saskatoon, 1988), particularly pp. 1-2.
67. PABC, McClung Papers, vol. 4(2); Nellie L. McClung, "Value of Social Life in Country Homes," *The Nor'-West Farmer*, 5 July 1911, pp. 845-46.
68. McClung, "Value of Social Life in Country Homes." Also see Georgina Taylor, "'Should I Drown Myself Now or Later?' The Isolation of Rural Women in Saskatchewan and their Participation in Homemakers' Clubs, the Farm Movement and the Co-operative Commonwealth Federation, 1910-1967," in *Women: Isolation and Bonding = The Ecology of Gender*, ed. Kathleen Storrie (Toronto, 1987), pp. 79-100.
69. McClung, "Value of Social Life in Country Homes," pp. 845-46.
70. Nellie L. McClung, "The Humor of Everyday Life," *The Western Home Monthly*, December 1924.
71. PABC, McClung Papers, vol. 30, [Fort William] *The Daily Times-Journal*, 20 December 1910.
72. PAM, Canadian Women's Press Club Papers, Winnipeg Branch, Minute Book, 19 June 1910.
73. PAM, Quill Club Papers, "Minutes of Meetings November 14, 1908–November 13, 1910."
74. PABC, McClung Papers, vol. 20.
75. Ibid., vol. 18, Manitou *Western Canadian*, 1 June 1911; PAM, *The Canadian Thresherman and Farmer*, August 1911, p. 80.
76. PABC, McClung Papers, vol. 18, Manitou *Western Canadian*, 1 June 1911.

Chapter 5—The Winnipeg Years: The Growing Spirit of Reform

1. James H. Gray, *The Boy from Winnipeg* (Toronto, 1970), p. 2; Alan Artibise, *Winnipeg: A Social History of Urban Growth, 1874-1914* (Montreal, 1975), pp. 130-31; W.L. Morton, *Manitoba, A History*, 2d ed. (Toronto, 1967), pp. 301, 322; Artibise, *Winnipeg*, p. 189.
2. Susan Jackel, "First Days, Fighting Days: Prairie Presswomen and Suffrage Activism, 1906-1916," in *First Days, Fighting Days: Women in Manitoba History*, ed. Mary Kinnear (Regina, 1987), pp. 53-75. For a biography of E. Cora Hind, see *Brave Harvest* by Kennethe Haig (Toronto, 1945).
3. James H. Gray, *Booze: The Impact of Whiskey on the Prairie West* (Toronto, 1972), pp. 71-72.
4. Nellie L. McClung, "Through the Eyes of a Visitor," *Organized Helpfulness: All People's Mission, 1911-1912* (The Winnipeg Church Extension and City Mission Association of the Methodist Church, 1912), pp. 3-8.
5. John Herd Thompson in *The Harvests of War: The Prairie West, 1914-1918* (Toronto, 1978), pp. 74-75, states that the western Canadian provinces contained the largest concentration of non-English-speaking immigrants and "the attitudes of English-Canadian Westerners toward minority cultures before the war were not as tolerant or as uniformly favourable as is sometimes implied." The Great War did nothing to change this situation.
6. Winnipeg, *The Voice*, 17 March 1911.
7. In fact, women wage-earners generally supported the family unit. "In many cases these women simply turned their entire pay envelope over to their parents or husbands and received a small allowance for necessities in exchange," in James D. Mochoruk and Donna Webber, "Women in the Manitoba Garment Trade, 1929-45," in *First Days, Fighting Days: Women in Manitoba History*, ed. Mary

309

Kinnear (Regina, 1987). See also "Women and Labour During World War I: Women Workers and the Minimum Wage in Manitoba" by Linda Kealey in the same book. Kealey deals with the wages, hours, and conditions of women workers, and the struggle to gain a "living wage." See, too, Graham S. Lowe's *Women in the Administrative Revolution: The Feminization of Clerical Work* (Toronto, 1987) where he speaks of women's low paid, "menial, dead-end jobs" in spite of the fact of their knowledge, which could be, at times, higher than the men they worked for.

8. Nellie L. McClung, *The Stream Runs Fast: My Own Story* (Toronto, 1945), pp. 101–106.

9. Carol Bacchi, "Divided Allegiances: The Response of Farm and Labour Women to Suffrage," in *A Not Unreasonable Claim: Women and Reform in Canada, 1880's–1920's*, ed. Linda Kealey (Toronto, 1979). Bacchi sees the motives for the vote of farm and city women as different, and documents a disagreement arising in Saskatchewan (p. 102).

10. Nellie L. McClung, *Purple Springs* (Toronto, 1921), p. 99.

11. Alison Prentice et al., *Canadian Women: A History* (Toronto, 1988), pp. 169–70. See also Nancy F. Cott, *The Grounding of Modern Feminism* (New Haven, 1987), Chapter I, "The Birth of Feminism"; also Nancy F. Cott, "Feminist Theory and Feminist Movements: The Past Before Us," and Deborah L. Rhode, "Feminist Perspectives on Legal Ideology," both in *What is Feminism? A Re-Examination*, eds. Juliet Mitchell and Ann Oakley (New York, 1986).

12. Linda Kealey, ed., *A Not Unreasonable Claim* (Toronto, 1979), "Introduction" by editor, p. 7, and in the same book, Wayne Roberts, "'Rocking the Cradle for the World': The New Woman and Maternal Feminism, Toronto 1877–1914."

13. Nellie L. McClung, *In Times Like These* (1915; reprint, Toronto, 1972), p. 77.

14. Nellie L. McClung, "The New Citizenship," [re Political Equality League of Manitoba, n.d.] in *The Proper Sphere*, eds. Ramsay Cook and Wendy Mitchinson (Toronto, 1976), p. 289.

15. McClung, *In Times Like These*, pp. 64, 86.

16. Ibid., p. 43.

17. Ibid., p. 33.

18. Mark McClung, interview with the authors, Ottawa, 25 June 1974.

19. McClung, *In Times Like These*, p. 33.

20. Nellie L. McClung, *The Next of Kin* (Toronto, 1917), p. 136.

21. Provincial Archives of British Columbia [PABC], McClung Papers, vol. 8, rough draft of article, n.d.

22. Ibid., vol. 17, newspaper clipping, Edmonton *Bulletin*, 27 February 1915.

23. Nellie L. McClung, "Speaking of Women," *Maclean's*, May 1916, p. 25.

24. McClung, *In Times Like These*, p. 52.

25. See Veronica Strong-Boag, "'Ever a Crusader': Nellie McClung, First-Wave Feminist," in *Rethinking Canada: The Promise of Women's History*, eds. Veronica Strong-Boag and Anita Clair Fellman (Toronto, 1986), pp. 178–81.

26. Nellie L. McClung, "Every Woman Is Not a House-Keeper," in *Be Good to Yourself* (Toronto, 1930), pp. 146–51.

27. McClung, *In Times Like These*, p. 86.

28. Ibid., pp. 64–66.

29. Ibid., pp. 85–86.

30. Ibid., p. 116.

31. McClung, *The Next of Kin*, pp. 102–11. See Georgina Taylor, "Should I Drown Myself Now or Later?" pp. 79–100.

32. Nellie L. McClung, "What Will They Do With It?" *Maclean's*, July 1916, p. 38.
33. Nellie L. McClung, "A Retrospect," *The Country Guide*, 2 December 1929.
34. McClung, *In Times Like These*, p. 62.
35. Ibid., p. 40.
36. McClung, "Speaking of Women," *Maclean's*, p. 26.
37. E. Cora Hind, "The Woman's Quiet Hour," *The Western Home Monthly*, February 1912; Winnipeg *Town Topics*, 14 December 1912; McClung, *The Stream Runs Fast*, p. 101. During her 1916 tour of Canada, Mrs. Pankhurst asked NLM to arrange two public appearances in Edmonton for her in June. Again, NLM held a reception for Mrs. Pankhurst in her home.
38. Provincial Archives of Manitoba [PAM], Newspaper Scrapbooks, 1914 provincial election, *Winnipeg Free Press*, 16 March 1914.
39. PABC, McClung Papers, vol. 34, newspaper clipping, Edmonton *Journal*, 19 January 1914.
40. PAM, Political Equality League Minute Book, Minutes for 27 June 1912 and 25 February 1914.
41. PABC, McClung Papers, vol. 34, newspaper clipping, Hamilton *Times*, 25 March 1914.
42. PAM, Political Equality League, Minutes of executive, 12 January 1914.
43. See Mary Kinnear, "The Icelandic Connection: 'Freyja' and the Manitoba Woman Suffrage Movement," in *Canadian Woman Studies* VII (Winter 1986). Kinnear analyses the Icelandic feminist philosophy in the periodical *Freyja* [Woman] and then relates it to ideas in the Anglo-Saxon women's movement.
44. Reports on the deputation quoted in the previous paragraphs taken from *The Grain Growers' Guide*, 4 February 1914; two unidentified newspaper clippings in the McClung Papers, vol. 34; editorial in the Winnipeg *Tribune*, 28 January 1914; PABC, McClung Papers, vol. 22(3).
45. McClung, *The Stream Runs Fast*, p. 116.
46. Accounts of the mock parliament as described in the above paragraphs are found in the Winnipeg *Tribune*, *Free Press*, and *Telegram* for 29 January 1914. See also McClung, *The Stream Runs Fast*, Chapter XIV, and a fictionalized version which NLM says is "substantially a matter of history" in Chapter XXII of *Purple Springs* (1921). There is also a MS version of Nellie's speech in the McClung Papers, vol. 20, though she apparently did not stick to this script.
47. PABC, McClung Papers, vol. 35, unidentified newspaper clipping, "People Flock to Hear Mrs. McClung"; Melita *Enterprise*, 18 June 1914.
48. *Winnipeg Free Press*, 29 May 1914.
49. *Winnipeg Free Press*, 3 June 1914.
50. PABC, McClung Papers, vol. 7, MS for a speech, n.d.
51. McClung, *The Next of Kin*, p. 234.
52. PABC, McClung Papers, vol. 35, unidentified newspaper clipping, n.d.
53. McClung, *The Next of Kin*, p. 231.
54. McClung, *In Times Like These*, p. 53.
55. Ibid., p. 55. See Gerald Friesen, *The Canadian Prairies: A History* (Toronto, 1984), pp. 351–54, especially for the ethnic side of the suffrage issue. See also, John Herd Thompson, "'The Beginnings of our Regeneration': The Great War and Western Canadian Reform Movements," in *The Prairie West: Historical Readings*, eds. R. Douglas Francis and Howard Palmer (Edmonton, 1985), pp. 450–65; and Veronica Strong-Boag, "Canadian Feminism in the 1920s: The Case of Nellie L. McClung," in the same book.
56. PAM, Newspaper Scrapbooks, 1914 provincial election, *Winnipeg Free Press*, 1 May 1914.

57. McClung, *In Times Like These*, pp. 57–58.
58. Winnipeg *Telegram*, 2 May 1914.
59. Winnipeg *Tribune*, 9 June 1914; Winnipeg *Telegram*, 9 June 1914.
60. PABC, McClung Papers, vol. 35, Neepawa *Register*, 11 June 1914.
61. PAM, Newspaper Scrapbooks, 1914 provincial election, *Winnipeg Free Press*, 3 June 1914; PABC, McClung Papers, vol. 35, Toronto *Globe*, 6 June 1914.
62. McClung, *The Stream Runs Fast*, pp. 127–29.
63. Ibid., p. 126.
64. PABC, McClung Papers, vol. 21, rough MS work for *The Stream Runs Fast*.
65. McClung, *The Stream Runs Fast*, p. 126.
66. Mark McClung, interview with the authors, Ottawa, 25 June 1974.
67. *Winnipeg Free Press*, 12 June 1914. Dateline reads: Hamiota, June 11.
68. Nellie L. McClung, "Can a Woman Raise a Family and Have a Career?" *Maclean's*, 15 February 1928.
69. PABC, McClung Papers, vol. 35, unidentified newspaper clipping, n.d.
70. *Winnipeg Free Press*, 7 July 1914.
71. *Winnipeg Free Press*, 10 July 1914.
72. Morton, *Manitoba*, p. 337. The number of constituencies had been increased from 42 to 49, including 3 new northern ridings that went to the Conservatives.
73. McClung, *The Stream Runs Fast*, pp. 136–37; McClung, *The Next of Kin*, pp. 22, 26.
74. PABC, McClung Papers, vol. 17, newspaper clippings, *Winnipeg Free Press* and the *Prairie Farmer*, 22 September 1914. NLM's account of the occasion in *The Stream Runs Fast*, pp. 141–42, is somewhat different.
75. Ibid., newspaper clipping, *The Statesman*, 24 September 1914.
76. Morton, *Manitoba*, pp. 341–47.
77. PABC, McClung Papers, vol. 12 (10), newspaper clipping, *Manitoba Free Press*, n.d.
78. Ibid., vol. 35, unidentified newspaper clipping, n.d. Dateline reads: Portage La Prairie, Manitoba, August 3 [1915]. The Macdonald Act, a prohibition act, was passed when Hugh John Macdonald was leader of the Conservative Party, but never proclaimed. When Roblin became leader, he held another referendum that went against prohibition so the act never became law.
79. PAM, Political Scrapbook, "Sir James Fails"; *Winnipeg Free Press*, 3 August 1915, dateline Manitou, 2 August; *Winnipeg Free Press*, 6 August 1915, "Election Eve Liberal Rally Great Success."
80. PABC, McClung Papers, vol. 17, *Winnipeg Free Press* "News Bulletin," 7 August 1915.
81. Ibid., vol. 35, unidentified newspaper clipping, n.d., "The Anomaly."
82. Ibid., collection of telegrams.
83. Ibid., unidentified newspaper clipping, n.d.

Chapter 6—The War Years: 1914–1919

1. Francis Beynon, "Country Homemakers," *The Grain Growers' Guide*, 18 November 1914.
2. Provincial Archives of British Columbia [PABC], McClung Papers, vol. 20, "Presentation on Leaving Manitoba," 27 November 1914.
3. Nellie L. McClung, *The Stream Runs Fast: My Own Story* (Toronto, 1945), pp. 142–43.
4. Ibid., p. 154.
5. Emily F. Murphy, "What Janey Thinks of Nellie," *Maclean's*, 1 September 1921, p. 15.
6. PABC, McClung Papers, vol. 17, newspaper clipping, Edmonton *Bulletin*, 27

Notes

February 1915. Earlier, while living in Winnipeg, NLM had been invited to speak at the founding meeting of the Edmonton Equal Franchise League.

7. Ramsay Cook and Craig Brown, *Canada: 1896-1920: A Nation Transformed* (Toronto, c. 1974), p. 212. For a more recent book specifically on the Canadian West, see Gerald Friesen, *The Canadian Prairies: A History* (Toronto, 1984).
8. McClung, *The Stream Runs Fast*, p. 139.
9. Nellie L. McClung, *In Times Like These* (1915; reprint, Toronto, 1972), pp. 14, 17.
10. Nellie L. McClung, *The Next of Kin* (Toronto, 1917), p. 211; *In Times Like These*, p. 18.
11. McClung, *In Times Like These*, pp. 18-19, 15, 12-13.
12. Thomas P. Socknat, *Witness Against War: Pacifism in Canada, 1900-1945* (Toronto, 1987), p. 45.
13. McClung, *In Times Like These*, pp. 24, 89.
14. PABC, McClung Papers, vol. 28, newspaper and magazine clippings: Toronto *Globe*, 1 November 1915, which also refers to her "delicately acid words"; Edmonton *Bulletin*, 10 November 1915, taken largely from the *Globe*; Calgary *Morning Albertan*, 20 December 1915; *Saturday Night*, 1 January 1916. And from the United States: Springfield, Mass., *Republican*, 1 November 1915; Baltimore *Sun*, 2 November 1915; *San Franciscan Argonaut*, 13 November 1915; Boston *Advertiser*, 4 December 1915, reviewed by an antisuffragist; *The Bookman*, n.d.
15. McClung, *The Next of Kin*, p. 45.
16. Public Archives of Canada [PAC], J.S. Woodsworth Papers, Vernon Thomas to Woodsworth, 11 December 1917; Provincial Archives of Manitoba [PAM], P191, letter from NLM to Mrs. A.V. Thomas, 1 April 1917.
17. McClung, *The Next of Kin*, pp. 47-51.
18. McClung, *The Stream Runs Fast*, p. 155.
19. John Herd Thompson, *The Harvests of War: The Prairie West, 1914-1918* (Toronto, 1978), pp. 97-98.
20. PABC, McClung Papers, vol. 17, Natalie Symons, "Nellie McClung of the West," *Canada Monthly*, February 1916, p. 232; also vol. 35, unidentified clipping, 3 August 1915.
21. James H. Gray, *Booze: The Impact of Whiskey on the Prairie West* (Toronto, 1972), p. 84.
22. Edmonton *Daily Bulletin*, 22 July 1915.
23. *The Canadian Thresherman and Farmer*, April 1916.
24. PABC, McClung Papers, vol. 25, typescript, speech to UFA Convention at Wetaskawin, 1919.
25. McClung, *In Times Like These*, pp. 98-99.
26. Lillian Beynon Thomas, "A Woman's Talk to Women," *The Canadian Thresherman and Farmer*, March 1916.
27. Catherine L. Cleverdon, *The Woman Suffrage Movement in Canada*, 2d ed. (Toronto, 1974), p. 63.
28. Information in the above two paragraphs from Cleverdon, *Woman Suffrage*, pp. 37, 114-21.
29. Francis Beynon editorial, *The Grain Growers' Guide*, 27 December 1916; and McClung letter, 24 January 1917. In the long run Nellie believed in, and supported, universal female suffrage on the same basis as male suffrage in Canada (before foreign-born male immigrants were disenfranchised).
30. PABC, McClung Papers, vol. 17, unidentified newspaper clipping, Calgary, 1917, "Mrs. McClung Agrees with Next-of-Kin Resolution."
31. Ibid., vol. 18, Nellie L. McClung, "What the Red Cross is Doing in the North

313

Notes

Country," *The Canadian Home Journal,* n.d.

32. Nellie L. McClung, "The Ukrainians in Canada," *The Canadian Home Journal,* October 1917, pp. 12ff.
33. Cook and Brown, *Canada: 1896–1920,* p. 295.
34. Nellie L. McClung, "Loyalty," *The Grain Growers' Guide,* 5 December 1917.
35. Toronto *Globe,* 12 October 1915.
36. PABC, McClung Papers, vol. 18, newsclipping, *Saturday Night,* n.d.
37. Ibid., vol. 17, Natalie Symons, "Nellie McClung of the West," *Canada Monthly,* February 1916, p. 232.
38. Toronto *Evening Telegram,* 14 October 1915.
39. PABC, McClung Papers, vol. 36, Paris, Ont., *Transcript,* 29 October 1915, letter to the editor.
40. Toronto *Evening Telegram,* 14 October 1915.
41. PABC, McClung Papers, vol. 13, unidentified clipping.
42. Ibid., vol. 36, newspaper clipping, Ottawa *Citizen,* 22 October 1915.
43. Toronto Public Reference Library, Biography Scrapbook, vol. 16, p. 10, newspaper clipping, Toronto *Telegram,* 16 October 1915.
44. PABC, McClung Papers, vol. 11 (4), in a letter from Joy Young, assistant editor, *The Suffragist,* to NLM, 10 October 1916.
45. Ibid., vol. 35, unidentified newspaper clipping, 11 May 1916; vol. 36, Minneapolis *Journal,* 8 May 1916.
46. Ibid., vol. 10(1), Thomas H. Johnson to Percy Anderson, Chicago, 10 May 1916.
47. Ibid., vol. 11(4), letter from Carrie Chapman Catt to NLM, 18 July 1916.
48. Ibid., typed itinerary from Nettie Shuler, Corresponding Secretary, NAWSA; letter from Schuler to NLM, 14 February 1917, mentions that National Headquarters paid for her time in West Virginia and that Maryland received her for two speeches for $75.00, but no dates are mentioned. See also McClung Papers, vol. 51, newsclipping from Parkersburg, West Virginia. Although there is no direct evidence that McClung visited Colorado, an account of the early suffrage movement and its organizing by means of women in varied women's associations "networking" makes for interesting reading. See Carolyn Stefanco, "Networking on the Frontier: the Colorado Women's Suffrage Movement, 1876–1893," in *The Women's West,* eds. Susan Armitage and Elizabeth Jameson (Oklahoma, 1987). The same kind of "networking" went on among women in Canada.
49. PABC, McClung Papers, vol. 17, Corsicana *Morning News,* 24 November 1916.
50. Ibid., vol. 11(4), letters from Dr. Effie McCullom Jones, Iowa, to NLM, 9 March 1917, and Maude Clark, Texas, to NLM, 5 July 1917; pamphlet, "Jane Brown," Copyright 1917, Little Book Shop, 634 Wilson Bldg., Dallas, Texas. Published by Special Arrangement with the Author, Nellie L. McClung, author of "Sowing Seeds in Danny," "The Second Chance," "In Times Like These." The poem was written in 1914, published in Canadian periodicals, and finally enshrined in NLM's *Be Good To Yourself* (Toronto, 1930), pp. 12–17.
51. PABC, McClung Papers, vol. 17, Corsicana *Morning News,* 24 November 1916.
52. Ibid., vol. 38, unidentified newspaper clipping.
53. Ibid., newspaper clipping, Youngstown, n.d.
54. See Eleanor Flexner, *Century of Struggle: The Woman's Rights Movement in the United States,* rev. ed. (Cambridge, Mass., 1975).
55. PABC, McClung Papers, vol. 11(4), Lucy K. Miller to NLM, 16 December 1916.
56. Ibid., Maria McMahon to NLM, 26 March 1917.
57. Ibid., Mary Dewson to NLM, 26 June 1917.
58. Ibid., Shuler to NLM, 2 March 1917.

Notes

59. *Woman Citizen.* (No further information available.)
60. PABC, McClung Papers, vol. 11(1), Shuler to NLM, 3 January 1918.
61. PABC, McClung Papers, vol. 11 (1), contains invitations mentioned, and many others.
62. Nellie L. McClung, "Preface," to *Three Times and Out: A Canadian Boy's Experience in Germany* (Boston, 1918).
63. Mark McClung, interview with the authors, Ottawa, 25 June 1974.
64. PABC, McClung Papers, vol. 51, unidentified newspaper clipping, 5 April 1918; vol. 38, Vancouver *Province* editorial, 5 April 1918; Nellie L. McClung, "Teachers Wanted in Alberta," *Everywoman's World*, May 1918.
65. PABC, McClung Papers, vol. 26, typescript, heading: "Mrs. Nellie McClung at First Baptist Church," 22 March 1918.
66. Nellie L. McClung, "The Mobilization of Canadian Women," *Everywoman's World*, March 1918; see also "Call to Arms: Women of Canada" in the same issue.
67. Provincial Archives of Alberta [PAA], Canadian Women's Press Club, Edmonton Branch, Minute Book No. 4, 28 June 1918; PAC, Robert Borden Papers, 52193, Emily Murphy and NLM to Borden, 11 February 1918.
68. PABC, McClung Papers, vol. 11(1), Newton Rowell to NLM, 19 February 1918.
69. All information on the Women's War Conference that follows, unless otherwise noted, is taken from PAC, Robert Borden Papers, vol. 105, *Report of the Women's War Conference Held at the Invitation of the War Committee of the Cabinet, February 28–March 2, 1918* (Ottawa, 1918). Except for "Mrs. Nellie McClung" and "Mrs. Irene Moody" (Vancouver), the report refers to delegates under their husband's name and, for consistency, this book follows that practice here.
70. PABC, McClung Papers, vol. 26, typescript, speech at First Baptist Church [Edmonton?], 22 March 1918.
71. Ibid.
72. PABC, McClung Papers, vol. 38, Toronto *Star*, 2 March 1918.
73. Ibid.
74. E. Cora Hind, "The Woman's Quiet Hour," *The Western Home Monthly*, April 1918.
75. PABC, McClung Papers, vol. 26, typescript, speech at First Baptist Church [Edmonton?], 22 March 1918.
76. McClung, *The Next of Kin*, pp. 211, 240.
77. PABC, McClung Papers, vol. 25, typescript, speech to the United Farmers of Alberta, n.d.
78. Nellie L. McClung, "What Twelve Canadian Women See as the Outcome of the War," *Everywoman's World*, April 1915.
79. PABC, McClung Papers, vol. 23(3), typescript, n.d., "Do We Want Women at the Peace Conference? Please—Yes."
80. PAC, Robert Borden Papers, Borden to Acting Prime Minister, "Secret," 11 December 1918. There are several letters to Borden from Calgary women and women's associations regarding the appointing of women to the Peace Conference—none from NLM personally.
81. PABC, McClung Papers, vol. 23(3), typescript, n.d., "Do We Want Women at the Peace Conference? Please—Yes."
82. McClung, *The Stream Runs Fast*, pp. 190–97.

Chapter 7—Alberta Politics: 1917–1926

1. Lillian Beynon Thomas, "A Woman's Talk to Women," *The Canadian Thresherman and Farmer*, March 1916.
2. Nellie L. McClung, *Everywoman's World*, October 1917. "McClung established

315

Notes

what might be termed an 'arms-length alliance' with the pro-reform Manitoba Liberals in 1914, on the basis of an agreement that the latter would introduce suffrage legislation once they defeated the governing provincial Conservatives." See Sylvia B. Bashevkin, "Independence Versus Partisanship: Dilemmas in the Political History of Women in English Canada," in *Rethinking Canada: The Promise of Women's History*, eds. Veronica Strong-Boag and Anita Clair Fellman (Toronto, 1986), pp. 246-75.

3. Provincial Archives of British Columbia [PABC], McClung Papers, vol. 25, MS speech to the UFA, n.d.
4. Carol Bacchi, "Divided Allegiances: The Response of Farm and Labour Women to Suffrage," in *A Not Unreasonable Claim: Women and Reform in Canada, 1880's–1920's*, ed. Linda Kealey (Toronto,1979), p. 105.
5. Public Archives of Canada [PAC], National Council of Women Papers, vol. 67, Emily Murphy to Mrs. Cummings, 7 February 1916.
6. PABC, McClung Papers, vol. 24(2), "Women's Place on the Band Wagon," typescript, n.d.
7. Ibid., vol. 4(2), typescript, no title, n.d.
8. Ibid.
9. PABC, McClung Papers, vol. 23(3), "The Winnipeg Strike," typescript, n.d.
10. Nellie L. McClung, "Peace on Earth," *Western Home Monthly*, December 1920, pp. 5, 15.
11. Calgary *Daily Herald*, 16 May 1917.
12. PABC, McClung Papers, vol. 17, unidentified clipping, n.d.
13. Calgary *Albertan*, 26 May 1917, editorial; 28 May 1917, letter to the editor; 2 June 1917.
14. Gerald Friesen, *The Canadian Prairies: A History* (Toronto, 1984), pp. 371-72.
15. Edmonton *Bulletin*, 4, 5, 7, 12, 16, 18 July 1921.
16. Edmonton *Bulletin*, 18 July 1921.
17. Edmonton *Bulletin*, 19 July 1921.
18. PABC, McClung Papers, vol. 11(4), file of telegrams and letters of congratulation.
19. Nellie L. McClung, *The Stream Runs Fast: My Own Story* (Toronto, 1945), pp. 175-76; PABC, McClung Papers, vol. 25, typescript, n.d.
20. Edmonton *Morning Bulletin*, 8 February 1922.
21. McClung, *The Stream Runs Fast*, p. 172.
22. Calgary *Morning Albertan*, 8 February 1922.
23. Edmonton *Bulletin*, 16 March 1922.
24. Edmonton *Journal*, 21 March 1922.
25. PABC, McClung Papers, vol. 22(4), MS; Edmonton *Bulletin*, 3 March 1923.
26. Edmonton *Bulletin*, 15 March 1923.
27. PABC, McClung Papers, vol. 25, typescript, speech to legislature, 16 February 1924.
28. Ibid., vol. 13, pamphlet, *Address Given by Nellie L. McClung at the Women's Institute Convention, 31 May 1923*, pub. by Alberta Prohibition Committee of Edmonton; vol. 18, clippings, *Calgary Eye Opener*, 23 October 1920.
29. Ibid., vol. 25, typescript, speech to legislature, 31 January 1924.
30. Edmonton *Journal*, 1 February 1924; Kennethe M. Haig, "Preface" to *Pathfinders*, by Miriam Green Ellis (CWPC, 1956). For a short biography of Irene Parlby, see *Perennials and Politics* by Barbara Villy Cormack (Sherwood Park, Alberta, n.d.).
31. Mark McClung, interview with the authors, Ottawa, 25 June 1974.
32. Edmonton *Bulletin*, 25 February 1922.
33. Edmonton *Journal*, 25 March 1924.

34. PABC, McClung Papers, vol. 20, "Votes and Proceedings of the Province of Alberta, April 1, 1924"; Edmonton *Bulletin*, 2 April 1924.
35. Edmonton *Bulletin*, 10 February 1922.
36. Edmonton *Bulletin*, 26 February 1926.
37. PABC, McClung Papers, vol. 17, unidentified newspaper clipping, n.d.
38. Calgary *Bulletin*, 4 June 1926.
39. Calgary *Bulletin*, 17 June 1926.
40. PABC, McClung Papers, vol. 7(15), MS draft of speech; vol. 20, typescript, n.d., Medicine Hat Liberal meeting.
41. Calgary *Bulletin*, 25 June 1926.
42. PABC, McClung Papers, vol. 17, unidentified clipping, n.d.
43. Calgary *Bulletin*, 29 June 1926.
44. Veronica Strong-Boag, "Canadian Feminism in the 1920s: The Case of Nellie L. McClung," *Journal of Canadian Studies* XII (Summer 1977): 62.
45. Nellie L. McClung, "How It Feels To Be A Defeated Candidate," in *Be Good To Yourself* (Toronto, 1930), pp. 45-55.
46. McClung, *The Stream Runs Fast*, p. 175.

Chapter 8—Women's Role in the Church

1. Provincial Archives of British Columbia [PABC], McClung Papers, vol. 11(4), Rev. T. Albert Moore to NLM, 3 June 1920.
2. *Proceedings of the Fifth Ecumenical Methodist Conference, September 6-16, 1921*, pp. 241-67.
3. Veronica Strong-Boag, *The Parliament of Women: The National Council of Women of Canada, 1893-1929* (Ottawa, 1976), p. 394.
4. PABC, McClung Papers, vol. 17, newspaper clippings, unidentified, n.d.
5. Nellie L. McClung, "Peace on Earth Begins at Home," *The Western Home Monthly*, December 1922.
6. Nellie L. McClung, "Spiritual Anaemia," *The Western Home Monthly*, January 1923.
7. PABC, McClung Papers, vol. 11(6), typescript, 1926; "What Religion Means to Me," *The Quest* V, 29 March 1942; "What Life Has Taught Me," *Onward*, 30 December 1951.
8. Nellie L. McClung, *In Times Like These* (1915; reprint, Toronto, 1972), pp. 103-104.
9. Ibid., pp. 102-27. For a modern United Church woman minister's dealings with these difficult and emotional problems, see Carol L. Hancock, "Between Love and Challenge in Company with Nellie McClung" (unpub. MSTh. thesis, St. Andrew's College, University of Saskatchewan, 1985), and *No Small Legacy* (Winfield, B.C., 1986), also by Hancock.
10. McClung, *In Times Like These*, pp. 113-15.
11. Ibid.
12. Winnipeg *Tribune*, 13 June 1914.
13. *The Christian Guardian*, 16 October 1918.
14. Ibid. There were 2,082 such boards.
15. Nellie L. McClung, *The Stream Runs Fast: My Own Story* (Toronto, 1945), pp. 218-23.
16. *Proceedings of the Fifth Ecumenical Methodist Conference, September 6-16, 1921*, pp. 241-67.
17. PABC, McClung Papers, vol. 17, unidentified newspaper clipping, n.d.
18. *Methodist Record*, 16 September 1921.
19. *Proceedings of the Fifth Ecumenical Methodist Conference*, pp. 241-67.

20. Mark McClung, interview with the authors, Ottawa, 25 June 1974. *Time and Tide* was subtitled "The Review with Independent Views on Politics, Literature, Art."
21. PABC, McClung Papers, vol. 26, journal.
22. Ibid., vol. 18, *The Canadian Gazette*, 15 September 1921.
23. Ibid., vol. 26, newspaper clipping, Glasgow *Daily Record and Mail*, 4 October 1921; vol. 7(33), notebook journal titled: "What I Wrote about Scotland, 1921"; vol. 26, Scotland journal. See also *The Stream Runs Fast*, p. 220.
24. PABC, McClung Papers, vol. 25, notes for a speech headed: "Public Service for Women," Forum Club, London, England, 2 November 1921.
25. Ibid., vol. 17, unidentified clipping.
26. Ibid., vol. 51, note on unidentified clipping. For an excellent short story depicting British immigrants who failed to thrive, see Nellie L. McClung, "O, Canada!" in *Time and Tide* XII (12 September 1931): 1059–60.
27. PABC, McClung Papers, vol. 17, unidentified clipping, 17 November 1921.
28. Ibid.
29. McClung, *The Stream Runs Fast*, pp. 234–35.
30. *Report of the Committee on the Ordination of Women*, Prepared by order of the General Council for submission to the Presbyteries, 1922, p. 3. In the Presbyterian Church, women had equal rights with men in congregational meetings, but they were not regarded as eligible for the eldership and did not have a place on the Session, and therefore had no place in the membership of Synod or Assembly. See *Acts and Procedures of the Presbyterian Church in Canada*, 1922, pp. 26, 279; 1927, pp. 98, 620; 1924, p. 254.
31. PABC, McClung Papers, vol. 3(20), MS, no title, n.d.
32. Dr. Ernest Thomas, "Shall We Ordain Women?" *The New Outlook*, 18 January 1928.
33. *Report of the Committee on the Ordination of Women.*
34. R. Edis Fairbairn, "Well! Why Not Ordain Women?" *The New Outlook*, 11 April 1928.
35. For a discussion of the work and professional status of deaconesses, see Nancy Hall, "The Professionalisation of Women Workers in the Methodist, Presbyterian, and United Churches of Canada," in *First Days, Fighting Days: Women in Manitoba History*, ed. Mary Kinnear (Regina, 1987), pp. 120–33. Deaconesses were considered to be "pastors' aids" working "in the shadow of the clergyman." By 1922, 26 deaconesses made their grievances public in a memorial to the Methodist General Conference. They wanted the order remedied or abolished. See John D. Thomas, "Servants of the Church: Canadian Methodist Deaconess Work, 1890–1926," *Canadian Historical Review* LXV (September 1984): 380–95.
36. Alice A. Chown, *The Stairway* (1921; reprint, Toronto, 1988). See also John Stuart Mill, *The Subjection of Women* (London, 1869).
37. Thomas, "Shall We Ordain Women?" pp. 5, 21; L.M. England, "The Ordination of Women," *The New Outlook*, 22 February 1928, p. 7; Fairbairn, "Well! Why Not Ordain Women?" pp. 5–6; letters to the editor of *The New Outlook*.
38. "Editorial," *The New Outlook*, 7 March 1928.
39. There are no minutes for committee meetings, but the controversy was renewed later in the exchange between Dr. Thomas and NLM, and in a letter, Campbell to NLM, 28 November 1929, in the McClung Papers, vol. 11(6).
40. *The United Church of Canada, Year Book and Records of Proceedings, 1928*, Report of the Sessional Committee on Ordination of Women, Thursday, Sept. 13, 1928, p. 120.
41. *The Free Press Prairie Farmer*, 19 September 1928.
42. Ibid.

43. Dr. Ernest Thomas, "Women in the Pulpit," *Chatelaine*, October 1928, pp. 6–7, 32.
44. Nellie L. McClung, letter to the editor, *The New Outlook*, 19 December 1928; NLM, letter to the editor, *Chatelaine*, December 1928.
45. Nellie L. McClung, "Shall Women Preach?" *Chatelaine*, September 1934, pp. 14–15.
46. PABC, McClung Papers, vol. 5(16), untitled MS, n.d.
47. Mark McClung, "Portrait of My Mother," text of a talk given at the Nellie McClung Conference, University of Guelph, 26–28 September 1975, p. 15.
48. Edmonton *Bulletin*, 31 January 1929; *The New Outlook*, 19 December 1928; *The Beaver, Canada First*, 21 February 1929.
49. Nellie L. McClung, "Our Present Discontents," *Canadian Home Journal*, March 1929, pp. 9, 30.
50. McClung, "Shall Women Preach?" pp. 14–15.
51. Nellie L. McClung, "A Retrospect," *The Country Guide*, 2 December 1929.
52. *Record of Proceedings of the Tenth Conference of the Saskatchewan Conference of the United Church of Canada*, 1934, p. 23.
53. Lydia Gruchy, interview with the authors, White Rock, B.C., 19 May 1980.
54. McClung, "Shall Women Preach?" pp. 14–15.
55. *The United Church of Canada Year Book and Record of Proceedings*, 1935.
56. Eva M. Ferguson, "Canada's First Woman Minister," *The New Outlook*, 4 November 1936.
57. Dr. Ernest Thomas, "Ladies—We Give You The Pulpit!" *Chatelaine*, May 1937.
58. PABC, McClung Papers, vol. 24(4), "The Long Road to Freedom," typescript, n.d.

Chapter 9—Living in Alberta: 1914–1932

1. *British North America Act, 1867*, 30 and 31 Victoria, c. 3, section 24.
2. Public Archives of Canada [PAC], William Lyon Mackenzie King Papers, NLM to King, 30 December 1921; McDougall to NLM, 6 January 1922; NLM to King, 27 February 1922; King to NLM, 26 July 1923; NLM to King, 4 November 1925; King to NLM, 11 November 1925.
3. Edmonton City Archives, Emily Murphy Papers, unidentified clipping, Calgary, 1926.
4. Manitoba *Free Press*, Ferguson quoted in editorial, 22 October 1927.
5. See Una MacLean, "The Famous Five," *The Alberta Historical Review* (Spring 1926). For a more detailed presentation of the event, see Rudy G. Marchildon, "The 'Persons' Controversy: The Legal Aspects of the Fight for Women Senators," *Atlantis* VI (Spring 1981): 99–113; see also Olive M. Stone, "Canadian Women as Legal Persons: How Alberta Combined Judicial, Executive, and Legislative Powers to Win Full Legal Personality for All Canadian Women," *Alberta Law Review* XVII (1979): 331–71.
6. Provincial Archives of British Columbia [PABC], McClung Papers, vol. 11(6), Murphy to NLM, 5 August 1927; copy of letter, Murphy to Stuart Edwards, Deputy Minister of Justice, 9 November 1927; Edwards to Murphy, 30 November 1927; Murphy to NLM, 2 December 1927.
7. Ibid., Murphy to NLM, 2 December 1927.
8. Cleverdon, *Woman Suffrage*, pp. 147–49.
9. Ibid., p. 148.
10. Ibid.
11. Record of Proceedings in the Privy Council, No. 121 of 1928, On Appeal from

Notes

the Supreme Court of Canada: In the Matter of a Reference as to the Meaning of the Word "persons" in Section 24 of the British North America Act, 1867. For legal implications, see Marchildon, "The 'Persons' Controversy," pp. 99–113.

12. Albie Sachs and Joan Hoff Wilson, *Sexism and the Law: A Study of Male Beliefs and Judicial Bias in Britain and the United States* (Oxford, 1978), pp. 38–41.
13. PABC, McClung Papers, vol. 29, MS for radio address, "Now That We are Persons," n.d.
14. Ibid., vol. 17, unidentified Winnipeg newspaper clipping, n.d.
15. Edmonton City Archives, Emily Murphy Papers, unidentified clipping, Owen Sound press release, 1929.
16. PABC, McClung Papers, vol. 17, Vegreville *Observer*, 23 October 1929.
17. Ibid., unidentified newspaper clipping, n.d.
18. PABC, McClung Papers, vol. 11(6), Murphy to NLM, 4 March 1930.
19. Nellie L. McClung, "Two Men and Five Women," *Farm and Ranch Review*, 1 March 1930, p. 34.
20. Byrne Hope Sanders, *Emily Murphy, Crusader* (Toronto, 1945), p. 258.
21. Caesar Smith, "Keep the Co-Eds at Home," Toronto *Star Weekly*, 20 October 1926, p. 35.
22. *Maclean's*, 15 March 1926, pp. 15, 55–56.
23. *Canadian Home Journal*, March 1929, pp. 9, 30.
24. PABC, McClung Papers, vol. 29, MS radio address, "Now That We Are Persons," n.d.
25. Nellie L. McClung, "Our Present Discontents," *Canadian Home Journal*, March 1929, pp. 9, 30.
26. Nellie L. McClung, "A Retrospect," *The Country Guide*, 2 December 1929, pp. 3, 58.
27. Margaret McClung, interview with the authors, Victoria, 22 May 1980; Winnie Fudger, interview with the authors, Calgary, 10 May 1977.
28. PABC, McClung Papers, vol. 39, newspaper clipping, Dundalk *Herald*, n.d.
29. Helen Lenskyj, "A 'Servant Problem' or 'Servant-Mistress' Problem?" *Atlantis*, vol. 7, no. 1 (Fall 1981): 3–11.
30. Marilyn Barber, "The Servant Problem in Manitoba, 1896 to 1930," in *First Days, Fighting Days: Women in Manitoba History*, ed. Mary Kinnear (Regina, 1987), pp. 112–13.
31. Nellie L. McClung, *The Stream Runs Fast: My Own Story* (Toronto, 1945), pp. 260–61. The Scots woman portrayed here was Jean McDonald. She was quite hurt by Nellie's description of her as a woman "who liked any fight better than no fight at all," but later she visited the McClungs at Lantern Lane, Vancouver Island, and forgave Nellie. Glenbow Archives, Jean McDonald Papers, M724, Memoirs (appendices by Molly La Frances).
32. Toronto *Star Weekly*, 21 May 1927.
33. *Maclean's*, 15 January 1931.
34. McClung, *The Stream Runs Fast*, p. 258.
35. Ibid., p. 259.
36. Ibid.
37. Mrs. P. Halvarsen, interview with the authors, Victoria, 26 May 1980.
38. Winnie Fudger, interview with the authors, Calgary, 10 May 1977.
39. Mrs. P. Halvarsen, interview.
40. PABC, McClung Papers, vol. 11(6), translation of review from *Canadian Uütiset*, enclosed in a letter from Korte to NLM, 18 November 1925.
41. McClung, *The Stream Runs Fast*, p. 242.
42. Nellie L. McClung, "Getting Acquainted," *Western Home Monthly*, February 1925.

Notes

43. PABC, McClung Papers, vol. 20(2), Canadian Authors Association, "Branches Make Report," 1930–31; and vol. 11(4), J.M. Gibbon to NLM, 28 March 1921 and 13 April 1921.
44. *The Authors' Bulletin*, April 1925.
45. *The Authors' Bulletin*, August 1925, pp. 32–33, 12; Lyn Harrington, *Syllables of Recorded Time: The Story of the Canadian Authors Association 1921-1981* (Toronto, 1981), p. 82.
46. *The Authors' Bulletin*: August 1925, pp. 30–31, and September 1931, pp. 30–31; Harrington, *Syllables of Recorded Time*, p. 140.
47. *The Authors' Bulletin*, November 1926.
48. Various issues of *The Authors' Bulletin*: November 1926, p. 27; December 1928, p. 16; December 1927, p. 34.
49. Reports from Calgary branch in *The Authors' Bulletin*: November 1926, pp. 27–28; August 1925, pp. 15, 4; December 1928, pp. 16–17; December 1927, p. 34.
50. Various issues of *The Authors' Bulletin*: November 1924, regarding the CAA president's address by Robert J.C. Stead, given that spring; November 1926; September 1932; September 1931; December 1927; December 1928; May 1932; September 1932; September 1930; and September 1932.
51. "Canadian History and Canadian Biography," *The Authors' Bulletin*, December 1928.
52. Glenbow Archives, Calgary Women's Literary Club, Minute Books, various minutes: Article 12 of the constitution regarding membership was read at the first fall meeting every year; 12 October 1926; 6 January to 26 May 1931; the Minute Book for 1925–1932 records the study programs for the period when Nellie McClung was a member.
53. Mark McClung, interview with the authors, Ottawa, 25 June 1974.
54. PABC, McClung Papers, vol. 17, Calgary *Albertan*, 9 July 1932.
55. Glenbow Library, vertical file, "McClung, Nellie," Calgary *Albertan*, 6 August 1932.

Chapter 10—Antiromantic Fiction of a Feminist

1. Nellie L. McClung, "An Author's Own Story," *Saturday Night*, 25 January 1913, p. 29.
2. Nellie L. McClung, *The Stream Runs Fast: My Own Story* (Toronto, 1945), pp. 7–8, 10–11.
3. United Church Archives [UCA], [Mrs. R.W. McClung], "A Novel Birthday Present," *East and West*, 7 May 1904. The name is written in ink across the piece, probably for editorial records.
4. Provincial Archives of British Columbia [PABC], McClung Papers, vol. 22(4).
5. Ibid., vol. 10(1), correspondence, W.H. Withrow to NLM, 4 November 1907 and 12 November 1907.
6. Ibid.
7. McClung, *The Stream Runs Fast*, p. 11.
8. PABC, McClung Papers, vol. 1(7).
9. Ibid., William Briggs to NLM, 13 July 1905.
10. L.M. Montgomery was exuberant when she got published in a "first-class" magazine like the *Delineator*. See *The Selected Journals of L.M. Montgomery–Volume I: 1889-1910*, eds. Mary Rubio and Elizabeth Waterston (Toronto, 1985), p. 270.
11. PABC, McClung Papers, vol. 10(2), letter from Dreiser to Henry W. Lanier, 5 May 1908.
12. Ibid., vol. 30, newspaper clipping from Toronto *Globe*, Saturday, [?] November, [likely 1910].

321

Notes

13. Ibid., vol. 10(1).
14. Ibid., vol. 10(1), letters of 24 February 1906 and 26 April 1906; 12 February 1907; 10 June 1907; 8 March 1906 and 27 February 1907. Curiously, NLM took exception to the phrase "What the devil" in Irene Baird's *Waste Heritage* (Toronto, 1939) and even more so of her use of "hells and damns, blasts and bloodies" in Baird's *He Rides the Skies* (Toronto, 1941).
15. PABC, McClung Papers, vol. 10(2), letter from the McClungs (senior) to NLM from Victoria, 12 September 1908.
16. Ibid., vol. 10(1), various letters from E.S. Caswell to NLM, 1906–1907.
17. Ibid., vol. 10(2), E.S. Caswell to NLM, 7 December 1908.
18. Dick Harrison, *Unnamed Country: The Struggle for a Canadian Prairie Fiction* (Edmonton, 1977), p. 154.
19. PABC, McClung Papers, vol. 4, "On the Reading of Books," n.d.
20. Nellie L. McClung, *Sowing Seeds in Danny* (Toronto, 1908), p. 138.
21. Ibid., pp. 118, 125.
22. Ibid., pp. 186–88, 191.
23. Dick Harrison, for example, in *Unnamed Country* considers the last half of *Sowing Seeds in Danny* "unbearably maudlin," even though the last half records such satirical romance material as "Egbert and Edythe," pp. 186–88.
24. McClung, *Sowing Seeds in Danny*, pp. 158, 153.
25. Susan Jackel, "The House on the Prairies," *Canadian Literature*, no. 42 (Autumn 1969): 46–55.
26. Clifford Geortz, as quoted in Carol Fairbanks, *Prairie Women: Images in American and Canadian Fiction* (New Haven, 1986), p. 31.
27. Nellie L. McClung, *The Second Chance* (Toronto, 1910), p. 58.
28. Nellie L. McClung, *Painted Fires* (Toronto, 1925; published in Finland as *A Finnish Girl in America* [1927]), pp. 251–52.
29. See Henry Nash Smith, *Virgin Land: The American West as Symbol and Myth* (New York, 1950).
30. Harrison, *Unnamed Country*, pp. 81–82.
31. Nellie L. McClung, *The Stream Runs Fast*, p. 237.
32. Nellie L. McClung, "Standards," Toronto *Star Weekly*, 21 May 1927.
33. Nellie L. McClung, "The Black Curse," *Chatelaine*, September 1931.
34. Nellie L. McClung, "The Girl From God Knows Where," *Maclean's*, 15 January 1931.
35. Nellie L. McClung, "Three Christmas Eves: 1938–1939–1940," PABC, McClung Papers, vol. 24(4), typescript [ca. 1940].
36. *The Authors' Bulletin*, September 1931.
37. Harrison, *Unnamed Country*, p. 97.
38. Nellie L. McClung, "The Way of the West," in *The Black Creek Stopping-House* (Toronto, 1912), pp. 209–24.
39. Harrison, *Unnamed Country*, p. xiii.
40. Ibid., pp. 72–79, 98, 81.
41. Nellie L. McClung, "The Neutral Fuse," in *All We Like Sheep* (Toronto, 1926), pp. 104, 107, 111–12, 113.
42. Nellie L. McClung, "Thirty Years," in *Be Good to Yourself* (Toronto, 1930), pp. 72–76.
43. McClung, *Painted Fires*, p. 93.
44. McClung, *The Stream Runs Fast*, pp. 237–41.
45. McClung, *Painted Fires*, pp. 3–8.
46. Ibid., pp. 22–24.

Notes

47. Emily Murphy, *The Black Candle* (Toronto, 1922).
48. McClung, *Painted Fires*, pp. 55–56.
49. Varpu Lindström-Best, *Defiant Sisters: A Social History of Finnish Immigrant Women in Canada* (Toronto, 1988), p. 13.
50. Klaus Peter Stich, "Immigration and the Canadian West: From Propaganda to Fiction," (unpub. Ph.D. dissertation, York University, 1974), p. 108.
51. McClung, *The Second Chance*, p. 203; McClung, "Carried Forward," in *All We Like Sheep*, p. 203.
52. PABC, McClung Papers, vol. 24(3), typescript, "The Writer's Creed," n.d.
53. In *Transactions of the Royal Society of Canada*, vol. VI, Series 4 (June 1968): 173.
54. McClung, "The Black Creek Stopping-House" in *The Black Creek Stopping-House*, p. 27.
55. Stich, "Immigration and the Canadian West."
56. McClung, "The Black Creek Stopping-House," in *The Black Creek Stopping-House*, pp. 27, 61–63.
57. Ibid., pp. 167–68.
58. Nellie L. McClung, "Carried Forward," in *All We Like Sheep* (Toronto, 1923), p. 204.
59. Johan Lyall Aitken, *Masques of Morality: Females in Fiction* (Toronto, 1987), pp. 14–15.
60. Nina Baym, *Women's Fiction: A Guide to Novels By and About Women in America, 1820–1970* (Ithaca, N.Y., 1978) p. 74.
61. Ibid., pp. 74, 11–12.
62. See Laurence Ricou, *Vertical Man/Horizontal World* (Vancouver, 1973); Dick Harrison, *Unnamed Country*; Eric Callum Thompson, "The Prairie Novel in Canada: A Study in Changing Form and Perception" (unpub. Ph.D. dissertation, University of New Brunswick, 1972); *versus* Patricia Louise Verkruysse, "Small Legacy of Truth: The Novels of Nellie McClung" (unpub. M.A. dissertation, University of New Brunswick, 1975); Tamara Palmer, "Ethnic Character and Social Themes in Novels About Prairie Canada and the Period from 1900 to 1940" (unpub. M.A. dissertation, York University, 1972); and Clara Thomas, "Women Writers and the New Land," in *The New Land: Studies in a Literary Theme*, eds. Richard Chadbourne and Hallvard Dahlie (Waterloo, Ontario, 1978).
63. Nellie L. McClung, *Purple Springs* (Toronto, 1921), p. 60.
64. Baym, *Women's Fiction*, p. 19.
65. Ibid., p. 168.
66. McClung, *Sowing Seeds in Danny*, p. 300.
67. Elaine Showalter, *A Literature of Their Own: British Women Novelists from Brontë to Lessing* (Princeton, 1977), pp. 100, 123, 181.
68. McClung, *Painted Fires*, pp. 94–95.
69. Aitken, *Masques of Morality*, p. 66, has noted that "there must be some kind of killing, however symbolic or ritualistic" to effect the heroine's release in women's fiction for "once domesticated it is difficult to learn to be free, to dare, or to remember how to be wild."
70. See the Calgary Business and Professional Women's Club Reports, 1926–59, Glenbow Archives, BD3/.C212/f.3. Emily Murphy in *The Black Candle* (1922) concurred.
71. McClung, *Painted Fires*, pp. 313–14.
72. Aitken, *Masques of Morality*, p. 66.
73. Stich, "Immigration and the Canadian West," pp. 102, 124, 127.

Notes

74. Baym, *Women's Fiction*, pp. 24, 26–27, 11.
75. E.L. Bobak in "Seeking 'Direct Honest Realism': The Canadian Novel of the 1920's," *Canadian Literature* LXXXIV (Summer 1981): 85–86, sees McClung as a "realist" in certain ways but points out that "the first steps of the shift from the rural romance of the twenties to the realistic novel were awkward and difficult, often only imperfectly achieved by writers and imperfectly understood by readers and critics. For example, Nellie McClung's *Painted Fires* (1925) shows a recognition that the turmoil of the post-war decade required expression. A Communist maid is included in the plot, but she is a flutterbrain mouthing slogans she does not understand. McClung shows little comprehension of the genuine social issues behind the slogans" (p. 86). Indeed McClung was familiar with the social issues behind the slogans, but would not have found Communism an answer to social unrest. What she is satirizing is the mindless parroting of slogans with little, if any, comprehension of the real issues, the mere jumping on the bandwagon of others.
76. Verkruysse, "Small Legacy of Truth," p. 180.
77. Baym, *Women's Fiction*, pp. 14–15.
78. PABC, McClung Papers, vol. 24(3), NLM, typescript, "The Writer's Creed" [ca. 1940].
79. Ibid., typescript [ca. 1909].
80. Ibid.; Nellie L. McClung, "The Humor of Everyday Life," *The Western Home Monthly*, December 1924.
81. PABC, McClung Papers, vol. 39, newspaper clipping, "Have Eyes for Heroism of the Common People Is Message of Mrs. McClung," in an address, "Heroes of Peace," delivered to the League for Peace and Freedom, Calgary *Albertan* (1934).
82. Nellie L. McClung, "Backgrounds in Canadian Literature," Victoria *Daily Times*, 4 January 1933; Nellie L. McClung, "Taking Books to the People," PABC, McClung Papers, vol. 43, scrapbook, unidentified magazine, n.d.; Provincial Archives of Alberta [PAA], a 1935 interview with NLM, in information file on NLM.
83. PABC, McClung Papers, vol. 23(3), typescript, "Speak Up! Ladies!" n.d.
84. Margaret Laurence, *Dance on the Earth, A Memoir* (Toronto, 1989).
85. Nellie L. McClung, *When Christmas Crossed the Peace* (Toronto, 1923); McClung, *Second Chance*, pp. 50, 99, 21.
86. PABC, McClung Papers, vol. 22(1), MS, n.d.
87. Ibid., vol. 22(3).
88. Nellie L. McClung, "Babette," *Canada West*, November 1907.
89. McClung, *Purple Springs*, pp. 126–37, 172–88.
90. Marilyn Barber, "Help for Farm Homes: The Campaign to End Housework Drudgery in Rural Saskatchewan in the 1920s," *Scientia Canadensis* IX (June 1985): 7–8.
91. Mary Kinnear, "'Do You Want Your Daughter to Marry a Farmer?': Women's Work on the Farm, 1920," in *Canadian Papers in Rural History* VI, ed. Donald H. Atkenson (Gananoque, 1988), 139, 148–49.
92. McClung, *Purple Springs*, pp. 130, 132; McClung, "Carried Forward," in *All We Like Sheep*, p. 228.
93. Gillian Beer, "Beyond Determinism: George Eliot and Virginia Woolf" in *Women Writing and Writing About Women*, ed. Mary Jacobus (London, 1979), pp. 18–19.
94. McClung, *Painted Fires*, pp. 3–8.
95. Melody Graulich, "Violence Against Women: Power Dynamics in Literature of the Western Family," *The Women's West*, eds. Susan Armitage and Elizabeth

Jameson (Oklahoma, 1987), p. 114.

96. McClung, *Painted Fires*, p. 39; McClung, "Bells at Evening," p. 241, and "Carried Forward," p. 226, in *All We Like Sheep*.

97. Veronica Strong-Boag, "Pulling in Double Harness or Hauling a Double Load: Women, Work and Feminism on the Canadian Prairie," *Journal of Canadian Studies* XXI (Fall 1986): 35.

98. Mary Jacobus, "The Difference of View" in *Women Writing and Writing About Women*, ed. Mary Jacobus (London, 1979), pp. 17–19.

99. McClung, "Carried Forward," in *All We Like Sheep*, pp. 185–86, 191–92.

100. Lorna Irvine, *Sub/Version* (Toronto, 1986), pp. 97, 11.

101. McClung, *Purple Springs*, pp. 165–88. It was not until 1920 in Alberta that women gained equal control with their husbands over their children. *Purple Springs* is set in Manitoba in 1914, but dower legislation was not introduced until after 1914, and under the English *Divorce and Matrimonial Causes Act, 1857*, then in effect, "many courts continued to recognize common law paternal rights over children and award custody to fathers." While there was legal diversity on this issue across Canada, "Manitoba courts were particularly sensitive to the strong paternal rights found at common law." *The Manitoba Dower Act*, S.M. 1918, c. 21; *The Divorce and Matrimonial Causes Act, 1857;* Alison Diduck, Faculty of Law, University of Manitoba.

102. Graulich, "Violence Against Women," pp. 113, 116–17.

103. McClung, *Purple Springs*, pp. 42–44.

104. Gisela Bock, "Women's History and Gender History: Aspects of an International Debate," *Gender and History* I (Spring 1989): 18.

105. McClung, *Painted Fires*, pp. 29–30, 129.

106. McClung, "Carried Forward," in *All We Like Sheep*, p. 217.

107. Annette Kolodny, "A Map for Rereading: Gender and the Interpretation of Literary Texts," in *The New Feminist Criticism*, ed. Elaine Showalter (New York, 1985), pp. 56–57.

108. McClung, *Painted Fires*, pp. 67–68; 71–74.

109. McClung, *Purple Springs*, pp. 180–83; McClung, "Jane Brown," in *Be Good to Yourself*, pp. 12–17.

110. Veronica Strong-Boag, *The New Day Recalled: Lives of Girls and Women in English-Canada, 1919–1939* (Toronto, 1988), p. 19.

111. McClung, "Carried Forward," in *All We Like Sheep*, pp. 184–234.

112. McClung, "All We Like Sheep," in *All We Like Sheep*, pp. 20–23.

113. McClung, "Carried Forward," in *All We Like Sheep*, pp. 193, 198, 202–203, 207.

114. McClung, "Babette"; "Red and White," in *All We Like Sheep*, pp. 128–75.

115. McClung, *Painted Fires*, pp. 220–21.

116. McClung, *Purple Springs*, pp. 242, 228.

117. PABC, McClung Papers, vol. 18, MS address, "Words and Imagination," n.d.

118. Eric Callum Thompson, "The Prairie Novel in Canada: A Study in Changing Form and Perception" (unpub. Ph.D. dissertation, University of New Brunswick, 1972). Thompson does not deal with McClung's short stories.

119. In *Unnamed Country*, Dick Harrison makes the astonishing statement that "novels devoted to an author's concern over social issues" are a rarity, although *all* of McClung's work can be so described.

120. Baym, *Women's Fiction*, p. 45.

121. PABC, McClung Papers, vol. 18, pencil MS, unidentified article; vol. 24(3), NLM typescript, "The Writer's Creed" [ca. 1940].

122. Elaine Showalter, "Towards a Feminist Poetics," in *Women Writing and Writing*

About Women, ed. Mary Jacobus (London, 1979), pp. 34–35.

123. Irvine, *Sub/Version,* p. 3; and Showalter, "Towards a Feminist Poetics," p. 25.
124. Misao Dean, "Voicing the Voiceless: Language and Genre in Nellie McClung's Fiction and Her Autobiography," *Atlantis* XV (Autumn 1989): 65–75.

Chapter 11—Life at Lantern Lane

1. Provincial Archives of British Columbia [PABC], McClung Papers, vol. 55, *News Letter* of Manufacturers' Life, 25 August 1946.
2. Nellie Letitia McClung, quotations in the preceding two paragraphs are from *Leaves from Lantern Lane* (Toronto, 1936), pp. 1–9.
3. *Leaves from Lantern Lane* was followed by *More Leaves from Lantern Lane* (Toronto, 1937).
4. Margaret McClung, interview with the authors, Victoria, 22 May 1980.
5. McClung, *Leaves from Lantern Lane,* pp. 127–28.
6. Ibid., p. 4.
7. Glenbow Archives, BD.3. 6646, J1, NLM to Louise [Dean], 20 October 1932.
8. McClung, *Leaves from Lantern Lane,* p. 192.
9. Ursula Jupp, "Nellie McClung of Gordon Head," Victoria *Daily Colonist,* 21 October 1973, p. 15.
10. McClung, *Leaves from Lantern Lane,* p. 22.
11. Ibid., p. 103.
12. PABC, McClung Papers, vol. 12, newspaper clipping, "Are We Disturbed?" Ottawa *Citizen,* 15 March 1937.
13. Ibid., vol. 15, newspaper clipping, "The Expert," *The Hamilton Spectator,* 19 September 1936.
14. Nellie L. McClung, "Remedies," *Edmonton Bulletin,* 20 May 1939.
15. Vancouver *Daily Province,* 9 November 1937, CP report of NLM address at Toronto Book Fair. PABC, McClung Papers, vol. 14, critical responses appear, for example, in editorials in the Vancouver *Sun,* 13 November 1937; the Grand Forks *Gazette,* 18 November 1937; and the Vancouver *Daily Province,* 10 November 1937, the latter titled "Lo! The Poor Douk!" Regarding deportation of unemployed immigrants, see John Herd Thompson and Allen Seager, *Canada 1922–1939: Decades of Discord* (Toronto, 1985), p. 226.
16. Among other restrictions in B.C., the Japanese were barred from pharmacy, law, police force, post office, public health nursing; they could not obtain logging licenses, and after 1930, there were quotas on their fishing licenses. Ken Adachi, *The Enemy That Never Was* (Don Mills, 1976), pp. 52, 145, and passim.
17. PABC, McClung Papers, vol. 17, two newspaper clippings, Vancouver *Daily Province,* 9 October 1935, and another identified and dated by hand as the Vancouver *Commonwealth,* 10 October 1935. Also, the Vancouver *News Herald* and Vancouver *Sun,* 9 October 1935, pp. 4 and 2, respectively.
18. Ibid., vol. 15, newspaper clipping, NLM, "Defensive Common Sense," in the Wiarton, Ontario, *Canadian Echo,* 27 August 1936.
19. Ibid., vol. 5(2), rough drafts of column: NLM, "Still There is Hope!" and unidentified newspaper clipping, 9 September 1939; Adachi, *The Enemy,* p. 184 and p. 390, n. 18.
20. Nellie L. McClung, "What Did 1941 Teach Us?" *Winnipeg Free Press,* 10 January 1942.
21. PABC, McClung Papers, vol. 15, newspaper clipping, NLM, "That We May Not Forget," *Winnipeg Free Press,* 14 November 1942.
22. Ibid., vol. 12(10), A.E. Archer, Lamont Clinic, to NLM, 18 October 1944.

23. Ibid., vol. 21, rough draft of letter, n.d. There are no B.C. Department of Education records for the 1940s.
24. Ibid., vol. 53, interview by Myrtle Patterson Gregory, Vancouver *Sun*, 20 November 1945.
25. Public Archives of Canada [PAC], Agnes Macphail Papers, NLM to Macphail, 15 April 1939; W.L.M. King Papers, vol. 253, NLM to King, 20 December 1938; King to NLM, 23 December 1938.
26. PABC, McClung Papers, vol. 15, typescript.
27. Ibid., vol. 14, newspaper clipping, *Calgary Herald*, 2 March 1939.
28. PAC, Agnes Macphail Papers, NLM to Macphail, 15 April 1939.
29. Irving Abella and Harold Troper, *None Is Too Many* (Toronto, 1982). The authors describe the non-Jews who sought to help Jewish refugees as "a handful of concerned, dedicated citizens across Canada" with little influence who were not taken seriously (p. 284).
30. PABC, McClung Papers, vol. 21, rough draft for *The Stream Runs Fast*.
31. Glenbow Archives, newspaper clipping, the Calgary *Albertan*, 6 August 1932, in information file on Nellie McClung.
32. PABC, McClung Papers, vol. 25, newspaper clippings report speeches on 24 September, 19 and 24 October, 19 November 1932, and one to the Women's Canadian Club, 4 January 1933.
33. Ibid., vol. 40, various newspaper clippings.
34. Ibid., vol. 7(20), NLM, typescript, "The Fellowship of Book Lovers," for release 7 November 1935 for Canada Book Week; vol. 40, two newspaper clippings, the *Calgary Daily Herald*, 22 October 1935 and the Calgary *Albertan* (1935).
35. Ibid., vol. 40, newspaper clipping, the *Calgary Daily Herald*, 22 October 1935; vol. 15, newspaper clipping, NLM, "Second Spring" in the Winnipeg *Prairie Farmer*, 23 October 1935; vol. 40, newspaper clippings, NLM, "The Adventure of Living" in the Winnipeg *Tribune*, 3 December 1935; the *Chatham Daily News*, 14 November 1935.
36. Ibid., vol. 40, NLM, "The Adventure of Living," in the Winnipeg *Tribune*, 3 December 1935; vol. 14, newspaper clipping, Saskatoon *Western Producer*, 9 July 1936.
37. Nellie spoke in Nelson and Cranbrook, British Columbia, on 19 and 22 February; in Lethbridge, Calgary (twice), and Edmonton (three times) from 24 February to 2 March; in Saskatoon and Regina, Saskatchewan, 3 and 5 March. She attended the Board of Broadcast Governors in Ottawa, 8–11 March. While there she spoke in Ottawa on 10 March, and nearby Kemptville on 11 March. From the 15th through the 19th of March, Nellie spoke in a different Ontario town every night: Toronto, Hamilton, St. Catherines, Strathroy, and Woodstock. Her last Ontario speech of the 1937 tour was in Sudbury on 24 March, and she concluded in Winnipeg on 30 March. [Newspaper clippings in McClung Papers, various files.]
38. Nellie L. McClung, "Are We Disturbed?" Ottawa *Citizen*, 15 March 1937, referring to her speech in Toronto.
39. PABC, McClung Papers, various files, newspaper clippings; Provincial Archives of Alberta [PAA], two unidentified newspaper clippings dated 3 November 1937 in information file on Nellie L. McClung.
40. PABC, McClung Papers, vol. 12(8), PC 2369, Governor General in Council, 10 September 1936, makes appointments of nine Governors according to the provisions of the Canadian Broadcasting Act, 1936; PAC, W.L.M. King Papers, telegram, NLM to King, 10 September 1936 accepting appointment. Presumably there was a phone call, King to NLM.

Notes

41. Mark McClung, "Portrait of My Mother," text of a talk given at the Nellie McClung Conference, University of Guelph, 26–28 September 1975.
42. University of British Columbia, MSS Collection, Alan B. Plaunt Papers, Claxton to Plaunt, 10 September 1936 and 11 September 1936.
43. Victoria *Daily Times*, 12 June 1937, "Mrs. Nellie McClung Addresses Gyros on CBC Development Plans."
44. Nellie L. McClung, "The Voice of Canada," *Ottawa Evening Citizen*, 6 February 1937.
45. CBC Archives, Minutes of the CBC Board of Governors, 19 December 1936 and 24 March 1938; University of B.C. MSS Collection, Alan B. Plaunt Papers, Plaunt to NLM, 30 September 1936, explaining why Toronto and Montreal must come first.
46. CBC Archives, Minutes of the CBC Board of Governors, from November 1936 to November 1940. McClung missed only a special meeting called in Toronto on 8 September 1937. She had just recently returned from a regular board meeting in Quebec City in early August. After 1940, ill health prevented Nellie from attending.
47. PABC, McClung Papers, vol. 12(8), letter from Robert England (member, CBC advisory council in B.C.) to NLM regarding her complaints about an objectionable item on a variety programme; NLM, "Voices on the Air," Saskatoon *Star Phoenix*, 7 November 1941, describes professors talking about Job as "intellectual twitter"; McClung Papers, vol. 12(9), Arthur Phelps, letter to the *Winnipeg Free Press* replies that NLM confuses "analysis with cynicism and thought with sabotage."
48. CBC Archives, Minutes of the CBC Board of Governors, 17 November 1937 and 22 March 1938.
49. Frank W. Peers, *The Politics of Canadian Broadcasting, 1920–1951* (Toronto, 1969), pp. 278–80.
50. Nellie L. McClung, *The Stream Runs Fast: My Own Story* (Toronto, 1945), pp. 64–65.
51. PABC, McClung Papers, vol. 16, newspaper clipping, *Witness and Homestead*, 4 January 1941.
52. Nellie L. McClung, quoted in Elizabeth Bailey Price, "It's Not a Man's World," *Liberty*, 11 October 1941.
53. CBC *Regulations*, Paragraph 6, subsection 2, section 11; PABC, McClung Papers, vol. 6(16), rough draft of letter, NLM to Brockington, n.d.; interview and report of NLM speech to Ministerial Association of Victoria, Victoria *Daily Times*, 3 July 1937.
54. University of B.C. MSS Collection, Alan B. Plaunt Papers, letter, Plaunt to NLM, 20 July 1937.
55. PAC, W.L.M. King Papers, NLM to King, 3 July 1937; King to NLM, 29 September 1937; NLM to King, 7 October 1937.
56. See, for example, Lotta Dempsey's "It's News" column entitled "Women Should Get On The Air," an interview with NLM in *Chatelaine*, December 1937, p. 88; "Eavesdrop . . . with Eva Reid," Calgary *Albertan*, 21 January 1970.
57. McClung, *The Stream Runs Fast*, p. 262.
58. Victoria *Daily Times*, 12 February 1938.
59. Nellie L. McClung, "Nellie McClung in Hollywood," *Chatelaine*, September 1932; and McClung, *The Stream Runs Fast*, pp. 273–74.
60. McClung, *The Stream Runs Fast*, pp. 273–75.
61. Ibid., pp. 270–76; PABC, McClung Papers, vol. 15, typescript, "Canadian Fiesta,"

for release 21 May 1938.
62. McClung, *The Stream Runs Fast*, p. 279.
63. Ibid., p. 285.
64. PABC, McClung Papers, vol. 43, unidentified newspaper clipping, hand dated, 15 April 1947.
65. Ibid., vol. 12(9), telegram, King to NLM, 15 August 1938.
66. Ibid., letter from Andrew Miller, Miller Services Limited, to NLM, 13 September 1938.
67. Ibid., Whitton to NLM, 26 August 1938. See also *No Bleeding Heart: Charlotte Whitton, a Feminist on the Right*, by P.T. Rooke and R.L. Schnell (Vancouver, 1987).
68. PABC, McClung Papers, vol. 26, notebook, Geneva, September 1938.
69. McClung, *The Stream Runs Fast*, p. 296.
70. PABC, McClung Papers, vol. 39, newspaper clipping, Calgary *Daily Herald*, 5 November 1938.
71. Veronica Strong-Boag, "Peace-Making Women: Canada 1919–1939," in *Women and Peace: Theoretical, Historical and Practical Perspectives*, ed. Ruth Roach Pierson (New York, 1987), pp. 170–75. See also Thomas P. Socknat, *Witness Against War: Pacifism in Canada, 1900–1945* (Toronto, 1987).
72. Walter Houston Clark, *The Oxford Group: Its History and Significance* (New York, 1951); Robert G. Stewart, "Radiant Smiles in the Dirty Thirties: History and Ideology and the Oxford Group Movement, 1932–1936" (unpub. M.Th. thesis, Vancouver School of Theology, 1974).
73. Mrs. Louise Dean, interview with the authors, Calgary, 10 May 1977.
74. Stewart, "Radiant Smiles," pp. 88–90.
75. Editorial, *Nation*, 20 May 1939; Marc A. Rose, "Buchman and Moral Re-Armament," *Christian Herald*, October 1939; in 1936 the Reverend Richard R. Roberts—moderator of the United Church—described Buchman as an "unilluminated ass" for his "blather" about saving the world through a "'God-controlled Hitler,'" cited in Stewart, "Radiant Smiles," p. 87.
76. Nellie L. McClung, "The Oxford Group" in *More Leaves from Lantern Lane*, p. 197; PABC, McClung Papers, vol. 5(6), undated MS, but internal evidence suggests it was written in 1937.
77. PABC, McClung Papers, vol. 15, newspaper clipping, *Edmonton Bulletin*, 31 December 1937; vol. 44, newspaper clipping, Saskatoon *Star Phoenix*, 18 January 1938.
78. Ibid., vol. 2(3), undated MS.
79. Ibid., vol. 15, newspaper clipping, Saskatoon *Star Phoenix*, 20 September 1937; vol. 12(9), Baxter to NLM, 5 October 1937.
80. Mrs. Louise Dean, interview with the authors, Calgary, 10 May 1977; McClung Papers, vol. 55, a poetic tribute dated 21 August [1946] to Nellie and Wes on their 50th wedding anniversary from an MRA member who recalls how welcome the light at Lantern Lane "often" was when he returned by bus in the evenings. The verse is simply signed "Michael" from the MRA centre "Mountain House. Caux Sur Montreux" in Switzerland. The same name appears on a card from the MRA group there on the same occasion that includes the signature of Frank Buchman.
81. PABC, McClung Papers, vol. 15, typescript, "What Are We Going To Do?" marked for release, 5 February 1938.
82. Ibid., vol. 13, newspaper clipping, *The New Witness*, 8 November 1938.
83. Ibid., vol. 26, small notebook, "Guidance," 17 September [1938].
84. Ibid., vol. 45, unidentified newspaper clipping, n.d.

85. Ibid., vol. 17, newspaper clipping, *The Varsity*, 25 October 1938; vol. 39, newspaper clipping *Calgary Daily Herald*, 5 November 1938; vol. 17, newspaper clipping, *The New Witness*, 8 November 1938.
86. Ibid., vol. 15, typescript, radio address under auspices of the Business and Professional Women's Clubs, 16 November 1939. There are two versions of this speech in NLM's papers. One stresses MRA more than the other. It is not clear which one she used.
87. Jupp, "Nellie McClung of Gordon Head." Jupp was a next-door neighbour at Gordon Head for the last 17 years of NLM's life (1934-51). Her article is a reminiscence written on the occasion of the NLM commemorative stamp in 1973. Other visitors Jupp recalls were Leonard Brockington and Emily Carr.
88. Material in the preceding three paragraphs on the Olympia, Washington, MRA conference in May 1940 is from PABC, McClung Papers, vol. 18, black notebook.
89. PABC, McClung Papers, vol. 16 (20), letter MS, various attempts to answer letter to "Vox Pop," *Liberty*, n.d., but internal evidence suggests fall of 1940.
90. University of B.C. MSS Collection, Alan B. Plaunt Papers, letter, NLM to Plaunt, 13 January 1940; PABC, Eugenia Perry Papers, letter, NLM to Perry, 27 October 1940.
91. PABC, McClung Papers, vol. 2(9), various draft letters to members of Board re findings of Parliamentary Committee to study the CBC. This committee was critical of the manager, Gladstone Murray. McClung defended him. In the CBC Archives, Minutes of the CBC Board of Governors, 15 September 1941, the chairman read letters from NLM with regard to various matters that were noted and discussed; chairman read letter of resignation from NLM, 28 September 1942; PABC, McClung Papers, vol. 10(10), letter, Donald Manson, Secretary of Board of Governors, to NLM, accepting resignation and expressing extreme regret of board, 3 October 1943.
92. CBC Archives, Minutes of the CBC Board of Governors, 11 August 1943; PABC, McClung Papers, vol. 10(10), letter, General Manager CBC to NLM, 1 September 1943.
93. PABC, McClung Papers, vol. 16, typescript for release 29 March 1941.
94. Carolyn G. Heilbrun, *Writing a Woman's Life* (New York, 1988), p. 17.
95. McClung, "Introduction" to *The Stream Runs Fast*, pp. vii-xiii.
96. PABC, McClung Papers, vol. 21.
97. Ibid., vol. 12(11), letter, John [?] to Thomas Allen, 3 December 1945.
98. Nellie L. McClung, "Are We Uneasy? We Should Be," *Canadian Home Journal*, January 1945; NLM, "A Child Remembers," *Farmers' Magazine*, December 1946; NLM, "Stay, Bright Spirit!" "Christmas With Your Heart In It," "Christmas Moonlight and Magic," *Family Herald and Weekly Star*, 24 December 1947, 21 December 1949, and 21 December 1950, respectively.
99. The Edmonton *Bulletin*, 17 February 1944, reported that J.W. McClung, K.C. "died suddenly about 6:00 p.m. on Wednesday " In *The Stream Runs Fast*, Nellie McClung says, of her son Jack, "But I knew there was a wound in his heart—a sore place . . . like a wound in a young tree. It does not grow out. It grows in," p. 195; see also pp. 311-13. PAA, Premiers' Papers, E.C. Manning, 69.289 (682), letters, Lillian McClung [Mrs. Jack McClung] to Manning, 12 November 1944, and Manning's reply, 16 December 1944. PAC, National Film, Television, and Sound Archives, T 1979-114/68, a taped interview of R.G. Reid, former Premier of Alberta, by Marjorie McEnaney. Mark McClung, interview with the authors, Ottawa, 25 June 1974. Candace Savage, *Our Nell: A Scrapbook Biography*

of Nellie L. McClung (Saskatoon, 1979), p. 198.

100. PABC, McClung Papers, vol. 21, early typescript of *The Stream Runs Fast*, pp. 195–97, added to original MS.
101. McClung, *The Stream Runs Fast*, p. 311; Margaret McClung, in an interview with the authors, Victoria, 22 May 1980.
102. McClung, *The Stream Runs Fast*, pp. 311–13.
103. PABC, McClung Papers, vol. 53, newspaper clipping, Vancouver *Sun*, 20 November 1945.
104. Ibid., vol. 12(10), letter, Hannah Sweet to NLM, 28 June 1945.
105. Ibid., vol. 12(10), typescript of inscription.
106. Ibid., vol. 15, typescript headed *Telegram*, February 1940.
107. Nellie L. McClung, "Mother's Day Is Here Again," *Victoria Times*, 9 May 1942.
108. PAC, Moving Image and Sound Archives, Mark McClung Collection, "Interview [1975] of Mark McClung, son of Nellie McClung, by an unidentified interviewer, about: Nellie McClung," 30 mins., acc, 1978–0191, no. 3a.
109. PABC, McClung Papers, vol. 63, newspaper clipping, *Victoria Times*, 13 December 1941.
110. Nellie L. McClung, "Letter to the Editor," *Victoria Times*, 3 July 1950.
111. PABC, McClung Papers, vol. 21, NLM, early typescript, *The Stream Runs Fast*.
112. Veronica Strong-Boag, "Peace-Making Women: Canada, 1919–1939," in *Peace: Theoretical, Historical and Practical Perspectives*, ed. Ruth Roach Pierson (New York, 1987), p. 171.
113. PABC, McClung Papers, vol. 55, scrapbook of newsclippings, telegrams, letters, and cards; vol. 56, scrapbook of greeting cards; vol. 18, CP newsclippings from several newspapers.
114. University of Toronto Library, letter, NLM to Mr. H. M. Corbett, Ontario College of Pharmacy, 15 March 1948.
115. Margaret Ecker Francis, "Nellie McClung," *Canadian Home Journal*, October 1947.
116. PABC, unidentified clipping, an editorial: reprinted by courtesy of *The Family Herald and Weekly Star*, 1951.
117. PAC, Mark McClung Papers, letter, Paul McClung to Mark McClung.
118. PABC, Eugenia Perry Papers, letter, Eugenia Perry to Wes McClung, 6 September 1951.
119. Mrs. Ruth Scott, Victoria, interview with Candace Savage in Wawanesa, Manitoba, n.d.
120. Jupp, "Nellie McClung of Gordon Head."
121. Mrs. Ruth Scott, interview with Candace Savage.
122. Carol Hancock, "Between Love and Challenge in Company with Nellie McClung" (unpub. MSTh thesis, St. Andrew's College, University of Saskatchewan, "Introduction" and p. 47).
123. PABC, McClung Papers, vol. 21, NLM, early typescript, *The Stream Runs Fast*.
124. Hancock, "Between Love and Challenge," p. 53.
125. Ibid., pp. 51, 42.
126. Ibid., p. 140.

Index

❖

Index

McClung, Nellie, birth, 1, 2; childhood, 15, 22, 26–28, 39; death, 298; domestic help, 76–77, 132, 216–21; education, 22–24;
Family life: and career, balancing of, 39, 116, 133; children (*see also* individual names): 76–77, 87, 114; attitude towards, 78, 86, 100–02; Margaret Laurence on Nellie McClung's, 253;
Feminist beliefs: 29, 36, 37, 82–83, 113, 116; development of, 22–23, 29, 36, 40, 65;
Fictional heroines: Babette, 255–56; Hilda Berry, 245, 247, 257, 262–63; Helmi Milander, 237–38, 243–45, 247–50, 260, 266, 269; Borska Taski, 239; Pearlie Watson, 72–73, 112, 234–37, 247–50, 254, 260, 262, 266, 269;
funeral, 298–99; future, Nellie's vision of, 84; health, xiii, 12, 277, 280, 292; humour, 4–5, 60, 73, 77, 96, 113, 125, 127, 155–56, 177, 182, 192, 291;
Literary influences on: Edward Bellamy, 98; Margaret Deland, 64; Charles Dickens, 44, 47–48; Charlotte Perkins Gilman, 116; Bret Harte, 230; Mackenzie King, 170–71, 276; Olive Schreiner, 116–17;
marriage (*see also* McClung, R.W. (Wes): 13, 43, 69; medical care, views on, 117; motherhood, 76–77;
Political life (*see also* Politics; Religion and Politics): defeat at the polls, 184, 187, 226; member of the Alberta Legislative Assembly, 180–81, 197; speaker to Liberal Party Convention, 127; suffrage (*see* McClung, Nellie, suffrage); temperance (*see* McClung, Nellie, temperance);
religious beliefs, 28, 64–65, 185, 188–89, 291, 294, 299; school teacher, 48–52; social reformer, xv, 37, 42, 69, 109, 175, 217, 228, 247, 253, 269;
Suffrage (*see also* Suffrage; Women's, suffrage): as unofficial leader of, xv; campaigns, xv, 118–19, 129, 133–34, 136, 39, 147, 49, 154, 55;
Temperance (*see also* Temperance; Prohibition; Alcohol): campaigns, 136, 147, 154, 172; education, 54, 80; efforts for, 54, 55, 81, 128; first public address to WCTU, 80; tract, 254;
teachers of Nellie McClung, 22–25, 41, 42, 226;
Tours: Alberta, 277, 279; Britain, 195–96; Manitoba, 73, 91, 96, 277; Ontario 73, 96, 97–99; Quebec, 277;

Saskatchewan, 277, 279; United States, 157–58;
trapping mink, 26;
Writing: 106, 227–28, 246–47, 258, 276, 292, 295; ambition, 40, 53, 55, 68, 91, 147–48, 228, 229; style, xiii, xiii–xv, 1, 22, 35, 73, 230, 251; themes, 143–44, 228, 258–60, 267, 269
McClung, Paul, 76, 78, 86, 181, 215
McClung, R.W. (Wes), xiii, 43, 56, 58–60, 63, 65–68, 72, 75, 83–84, 90–95, 97, 104, 135, 176, 179, 181, 217–18, 227, 229, 270–71, 283, 297, 298; drug store, 69, 70, 85, 89–91; marriage, 69, 87–89; support for Nellie, 68, 82, 114, 124, 216
McKinney, Louise, 173, 175, 197, 209, 258
McNaughton, Violet, 26, 169
Macphail, Agnes, 212, 216, 276–77
McPherson, Aimee Semple, 284–85, 299
Manitoba (*see also* Politics; McClung, Nellie, political life): prohibition campaign (*see also* Alcohol; Temperance): 107, 113, 129; suffrage campaign (*see also* Women's Parliament): 107, 112, 119, 127, 131, 133, 138; Legislative Assembly, 119; tours (*See* McClung, Nellie, tours); Winnipeg Quill Club, 103
Martin Chuzzlewit (Charles Dickens), 47
Meighen, Arthur, 207–08
Methodist: Book and Publishing House, 84, 97, 98, 119, 231; Church, 73, 193; missionary, 195; Sunday School publications, Nellie's, 229
Methodist Woman's Missionary Society, 141
Military Voters' Act, 152
Ministry, women in the. *See* Women, Ordination of
Mock parliament. *See* Women's parliament
Mooney, Elizabeth (Lizzie), xiii, 3, 4, 17–18, 30, 38, 39, 41, 67–68, 92
Mooney, George, 3, 12, 26, 30, 38, 40, 41, 67
Mooney, Hannah, xiii, 3, 4, 12, 23, 25, 27, 31, 38, 58, 62, 67, 84, 295
Mooney, Jack, 3, 26, 27, 34–39, 52, 61, 67
Mooney, John, 2, 9, 11, 12, 14, 19, 20, 35, 36, 37, 60; attitudes towards Nellie, 5; character, 6, 16; religious beliefs, 5, 64
Mooney, Letitia (McCurdy), 2–4, 7–9, 11–12, 13, 14, 23, 26, 31, 33, 39, 49, 54, 59, 61, 69, 86, 103, 298; attitude towards Nellie, 22, 29, 30, 35, 36–38, 46, 48, 52, 56, 69; character, 5, 6, 12, 13, 27, 46, 50, 57; religious beliefs, 5, 28, 63–64
Mooney, Will, 3, 8, 9, 10, 12, 14, 17, 18, 19, 26, 30, 38, 40, 46, 47
Moral Re-Armament (MRA) (*see also* Religion and Politics): 286–91

Index

More Leaves from Lantern Lane, 271
MRA. *See* Moral Re-Armament
Murphy, Emily Ferguson, 119, 142, 150, 160, 163, 180–81, 207–10, 212–14, 244, 251
"My Religion," 189

Nash, Mrs. Claud, 110
National American Woman Suffrage Association (NAWSA), 155–57
National Council of Women of Canada, 76, 110–11, 169, 188
National Equal Franchise Union, 169
NAWSA. *See* National American Woman Suffrage Association
"Neutral Fuse, The," 224, 242, 267
"New Citizenship, The," 119
"New Year's Message 1938," 276
Next of Kin, The, 106, 143, 145, 157
Normal School, 24, 36, 37, 38, 40–42, 45, 46, 49, 52, 68, 73, 249
Norris, T.C., 130, 141
Northfield School, 22–23, 26, 31, 34, 42, 67, 285
Novels. *See* individual titles; McClung, Nellie, writing

"O, Canada!" 240
Oliver, Rev. H.E., 199, 205
"One of the McTavishes," 255, 267
Ontario tours. *See* McClung, Nellie, tours
Ordination of women. *See* Women, ordination of
"Our Present Discontents," 215

Pacifism, 144
Painted Fires, ix, xiv, 44, 221, 237, 240, 243–44, 248, 250–52, 255, 257, 260, 266, 269
Pankhurst, Emmeline, 118, 186
Parlby, Irene, 169, 175, 180, 182, 185, 209
PEL. *See* Political Equality League
"Perils of Heroism, The," 254
Pharmacy. *See* McClung, R.W. (Wes), drug store
Pioneer life (*see also* Women, Farm work; Women, pioneer hardships): 11, 16–17, 19, 25–26
Political Equality League (PEL), 82, 111–12, 115, 119–20, 127, 140, 149, 168
Politics (*see also* Religion and Politics; McClung, Nellie, political life):
Alberta: Conservative Party, 172–73; elections, 172–73, 175, 184–86; Legislative Assembly, 169, 176; Liberal Party, 172, 175, 182, 228; Suffrage bill, 169; United Farm Women of Alberta, 185; United Farmers of Al-

berta (UFA), 173–82, 187;
Federal: Conservative Party, 151–53, 214; elections, 134–38; Liberal Party, 151–53, 274;
Manitoba: Conservative Party, 109, 127, 129–34, 136; Liberal Party, 127–34, 137–38;
Senate, women's admission to, 203, 206–08, 210, 212, 214
Prohibition (*see also* Alcohol; McClung, Nellie, temperance): xvi, 79, 81–82, 83, 103, 107, 108, 109, 117, 136, 142, 146–49, 154, 158, 167, 169, 172, 175–76, 178–80, 183, 187, 253, 282; bill, 147; campaign, 136, 147, 154, 172; repeal of, 281, 294
Prohibitionist, 135, 146, 169, 175–76, 181, 184
Purple Springs, xiv, 195, 249, 260, 266

Rae, Elizabeth (Lizzie). *See* Mooney, Elizabeth (Lizzie)
"Red and White," 243, 264–65, 267
Religion. *See* Methodist Church; United Church; Women, ordination of
Religion and Politics: Moral Re-Armament, 286–91; Social Gospel, 299
Religious beliefs. *See* McClung, Nellie, religious beliefs
Riel Rebellion, 24, 31
"Right of a Child to a Good Start in Life, The," 100
Robert Elsmere (Mrs. Humphrey Ward), 64
Roblin, Sir Rodmond P., 109–11, 120–32, 135–36, 142, 170
"Romance in Everyday Life, The," 224, 277
Ross, Sinclair, 61, 101
Rowell, Newton, 210–11, 290

Schultz, Mr. Frank, 22–25, 42, 226
Second Chance, The, 72, 96, 237, 242, 245, 249, 254
Second World War. *See* World War II
Showalter, Elaine, xiv, 248, 268
Sifton, Clifford, 142, 172
"Silver Linings," 277
"Six Weeks Vacation: Truth is Stranger than Fiction," 59
Sowing Seeds in Danny, 74, 85, 91, 95–96, 98, 231, 234, 248, 249
Speaking tours. *See* McClung, Nellie, tours
Stream Runs Fast: My Own Story, The, xii, xvi, 15, 81, 104, 166, 196, 238, 292–93
Strong-Boag, Veronica, 82–83, 258
Suffrage (*see also* McClung, Nellie, suffrage; Women's, suffrage; Franchise): 120, 121, 124, 130, 137, 154, 172, 197; Alberta bill, 169;

335